Battling for News

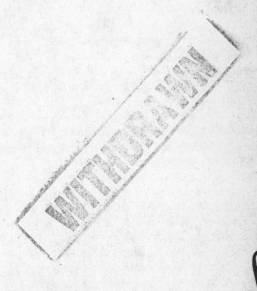

SCEPTRE

Battling for News

The Rise of the Woman Reporter

ANNE SEBBA

SCEPTRE

Copyright © Anne Sebba 1994

First published in 1994 by Hodder and Stoughton
A division of Hodder Headline PLC
First published in paperback by Hodder & Stoughton, 1995
A Sceptre Paperback

A John Curtis Book

The right of Anne Sebba to be identified as the Author of
the Work has been asserted by her in accordance with
the Copyright, Designs and Patents Act 1988.

10 9 8 7 6 5 4 3 2 1

A CIP catalogue record for this title
is available from the British Library
ISBN 0 340 63261 5

Printed and bound in Great Britain by
Cox and Wyman Ltd, Reading

Hodder and Stoughton
A Division of Hodder Headline PLC
338 Euston Road
London NW1 3BH

FOR
ADAM LEO

Contents

Acknowledgments

I am greatly indebted to many people for help in my research, or for giving me insights, assistance, hospitality or general advice, or for granting me permission to quote from their published works (as documented in the Notes and Select Bibliography). My thanks go to: Patsy Adamski, Kate Adie, Isabel Allende, Joan Astley, Lynne Reid Banks, Brian Basham, Nicola Beauman, Sybille Bedford, Adrianne Blue, Nan Bowman-Albinski, Heather (Baroness) Brigstocke, Victoria Brittain, Helen Callaway, Peter Calvocoressi, Peter Castle, Patricia Clough, Richard Collier, Fidelma Cook, Gerry Cook, Chris Cramer, Aidan Crawley, Harriet Crawley, Caroline Davidson, Phyllis Deakin, Michael and Della Fathers, Robert Fox, Rosemary Friedman, John Gau, Martha Gellhorn, Frank Gillard, Shiela Grant Duff, Frank Goldsworthy, Diana Goodman, Jean Goodman, Bernard Hall, Peter Hancock, Jeremy Harding, Shulamit Hareven, the late Harold Harris, John Haslam, John Hatt, Tim Heald, Dorothy Helly, Clare Hollingworth, Fred Hunter, Evelyn Irons, Raymond ('JAK') Jackson, Mary Kenny, Phillip Knightley, Julia Langdon, Edie Lederer, Honora ('Honey') Lorenzo-George, Sir Fitzroy Maclean, Franca Magnani, Rob Matthews, Roisin McAuley, Angus McGill, Caroline Moorehead, Trish Morrissey, Nigel Nicolson, Mollie Panter-Downes, Gordon Parker, Eve Perrick, Tom Pocock, Elizabeth Pond, Ali Porteous, Rosalie Sebba, Christopher Seton-Watson, Julian Shuckburgh, John Simpson, Elise Smith, Claire Sterling, Mary Stott, Andy Thompson, Claire Tomalin, Ion Trewin, Hugo Vickers, Marina Warner, Richard West, Helena Whitbread, Monica Dehn Wilson, Justin Wintle, Charles Wintour, John Young and Tullia Zevi.

I am most grateful to the following owners of unpublished works or letters for allowing me access to their material (details of which are shown in the Notes) and for giving me permission to quote from them: Joan Astley (Astley Private Papers); Aidan Crawley (Virginia Cowles: War Correspondent 1935–45. Memoir of his wife); Fred Hunter ('W. T. Stead's Encouragement of Women on The National Press', to be published shortly in *Victorian Periodicals Newsletter*); Honora ('Honey') Lorenzo-George (owner of the autobiography of Emillie Peacocke); Mary Stott (autobiographical memoir).

I am also indebted to staff from the following institutions or companies who have responded to my queries and helped me with my research: Article 19, the BBC, the British Library, the British Newspaper Library, the *Daily Express* Library, the *Daily Mail* Library, the Equal Opportunities' Commission, the Fawcett Library, the Imperial War Museum, *The Independent*, the Institute of Journalists, the John Rylands University Library of Manchester, the London Library, the Ministry of Defence, the *New Yorker*, the Public Record Office, Richmond-upon-Thames Library, the *Spectator*, News International Library (where Melanie Aspey and Eamon Dyas were particularly helpful) and TV-am.

I would also like to thank my publisher, John Curtis, in whose stimulating company the idea for this book first took root; my agent, Gill Coleridge, for help, friendship and advice; my editor, Linda Osband, and my indexer, Douglas Matthews, who have all contributed in myriad ways. My deepest gratitude is for my husband Mark, who has, as usual, been unflagging in his encouragement and unstinting with practical assistance.

Anne Sebba, London, 1993

'Though perhaps we do not say so we leave it to be inferred that of the dwellers in Fleet Street there are, not two sexes, but two species – journalists and women journalists – and that the one is about as far removed organically from the other as a dog from a cat.'

ARNOLD BENNETT, *Journalism for Women*, 1898

Introduction

When the American reporter, Henrietta Stackpole, makes her appearance in Henry James's *The Portrait of a Lady*, she is introduced as a woman 'in the van of progress... [with] clear-cut views on most subjects'.

Miss Stackpole was employed to send regular reports, or 'letters' as they were called, to a New York-based paper, *The Interviewer*. She possessed not only considerable ability but also 'courage, energy and good humour... without parents and without property [she] had adopted three of the children of an infirm and widowed sister and was paying their school bills out of the proceeds of her literary labour.' And yet this intelligent, independent young lady is viewed as an object of extreme curiosity by her hosts in England, an American expatriate family.

'She must be a kind of monster. Is she very ugly?' asks Ralph Touchett. 'A female interviewer – a reporter in petticoats? I'm very curious to see her.'

It is not long before Ralph comes to admire Miss Stackpole for her bravery, but persists in being made uncomfortable by many of her other attributes necessary for her work. By the time *The Portrait of a Lady* first appeared in 1881, women reporters were hardly commonplace, yet there were enough of them, especially in Italy where much of the book is set, for James to have been confident that he was not creating an unbelievable character.

Yet who was the first woman reporter? Almost all the women I have interviewed for this book have, quite rightly, claimed the distinction of being first in a particular field – the first to be sent abroad by a newspaper; the first to cover a war; the first to run her own bureau abroad; the first to report a war live. The list is long as, one by one, a different barrier is broken down.

The first reference to the word 'reporter' in a professional sense – as a person specially employed to take notes of an event for publication – is given by the Oxford Dictionary as occurring in 1813 in relation to the Press Gallery. The history of the *Yorkshire Post* refers to reporters at Peterloo in 1819 and William Cobbett referred in 1826 to 'a lying Irish reporter' at Preston.

Given my personal definition of a reporter as someone who has witnessed an event which they then describe, and perhaps also analyse for others, women have been acting as eye-witnesses, describing horrific or vivid scenes from life, for several centuries. In 1301, the Prioress of Clerkenwell, distraught over the vandalism caused by rowdy playgoers, wrote to the King begging him to put a stop to such behaviour. What a vivid picture of London life the Prioress depicts when she complains that 'the people of London lay waste and destroy her corn and grass by their miracle plays and wrestling matches so that she has no profit of them . . . they are a savage folk and we cannot stand against them. . . .'[1] In the early eighteenth century, the letters of Lady Mary Wortley Montagu, wife of an English ambassador, contain many descriptive gems from her travels and life abroad. Fanny Burney's retelling of her own mastectomy in 1811 describing 'the most torturing pain . . . when the dreadful steel was plunged into the breast – cutting through veins – arteries – flesh – nerves', is among the most graphic pieces of reportage one might ever come across. Flora Tristan, a French feminist 'with the firm resolve to discover everything for myself', wrote some memorable descriptions in 1839 of London prostitution and the debauchery of the British aristocracy, after closely observing its activities in London's Waterloo Road.

Perhaps the first woman who recounted world events for posterity, if not for a newspaper, was Christine de Pisan, medieval chronicler and author of *The Book of Fayttes of Armes and of Chyvalrye*, written in 1408–9. Christine was not, however, an eye-witness reporter. She was a poet, prose writer and biographer caught up in the wars of her time – the latter stages of the Hundred Years War, the civil wars of Orléans and Burgundy, and the catastrophe of Agincourt. In her poetry especially, Christine championed the cause of women against the degradation and oppression imposed on them by men. Although she was largely a compiler, marshalling a mass of information about warfare, she also included numerous original passages, furnishing detailed information about the victualling of a garrison and a castle, as well as the weaponry needed for the siege of a fortress. Her sources were 'wise knights', whose anonymity she maintained. She was capable of grasping so unfeminine a matter as warfare since her father had personally supervised her education, teaching her Latin, philosophy and science, subjects rarely imparted to girls in the Middle Ages.

She must, too, have possessed the essential quality necessary for all reporters: the burning desire not only to find out but also to tell; in other words, to communicate. Women are trained to be good listeners – there are many examples in this book of men revealing more to women simply because they appear more relaxed and adept at receiving the information – and women have a natural facility for recounting what they have heard or seen. Although there are also occasions when men relate better to other men. In June 1944, a male reporter accompanied the British troops crossing the Channel in gliders. Chester Wilmot, correspondent of the Australian Broadcasting Corporation (ABC), trained as a parachutist and shared some of the men's most intimate thoughts about patriotism and fear. But the best reporters also need to be observant, determined, open-minded, brave and hard-working, qualities which men are just as likely to possess as women.

Whether or not our attention is gripped depends not so much on the story as on the person who saw it happen. We rely not merely on their objectivity but on their ability to see clearly and understand what they are seeing, their memory in recapturing facts and atmosphere, their resourcefulness in relaying the story, their technical skills such as knowledge of foreign languages and shorthand and, above all, their ability to craft words and phrases that fit the narrative.

Women have long been attracted to journalism and writing for newspapers has proved a more welcoming career for them than almost any other profession. Becoming a journalist in Victorian times was one of the very few routes open to intelligent women with some education to rise beyond humble origins or out of a failed marriage. Margaret Bateson – a journalist herself – editing a book in 1895 entitled *Professional Women upon Their Professions*, wrote:

In journalism women have a more assured position than in almost any of the great arts and professions. Between men and women there is no question of rights and, I trust, very little of rivalry. If proof were needed of the good fellowship that exists, it is found in the absolute equality of treatment meted out to both sexes in the Institute of Journalists.[2]

Is there any evidence that women report happenings differently from men? There are, of course, no statistical surveys and so any opinion is bound to be subjective. In an 1898 book – the first in English to be devoted to the subject – Arnold Bennett, the novelist, posed a similar question. In his small volume, entitled *Journalism for Women: A Practical Guide*,[3] he asked: 'Is there any sexual reason why a woman should be a less accomplished journalist than a man? I can find none.' Bennett did not shirk from criticising women for what, in his view, were their revealed shortcomings. He catalogued these as inattention to detail, especially where punctuation, spelling and grammar were concerned, lack of restraint or a tendency to over-emphasise and, finally, a failure to understand that business is business; he cites the example of a woman journalist who asked for a commission to report a royal visit and then did not feel up to writing it because she was too tired.

None the less, Bennett, who together with literary giants such as H. G. Wells, Oscar Wilde and Bernard Shaw was a vociferous supporter of women writers, was adamant that, 'despite a current impression to the contrary implicit in nearly every printed utterance on the subject, there should not be any functional disparity between the journalist male and the journalist female'.

And yet, during the intervening hundred or so years, women's suitability or otherwise as reporters has been constantly debated. Today, women are no longer expected to report only feminine topics; war and politics are on their agenda just as frequently as fashion and royal babies. But the debate usually focuses on two aspects: are women more emotionally biased than men and therefore partisan, and is this necessarily a bad thing? And do women report, especially in wartime, so-called soft news, oriented towards people rather than statistical facts?

In this book I have discussed the work and lives of some women who are unashamedly partisan and others who prize objectivity above all else. But equally there are women who elude categorisation. Florence Dixie would never have written so movingly about the Zulu king, Cetshwayo, had she not been emotionally stirred by his cause. Shiela Grant Duff never hid the fact that the only reason she wanted to report from Europe in the 1930s was because she felt so passionately concerned about the world situation, an emotion fostered by the death of her father in the First World War. Martha Gellhorn believes that being partisan is an essential prerequisite to good reporting. On the other hand, Virginia Cowles was determined to be as objective as possible and always tried to give the argument on both sides a fair hearing. The scholarly training and intellectual rigour of Elizabeth Wiskemann prevented her from being influenced by her emotions however passionately she may have felt.

The soft versus hard news argument is complicated in that more women reporters than men do concentrate on writing about the hospitals, orphanages and dislocation to the population in wartime; but many would argue that this is the real and, therefore, the hard news. Nothing else really matters. Writing about numbers of aeroplanes shot down and military hardware, they say, is the soft option male journalists often go for because it is easier and less taxing to one's emotional being. This argument was particularly well aired at the time of Vietnam during which more women reporters were given freer access than in any previous world conflict. There are, as ever, exceptions. Clare Hollingworth, who has been fascinated by battlefields and warfare since childhood, believes that the only issue in times of war is who is dominating the front line. Strategy and understanding the armies' relative strengths is all. Anything else is 'sidebar' material. Kate Adie, perhaps because she is often with the military, has, like Hollingworth, also been dubbed a 'macho male reporter'.[4] In fact, she is as much at home with both types of story. And it is important to point out that several male reporters today also write heart-wrenching stories about the victims of war.

None the less, it often seems that the background stories to a particularly violent or tragic situation are provided by women. 'Perhaps society does allow women more freedom to operate using their feelings,' explained Elizabeth Pond, an experienced, international political reporter.[5] A good example of this was a thoughtful piece written by Geraldine Brooks, who covered the Gulf War for the *Wall Street Journal*, about breaking bread with displaced Kurds in the aftermath of war. It was clear that the family, living in daily fear of Saddam Hussein's helicopters thudding over to crush what little remained of their mountainous homes, had offered hospitality to Brooks, treating her as one of them. The date, if not the occasion, was the eve of Passover and Brooks, in an extended metaphor, compared the Kurdish situation with that of the Jews who had been slaves unto Pharaoh until they escaped.[6]

In April 1991, journalist Carol Thatcher, discussing on *The Frost Programme* newspaper coverage of the Kurdish plight, commented on 'how good some of the women reporters, rather better than their male counterparts, have been at communicating just the horror in some of the refugee camps'. According to Sue Lloyd Roberts, reporter, camerawoman and mother, 'women do have a greater sensitivity to the subject. They have more access because they can be like a fly on the wall and they are not so threatening. I can get closer to the human aspect of war.'[7]

The Israeli novelist, Shulamit Hareven, began life as a reporter, covering several of Israel's wars as a front-line correspondent. But her motivation was always the urge to understand rather than to report to the public. She insists that she has never gone to war because of the excitement. 'War is the stupidest and saddest thing in existence, but it, too, has to be understood in order to talk about it intelligently.' Hareven is convinced that being a woman, especially an older woman, has helped her to communicate with those involved in fighting the wars. They see her as 'an older sister or mother figure for whom they don't have to translate, or censor themselves including the fantasies, the fears, the illogic of it, the ultimate ignorance and improvisation. Not to speak of the authentic language and metaphor.'[8]

Today Hareven is actively involved in the Peace Now movement and has developed good contacts with Palestinians:

The things I hear are sometimes things I believe people – certainly most Palestinians – would not tell a man; surely not a foreign reporter at the American Colony Bar. When you sit down with the family in the kitchen, and help cut the beans, you hear some truths, rather than political declarations. Especially about the PLO . . . . I think a woman is less threatening to some people, less suspected of belonging to some kind of agency. More like family. More humane.

Nevertheless, she accepts that while making contacts may be easier for a woman, the quality of reporting is less a question of gender and more to do with the degree of perception and intelligence. 'Good reporters, men or women, want to understand; bad ones are after "scoops", significant or not.'[9]

Perhaps it is no coincidence that Hareven is today a prize-winning fiction writer. Several other women in this book have moved on from fact to fiction, such as Lynne Reid Banks and Marina Warner, the latter freely admitting that a particularly horrific scene she witnessed in Vietnam is one she has revisited both in a novel and in a short story. Others, such as Martha Gellhorn, Sybille Bedford and Rebecca West, have managed to combine fiction and reporting, Gellhorn viewing fiction as the more pleasurable, if more difficult, task; an indulgence to be paid for by her journalism. The link between the two crafts is not as obvious as it may appear. A good reporter must know how to stand back from the events to be described while a novelist must be able to thrust forward into the heart of his or her character and think for them. Imagination is the prerequisite for one and an encumbrance for the other, but the experience of reporting may provide the stimulus to unlock the imagination.

'Being a novelist definitely helps with law reporting,' according to Sybille Bedford. 'You sense, even if you cannot change facts. You can, with a novelist's eye, trim them or present them or shape them into a story.' But she knows that, with any truly dramatic situation, one should never invent: 'It's value is that it's true.' Both reporters and novelists need insight through imagination, she believes. 'A good novelist has to know the world and see the sunrise, but then some people write wonderful books who have never been beyond their own, Kentish village . . . . The springs of writing are very mysterious.'[10]

But if feminine intuition gives an edge to women reporters, surely the fact that many are still trapped by domesticity hampers them? Some media organisations, including the BBC, are, gingerly, trying to make practical arrangements so that women who wish to report from trouble spots at short notice can do so without fear of domestic concerns preventing them. Not many of the reporters in this book have had children during the period when they were actively working as reporters, but enough do to show that children do not have to be a bar to a reporting career. Florence Dixie in the 1890s thought nothing of leaving her two young sons behind when she went off to Africa for the *Morning Post*. Of course, it was different then as she was leaving them to a retinue of nursery staff. In the 1950s, Claire Sterling faced some of the most agonising decisions of her career when she was plunged into danger zones which meant not merely risking her life but that her children might be left motherless. Victoria Brittain, a single parent, took her son with her to war and through involvement with his activities managed to become part of the native Saigon community in a way that would not have been possible without him. Martha Gellhorn has also managed to maintain a reporting life as a single parent as has Patricia Clough, although she freely admits her life has been much harder because of constant worries about bringing up her child. To quote Elizabeth Pond again:

You have to keep working and supporting yourself until someone notices your work. This takes an enormous amount of time and energy and it best happens when you are young, exactly the period in your life when most women are starting families and devoting much of their time to that.[11]

Libby Purves, a journalist and editor, commented in an article about women war correspondents, 'worth recording is that Jane Peel – like Kate Adie, or Lee Miller at the time of her war work – is unmarried and without children. It is easier to feel like a young man, like a soldier even, at that time of a female life.' She continued:

The psychological changes of pregnancy are great: I carried a child through the months of the Falklands war and was glad not to be there. Even within the bounds of professionalism, by the end of that war and that pregnancy I would not only have been less willing to risk my life, but would have been reporting in different words than I would have chosen at the beginning. But that is one personal view; and it is unfair for mothers to claim a monopoly on compassion.[12]

Domestic distractions apart, there is still a real but not insurmountable difficulty facing those women who wish to report from Arab countries. When Victoria Brittain went to Algiers in the early 1970s, her journalist second husband having been posted there, she found her professional life cramped to the point of sterility. Algeria may have been the leader of the Third World movement, 'but as a woman I couldn't get an interview ... women were totally excluded from political life'.[13]

Claire Sterling was in Rabat in the early 1950s trying to secure an interview with the Chief Imam in Fez. This she eventually managed only to be told: 'I detest American women especially American women journalists. I think they are all whores.'[14] The interview was swiftly terminated, but not before he had shown her his beautiful collection of Korans. Forty years later, American agency journalist Edie Lederer reporting from Saudi Arabia first had to acquire an 'I-am-not-a-whore' pass before she could travel.

There have been many other fictional portraits of women reporters – or, occasionally, Ace girl reporters – in the wake of Henry James's creation of Henrietta Stackpole. In 1984, the Peruvian-born writer Isabel Allende wrote a brilliant and disturbing novel entitled *Of Love and Shadows*, in which the heroine, a reporter called Irene Beltran, suffers unbelievable torments and torture in pursuit of her job and the truth. Beltran may have been a fictional creation but her experiences were based on a true story Allende knew only too well. 'I had several models,' she explained. 'My colleagues in Chile in the seventies, courageous women journalists who defied the dictatorship to do their job.'[15]

Some reporters are motivated by an urge to understand; others by a desire to tell; one or two, like Agnes Smedley, by the conviction that if they understand and tell the world they may even influence the course of events. And there will always be some attracted by what they think is a glamorous lifestyle – although most of the women in this book convincingly give the lie to that assumption. Sybille Bedford's definition of a truly professional reporter is one who is prepared to stand out in the rain for hours, armed, of course, with a pencil rather than a pen. Irene Beltran was motivated by the same passionate outrage against injustice that has kept Martha Gellhorn in the forefront of reporting for nearly seventy years. Old age has, if anything, increased her fearlessness and mistrust of those with power. She now recognises that perhaps she cannot influence world events and is only

one small voice telling the truth about one small part of large events. On the other hand I have always felt that this business of telling your little section of the truth becomes effective when enough reporters are doing it.... I think I always wanted to get on the record somehow what I had seen, on behalf of those who were being hit by history.[16]

What follows in this book is an account of what many women have witnessed in the last 150 years. The events themselves are not always different from those that men have seen, but, frequently, they appear to have been. It is also an account of the battles women have fought in order to be able to tell these stories. Nowadays such battles are rarely with editors, who frequently recognise advantages in using women to report on many situations. More often the battles are with male colleagues, some of whom may feel themselves threatened by the star status accorded to several women reporters, others of whom resent what they see as special privileges granted them; a few merely patronise their female colleagues. The women in this book have reported much more than just war. They have investigated many a horror of peacetime society from prostitution, drug abuse and sexual deviation to riots, strikes and criminal trials.

But inevitably the major arguments still focus on women's suitability to be in the thick of war. War is too dangerous for women, it is said. They do not have the same basic knowledge of guns or ballistics as men and may, therefore, represent a hazard for others. Or, young women reporters are so eager to prove their prowess in war zones that they will take unnecessary risks – a view scorned by the women reporters I interviewed, who all insist that they weigh up the dangers with calculated realism. A further argument used by the military is that the presence of a woman in the midst of battle can inhibit nervous young soldiers or lead older ones to acts of chivalry when they should be concentrating on fighting the enemy.

Women reporters argue that knowledge of military hardware can be acquired and many of them have set out to do this. In addition, the increasing numbers of female military personnel invalidate the old canard about the dangers of having women in the midst of an army. The military accepts, of course, that war and civil conflict are dangerous and are becoming increasingly hazardous for all journalists, who are now often viewed as legitimate targets, in particular by a partisan or terrorist enemy. But it is no more dangerous for a woman than a man. 'It is not as if there are special, women-only grenades,' commented Diana Goodman.[17]

The last twenty years have seen dramatic changes for women in all branches of society. No one can seriously argue any longer that women have smaller brains, weaker personalities or deficient characters; all of which had been said in the not so distant past. The 1990s have been designated in the United Kingdom 'The Decade of Women', but, in the field of news reporting, there is not a great deal left for women to accomplish. Yet as the difference between the sexes diminishes and men and women experience more of each other's pleasures, traumas and responsibilities, so the way they report news grows more alike and is, today, largely indistinguishable. Although diversity will always persist, nowadays the treatment a reporter lends to a story is determined largely according to temperament rather than gender.

Perhaps the most notable achievement will be when women reporters are working in sufficient numbers that they are no longer judged by their looks, their personalities or their private lives and when we, the audience, are able to absorb merely the news they are reporting.

This book does not attempt to offer a comprehensive history of women reporters. I hope it shows, by focusing on individuals many of whom have set precedents and all of whom have had experiences beyond the imagination of most of us, how the role has developed in Britain from the pioneer reporters of the mid-nineteenth century to the true professionals of the late twentieth. Inevitably, people learn from each other and build on past experiences to reach new ground.

My choice of subjects has been personal and, in some cases, arbitrary and I have, mostly, limited myself to English-speaking reporters based in the United Kingdom. I have not included photographers, although I know that their brand of eye-witness reporting has contributed no less significantly to recording the news; they deserve a book in their own right. I was concerned neither to accord equal length to each reporter, nor to use only those who fitted a particular pattern or theory, nor those who held a particular set of political beliefs. Some excelled at news-gathering but had few literary skills; others wrote beautifully but were less enamoured by the chase. They are often very different 'types' and personalities, but they all have a shared interest. I believe the ones I have chosen are also those who have shaped the profession, but, above all, I wanted to write about those individuals who intrigued me.

I

Sisters, Wives and Nurses

'The impossibility of saying "no" to a lady.'

That, however, is precisely what the manager of *The Times* in 1861 went on to do. The lady in question, sister of *The Times*'s resident correspondent in Italy, Henry Wreford, and known to history only as Miss Wreford, had usefully covered for her brother two years previously when he had fallen ill. Then, as the Italian revolutionaries were straining for action, Mr Mowbray Morris of *The Times* had been glad 'to receive from you whatever information you can gather from Mr Wreford's friend and your own observation'.[1] Bolstered by her experience, and doubtless not averse to some financial reward for writing, Miss Wreford requested further commissions, only to be met with the following polite rebuff:

My Dear Madam, Your letter did not find me on duty and my colleague who was acting in my absence very wisely skirted the impossibility of saying 'no' to a lady – for that is what I am obliged to say, though I do not doubt your ability to do well what you propose.[2]

Miss Wreford, although not posted abroad by a newspaper, can none the less claim her place as one of the first women foreign correspondents; but not the first. In 1846, after living in Australia for five years for health reasons, the redoubtable Mrs Caroline Chisholm was invited, on her return to Britain, to write a regular column in Douglas Jerrold's *Weekly Newspaper* on the subject of 'life in the colony'. Mrs Chisholm, a Roman Catholic philanthropist known as The Emigrant's Friend, worked tirelessly to help newly arrived immigrants find homes and jobs. She knew many of them personally and used the material from hundreds of interviews to give a powerfully direct voice to her pamphlets and articles. She aimed to give women who were contemplating emigrating to Australia as much information and advice as she could, based on her own experiences. In 1853, she returned to Australia and continued her reports about colonial life for a further twelve years.

But while Mrs Chisholm was clearly motivated by a desire to help women, not all women writers were in favour of the emancipation of their sex and some wrote in praise of domestic virtues. Mrs Eliza Lynn Linton was a self-educated, determined young woman from the Lake District, who took herself to London in the first half of the century in search of the literary lifestyle. There she studied in the Reading Room of the British Museum until she had gathered enough material for two historical novels. But when she discovered that these did not pay enough, she turned to journalism. In 1848, she was taken on by the *Morning Chronicle*. For a woman to be given regular employment on a daily newspaper rather than having occasional freelance work accepted was a real breakthrough. And three years later, when she went to Paris, although she may have been required to do little more than write letters describing the Parisian social scene, she titled herself the *Morning Chronicle*'s Paris correspondent for a few years. Returning to London in the 1860s, and still writing for the *Morning Chronicle*, she became the first – and only – full-time woman journalist in Fleet Street, paid the princely sum of twenty guineas a month.

In 1868, she married. Although the marriage failed within a short time, there remained a need to support a penniless husband and family. It was then that she turned to writing novels and short stories, which, in spite of her own youthful independence, were strongly reactionary in tone. There was a contradictory element to these, well illustrated by her autobiographical novel *Sowing the Wind* (1867), which identifies a woman journalist fighting for success in a man's world as its heroine. Yet it was Mrs Lynn Linton who attacked George Eliot as unwomanly and immoral, and one reviewer described her as 'a thorough mistress of English' through whose pen 'the shallow pretences of the "New Woman" are ruthlessly torn aside'.[3]

But in the middle of the last century, the New Woman was not yet talked about. It was clear, however, that for a well-educated woman who wished to use her mind and had a lively appreciation of world events, journalism was an obvious outlet. Since it also offered a wide scope for freelance and part-time work, it had considerable appeal for women. Thanks to the broad-minded approach of her dissenting businessman father, Jessie White was encouraged from an early age to break out of the conventional middle-class mould. He ensured that she had a sound education and, in 1854, sent her to Paris when she was twenty-two to study at the Sorbonne. Strikingly good-looking with long, golden hair, Jessie was immediately drawn into a circle of Parisian liberals. Although she had already heard much about the Italian patriot, Giuseppe Mazzini, and the problems facing Italians working for unification through her father's business contacts, it was a heady six weeks spent in Sardinia, where she met the revolutionary leader, Giuseppe Garibaldi, and was then introduced by him in Rome to Robert and Elizabeth Barrett Browning, both fervent advocates of the Risorgimento, which was to shape the rest of her life. In the spring of 1855, Jessie returned to England, accompanied by Garibaldi's eight-year-old son Ricciotti, who needed an operation on his legs; searching for a challenge that would maintain her involvement in Garibaldi's cause, she was drawn into the Friends of Italy Society.

Her original intention had been to study philosophy, but now, imbued with a real purpose, she tried to enrol at several London hospitals to train as a doctor, believing that she could best devote herself to the Italian cause if she had some medical knowledge. She was refused admission. Instead, she immersed herself in Mazzini's political theories and acquired some elementary knowledge of nursing. In November 1856, she wrote her first article for the *Daily News*, England's most pro-Italian newspaper and an authoritative but popular journal with liberal sympathies, as part of a series called 'Italy for the Italians'. It was an unsigned, emotional appeal to the 'English love of justice and liberty', which she hoped would be used on behalf of struggling nationalities such as the Poles, Hungarians and Italians.[4] Less than a year later she applied to the paper's editor asking to be appointed the Italian correspondent.

Although there was no definite commitment by the newspaper to consider the young and inexperienced Miss White as its official correspondent, she left for Italy convinced that this was indeed her position. Within a month she was disconcerted to discover that the *Daily News* had despatched a man, Luigi Mariotti, as its official representative. Jessie was always blatant about her sympathies for the cause and appears never to have seen a need to act as an impartial observer or news-gatherer. She engaged immediately in pro-Mazzini activities and, after a conspiracy to seize a Piedmontese ship failed, found herself imprisoned. The British ambassador, called upon to work for her release, said that he found it extremely difficult since she would not promise to return to England immediately. He added, notwithstanding the fact she was a woman, that she was a 'perverse and obstinate spirit'. In official despatches she was always described as 'one of Mazzini's assistants' – a tag she vehemently objected to – not as 'an English newspaper-woman'.

But her four months in jail were not entirely wasted. There she met and became engaged to an Italian fellow-radical, and prisoner, Alberto Mario, eight years her senior. The two were married on 19 December 1857 and, shortly after, departed for the United States on a lecture tour. Jessie made some valuable contacts during this trip and was given several commissions to write about the Italian situation for American journals. On their return to Europe they found themselves arrested twice, the first time on suspicion of being Austrian spies, the second on suspicion of being involved in a Mazzinian plot again.

On 11 May, Garibaldi made his famous landing at Marsala, Sicily, with 1,000 red-shirted volunteers and within a few weeks, riding the crest of a peasants' revolt, had reached Palermo, where he set up a provisional government. Alberto was then invited to run a local school for about four thousand children of the poorest classes and Jessie's chief task was to nurse those wounded in battles along the way. She took over a monastery as her hospital base, but suffered from shortages of all essential supplies such as opium, quinine, chloride of lime and bandages. They lacked even straw for mattresses. A letter to the English press did, however, result in an avalanche of medical materials, including artificial limbs. Her task was made still more difficult by the ubiquitous dirt and lack of sanitary conditions; in the hot, Sicilian summer it was hard to control the spread of gangrene and typhus. Jessie worked long hours to alleviate what suffering she could and showed enormous compassion. Human comfort was the only sort of anaesthetic available and, in the case of a twelve-year-old boy whose arm was being amputated, she held him on her lap throughout the operation weeping, according to her husband, more than the boy himself.

Jessie's toiling as a nurse in the autumn of 1860 earned her the epithet of the Red Shirts' Florence Nightingale. She was, for a time, more nurse than correspondent and Garibaldi joked that, although the ambulance in which she rode should have been behind the leaders, it was often near the front as she went in search of food or medicines. Nor did she lack for courage as she dashed on to the field of battle to collect the wounded or as she engaged in competition with several English reporters sent to cater for the large English appetite for Italian news.

But her position with the *Daily News* was more tenuous than she originally realised since it had now appointed another correspondent, Carlo Arrivabene, a Neapolitan who spoke fluent English. Jessie soon became a friend of Arrivabene and, in her overriding aim to propagate news of the Italian situation, would often share her would-be scoops with him or other English reporters. Henry Wreford of *The Times* was so impressed by Jessie's bravery in making no less than fourteen trips from the hospital to the field under fire that he wrote about her in his own despatches.

In 1861, Victor Emmanuel was proclaimed King of the new Kingdom of Italy. Jessie, an outspoken propagandist in favour of both republicanism and unification, was now commissioned to write three articles per week for the *Morning Star*. For the next few years she supported herself as a professional writer, translating some of Mazzini's essays, reporting for other English newspapers and, from time to time, returning to England to give lecture tours. She even bought herself a typewriter. A turning-point came in 1866 with the death of both her parents; from then on she looked upon Italy as her home and also began an important assignment as Italian correspondent for a new American periodical, *The Nation*. Both its founder, E. L. Godkin, and its editor, William Lloyd Garrison, had been impressed by Jessie when she had visited in 1858; six years later they had not forgotten her.

Her war articles were all the more vivid for the amount of time she spent behind the lines, witnessing at first hand how wretched life was in the poverty-stricken southern Italian towns and seeing the desperation in the hospitals and schools. This humanity gave her campaigning despatches an edge over her rivals. In addition, she had the ear of Garibaldi and could embroider her articles with many personal anecdotes. In 1866, when ordered not only to halt but to give up much of their conquered territory, the Garibaldini were enraged after all they had fought for. Jessie, witnessing the scene, wrote of how the order was received: 'I saw them break their swords, shatter their bayonets, many threw themselves to the ground and rolled in earth still soaked in their brothers' blood.'[5]

Jessie accompanied Garibaldi and the Red Shirts again in 1870, when he formed a volunteer corps against the Prussians. This time she went as the properly accredited military correspondent of several English and American papers (including *The Scotsman*, *The Nation* and *The Tribune* in New York), but she still undertook nursing duties as and when required. Conditions were primitive and Jessie was often frozen, wet and exhausted. She was usually up all day and night, determined to share the rigours of the soldiers' experiences and undergo the same deprivations of food, sleep and home life. None the less, because this time she was able to concentrate on reporting, because she had matured politically and because Garibaldi's trust enabled her to attend many secret meetings of his high command, her articles provided a unique coverage of Garibaldi's participation in the Franco-Prussian War. Although still in awe of Garibaldi's heroic qualities as leader, she was also aware of his fading charisma. Nor were her reports overly emotional as she included detailed statistics of the dead and injured, descriptions of battlefields, tactical analyses and accounts of minor skirmishes.

According to Mazzini, in one of his letters to an English woman friend,* 'Jessie speaks like a soldier, insults everybody and is dictatorial in her tone far worse than Garibaldi himself.'[6]

After this campaign, Jessie devoted herself to peacetime reporting. She and her husband were perpetually short of money and depended largely on what Jessie could earn from her articles and books on a variety of subjects. She was known to drive a hard bargain with her editors and publishers, but, in return, scoured the country, even in old age, searching for interesting and unusual material. It was not mere coincidence that so many British journalists reported on Italy for their readers. The warm climate, classical allusions and romantic nature of its inhabitants all contributed to making Italy the focal point of the grand tour. Thus many English men and women were more familiar with it, as tourists, than with any other part of Europe.

In 1881, Jessie was dredging her memory to write a life of Garibaldi, which, perhaps because of her close association with the protagonist, was not always as accurate as her on-the-spot reporting. Some passages have been criticised by one historian as 'quite wrong', 'mistaken' or even 'nonsense'.[7] In 1883, a year before the book was finished, Alberto died, which left her totally dependent on income from her own writing. For the next twenty-three years, until her own death aged seventy-four on 5 March 1906, she worked indefatigably.

History may remember Jessie White Mario as Garibaldi's friend and sometime nurse, but her most lasting achievement should be the series of articles she wrote between 1866 and 1906 for *The Nation*. An obituary in that journal, written by the editor himself, praised the wide choice of subject matter in her columns, from Florentine mosaics

---

* See chapter 4, page 49. The friend was Emillie Peacocke's grandmother.

to Venetian glass and the opening of the St Gothard Tunnel. 'Our readers will recall her exposition of the horrors of the subterranean life of Naples, of the sulphur mines of Sicily. She was responsive to every proletary [sic] movement for the relief from oppression or distress.'[8]

Benedetto Croce, in his 1929 history of Italy, refers to White Mario, whom he assumes to be a man, as one of the few people not to look with pessimism on Italian affairs in the 1870s. Croce then quotes a comment of Jessie's that if the Italian Risorgimento had been 'a beautiful poem', the prose translation of it, which had been made after 1870, was 'faithful to the original. "He" showed how far Italy had travelled since 1848 and argued from the philosophical basis that Italy and Italians were together in the making.' Jessie was particularly good at explaining to her American readers the difficulties of welding such a diverse country into one. She saw clearly the enormous problems which beset the backward and primitive south because she spent much time walking around talking to slum dwellers and miserable mine workers. Her biographer wrote:

The ignorance and degradation of this part of Italy haunted her, and publicising the truth about it became a compulsion. She collected evidence in which no other writer was yet professionally interested; statistics on the birthrate; on the rate of infant mortality and on the incidence of disease. She pleaded for the provision of elementary public hygiene. The sense of urgency and immediacy that sharpened her detailed reports on conditions in Southern Italy makes these articles stand out as some of her most successful work.[9]

Jessie White, reporter, shared many of the characteristics seen in later women reporters. In the first place, she had an international outlook gained from travel abroad when young and from her father's business background. She enjoyed access to excellent contacts, and wrote vividly and emotionally about war and other horrors of human existence with particular sympathy for and understanding of its victims in hospitals or slums. She was highly motivated by a cause and by the human leader of that cause, to the point where objectivity suffered. She had enormous energy, vitality and physical stamina – crucial attributes given the amount of travelling, and uncomfortable travelling at that, involved – and she was unafraid of adverse public opinion. She was neither academic nor thinker, but a doer with a sound practical bent. Above all, she was a crusader motivated by a deep-seated need to help society reform itself, especially the emerging Italian society which she had played a part in founding.

While Jessie White was on the march with Garibaldi through France, Mrs Emily Crawford was often to be found doing the rounds of Parisian hospitals, where she too gleaned information for the *Daily News*. Even when Paris was overwhelmed by a dreadful cholera epidemic, Emily Crawford was visiting hospitals for news. But her most famous scoop was on 23 March 1871, when the communists seized Paris. Mrs Crawford made her way alone at nightfall through the barricaded city and obtained an interview with the communist leaders as they sat in council. 'Many a time when shots were falling around she set forth on some journalistic enterprise, carrying no arms, her ready wit and quick perception proving her surest weapons of defence.'[10]

Emily Crawford, *née* Johnstone, was born in Ireland to a middle-class family, but moved to Paris when her father died leaving the family in straitened circumstances. Emily was imbued with a tremendous enthusiasm for work and when an invalid lodging in the same house gave her, at eighteen, her first journalistic introduction, she seized the chance. This was a time of great social exhibitionism in Paris and Emily found the serious tones used to report most of the stories extremely boring. She wrote with few restrictions her impressions of life in the Champs Elysées, the Boulevards and the Bois de Boulogne. She married a journalist, G. M. Crawford, and the pair worked in tandem as Paris correspondents for the *Daily News*.

It was no coincidence that both Emily Crawford and Jessie White had their work published by the *Daily News*. This newspaper had, in the past, given platforms to Harriet Martineau and Frances Power Cobbe, both outspoken feminists. From 1868, Sir John Robinson, the manager of the paper, restored its fortunes largely by his realisation that the public wanted not so much bare facts but rather details with as much description as possible. His upbringing as the son of a Congregational minister no doubt made him more receptive to employing women as one way of achieving this.

Even the arrival of two children did not stem Emily's desire to report the news and, during the siege of Paris in 1870, she and her husband sent their children back to England to be looked after by friends so that they could remain in the city. In spite of having stocked their cellar for a long siege, they were soon forced to leave for Bordeaux. It appears that Henry Labouchère, one of the proprietors of the paper, had journalistic ambitions of his own. Finding himself in Paris in 1870, he went to see Crawford and told him that he intended to replace him as correspondent of the *Daily News*. 'As I am a proprietor of the paper Robinson won't object,' he is alleged to have told the bemused Crawford. Perhaps his actions also had something to do with the *Daily News*'s attempt to become a mass circulation paper. It had just reduced its price to one penny and was re-equipped with new printing machinery. The Franco-Prussian War and siege of Paris were obvious opportunities to attract new readers, always more excited by stories about war rather than peace.

The Crawfords had half an hour to pack before the last train left the city. Immediately after they had crossed the Seine, Emily heard a terrific explosion. Looking back, she saw that the railway bridge had been blown up. There were many other hazards on the journey, as Emily was to report for several English and American newspapers. After being detained for many days on the line, another train ran into theirs killing eighteen passengers. She and her husband were spared only because, minutes before the crash, they had moved to the rear of the train. Once they arrived at Bordeaux they had to sleep on the kitchen floor of a small inn, along with scores of other fugitives. These bare boards were their only bed for many months, 'but in the midst of these privations the gallant couple found magnificent opportunities for observation of the stirring events of those times'.[11]

According to a contemporary observer, Mrs Crawford always maintained that 'there was nothing that a man can do that a woman cannot do also', and set out to prove this in 1889 by climbing the as yet unfinished Eiffel Tower by the dizzy spiral staircase which was barred to the public from the second floor onwards.

She was aware of the twin requirements of resourcefulness and good contacts. Through her friendship with the veteran French politician, M. Thiers, she had access to his inner Cabinet and, at a time when not a single English journal was connected with Paris by private wire, telegraphed her news to England. She displayed even greater initiative when covering the Versailles conference in May 1871, sitting from seven in the morning until midnight in the front row of the *loge grillée* to which she had been admitted by special favour. She was allowed neither to move nor to take any notes, but she had a remarkable memory and as soon as it was over she left for Paris, sat up all night writing and sent her despatch to London on the first mail. Hers was the first full account of the debate and defeat of the French Government to reach the English press. Meanwhile, her husband and numerous other correspondents, unable to gain admittance, could only mingle with the crowd and write 'colour' pieces about the state of popular feeling.

No less revealing of her stamina was an incident when, during the night of a terrifying thunderstorm, she rushed out of a grand state ball in her satin shoes and delicate gown to find the streets deserted of cabs. She ran to the telegraph office, where she despatched her dripping description of the ball to London.

Emily Crawford, who was a firm believer in radical and republican principles, declined several offers to file for conservative papers and wrote chiefly for the *Daily News* and *The Tribune* in New York. Of her two children, one became a journalist who achieved some fame as a special correspondent from Lisbon during the Dom Pedro crisis.

By 1870, a handful of women had proved their ability to write descriptive copy, which, crucially, helped sell newspapers. When offered more demanding work, women such as Mrs Crawford, during the siege of Paris, also proved that they could not only rise to the occasion but could even score over their male rivals. One of the main difficulties women faced at this time was in being taken seriously, especially in matters of politics or economics. Several novelists wrote under a male pseudonym to overcome this hurdle. Mrs Lynn Linton was, of course, well aware of the prejudice, but, as she explained in *Sowing the Wind*, one distinct advantage offered by women journalists was that they were cheaper and more ready to turn their hand to the most humble tasks – from book reviewing to descriptions of garden fêtes – looked down upon by men. Even so, they were never offered political work. Given that bylines did not exist, the newspaper audience might not have known, but for the personalised flavour of the report, whether the author was a man or a woman. But few serious reports were written by women since most senior journalistic appointments in the latter half of the nineteenth century went to men with high academic qualifications, usually university graduates and often from Oxbridge. This was not only because they were expected to write better and have a sounder grasp of political and economic realities, but also because they would have better contacts in the political and administrative worlds. Naturally women, however great their intellect, could not compete until universities opened their doors, which they did only in the mid-1870s.

2

The First Professionals

'Many of the most skilful pens in England were handled by ladies.'
MR GROSER OF THE NATIONAL ASSOCIATION OF JOURNALISTS

One of the major changes affecting the work of a foreign correspondent in the 1870s was the development of technology. Shortly after the middle of the nineteenth century, telegraphic links had been established to the Black Sea and to India; in England, the *Daily News* was the first to grasp the significance of using telegraphy in speeding up, if curtailing, the length of its correspondents' reports during the Franco-Prussian War. One unwelcome by-product of the open telegraph wire, however, was that foreign powers could control and censor what was transmitted. Sending a long letter by post at least had the merit of being private. As telegraphy was expensive, too, the long and highly personalised letter did not immediately disappear. The increase in circulation experienced by most newspapers from the 1860s onwards went some way towards paying for this, but there were other demands for money to be invested in new machinery.

The foreign correspondent was also hit by the temporary lull in wars on European soil after the Franco-Prussian War. While there was still plenty of scope for the diplomatic correspondent, the war correspondent had to travel much further for a story: South Africa, the Balkans or the North-West Frontier being the main theatres of war in the 1880s and 1890s. For English readers, events in South Africa were of primary importance.

When Lady Florence Dixie, aged twenty-six and married to Sir Beaumont Dixie, a weak-minded aristocrat whose gambling habits threatened his family with ruin, was invited in 1881 by the *Morning Post* to report on the situation in the Transvaal, most commentators considered the episode a stunt. It was assumed that the Zulu Wars would be but a brief flurry and many of the popular papers were quick to scorn one whom they imagined was a brainless socialite who would have trouble keeping up with the troops.

As a rival paper commented:

The action of our contemporary in choosing not only a feminine 'special', but one with a handle to her name is most enterprising and spirited and for the time it can point with pride to its originality, but it must not expect to be left alone in this particular respect.... Even now, we understand, overtures are being made to a Countess in her own right to proceed to the Transvaal; and we may mention, with reserve, that it is on the cards that an aristocratic contemporary of ours has hopes of securing a real dowager duchess to represent it at the seat of war, though, for the present, she is holding out on the question of ladies'-maids, of which, she declares, she must take four.... '

But such lampooning had little effect on Florence Dixie, the youngest child of the Marquess of Queensberry, who was a most forceful and courageous woman. She had a twin brother, James, and had always determined to do whatever he could. She was an eccentric, a tomboy and a fearless and experienced horsewoman who had spent much of her childhood racing ponies across Scottish moors, but at the same time a romantic who loved poetry. When the *Morning Post* commissioned her to go to South Africa, it did so partly on the strength of one travel book, *Across Patagonia*, which had been published with great acclaim the year before, but also on account of her personality. She had travelled to Patagonia a scant three years after her marriage and two months after the birth of her son because she needed to satisfy a craving for adventure; she wanted to be the first white woman in Patagonia. Then, on discovering her husband's enormous gambling debts and speculative losses resulting in debilitating mortgages and diminished rents, she realised some action was needed to save the family home for the children's sake. One way of responding to the situation was to go to South Africa as a war correspondent, even if it meant leaving her two small sons and a comfortably grand home. Goaded by the knowledge that her twin, James, had been posted to South Africa on active service, she went to see Sir Evelyn Wood, overall commander of British troops, before his departure for the Cape and extracted from him a promise that he would get her husband a commission in the Irregular Force and provide her with a tent and some rations at his headquarters, if she could get an appointment as a newspaper correspondent.

'I cannot say more than that I will live with the troops, go out with them when they fight and in fact never shirk danger, fatigue or trouble,' Florence wrote to Thomas Bowles, the founder of *Vanity Fair* and a friend. 'All I ask is for my expenses to be paid out there and back ... and the few horses I shall require bought.'[2] Bowles mentioned her to Algernon Borthwick, editor of the *Morning Post*, who recognised her talent and energy and, in agreeing to her proposal, made her the first woman appointed and sent by a newspaper to cover a foreign war.

However, Florence suffered a major disappointment by the time she and Beau arrived in Cape Town as it appeared, following the enormous British defeat at Majuba Hill, that the war in the Transvaal was virtually finished. They immediately acquired some horses and made for the front with all haste, but on the way learned that a peace treaty had been signed. When Florence left Britain her native imperialism had led her to believe that she would be reporting important victories. She could not hide her overwhelming regret at the prospect of 'this wretched peace', that the war might be over before she saw any fighting. 'Will England disgrace her name and prestige by allowing herself to be defeated on all sides by men of this sort; and then calmly, without one victory, come to terms?' she wrote in her first despatch from Durban.[3] The report, in the form of a highly personal letter in florid style, went on: 'Can we hide from ourselves, much as we would like it, that if we do this we are disgraced? Shame must indeed fill the heart of all Englishmen if such things are to be.'

One day on her journey to the front, Florence was invited to dine with Sir Evelyn Wood, thus renewing the contact made in London and now eased by the fact that James was a captain in the 15th Hussars, based at Signals Hill near Newcastle. By May, Florence and her party had made it to Majuba Mountain, 'the melancholy spot which must ever remain as a sad memory to England', passing on the way only the remnants of war – a pathetic procession of wounded men crawling south amid the numerous skulls and skeletons of man and beast.

At the start of her trip, local papers had been quick to jibe at Lady Florence, the war reporter, but it was not long before they were impressed by her experienced and graceful horsemanship and her evident disregard for being covered in mud, or crossing narrow, dangerous streams or crevices. Her energy was impressive by any standards as she could ride all day and then climb a mountain in the evening. As she told her readers in England, when they once came across a hotel in a shanty town, after a long day's travelling, there was only one bed available which the proprietors offered to Florence. But she was insistent on sleeping outside, with her saddle as support, as

much to share the life of the men in the party as because she believed
the hotel room was infested with fleas. Sleeping outside did not worry
her at all; in fact, she preferred it. She soon won the respect of her
travelling companions; she never complained about the hard ground
or the leaky tents, the lack of privacy or washing facilities, but, most
important of all, she could hold her whisky. She was usually up at
dawn grooming the horses, leaving her husband to attend to the
cooking unless they were eating at the officers' mess. On one occasion
the convoy prepared for what they thought was a group of Boers about
to attack. When the opposition turned out to be harmless Kaffirs and
a herd of cattle, Florence was visibly downcast.

Florence always insisted in her reports for the *Morning Post* that it
was her duty to reflect as faithfully as possible public feeling in South
Africa. 'It is not for me to judge, neither is it my place to send home
accounts of what never took place. My object is to speak the truth of
what I have seen and faithfully recount what I have heard from
authentic and undeniable sources.'[4] Sometimes, lazily, she bolstered
her pieces by quoting chunks from local papers, such as the *Natal
Mercury.* But her articles lack any real political depth. Some were
nothing more than forceful statements of her own opinion, with no
reporting at all. For example, when she attacked the British Prime
Minister, Mr Gladstone, she none the less couched it in terms of
representing public opinion 'out here':

Mr Gladstone and his government have given in to the Boers on all points . . .
much blood will be spilt and the whole tragedy that must come sooner or
later will be the result of the cowardly bungling of the present government. . . .
England has forsaken her countrymen in their time of need and many will
try to forget that they are Englishmen – most are ashamed of the very name.[5]

But she did manage to capture the atmosphere of the final battles
in spite of not having watched them, and her physical descriptions
gave a vivid picture of an intensely beautiful country laid waste by the
devastation of war. She was evidently struck by the vastness of the
country and its kraals, 'the great sweep of hill and valley, so beautiful
in its wild, untamed grandeur'. Little wonder then that her highly
personalised reports were often more popular and interesting than the
dry Reuters telegrams on which newspapers depended.

When Florence and Beau finally arrived at Government House,
Pretoria, Florence's appearance caused something of a stir. She may
have been unbothered by her dirty, crumpled and mud-caked clothes

but others were not. New ones had to be ordered.* In Pretoria, Florence was to report on the Transvaal Royal Commission and, although she found the everyday bureaucracy rather boring, discovered one considerable advantage of being a woman reporter in 1880: she could walk aimlessly along the verandah and sit under a window to listen to the proceedings without any of the commissioners having the courage to remove her.

Pretoria, theoretically the end of her assignment, was far from being all work. At Government House she could indulge in lawn tennis, picnics, polo matches and grand dinners. But something about the South African story had ensnared Florence's imagination and she was propelled by an overpowering impulse to understand for herself and to convey what she discovered to others in England.

When she left home, it is doubtful if she had more than a rudimentary grasp of the prevailing situation or the history of South Africa. She undertook the commission for money but also to escape her empty lifestyle. Now she began to study books on Zulu history and, as she recognised a cause and fought for it doggedly, an enthusiasm informed her writing from then on.

The spark which ignited this enthusiasm was a deputation of 300 African tribesmen to Government House. After her meeting with the chiefs, she asked to visit the Zulu king, Cetshwayo, then in exile. Such a visit was not possible immediately, Florence was told, because of a threatened Zulu uprising. However, by August she received permission and went immediately, even though this meant travelling in the rainy season. To reach Zululand, she put up with three days of incessant and drenching rain accompanied by cold so extreme that it killed 100 oxen.

She was, in an aristocratically patronising way, immediately struck by the Zulus she met. 'The Zulu is transformed from ugly Kaffir into a black adonis. I found in them an intelligence and quickness of perception which was truly surprising and their good nature and high spirits never for a moment flagged.' She made an immediate appeal on behalf of King Cetshwayo: 'England, who pretends to love justice, would do well to accord some of its mercy to a man who has appealed to the country for justice and who, if he were reinstated, would, I am

---

* It is interesting to compare her disinterest in clothes with that of her male colleague and friend Thomas Bowles. In 1866, he concluded that a suitable campaign outfit should include:

long, soft, Mexican boots up to the thigh – thick cloth breeches, short jacket – blanket with a hole in the middle – waterproof sheet ditto – blanket for a saddle cloth to be folded in four – two horseshoes – field glass – revolver (in a belt round the waist) – curry comb – paper and pencil and a tooth brush – with perhaps one spare flannel shirt.[6]

convinced, become her firmest ally and friend.'[7] She was, from the first, emotionally involved in his cause.

Although there was pity in Florence's eloquent defence of King Cetshwayo – his plight troubled her – at the same time she was moved by vague aspirations for the independence of the Zulu people and by the King's 'nobility of soul, dignity and courage in misfortune'. They spoke through an interpreter, but she was aware of all his nuances of voice and did not shirk eye contact. The King was already known to the British public, but Florence's pleas on his behalf helped to create the desired effect. By September, he learned that he was to go to England, where he found himself a hugely popular figure. He had lunch with Queen Victoria at Osborne on the Isle of Wight and was then offered by the Colonial Office generous terms to restore him to his kingdom. But the complex situation in Zululand could never allow for their implementation and, in February 1884, Cetshwayo was found dead, possibly poisoned.

Lady Florence Dixie's assignment formally ended on her return to England in early 1882. But so impressed was the *Morning Post* editor by her courage, her reporting and the distances she had covered that he was happy to offer her further commissions, telling her that she did credit to any of the war correspondents of the British press.

For the next twenty-five years Florence regularly aired her views in print and for payment, writing on a wide variety of subjects. She covered the Irish problem, women's position, Scottish home rule, married women and the vote, vegetarianism, sex and health. Her most deeply felt subject was the inferiority of women in late-nineteenth-century society and, with more than a hefty nod to her own situation, she could write convincingly of the enormous importance of giving girls exactly the same education and training as boys. In an article full of polemic and rhetoric, she examined the causes that made women's position one of

degradation, injustice and wasted existence. Men have had a great advantage through athletic training and women were kept weak . . . the laws that have established such a state of things are utterly at variance with nature and, as such, unnatural and unjust. The key to helping women is education, physical and moral.

She issued a rallying-cry to women to realise what their true position should be and fight for it: 'At present woman's worst enemy is herself . . . born of ignorance and brought up in ignorance.'[8]

By the time these articles appeared women journalists were a recog-

nised phenomenon. There were dozens of new journals and periodicals being launched and some magazines were starting to give
careers advice for girls who wanted to write for a newspaper. Journalism was one of the few professions which had always welcomed
women writers and was much more open than almost any other career
women were now considering. Much depended of course on the
individual proprietor or editor, one of the most sympathetic of whom
was W. T. Stead. Stead, whose non-conformist upbringing in the
provinces helped to guard him from the prejudices affecting so many
of his contemporaries, took over as editor of the *Pall Mall Gazette* in
1883. He had left school at fourteen and rose quickly to become editor
of the *Northern Echo* in Darlington aged only twenty-two, from 1871
to 1880. Stead learnt his journalism through experience, and had a
sincere belief in the need for women's suffrage and complete social
equality. Not only did he believe women were more dependable as
journalists than men, but he was also prepared to pay them at the
same rate as men, an unusually enlightened attitude at the time. He felt
that women writers had a particular talent for interviewing, perhaps
because of their ingrained capacity to listen, and instituted a regular
and ground-breaking series of interviews in the *Pall Mall Gazette*. He
employed as chief interviewer a woman called Hulda Friedrichs, whose
interviews were wide-ranging, lengthy and light.* Hulda Friedrichs worked for Stead for twelve years before becoming editor of the
Westminster Budget. Most of the women who worked for Stead were
journalists (rather than reporters), to whom he was always ready to
offer advice as well as practical support of a non-judgmental nature.

In 1886, Lady Colin Campbell emerged from one of the longest,
most sensational divorce cases in British history. As the trial showed,
Lady Colin was never the sort of woman to be content with the limited
role offered her by upper-class Victorian society. After the trial she
became an outcast and moved into a dreary, first-floor flat in Pimlico,
determined in future to live off her writing. She had already published
one novel and a second was to appear in 1889. But in her attempt to
create a new world for herself, Stead played an important role by
giving her commissions for the *Pall Mall Gazette*. She also contributed
to the *Saturday Review*, the *World* and *Ladies' Field*. In 1894, she and

---

* In 1899, an article appeared in the *Englishwoman* which said: 'Interviewing is another branch
of lady journalism – one that calls into play that subtle tact, which is the secret cause of many
successful careers; a quick sympathy and keen powers of observation are also necessary qualities
in a good interviewer.'⁹ Jerome K. Jerome gave up interviewing after he found himself always
interrupting and arguing with his interviewees.

a friend founded a short-lived weekly magazine to compete with the
Saturday Review called the *Realm*.

Mrs Virginia Crawford was another notorious divorcée to whom
Stead offered work. She was ostracised from society after her husband
divorced her citing, on her admission, Sir Charles Dilke, for adultery.
Maria Ternan, the spirited and energetic sister of Charles Dickens's
mistress, Nelly Ternan, similarly discovered that journalism offered
one of the few avenues open to divorced women with intellectual
capabilities and the need to earn a living. After ten years of less than
happy marriage she opted for an independent life, enrolling first at
the newly established Slade School of Fine Art in London. She then
moved to Rome, a city where a single woman could live unmolested,
working both as artist and journalist. Her friendship with Tom Trollope, brother of the novelist Anthony Trollope, gave her her first
chance as he asked her to deputise for him on the London *Standard*
whenever he and his wife travelled, which was often. Maria loved the
work and soon developed her own network of contacts as well as a
good grasp of the language. She was, like Jessie White, not afraid to
travel all over the country discovering information, or pursuing her
other interest, painting.

In 1886, on Tom's retirement, the *Standard* asked her to take over
his job permanently. For twelve years, until she was sixty-one, she
wrote a series of articles about life in Rome, including the usual staples
of cholera scares, the Pope's health, the eruption of Mount Etna or a
strike of cabmen and carters. Mostly these were signed 'from our
correspondent', but, occasionally, especially if the subject were
fashion, they were 'by a lady'. Dull though many of the *Standard*
pieces were, Maria's spirit, sparked by a restless and imaginative
nature, is best seen in a book she wrote about a journey to Tunisia in
1881. Called *Some Old Letters from North Africa* and published under
her married name, Maria Taylor, it evokes not merely the smells,
curious customs, dress and political system of late-nineteenth-century
Tunisia, but also tells of a harem she was taken into 'which no King
or Prince in Europe would have been allowed to enter.... This was
one of the few occasions in one's life in which it was a distinct advantage
to belong to the weaker sex.'[10] The climax of the book is her description
of a journey to, and overnight stay in, the Holy City of Kairouan. 'I
believe I am the only Christian woman who has done so hitherto,' she
wrote in great excitement. 'The only guarantee for my safety in the
fanatical city lay in the fact that (my escort) was well known and highly
respected among the tribes and was supposed by many of the Arabs

to be a Mohamedan, though in fact he was not so.' She admitted that her motivation was not merely to explore the ancient Arab city, and buy carpets in the thriving market, both of which she did, but to do something that no one else had ever done and to see things with her own eyes. 'I resolved to accept the attendant risk.'[11] The contrast between this and her routine journalism is evidence that the latter was undertaken to pay the bills but was not sufficient outlet for her obvious creative talents and curiosity. Travel to outlandish places could sweep away many of the barriers hedging women's lives in England at the time and satisfy many of their cravings.

Marie Belloc, sister of Hilaire and daughter of Bessie Parkes Belloc, who founded the *Englishwoman's Journal*, was another who found herself the recipient of Stead's kindness and trust for a different reason: none of her immediate family believed in her ability to write and tried to persuade her to give up. Stead gave her an opportunity by sending her to Paris to report on the Exhibition of 1889 at a salary of £10 a week. Although not employed by the *Pall Mall Gazette*, she often wrote for them after this, continuing to produce both books and articles after her marriage in 1896 to Frederick Lowndes, of *The Times*.

Thus women working for newspapers, although not legion, could, by the 1880s, no longer be ignored. In 1885, the National Association of Journalists (NAJ) had been set up by working provincial 'pressmen' to agitate, among other things, for better pay and conditions. Three years later, there was a demand for women journalists to be admitted, a demand of which Mr W. Collins, a London member, approved. Trying to scotch fears of women taking away men's work, he insisted that there was no need to fear competition from women as they were simply not able to

work in the Law Courts from ten in the morning and then go to the House of Commons and work till four or five in the next morning... but of late there had arisen various branches of press work which afforded excellent employment for lady journalists. There had, for instance, been a great increase in the publication of fashion articles in the newspapers and fashion journals and ladies' papers had multiplied very rapidly all of which required the services of ladies possessed of aptitude for journalistic work.

Mr Collins went on to cite Mrs Emily Crawford in Paris as a very desirable member of the Association. Mr Groser of Plymouth argued that 'many of the most skilful pens in England were handled by ladies, who', he thought, 'should be able to enter any profession where they could earn a legitimate livelihood.' The motion was adopted.[12] Thus women were accepted on the basis of equal membership with men, as long as their work experience was equal to that of the male applicants.

However, by 1890, the NAJ was transformed into the Institute of Journalists, which had a Royal Charter but no control over standards of entry into the profession. This change signalled a loss of power by the reporters to the journalists, editors and proprietors and so, in 1907, the reporters broke away to form the National Union of Journalists (NUJ). In 1894, some of those women – few of them reporters – working in a heavily male-dominated profession and feeling the need for a separate identity and protective organisation, formed The Society of Women Journalists. But by 1900, this organisation boasted a mere sixty-nine members and by 1905 236, when the 1891 Census listed 661 women as 'authors, editors, journalists'.[13] Presumably, most of the latter remained independent operators.

3

The Remarkable Flora Shaw

'It is sufficient gratification for most ladies to see themselves in print.'
UNNAMED EDITOR TO GRACE BENEDICTA STUART

When Flora Shaw visited Gibraltar in the winter of 1886, she took with her only a cool offer from W. T. Stead that he would publish any articles from there which he considered worthwhile. But he could give her no definite promises of a commission.

Yet, on 28 June 1887, her first article appeared in the *Pall Mall Gazette*. Before the trip she had read assiduously everything she could about the geography, history and geology of Gibraltar. From Gibraltar she went to Morocco, her first visit to Africa, and from there too managed to write authoritative stories which Stead, who found her an accurate reporter with a sound grasp of the facts, published in the *Pall Mall Gazette*.

Flora had gone to Gibraltar to accompany some elderly friends of her parents, the Younghusbands, in need of a warmer climate. She was confident that she could produce articles editors would want to pay her for and that this would cover the cost of her trip. But she was, after all, an unknown and an amateur. Nevertheless, after just a few months she returned with a small reputation established as a serious and capable journalist. She had worked hard during her stay in Gibraltar trying to understand every aspect of the colony's life. She became fascinated by the Jewish quarter and insisted on being taken to a synagogue service even though her guide told her that this was a special privilege since women were 'spared the burden of prayer'. Her curiosity to discover all of Gibraltar also led her to the cottage being used to detain Zebehr Pasha, the former ruler of huge tracts of Sudan, then a political prisoner exiled from Egypt by the British army of occupation, and she scored a minor reporting success through her interviews with him. He was eventually released and sent back to Cairo, which he believed had come about because of Flora Shaw's articles, several of which appeared in the *Contemporary Review* in the autumn of 1887. The *Pall Mall Gazette* now gave her more work on a variety of topics and other newspapers and magazines wanted her to write for them as well.

Flora Shaw was born into an upper-middle-class military family with colonial connections at Kimmage, near Dublin in Ireland. Her French mother, Marie de Fontaine, was daughter of a governor of Mauritius and, as Flora often stayed with her mother's sister in France, she soon became fluent in French. But her mother, who gave birth to fourteen children, died when Flora was just thirteen, leaving her as head of a sizable household. Only her father's remarriage in 1872 freed her from the perpetual restraints of this role. Flora had always been a good story-teller and, provoked by the need to make money, she now began writing stories for children which earned her good reviews but little cash. However, *Aunt Judy's Magazine*, a popular children's magazine, commissioned her to write some serials and stories, most of which were based on her childhood adventures with her aunt in France. She became further immersed in the world of print when she went to live with the Brackenbury family in Waltham Abbey as tutor to the children. Charles Brackenbury had been *The Times*'s correspondent during the Franco-Prussian War and he encouraged Flora's interest in foreign affairs. However, her drive for closer involvement led her to try working among the poor children in East London slums, but the poverty she now witnessed at first hand could never be fully alleviated by the well-meaning attentions of women such as herself. As she read and studied all the available literature on colonial affairs, she came to believe that emigration offered the only real solution to over-population in London and that she could help propel this solution better through her writing than through charity work. At the age of thirty and with no formal education, Flora took a room in a cottage in the Surrey countryside so that she could think and write alone.

It was here that she met the journalist and novelist George Meredith, who in turn introduced her both to Robert Louis Stevenson and, more significantly for her, W. T. Stead, just before her trip to Gibraltar.

For someone of Flora's background, the idea of travelling to exotic outposts of empire alone was not inconceivable but none the less posed some difficulties. It was made possible for her only because of her relationship with the Younghusbands, a sad and lonely couple who had not only been close family friends of the Shaws but whose son Charles had proposed marriage to Flora, which she had declined. None the less, after Charles's death in India, his parents continued to look on Flora with the warmth and affection of a daughter-in-law manquée rather than as a companion. When they invited her to travel with them first to Gibraltar and now Cairo, she accepted immediately. Once abroad, she knew that she could lead as independent a lifestyle as she needed for her work, which she viewed as her mission. This time, she went as the accredited correspondent of two papers, the *Pall Mall Gazette* and the *Manchester Guardian*, whose editor, C. P. Scott, was an admirer of her reporting skills. Flora was fascinated by the history of Egypt both before and after the British occupation in 1882 and again read everything she could find on the subject. Once arrived, she was well placed to attend all the official receptions and fashionable parties, where she made useful contacts, and she could behave as a tourist, wandering around and discovering the feel of the place for herself. Her fluent French was a great asset, but she also spoke some Italian and had managed to acquire a smattering of Arabic. She rarely took notes during an interview as she thought that this would interrupt the flow of conversation, but relied on her retentive memory when she wrote up her account immediately afterwards. Zebehr Pasha was helpful in effecting introductions for her to Muslim life in Cairo, but meeting the local correspondent of *The Times* was, she decided, a priority.

Charles Moberly Bell, *The Times*'s special correspondent in Egypt since 1865, proved an invaluable friend to Flora. He was on good terms with Sir Evelyn Baring, the British Administrator, and was happy to share not only this contact with his new rival but also all his knowledge and information. Baring was delighted with the introduction, hoping that he might use Flora to steer the *Pall Mall Gazette* towards what he considered a more rational, less emotional view of Egyptian politics. He met her at least twice a week for background briefings and offered her a great deal of written material – including some confidential despatches – to help her understand the situation. It was largely thanks to Baring's tuition that she acquired such a sound grasp of Egyptian finance, particularly where it concerned the construction of the Suez Canal.

Just how ready would Baring and Moberly Bell have been to help a male colleague? Flora may not have been one to flaunt her femininity but as her first biographer Enid, the daughter of Moberly Bell, wrote in

1947, '[her] pleasant, open manner and her readiness to be instructed inspired an eagerness to instruct. There are, after all, very few men who are not susceptible to the flattery of being given the whole attention of a charming and intelligent young woman.'[1] She was, by all accounts, elegant, attractive, forthright and dignified. She always wore black. 'Shaw's gender strategies show a double consciousness,' according to the authors of a new study on Shaw:

While following the code of feminine decorum in her social life, she deliberately undertook professional work not considered suitable for a woman. She studied political economy, developed sharp analytical skills, and through journalism moved into male public space.... As a woman she understood that her journalism provided the means she otherwise did not have for influencing public affairs.[2]

Or, as an earlier commentator described: 'Public men, however cautious, found it surprisingly easy to give away official information to such an interviewer.'[3]

Flora's work in Egypt, which included not only articles about finance and politics but also some more traditionally female stories such as writing about a home for freed women slaves, soon brought her to the attention of Britain's Colonial Office. They helped her enormously with her research and began to look on her as an authority on Mediterranean problems once it became clear she could write on complicated subjects with rare lucidity. In 1889, the *Manchester Guardian* asked her to represent them at a Brussels conference intending to eliminate slave trading. She was not merely the only woman attending the conference but, after just a few days' intensive research and preparation, probably one of the best-informed reporters.

There was no shortage of work for Flora now with regular commissions from both the *Manchester Guardian* and the *Pall Mall Gazette*. But, increasingly, she felt her views deviating from those of C. P. Scott, who opposed imperial expansion and the use of the colonies for emigration, but converging more closely with those of Stead, whom she admired and respected enormously. While praising Flora's judgment and clarity of vision, Stead none the less once commented that she failed the test of being a 'supremely good journalist because she did not bring a lump to the throat'.[4] Flora, of course, never intended to do this, other than in her children's stories. She was a persuasive communicator, but her appeal was to the intellect.

In 1890, Moberly Bell was recalled to London as assistant manager of *The Times* and promptly invited Flora to meet George Buckle, the editor, a meeting which has become clouded by mythology. Mr Buckle agreed, in theory, to Flora writing articles for him, but said that in practice there was no space, either in the office or the newspaper. Flora argued powerfully in favour of the need for *The Times* to print more colonial stories, but Buckle countered that there was no one competent on the staff to write them. She then suggested asking the Colonial Office for the name of someone suitable. Sir Robert Herbert of the Colonial Office told Buckle that he knew of no man suitable but he did know a woman and *The Times* could not possibly do better than engage her.

At all events *The Times* could not offer her a formal job since employing a woman was expressly forbidden, although Bell admitted to her, 'If you were a man, you would be Colonial Editor of *The Times* to-morrow.'[5] But it was agreed that she could write a regular fortnightly column, beginning in May 1890. This was to be unsigned; she had no desk and no office space allotted her so she took to sitting on the floor. In spite of these restrictions, her articles on Egyptian finance were read avidly by the chief proprietor, John Walter, who commented that they were exactly what the paper had long wanted. Still Buckle and Moberly Bell felt that they could not admit that the articles were a woman's work.

After a year of this, and having undertaken to fund the education of some nieces and nephews, Flora was painfully aware of the need to earn money on a secure basis. Yet she found herself in an awkward position with both Scott and Stead now questioning whether her work for them was compatible with her work for *The Times*, yet *The Times* was obstinately refusing to give her a full-time position. This situation threatened to turn into a crisis for her when she fell ill early in 1892. Moberly Bell's decision to send her on a tour of South Africa in the winter of 1892 not only restored her health but also transformed her career.

Like Florence Dixie before her, Flora investigated the diamond mines of Kimberley and the gold mines at Johannesburg and crowned these with an interview in Pretoria with President Kruger. Unlike Florence she travelled alone, unaccompanied by a man, and undertook a far more rigorous examination of South African society than Florence was commissioned to provide. Her reports were written in the form of letters and gave readers in London 'an overwhelming sense of first-hand knowledge about conditions of mining, prospects for agriculture and problems of labour, white and black. She reiterated the theme that South Africa was "nothing less than a continent in the making".'[6] Her letters were greeted with huge enthusiasm by Moberly Bell, who told her: 'I think I can honestly say that nothing of the sort published in the paper since March 1890 (when I arrived) has created such comment... never have I so often heard the term "remarkable" applied so generally and by so many different sorts of people as to your letters.'[7] Moberly Bell now asked her to sail on to Australia, New Zealand and Canada, where she was to talk to as many people as possible from politicians to farm labourers and factory managers.

She was away for over a year and this time her reports had earned her not merely acclaim but also title. Her appointment as colonial editor in 1892 made her the first woman on the permanent staff of *The Times*. By July 1893, she was being paid £66 13s 4d per month, far more than other women journalists at the time.[8] Flora had had to fight for her position and eventually won through by dint of hard work and powerfully arguing her corner and because three male editors recognised the intellectual vigour of her arguments, which shone through her work. C. P. Scott, while disagreeing with some of her views, was an early convert to women's talents as reporters of serious news. His wife, Rachel Cook, was one of the first female recruits to journalism from university and, although there were some who snidely attributed her success at the *Guardian* to her husband's position, she helped persuade him to make use of the intellectual capacities of several female contributors.

Two years after Flora's appointment at *The Times*, the London district of the Institute of Journalists elevated two women to its committee: Catherine Drew, an Irishwoman, and Grace Benedicta Stuart, the more feminist of the pair. Catherine Drew began writing on architectural matters as her father and brother were both architects and she became assistant editor of *The Irish Builder*, but when she came to London in 1871 the *Belfast News Letter* invited her to write a women's interest column – an innovation in 1871 – which they called the 'Ladies' Letter'. In 1895, she lectured on 'Journalism' at a gentlemen's club.

Grace Stuart might object to her inclusion in this book as she once protested angrily to *The Journalist* about the patronising attitude of the phrase 'lady journalist'. She wrote on a variety of topics for several magazines, but her knowledge of French and German politics and literature, fostered by relatives and residence on the continent, led to her often being sent by the *Daily News* as its special correspondent to report on Germany. Grace liked to tell a story about one editor who, even though he had commissioned a series of articles from her, then

declined to pay for them on the grounds that it was 'sufficient gratification for most ladies to see themselves in print'.

'Perhaps for your usual lady contributors; not for a member of the
Institute,' Grace replied. The editor then handed her the cheque and
proposed a second series of articles. 'I am afraid you must apply to
some of the ladies who like to see themselves in print for the second
series,' was Grace's riposte.[9]

It was not only London newspaper editors who were beginning to
see the advantages of employing women reporters. In February 1894,
the proprietors of the *Dundee Weekly News* and *Dundee Courier* sent
two women on a round-the-world trip 'for the purpose of gleaning
information as to the conditions of female labour in various countries'.[10] Their brief was to examine the operations of the numerous
missions, religious and charitable, and to study the different forms of
social life in these countries, in which it was assumed Dundee's women
readers would have a particular interest. Among the countries on their
itinerary were Egypt, Arabia, India, China, Japan, Canada and the
United States.

On 17 April 1897, Turkey declared war on Greece in answer to the
Greek Government's attempts to annex Crete. The war was short but,
as the major European powers were involved in blockading the island,
reporters soon flocked to the scene. Among these was Stephen Crane,
American author of *The Red Badge of Courage*. Accompanying him
was a woman with the assumed name of Cora Taylor, who posed as
his wife. Cora Taylor was a handsome woman, some five or six years
older than Crane, with a mane of golden hair and a dubious past.
When she first met Crane she was proprietor of a hotel and nightclub,
romantically called the Hotel de Dreme, and still married to her last
husband, an Englishman called Captain Donald William Stewart,
who refused to divorce her. This prevented Taylor and Crane from
marrying, but Crane always maintained that they were man and wife.

Cora had no experience of journalism, but, on meeting Crane, had
a sudden revelation that writing was to become her profession. In spite
of her total lack of experience of either wars or journalism, she was
hired by the *New York Journal* as their so-called 'first and only woman
war correspondent'. A despatch signed pseudonymously 'Imogene
Carter', which she wrote for them on 26 April 1897, was headed, 'War
seen through a woman's eyes'. She wrote of how she had seen the
Greek volunteers 'amid flowers and tears', and that she had seen the
wounded come in 'hastily and clumsily bandaged, unwashed and wan
with rolling eyes that expressed that vague desire of the human mind

in pain for an impossible meadow wherein rest and sleep and peace
come suddenly when one lies in the grass'. It was a moving piece; but,
as Crane scholars have pointed out, the tell-tale phrase 'impossible
meadow' suggests that its author was probably Crane himself.[11]

Richard Harding Davis, a fellow American and Crane's rival covering the war for *The Times*, had a low opinion of Cora. 'She is a
commonplace, dull woman, old enough to have been his mother and
with dyed yellow hair,' he wrote piously to his mother.[12] Such a
prejudiced comment may tell us more about the rivalry between the
two American male reporters than about Cora herself, who, whatever
her other faults, was certainly not dull. Davis, in short, did not approve
of women covering wars. During the battle of Valestino, Cora found
herself under heavy fire with shells screaming all around her; the
soldiers expressed amazement at the presence of a woman during the
fighting, all of which she wrote in her article which the *New York
Journal* headed, 'Imogene Carter's pen picture of the fighting at Valestino'. Perhaps Davis thought that she offered unfair competition. In
another letter home, describing the battle, he wrote that Crane was

never near the front, but don't say I said so. He would have come but he had
a toothache which kept him in bed. It was hard luck but on the other hand if
he had not had that woman with him he would have been with us and not at
Volo and could have seen the show, toothache or no toothache.[13]

A year later in 1898, Flora Shaw, who was by then a renowned
journalist of forty-five, was preparing to undertake a journey potentially far more hazardous than any war. For some time there had been
many tales in the popular press about wild behaviour in the mining
camps of the Yukon: gambling, drinking, prostitution and murder all
featured. In 1897, Moberly Bell asked Flora to make a second tour of
Canada so that *The Times* could have its own reports, or letters, on
the situation. On 10 August 1898, the following short paragraph,
headed anonymously 'from our own correspondent' and datelined
Dawson City, 23 July, was printed: 'I reached Klondike this morning
completing the journey from London in thirty-one days. This time
included four days' accidental delay on the rivers.'

The journey, although concluded with record speed, had been
momentous. After Flora's transatlantic crossing, she had taken the still
new Canadian Pacific Railway to Vancouver and had then transferred
to a steamboat for the 900-mile voyage north to Skagway. After landing
at this primitive port, on disputed territory, Flora still had another 600
miles to go, a journey which involved crossing mountains by a steep

track through a high pass before she could pick up a steamer to Dawson. She walked the major part of this trail carrying a light pack while her baggage and provisions were taken by pack train. 'The walking was at times very heavy. If rain had lately fallen it was through pure swamp. Sometimes ankle deep, sometimes knee deep, one was forced to wade along the valley bottoms, the summer sun beating hot upon your head.'[14]

Flora walked some twenty miles every day, encountering numerous other natural hazards along the way. When one day she saw what she thought was a hotel, it turned out to be little more than a smelly hut and she preferred to sleep outdoors. Finding herself the only woman on the steamer, which she eventually picked up from Lake Bennet, gave her some dubious privileges. 'The captain, who has to be up all night, allows me to share his cabin, sleeping in it when he is not there. I have borrowed a galvanised iron pail and a tin basin from the cook and can just manage to shut myself in so as to secure privacy for a wash.' Once she arrived at Dawson, her energy undiminished, Flora walked about talking to everyone she could, collecting information which she would write up at night and send back to The Times. Her long letters were given several columns, so important were they considered. Once she had formed a full impression of the Klondikers' situation, her reports gave the lie to the version which the popular press had put out, namely the bad behaviour of the Klondike miners. Flora began to sympathise with the men, who, she said, 'remain on the whole orderly and law-abiding', and she criticised the Canadian Government not only for its bad laws but also because 'the officers through whom they are administered are corrupt'.[15]

After this journey Flora proposed further trips to The Times: 'When I slept soundly on shingle in the Klondike the men told me that I ought to try sand, which they say, is the hardest thing there is. Obviously the desert is required to complete my experience.' However, the idea was turned down.

In 1902, she married Sir Frederick (later Lord) Lugard, High Commissioner of Northern Nigeria, six years her junior and with a view of Empire every bit as lofty as her own. Upon marriage, Flora gave up full-time journalism, but then felt doubly isolated in the humid malarial climate of Nigeria: no longer did she have contact with the London political scene, and she saw her new husband only at meal-times. She became low, depressed and irritable until, after little more than a few months, she was sent home on doctor's orders.

For another twenty-five years Flora worked on her husband's behalf, helping to advance his career as colonial administrator for which he was awarded a peerage, but also continuing with her own prodigious output of articles on imperial affairs. In all, she produced more than five hundred articles on economic and political issues in the colonies. In 1914, with the outbreak of the First World War, Lugard returned to Nigeria while she remained in England, helping Belgian refugees who were fleeing from the German advance. For this work she was created a Dame of the Order of the British Empire in her own right. Dame Flora fought shy of having her biography written, arguing that any woman who had not borne a child was a failure and her life not worth recording.[16]

Flora Shaw had blazed a hugely significant trail for other women reporters. Not only had she shown that women could write convincingly on international politics and economics, but she had also responded well to being sent abroad, living in unpleasant, dangerous conditions among a group of men and sending back vivid and perceptive reports. Most importantly, she was paid a fair rate for the job, a crucial step on the way to women's professionalism and self-esteem. Many women journalists at this time often faced severe difficulties in making ends meet, partly because of the sporadic nature of payment for their articles but also because of the crucial social obligation on them to preserve an outward appearance of being respectable. This imposition deserves to be emphasised because the job itself was still deemed unladylike by popular opinion. In 1898, an article on 'Bachelor Women' suggested that if women did not conform in matters of dress, they were likely to be ostracised socially since the attractions of a job which made easy relations with the opposite sex more possible, at the same time diminished their attractions to more conventional sectors of society.[17] As Grace Benedicta Stuart insisted, women were no longer prepared to write for the glory of it.

Shaw had always dressed immaculately, to the extent that when she had to appear in court in 1897 to explain her personal involvement in supporting Cecil Rhodes at the time of the Jameson Raid, she received a letter afterwards from Sir Herbert Stephen commenting: 'I observed with some amusement the mild astonishment of the ingenuous reporters at discovering that you were not a frump.'[18] She was no frump but no feminist either. Her career was pursued not for the benefit of other women who might be following in her footsteps, but because she believed implacably in the mission to spread colonial benefits and because of her need for financial independence to support herself, her sister and her sister's family.

Few of the women who succeeded in journalism up to this time had much sympathy for the parallel women's rights movements, but preferred to believe that if they had succeeded, others could too. Whereas Emily Crawford could continue her career after marriage because she was working alongside her husband and the domestic routine was hardly interrupted, Flora Shaw retired when she married as she did not believe her new status was compatible with a career. After all, the prevailing ethos of the period was that to have any career, other than marriage, was abnormal.

4

The New Woman

'We already have our lady.'
UNNAMED EDITOR TO EMILLIE PEACOCKE

The new century began with the explosion of a conflict that had been simmering for two-and-a-half centuries, together with a radical reappraisal of Britain's role in it. In fact, the Boers had declared war on 11 October 1899 and the British confidently expected any fighting to be over by Christmas. But this last, great imperial war, involving not merely Boers and British but black Africans too, took two-and-three-quarter years, cost thousands of lives and was, in the end, a most humiliating débâcle.

While the men could fight, what opportunities were there for women who felt strongly about the cause? Lady Sarah Isabella Augusta Wilson, the sixth daughter of the Duke and Duchess of Marlborough, was born in 1865 and for many years led the typical life of an English-woman of her class. Married to Captain Gordon Wilson, aide-de-camp to Colonel Baden-Powell, she was an excellent horsewoman, but was also widely read with a defined intellectual taste and natural ability as a writer.

At the outbreak of the South African War, Captain and Lady Sarah Wilson were travelling in South Africa and arrived at Mafeking just before the siege began. Captain Wilson, believing that the campaign would be very short and his wife in no particular danger, raised no objection to her making arrangements to represent the *Daily Mail* at the front. In any case, Lady Sarah had no intention of going home; she had come largely to escape the boredom of 'the season' and the tension of the situation fascinated her. But she was aware that,

Colonel Baden-Powell did not look upon my presence with great favour, neither did he order me to leave and I had a sort of presentiment that I might be useful, considering that there were but three trained nurses in the Victoria Hospital to minister to the needs of the whole garrison.[1]

Before the siege got under way, Lady Sarah was sent away for her own safety to the Kalahari Desert, but she was restless for news and soon became involved in sending important despatches to and from Mafeking. She discovered that the centre of official despatches and news was Vryburg, then in Boer hands. At first, she travelled there under the escort of a Dutch colonist, who, at critical moments, spoke to her as his sister; together they passed through sixty miles of rough country without being stopped by Boers and stayed in the town for some time. Buoyed by her success and safe return, and having been able to gain a fair idea of the progress of the war, she sent a messenger with the information she had discovered to Mafeking, where the garrison had received no news of the events of the war in the rest of the country. Then she repeated the escapade. But her activities became known to the Boers and, on trying to leave Vryburg after a visit, she was captured by Snyman, the Boer leader. She was detained for several days before being exchanged for a horse thief.

She spent the following eight months in beleaguered Mafeking, which enabled her to report, both in despatches for newspapers and later for a book, on daily life in the garrison during the last few months of the siege. Her description of incidents, 'by their diversity, give to the non-technical reader a better idea of what a siege has been and may be under modern conditions of warfare than any quantity of military reports,' was how a rival newspaper, the *Morning Post*, praised her work while reviewing her book.[2]

Inside Mafeking, Lady Sarah became an immensely popular figure. Young, spirited and extremely pretty, she soon established a 'bomb-proof' shelter to which staff officers fought for an invitation. This elegant shelter, 'a white-panelled hole carved out of the red soil of Mafeking',[3] boasted walls decorated with African spears from the Matabele War, a large Union Jack and a roof with small portholes. But although she was sending regular reports to the *Daily Mail*, she was offended when, on 2 January 1900, Baden-Powell's staff and other correspondents were invited to a large dinner from which she, without doubt because she was a woman, was pointedly excluded.

The *Daily Mail* was aware of the importance to their readership of their Lady correspondent, who was enduring the incessant noise of bullets and shells with little sleep and food. When the siege was over, they published an impressive picture of her, wearing a large, black hat topped with a multiplicity of plumes and bows; rather ridiculous in the circumstances. On 23 May, they printed her report, sub-headed 'Stirring Description by Lady Sarah Wilson'. She wrote a long piece with some personal details: 'I made my way to the hospital nearby and had a most disagreeable walk under a hail of bullets from two sides which luckily were all aimed high.' She then calmly set out the facts as she had heard them, but included several 'literary' descriptions of the way the light affected the scenery and the cacophony shattered the atmosphere.

Rudyard Kipling wrote that, during the campaign to relieve Mafeking, war correspondents had to have 'the constitution of a bullock, the digestion of an ostrich and an infinite adaptability to all circumstances',[4] a description which may well have fitted Lady Sarah Wilson. But on her return to England she became involved in philanthropic activities and society gatherings and, aside from a book of South African memories, she abandoned professional writing. When her husband was killed in the Great War, she embraced nursing fulltime, but such was her Mafeking fame that she was, for many years, Vice-President of the Society of Women Journalists. She died in London on 22 October 1929.

The 'career' of Lady Sarah Wilson is a clear indication that the life of a foreign correspondent, and particularly a war correspondent, was considered to be one of glamour and excitement. Although both Flora Shaw and Florence Dixie needed the money, Lady Sarah undertook her brief stint of reporting for purely quixotic and imperialistic motives.

Neither was Emily Hobhouse a professional reporter, but rather a single woman whose grave conscience was aroused in a different direction by events in South Africa. She spent her early life in Cornwall, in a provincial parsonage, where she was occupied with parish work far removed from major events of world history. But, on moving to London in her thirties, she found herself passionately motivated by reports of the situation in South Africa and, particularly, by the neglect and disease faced by thousands of women and children forced into concentration camps. Her reaction was instinctive, emotional and non-political; some might add feminine. Within a few years she had helped found 'The South African Women and Children Distress Fund' and, on 7 December 1900, this unworldly forty-year-old sailed 'quite alone and second class'[5] for The Cape as the Fund's representative, hoping to distribute food and clothes.

On arrival, she consulted with many influential leaders including Sir Alfred Milner, the High Commissioner, to whom she had been given an introduction as a friend of the family. After a long interview with Milner, he arranged for her to visit some of the camps. The misery, overcrowding, lack of food and insanitary conditions shocked her profoundly. 'It is such a wholesale cruelty and one of which England must be ashamed,' she wrote to her aunt, Lady Hobhouse. 'The whole system is a mistake and has placed thousands physically unfit in conditions of life which they have not strength to endure.'[6] Emily, well knowing that the small amount of charity she had to distribute could do little to help, was now determined to make the British public understand the inhumanity being practised in its name and to force it to address the issue of what should be done with these people.

She returned to England in the spring of 1901 and immediately sent a detailed report to the Secretary of State for War outlining the gross mismanagement in the camps and the appalling death toll. After an exchange of letters and meetings with government ministers seemed to be making little progress, extracts from her letters home were printed in newspapers and circulated in Parliament. The publicity caused a huge stir and shortly thereafter most of the recommendations in her report for the running of the camps were adopted by the Government.

None the less, much work remained and Emily was bitter when the British Government turned down her application to return to South Africa. In October 1901, she determined to go in any case, but was arrested on arrival at Cape Town and deported. She spent 1902 writing a book about her experiences and the following year managed to return to South Africa. From this time on her health deteriorated and although she continued to fight wherever she saw injustice, her fame rested on her courageous investigation and report in 1901.

That women were clearly developing an appetite both for news reporting and reading about news was recognised by Alfred Harmsworth (later Viscount Northcliffe). In 1903, he founded the *Daily Mirror* as a paper to be produced by women for women, believing that women could attract large audiences partly by their ability to elicit intimate details in interviews with well-known personalities. As Margaret Bateson, a journalist, had written a few years earlier: 'Women have a natural ability, superior to men, to make work livelier and more interesting. Perhaps she may be too colloquial but she imports into her work conversational ideas and the conversational method.' According to Bateson, the newspapers of thirty years before had failed to cater to women's interest because, 'The average woman, when reading them, felt almost as much an outsider as a young girl does who finds herself at table with a party of old gentlemen ... the editor of today, fulfilling the primary duty of enlarging his paper's circulation, takes care not to forget women.'[7]

Northcliffe's experiment, undertaken for commercial reasons rather than through any chivalrous notion of supporting women's talents, was short-lived, partly because the women, though industrious and willing, lacked experience or knowledge of the world. After a few weeks the 'women only' idea failed. Meanwhile, although the number of women writing for a wide variety of newspapers and journals was steadily increasing, the often unpleasant routine grind of becoming a reporter for a Fleet Street daily was still deemed a highly unsuitable female occupation. Fleet Street was considered a dangerously degrading environment whose inhabitants, once there, sank ever deeper into its mire and mud. A woman reporter in Fleet Street was bound to lose her femininity, so the argument ran, 'because she saw and knew and said things which were outside the range of the domestic woman's knowledge. They are despised, perhaps a little feared ... by men as well as women. And that is apt to make (them) bitter and rather hard .... You can't wash off the stains of Fleet Street,' wrote Sir Philip Gibbs in his 1909 novel, *The Street of Adventure*.

The heroine of that novel, the beautiful and talented Miss Katherine Halstead, was based on a young girl born into a journalistic family who came to Fleet Street just as the Edwardian era dawned. For Emillie Marshall, Fleet Street 'loomed ahead ... not as a street paved in gold ... but ankle deep in slush from the horse-borne traffic of its narrow roadway, but still siren of all streets'.[8]

That a newspaper office should hold only excitement rather than fear for Emillie was not unanticipated. Her maternal grandfather, father, several uncles and innumerable close family friends all worked on daily papers and Emillie frequently visited her father in his office. John Marshall, formerly chief reporter of the *Northern Echo* in Darlington, took over the editorial chair of the paper soon after Emillie's birth. It was the newspaper W. T. Stead had edited before he moved on to Fleet Street. Emillie's training in journalism consisted largely in being allowed to absorb the constant newspaper gossip which filled her house. 'The grown-up talk ... and what good talk it was, was mainly of newspapers and newspaper men and of the then all absorbing highly controversial world of politics,' wrote Emillie in an unpublished autobiography.[9] In addition, she had access to all the latest sensational 'New Woman' novels of the day as the *Northern Echo* appeared on every publisher's list and the latest fiction, however avant-garde, poured into her home throughout the year. She had another, unusual link with reporting: her grandparents had been friends of Jessie White Mario over a long stretch of years, since they had been thrown together in active conspiratorial work for the United Italy Movement. Emillie Marshall herself was in correspondence with and in awe of Jessie.

But there was also a more practical aspect to Emillie's training for journalism. At fifteen, she spent a year acquiring a thorough knowledge of Pitman's shorthand, after which her father devised a unique training plan, giving her a good working knowledge of the editorial, business and production side of a morning newspaper. Such technical training for a woman was entirely new and was to be crucial later; '... it enabled me to arrive at quick decisions and abide by them, qualities much appreciated by the responsible printer always working against the clock.' Her day was as often filled with routine sub-editing as with exciting reporting and no exception was made for the fact of her gender or her age – just sixteen. Her hours of duty six days a week did not end until after 3 a.m. when the GPO closed down and the flow of inky flimsies in their orange envelopes ceased for a while. Emillie explained the intoxication she felt:

Six times a week in the dawn I mounted my new safety bicycle to make the journey along the Great North Road to my home, filled with pride in the thought that I was already in possession of the news of the day that the people still asleep in the dark, silent houses would not learn till breakfast time.[10]

This girl reporter on her bicycle at dawn was not merely a novelty in the towns and villages of County Durham, but a sensation.

She was ambitious, too, and studied diligently the discreet advertisements offering editorial vacancies. In 1902, greatly daring, she ventured to reply to one small advertisement for a sub-editor on a provincial morning newspaper, giving a statement of her qualifications and experience but not mentioning her age, which was not yet twenty. A few days later she received the following polite reply from the *Yorkshire Daily Observer*:

Dear Madam, We regret we cannot possibly see our way to offering a position as sub-editor to a Lady. The difficulties and objections are in our view insuperable. ... But we do wish to say this, that, on the merits, your application is perhaps the best of a great number, about a hundred, which we received in reply to our advertisement.[11]

However, soon after this, Emillie's father left the *Echo* because of his long-standing opposition to the South African War; abandonment of a pro-Boer attitude was essential if the withdrawal of advertising was to be stemmed and the decline in circulation halted. The Marshalls were desolate, but moved to start a new life in London. A year later, John Marshall died aged forty-seven, exhausted and worn down.

Emillie now began the depressing trail of newspaper offices, offering her services as a highly trained sub-editor and verbatim reporter. She was good-looking, with long, fair hair and well turned out; her introductions were excellent. But editors were sceptical of her ability. 'Some of them mildly expostulated "but we already have our lady" with a half apologetic air of finality,' Emillie recalled. 'This, as I soon discovered, was literally the case. In the first years of the century a solitary woman staff reporter, ill paid and overworked, was regarded as all that was requisite and seemly in the way of feminine infiltration.'

Although women had, for the previous sixty years, been making considerable inroads into newspaper life, this was almost exclusively as journalists and not, according to the narrow sense in which the term was then used, as reporters. There was, in the Victorian era, a much clearer distinction between the term 'journalist' and 'reporter'; the former included those who submitted articles to newspapers or magazines, reviewed books, criticised plays or composed leaders or opinion pieces. Even foreign or war correspondents were referred to as 'journalists'. Reporters, however, covered small local or national events such as fires or accidents, as well as the routine reporting of births, marriages and deaths.

According to Fred Hunter, author of an authoritative study of women in journalism,

Until the 1890s, one could be sure that the reporter was someone who had left school by the age of fourteen, if not earlier, and had been apprenticed or indentured to a local small-town newspaper to learn the basics of his trade. From there he could go on to a newspaper in a larger town, or provincial city, then, if he was lucky, on to Fleet Street and a national newspaper in London.[12]

The journalist, however, was altogether a superior being. Frequently, male journalists, after the 1860s, had a university degree. It was from the ranks of the latter, not the reporters' room, that editors were drawn. Not surprisingly, in view of such limitations, only a handful of women determined to become reporters. Emillie Marshall was one of the very few who made it as a London reporter.

She was offered her first job on Fleet Street working for the *Church Family Newspaper*. Although this involved mostly sub-editing during the week, on Sundays she was given the chance to report sermons verbatim from St Paul's Cathedral, Westminster Abbey, the Temple Church or St Margaret's Westminster and others. In a way it was surprising that the *Church Family Newspaper* should offer a job to a female reporter since the position of women in regard to a National Church Synod for the Anglican Church was at the time a highly contentious question. None the less, the paper sent her to report on the meetings of the Joint Convocations of Canterbury and York at which a lively discussion of the subject was anticipated. But there was trouble for Emillie at the very outset of the proceedings. A woman at the press table was a strange sight and someone immediately questioned its propriety. 'The prolocutor, I think that was the correct title of the official who was instructed by the Archbishop to inform me that I could not be allowed to remain, courteously explained that no woman had ever attended such a gathering.'[13]

Awed though she was by her surroundings, Emillie stood her ground, vigorously protesting that she was not there as a woman but as the invited representative of the British press. She claimed the right under these circumstances to carry out her professional duties, asserting that either she was allowed to report the occasion or it would not be mentioned at all in her paper. Eventually, an ingenious if rather ludicrous compromise was reached. She was permitted to remain and report the proceedings as fully as she wished but only on condition that a red silken cord ('not mere common red tape') was placed between her and the assemblage denoting that she was, officially, non-existent. But Emillie had won an important battle.

Such frissons gave Emillie's reporting life an extra piquancy, but otherwise her work for the *Church Family Newspaper* was rather dull. Moreover, her weekly wage of thirty shillings did not stretch very far. When Emillie heard that W. T. Stead was to start a new daily paper, she immediately went to visit him in her lunch break, calling without an appointment in her excitement. Stead, 'a tall, wild, untidy but still impressive looking figure', burst out of his editorial room to greet her. 'The Northern Echo girl!' he exclaimed. 'I have been waiting for you. You got my wire?'[14]

It mattered little that Emillie had never received any telegram. Stead engaged her on the spot as a reporter on the forthcoming new paper at a starting salary of 'two pounds ten shillings – riches indeed'. He also offered her the exciting assurance that she would, before long, be the first woman reporter in the Press Gallery of the House of Commons.

Stead's project for a morning newspaper had been germinating for almost ten years, but the start-up capital he finally gathered was obviously inadequate and his plans for circulation and production both unworkable. *The Daily Paper* had no publishing office of its own but made use of various offices in and around Fleet Street during their hours of inactivity. The experiment died after five frenetic weeks and Emillie had to look for a new job. By the end of March 1904, and within a week of the demise of Stead's paper, she had been engaged by the infant *Daily Express*, started in 1900 by Cyril Arthur Pearson, as its first woman reporter on the regular staff.

Her arrival was a cause of some embarrassment for the young news editor, who was not inclined to let his new member of staff share the reporters' room, large though it was, with a dozen men. Instead, he suggested that she set up on the top floor of the building, sharing an office with a staid, married woman fashion editor who pasted up pages for the various provincial papers in the same group. After a few days, however, the news editor concluded that the arrangement was too inconvenient for him; any reporter must be accessible to the news department.

Most of the stories Emillie was asked to report would today be categorised as human interest. Politics, fashion and sport were all in another sphere; women, food and weather were her province. One day she might be sent to report on the death of a pet lemur who had been used by the theatrical profession for many years; on another occasion to interview a philanthropic lady about her scheme for sending pauper children to Canada, where they could be trained as farmers.

Stunt stories, too, which it was hoped would boost circulation, fell to Emillie to organise. But it was her tenacity in securing an advance copy of a new edition of *Hymns Ancient and Modern* – a target of investigative journalism unimaginable today – which drew her to the proprietor's attention. The paper's male reporters had all, so far, failed as the publishers and ecclesiastical editorial committee resolutely refused to co-operate. Emillie's ruse, which won her a full set of advance proofs, was to dissemble to an aged church organist that she was checking on behalf of devout churchwomen, deeply concerned as to the fate of hymns that meant so much to them. This scoop resulted in a page-one exclusive for the *Daily Express* the following day. Sir Arthur Pearson, the son of a clergyman, was particularly keen to know the details of the new hymn book and was, therefore, delighted with the success of his new reporter, who was awarded a rise of £1 a week.

In 1905, there was wild excitement in Fleet Street at the prospect of a new liberal daily, the *Tribune*, launched by a young Bolton mill owner, Franklin Thomasson, to carry out his father's last wishes. The *Tribune* appealed to Emillie not so much because of the handsome increase in salary it offered her – the *Express* matched this when it heard – but because it appeared as a great adventure in journalism. This newspaper 'of high hopes and rich promise'[15] was transmuted into the *Daily Rag* in Sir Philip Gibbs's novel.

Through her work at the *Tribune*, Emillie came to know many of the pioneer fighters for women's rights, such as the Rt Hon. Margaret Bondfield MP, the first woman Privy Councillor, and Mary Macarthur, the young Scottish trade unionist. Emillie occasionally posed as Mary's secretary for the sake of a story. The contacts forged by these two friendships included an introduction to the Labour leader, Keir Hardie, and to several other Labour intellectuals and politicians. These were important links for Emillie as the 'new journalism' had an almost insatiable appetite for women's stories, whether they concerned suffrage, organised labour or women battling for greater freedom from domesticity, all critical issues in the early years of the century. 'The woman's story had to be something piquant calculated to attract the attention of men as well as women readers,' Emillie had been taught.[16]

Emillie's personal friendship with Keir Hardie soon gave her a world scoop for the *Tribune*. Hardie told her of a women's suffrage resolution he was introducing in the House of Commons. His offer to get her tickets for the Ladies' Gallery was naturally accepted and it was thus as a result of her eye-witness account that one of the best-known incidents in the women's suffragette movement became known. As the night wore on, tension mounted when it became clear that the member then standing, Mr Sam Evans – a fierce opponent of women's suffrage – was determined to talk out the resolution. Suddenly the other women in the Ladies' Gallery tore off their disguising veils, ripped away the grille in front of them and threw a shower of 'Votes for Women' leaflets on to the heads of the MPs below. The Gallery was quickly cleared, but Emillie was the only press representative of either gender to have witnessed the scene, which she spent much of the night writing, to be quoted all over the world.

The disturbance was, she insisted in her report, 'a spontaneous thing'. She wrote sympathetically of how the women, 'however mistaken their tactics may be, have thrown themselves heart and soul into the agitation of votes for women', yet had to listen to themselves 'lightly dismissed in a few cursory and unsympathetic words' by Evans. They were only stirred to action under extreme provocation, Emillie explained. As they were forcibly escorted out, one policeman to every woman, Emillie noticed that one of the famous white flags, bearing the words 'Votes for Women', was left fluttering in the Gallery.[17]

Although Emillie's feminist and left-wing friends often tried to persuade her to work full-time campaigning for them, she was fully inspired and fulfilled by journalism, which was, for her, sufficient 'cause'. It gave her not only excitement but also a purpose. She was using the skills she had developed in the best way she could to effect changes in society.

In spite of all the enthusiasm, the *Tribune* never managed to generate sufficient advertising revenue and after two years the paper had to close. The future was grim for most of the journalists thrown so precipitately out of work. Many, however, did find new assignments and Emillie herself became the first woman reporter to be engaged on the *Daily Mail*. This new paper had a good record for employing women albeit mostly in an executive capacity; Mrs Mary Howarth, editor of the Woman's Page, was a redoubtable figure, and the exploits of Lady Sarah Wilson, its first woman war correspondent, were proudly related.

Less than six years after Emillie's initial arrival in Fleet Street, she no longer encountered any restrictions to her having free access to the shabby reporters' room of the *Daily Mail* with its ink-bespattered, sloping-top desk and motley collection of broken chairs and stools. There were never enough of these in the busy hours of the early evening, but the reporting staff 'must have been a chivalrous band for there always seemed to be a chair available when I returned to write my stories for the night'.[18] As the *Daily Mail*'s only woman reporter, Emillie's beat included the rampaging suffragette movement, whose militant members now often had recourse to raids on political meetings and persistent attacks on Cabinet ministers. Emillie was well served by her contacts within the movement, who trusted her.

Her day regularly began at dawn with the release of hunger strikers from Holloway Gaol. As the militant antics of the suffragettes were often front-page news, Emillie was in great demand and made a name for herself. But she was not given exclusively women's interest stories;

if she was the first reporter on duty when a particularly gruesome murder needed to be covered, she would be despatched regardless of her sex.

But the exciting days at the *Mail* lasted little more than a year for Emillie. In 1909, she met a reporter on the *Express*, Herbert Peacocke. When they decided to marry, they had to do so secretly, knowing well how a married woman reporter would be frowned upon. 'It was thought', Emillie wrote later, 'that she would be unreliable and that home affairs would interfere with her powers of concentration on the newspaper's interests. It was, moreover, an unforgivable breach of convention for members of rival staffs to marry.'[19] Emillie and Herbert's wedding was as small as possible, with only one of their Fleet Street colleagues in attendance and virtually no presents; afterwards they moved quietly into a flat in Chancery Lane. Some thirty years after Herbert's death, Emillie wrote:

If my own experience is anything to go by I would say that marriage between understanding journalists who know at first hand of the stress, struggle, the temperamental no less than the economic ups and downs of its exacting calling, can go a long way towards ensuring true happiness over the years.[20]

Once the *Daily Mail* learned of Emillie's marriage to an *Express* man, it concluded, 'reluctantly I believe', that she had to move to a journal that was not in direct competition. The prospect of working on a weekly periodical once more was not a stimulating one for Emillie, who loved the excitement and tension of a daily newspaper. But there was much goodwill towards Emillie and she was offered freelance work reporting for the *Observer* and for *The Times*, particularly on articles relating to women's increasing roles in public life. Emillie had had the good fortune to work at three newspapers all of which had been prepared to ride roughshod over many outdated conventions concerning women. None the less, she still had to labour under many disadvantages, principally the regular practice of paying male reporters as much as double that received by their female colleagues.

One of the greatest difficulties faced by a woman at the time was the style of dress she was expected to wear. Long trailing skirts often finishing in a dip or tail at the back invariably sloshed around in the mud of Fleet Street. Emillie herself recalled wearing high buttoned or laced boots possibly with patent leather vamps, felt hats in winter, flower-trimmed straw boaters in summer, 'speared to the hair by two stiletto-like hat pins with murderous protruding points. . . . This ludicrous fashion of dressing continued far into the stormy days of militant suffrage street battles, a sore handicap to news-gathering.'[21] She was also aggrieved by restaurants which served 'ladies' portions' for no reduction in price, assuming that a polite woman merely toyed with her meal when she ate in public. Emily had a good appetite and liked her food, so much so that she wrote an article proclaiming 'Women's right to eat'. More significantly, office lunches and dinners were invariably wholly masculine affairs 'even at such modern, go-ahead establishments as the *Daily Mail* and *Daily Express*'.

The reason given was usually custom. There never had been women attending such functions because no women worked on the papers and when there was only one woman it was considered embarrassing for her to be on her own in a roomful of men. It was partly to counter the one-sidedness of the public dinner table that several women's clubs were started in those years. Although the Press Club itself still barred its doors to women members, Emillie was not alone among her peers in realising how great was the disadvantage faced by women reporters because they could not meet the right people socially at clubs who could give them background or even a lead on a story.

It was several years before women had a choice of clubs to attend,* but among those started in the early twentieth century, the most famous included the Pioneer, the Writers of the Strand and the Lyceum, in a commanding clubhouse in Piccadilly itself. All these counted many women journalists among their members.

Emillie continued to write for a variety of outlets until 1915, when her daughter Marguerite was born and she gave up full-time work. After the war she went back to the *Daily Express* and was soon appointed editor of the Woman's Page of the *Sunday Express*, a post which she held until 1928. She commented wryly in her old age that if she had been offered to edit the despised Woman's Page, the Cinderella of journalism, when she first arrived in Fleet Street, 'my journalistic ambitions would have been sadly dampened. But now, in the 1920s, the control of the new Woman's Department was from every point of view a tempting proposition, calling for a new appraisal as opportunities for women were opening on every front.'[22] She found the work hugely satisfying, but in 1928, after a long association with the *Express*, was persuaded to move to the *Daily Telegraph*, then enduring a period of comparative decline, where she established a modern woman's department.

* The Women's Press Club was founded in 1943; see chapter 11.

In a small way, women of talent were beginning to be able to set their own terms as the story of Madame Clemence Rose, foreign correspondent, illustrates.

Clemence Rose was 'an exceedingly clever woman',[23] fluent in several languages, with a firm grasp of all the nuances of the then burning Austro-Hungarian question, as well as Balkan affairs and some excellent contacts, some of which included royalty. After moving to Rome for the *Morning Post* at the turn of the century, she developed a nervous disease which threatened to render her bald within a few weeks and, accordingly, asked the paper for permission to move to Vienna, where the more bracing climate would, so her surgeon advised, help to shake off the malarial fever which was complicating her nervous illness. In her mid-fifties and dependent on work, she asked rather pathetically, 'If I went to Vienna could I continue to be of any use to the paper?'[24] She pointed out to the editor that several other London newspapers were planning to send their Rome correspondents to Vienna and that, with her knowledge of German and understanding of the Italian side of the Austrian question, the paper should not suffer. Madame Rose became the Vienna correspondent of the *Morning Post*, staying for a time in the apartment of *The Times*'s correspondent, Wickham Steed. Steed, some twenty years younger than Clemence, had formed a close friendship with her years previously, but their relationship was more that of a foster mother and son than anything more romantic.

Not long after this move, Madame Rose made an even bolder suggestion. Steed had built up a reputation for being the best of *The Times*'s correspondents, but, in 1909, his relations with his newspaper became strained and he considered resigning. According to an internal memorandum at the *Morning Post*, which was hoping to win him over, both Moberly Bell and Lord Northcliffe were actively engaged in persuading him to stay. Madame Rose proposed that she and Steed should go to Paris as joint correspondents. 'Such a combination would put the *Morning Post* in front of every other paper for its Paris correspondence and would moreover be a nasty knock for *The Times*', the *Morning Post* memorandum continued. 'On every ground except that of expense' – the additional cost of hiring Steed was put at £1,500 a year – 'the arrangement would be a most desirable one and in the long run the expense would probably justify itself in the increased attractiveness and prestige of the paper.' Steed, however, remained with *The Times*, becoming foreign editor in 1914 and editor from 1919 to 1922. When he returned to England, Madame Rose followed, acting as hostess for him when he entertained important foreign visitors at his flat in Holland Park.

One other woman reporter who managed to establish herself in Fleet Street in the early years of the century worked under a man's name. Ada Jones was a good-looking woman who took the pen-name, John Keith Prothero – known to her friends as Keith. In 1911, this prolific 'lady journalist' attracted the attention of Cecil Chesterton, younger brother of G.K., who not only wooed her for many years but also employed her on the weekly magazine he started that year with Hilaire Belloc, first called the *Eye-Witness*, later the *New Witness*.

From about 1915 onwards Ada Jones ran the office. Then, when Cecil Chesterton was passed fit enough to enlist, Ada agreed at last to marry him in 1917. But the marriage lasted only a few months as Cecil died in France after enduring a twelve-mile march from Ypres while already severely ill. After Cecil's death, Ada decided that she could no longer take charge of the office but continued to write for other newspapers. Her most notable piece of reportage was a series of articles she wrote originally for a Sunday newspaper but later turned into a book about the life of London's destitute women and prostitutes. *In Darkest London*[25] is an account of Ada's time among London's outcast women. To research the book, she donned shabby clothes and, for several days and nights, walked around with nothing but a brown paper package containing a toothbrush and nightdress. For her first night the Salvation Army shelter in Hackney took her in. On other nights she went with little or no sleep, endured bitter cold that made her cry, and by day learned to sell matches or scrub stone steps before she could afford to eat. True reporter that she was, she wrote of nothing that she had not personally seen and felt, but she backed up the entire work with myriad statistics as well as a wide variety of interviews. It was a story no man could have written, overlaid with deep sympathy for the prostitutes she encountered whose work she recognised as 'the result of the will to live: they are unable to keep themselves in any other manner'.[26] When she revealed the disgusting conditions forced upon women who had fallen on bad times, she knew that she was describing a world about which her audience knew nothing: 'I had experienced actual physical privations which women of the middle class may weep over but cannot comprehend.' She nursed the hope that her crusading and vivid reports would 'awaken public opinion to the shameful inadequacy of public lodging-houses for women'.[27]

Emillie Peacocke died on 27 January 1964, aged eighty, after sixty years in Fleet Street at a variety of newspapers, during which time she had witnessed profound changes in the employment of women in journalism generally, but especially as reporters. As she, Ada Jones, Clemence Rose and one or two others like them had proved, there were no stories women were afraid to tackle, however dangerous, demeaning or demanding of intellectual rigour. Male editors were being freed to make use of the talent.

5

War and its Aftermath

'I have had but one loyalty, one faith and that was the liberation of the poor and oppressed.'
AGNES SMEDLEY

When the Archduke Franz Ferdinand, heir to the throne of Austria-Hungary, was assassinated at Sarajevo in 1914, Europe held its breath, but not for long. The shots fired by the Serbian student, Gavrilo Princip, were soon to plunge much of the world into one of the most devastating wars yet experienced. British newspaper editors did not, however, rush to send their new army of women reporters to cover events at the front line. In fact, they encountered major difficulties sending any correspondents at all to report the news.

'The war correspondent of 1914–1918 was ... a sort of glorious disseminator of official military propaganda,' wrote Wilbur Forrest, the correspondent for United Press International (UPI).[1] 'The critical correspondent was outflanked, decimated, routed,' he added in his memoirs. Following the introduction of the Defence of the Realm Act (1914), British war correspondents found themselves used to promote the official line and gagged as never before.

In 1916, a Department of Information was created which became, two years later, the Ministry of Information. This was headed by Lord Beaverbrook and drew upon the services of the editors of *The Times*, the *Daily Express*, the *Daily Mail*, the *Evening Post* and the *News Chronicle* as well as the managing director of Reuters, Sir Roderick Jones, knighted in 1917 for his efforts at the Department. As a result, the war correspondent was left with less freedom of action than ever.

Emillie Peacocke was seconded to this organisation in the last years of the war. Her brief was to write feature articles on the role of British women in wartime 'to impress neutral nations with the fine spirit, courage and capability of our resourceful womenfolk'.[2] She recognised that she had now been transmuted from reporter to civil servant, but it was a role she adopted cheerfully, motivated by patriotism.

Thus British newspapers appeared to accept government strictures which prevented them from publishing anything which could be construed as helping the enemy. At the same time, the proprietors, well recognising how war sells products, naturally wanted to send their own special correspondents to cover the hostilities. Lord Kitchener, who had a long-standing and deep-seated mistrust of all reporters, determined from the outset to prevent their going. Lord Northcliffe thought that the most acceptable type of correspondent in the circumstances would be a sportsman, an accomplished rider who might therefore appeal to the cavalry officers. As Phillip Knightley recounts,

Accordingly he ordered the Sporting Editor of the *Daily Mail* to buy a horse and report at the War Office. The War Office told the editor that there were no immediate plans to accredit war correspondents and sent him off to exercise his horse in Hyde Park, where he met five or six other prospective correspondents doing the same thing.[3]

Given an atmosphere of virtually total acquiescence in censorship, the behaviour of Emily Hobhouse, veteran scourge of the Boer War, appears particularly courageous. Emily, imbued with an intense hatred of all war, was immediately roused by the suffering and cruelty she now saw unfolding to use all her energies to promote peace, even when this went entirely counter to public opinion. She sent an impassioned plea to C. P. Scott, editor of the *Manchester Guardian*, a paper which had at first opposed the war, where her brother Leonard was both a director and leader writer and which she knew was a newspaper read in Germany. 'The War is crushing helpless millions. These are mostly women and children,' she wrote in an open letter to 'Fellow Women throughout Europe', which she hoped he would publish. 'Daily the cry of perishing childhood comes from the frozen marshes of Poland, the snow-bound Carpathians, the wastes of Belgium, France and Serbia – a cry that pierces even the censored press, a famine-stricken cry.'[4]

In spite of the writer's fame and personal connections, Scott declined to print the emotional outcry. 'It is, I fear, useless to try and stop the war at this stage,' he told her, adding that he had 'only admiration for your spirit'.[5] Emily then told Scott that she and her fellow radicals were disillusioned with the *Guardian*, as 'it no longer gives expression to their feelings and has just become like any other paper and follows the government'.[6] In 1915, Emily decided to take more direct action and spent three months working at the Women's International Bureau in Amsterdam; then she went to Italy. While abroad she seized an opportunity to visit Germany, naïvely believing that she could act as a messenger of peace and goodwill to the German people. Escorted by German officials, she was removed to Brussels and wrote, for the *Daily News*, an account of people waiting in food queues: 'In these queues one faced a bit of war in everyday garb stripped of glory – war in its ultimate effect upon a civil population, misery and broken lives.'[7] On her return to England, her action in visiting enemy territory was publicly called into question. But she always insisted that her visit was undertaken spontaneously, purely to help non-combatants, the victims of warfare. In general, no one doubted her motivation whether propelling her to write or to act.

Throughout the First World War, potential women war correspondents had little scope to report either about front-line battles or on the atmosphere behind the lines. Many became VAD nurses in England or served in France as part of the First Aid Nursing Yeomanry (FANYs). Enid Bagnold, who had worked for the philanderer, writer and editor, Frank Harris, on his short-lived ladies' weekly journal, *Hearth and Home*, and described herself as a 'sort of' journalist at the outbreak of the war, did both and used her experiences to more potent effect than any newspaper article she might have written. Her *Diary without Dates* chronicled the human suffering in the Royal Herbert Hospital, Woolwich, and showed with devastating simplicity the price paid for winning the war. As H. G. Wells wrote, 'While the official war histories sleep the eternal sleep in the vaults of the great libraries, probably you have all read one or two such war books as Enid Bagnold's *Diary without Dates*.'[8] The price Bagnold herself paid was the sack.*

Philip Gibbs, knighted after the war, was one of the most sensitive of the male war correspondents, who, at one point, obtained an appointment as a Special Commissioner of the Red Cross to report on field hospitals in France. One or two American women, denied formal accreditation, also worked from Red Cross or similar voluntary organisation assignments. Such stalwarts included Rheta Childe Dorr, Sophie Treadwell, Mary O'Reilly, Maude Radford Warren and Sigrid Shultz, an American by birth who travelled as a child throughout

---

* For Enid Bagnold, the description of herself as a reporter was unflattering. She saw herself as a journalist, writing up interviews or book reviews, but resented covering routine events because then 'I only feel reporterish and not at all important'.

Europe and was virtually fluent in five languages. In 1919, she joined the *Chicago Tribune*'s Berlin bureau as an interpreter and general factotum. By 1926, Shultz was appointed bureau chief and wrote many stories on political and social issues.

Peggy Hull was the only woman war correspondent of the First World War to approach professional recognition, although even she was not formally accredited. Initially Peggy, an American, paid her own way to Europe because her newspaper, the *El Paso Times*, could not afford to send her. But Peggy, an attractive blonde, was confident of success because of a contact she had made previously with General Pershing, Commander-in-Chief of the American Expeditionary Force, while covering his border skirmishes with Pancho Villa. She had impressed him by her uncomplaining ability to keep up with troops on the march and to sleep on the ground covered by nothing more than a rough blanket. The story goes that, when she reported to this fearsome General's headquarters in France, he, known for his aloofness and insistence on discipline, broke into a big smile, put out two welcoming hands and said, 'Well, well Peggy! You're like a breath from home.'[9] Soon after her arrival, Peggy was producing stories about visits to army training camps and events in the lives of ordinary soldiers. These were bylined, simply, 'Peggy', appeared in the Paris and US editions of the *Chicago Tribune*, and were greeted with considerable anger and envy by the other correspondents grounded at the press division headquarters at Neufchâteau. When they protested that an unaccredited writer was being shown favours and privileges denied them, a major row ensued and Washington was even involved. Peggy stayed a little longer, protected partly by her winning ways with the troops and General Pershing, and partly by a crucial pink pass which she had managed to persuade a business representative of the *Chicago Tribune* to share with her. But eventually the army forbade this ruse and Peggy, 'a victim of her male rivals',[10] was forced to spend the rest of the war in Paris.

In 1919, the peace conference assembled at Versailles. The *News of the World* sent a woman special correspondent, Elinor Glyn, to report on the historic scene. Glyn was a bestselling novelist whose most famous book, *Three Weeks*, published in 1907, had sold five million copies by the early 1930s. Unusually for the time, she wrote quite openly of the power of sex, coining the word 'it' as a shorthand for sex appeal but framing her stories in remote or exotic locations in an attempt to avoid the criticisms of reviewers or official censorship bodies. She used her fictional skills now to write of the 'hushed hum of voices, the grave faces of the statesmen and... the only note of brightness, the helmets of the National Guard'. She described the mien of the 'five plebeian German men... one whose lips were trembling, another with his eyes close together, frowning, another with a cynical look in his eyes'.[11] The piece, though short on facts, succeeded in its flowery way to conjure up the atmosphere and character of the protagonists. Rosalind Toynbee, daughter of Professor Gilbert Murray, the brilliant Greek scholar and long-standing champion of women's rights, was assistant to the *Manchester Guardian's* representative at the conference and thus found herself occasionally involved in reporting proceedings. Since her husband was in the Middle East section of the British peace delegation, she was particularly well served by a number of good, easy contacts.

Inglorious though the war may have been for women writers, few of their male counterparts emerged with much honour either. As Europe settled into its uneasy truce, with Versailles the breeding-ground for the German myth that its armies had, in fact, never been defeated but were stabbed in the back, it soon became obvious that the tension could snap at one of a number of pressure points. Given that the other lasting legacy of the war was the revelation of women's usefulness and ability to cope with what was hitherto seen as men's work, the stage was set for a number of well-educated, independent-minded women to report on a volatile world scene.

It was not entirely coincidental, therefore, that in 1919 a journalistic diploma course was initiated at King's College, London. For many years, with no similar course of instruction or preparation in Britain, this offered one of the few routes available to women wishing to train as journalists. There they were taught a specially concocted mix of practical journalism together with some background to modern history, literature and society. The course nurtured a diversity of talents and although several of its students went on to high positions in British newspapers, others turned to purely literary pursuits, such as Stella Gibbons, author of *Cold Comfort Farm*.

Mary Stott, the veteran journalist born into a newspaper family in 1907, needed no such course because she was able to learn on the job. Like Emillie Peacocke, her mother, uncle and brother had all worked in the press – at the *Leicester Mail* – and one day, when several of the staff fell ill, she received an urgent call to go in and 'help'. Initially, she worked in the proofreaders' room, where, 'holding the copy, not marking it, for Trade Union rules would have forbidden that, I learnt a great deal about how newspapers are written and put together'.[12] Not long after, in the summer of 1925, she moved down to the reporters' room; she was eighteen. A regular routine was soon established of doing the 'calls' – visiting the police and fire station and picking up the prices in the local market. Occasionally, she would be allowed to accompany an older, male reporter to a police court case or city council meeting. But, at first, her most important task in the reporters' room was making the chief reporter's tea and writing his notes for him as he suffered from arthritic hands. It was not long before he dictated less and less and let her write most of the story herself. She did not object to the writing, but she rebelled fiercely against making the tea for all the men. 'They presented me with a petition, but I didn't give in, and we sorted it out amicably,' Mary recalls.[13] Apart from that episode, she was not conscious of any hostility to her as a woman in a man's world and believes that her life as a female cub reporter was much safer than it could be today. 'Often I would walk home alone quite late at night after a theatre or concert, without any fear of being accosted. Even my mother was not nervous for me as, my goodness!, any mother would be in similar circumstances today.'[14]

But after two short years, Mary was taken off the reporting beat and promoted to 'women's editor'. This, she says, was a cost-cutting exercise as she was not old enough to be even on the lowest rung of the union scale. But, far from being thrilled, she was distraught and returned to the reporters' room to cry, overwhelmed by a sense 'that I had lost all hope of becoming a *real* journalist, a news reporter, a drama critic, a sub-editor. And I was pretty nearly right.'[15] From then on, however, this cub woman's editor had a daily column dealing not merely with women's local issues but also with interviewing visiting celebrities. Most importantly, she managed to develop a good working relationship with the printers and stone hands, notorious for their opposition to co-operation with women whom they tried to prevent from visiting their territory. Mary built up a rapport by making herself knowledgeable about type faces and how to make up the page 'on the stone' – standing on one side of the long table in the composing room where the type-filled frames of the pages were laid out, to work with the printer on making the necessary cuts and adjustments so that everything fitted.

Rewarding though that job was, it was not the career she had mapped out for herself, but, in the 1920s, it illustrates some of the unexpected difficulties young women faced, even those, like Stott, whose families had been journalists for generations. 'Not being allowed to be a reporter was one of two awful things that happened to me in my professional life,' Mary recalled recently.[16] The other occurred several years later on the *Manchester Evening News*, when, as the paper's first woman news sub-editor, she had risen to become deputy copy taster (or assistant chief sub) yet suddenly found her name dropped from the daily list for Saturdays – when the chief sub had a day off. The editor assured her that this had nothing to do with the excellent quality of her work. 'But we have to safeguard the succession,' he told her, 'and the successor has to be a man.'[17]

Denied the opportunity of being either reporter or chief sub-editor, Mary Stott 'drifted back into women's page journalism'.[18] When she was young her brother and other men had always teased her that she would never be able to stand the pace or the foul language involved in sub-editing; she had proved them doubly wrong yet still found her way barred. She wrote in her autobiography:

I have never liked attributing virtues and vices to one sex or the other and yet I feel that, whether by nature or nurture, some women are particularly fitted for subbing. We tend to be patient and meticulous, and an essential, absolutely vital, part of subbing is checking.... And keeping one's cool when the heavens open and copy rains down from every quarter isn't unlike the ability a woman at home develops in keeping a grip when the doorbell rings as the milk boils over, the toddler demands the pot and the awful thought strikes her that her husband asked her to 'phone the garage urgently.[19]

As an active feminist, Stott had always been passionately interested in women's affairs and organisations and from 1957 to 1970 held a pivotal job as editor of the *Manchester Guardian*'s Women's Page. Under her stewardship, this page broke new ground and sparked off a number of lively debates on several topics, including one which culminated in the foundation of the National Housewives' Register.

The story of Agnes Smedley, the American radical reporter, is far removed from that of Mary Stott.* Smedley was born fifteen years before Stott, in 1892, into a poor, illiterate family in northern Missouri. Her mother took in washing, her father was frequently absent or drunk. Becoming a writer seemed a ridiculous aspiration for anyone from such an impoverished farming community, yet Agnes was imbued from an early age with a passionate desire to learn and a desperate drive to speak out for the world's poor and oppressed,

* Yet, interestingly both received important support at a crucial time in their careers from the *Manchester Guardian*.

among whom she numbered herself. Throughout her life she faced huge battles singlemindedly not only with newspaper editors, who, because of her political views, from time to time refused to commission her, and with the British and then American establishments, who came to regard her as a spy, but even with many of her closest friends, who occasionally wished she might moderate her highly individualistic outlook.

Until the age of fifteen, Agnes Smedley lived an itinerant life of great hardship as her father dragged the family across the country in the illusory hope of finding his fortune. At sixteen, shortly after her mother died, she decided to make her own life and, by 1911, had managed to spend a year as a special student at the Tempe Normal College (now Arizona State University), where she became editor of the college magazine. After a brief, disastrous marriage, she went to New York, where she immersed herself in study and political activity, writing for the *Call*, a struggling, socialist daily, and the feminist *Birth Control Review*. The second decade of the twentieth century was a time of tumultuous political thought and Agnes became deeply involved with a group of Indian nationalists, which led to her arrest in 1918 and imprisonment without trial for six months in New York's Tombs Prison. When she was released, she continued her reporting career and renewed her intense activities with the Indian movement. However, in 1919 she left for Europe and, from 1921, for the next seven years lived in Berlin with an Indian revolutionary, Virendranath Chattopadhaya, known as Chatto. Chatto fostered Agnes's revolutionary consciousness and her anti-imperialistic instincts. While living in Germany she also sharpened her writing skills and, stirred by the misery of the working classes as her raw material, wrote some moving, but clear-sighted articles which were published in the United States, chiefly by *The Nation*:

The week has witnessed looting of many shops in various parts of the city, unrest in most cities throughout the country and actual street fighting in many. Looting and rioting are regarded as so much grist to the mills of the communists and revolutionaries alike. The communists take advantage of it and preach their dogma; the monarchists do the same. They smile cynically when they read of the frightful increase in the cost of living and say, 'It has not yet gone far enough. It must be worse still before the masses realise the mistake they have made in establishing a republic! We shall wait a bit longer.' But most of the townspeople are so weary, so destroyed by uncertainty and long years of nervous strain, that they do not care what happens. They are tired of it all.[20]

But on a personal level, the relationship between Smedley and Chatto was always flawed. He, still married, was intensely jealous of Agnes's men friends from before they met and initially refused to let her write for publication, describing this as 'showing off'. In addition, he refused to let her take a full part in his Indian work on the grounds that public knowledge of her earlier sex life would ruin him. Not surprisingly, such attitudes led to a radicalisation of her anti-marriage beliefs and she became fervent in her feminism. But many of her views far outstripped what the public was ready to hear and, although she experienced reluctance from editors to accept some of her work, she would rarely agree to change it. When, in 1927, she wrote about sexual problems and homosexuality, albeit anonymously, neither the editor of *The Nation* nor of the *American Mercury* felt able to publish, although they admired the frankness of the author.

However much Chatto insisted he loved Agnes and could not live without her, their impossible life together, which included occasional physical abuse, led Agnes to a nervous breakdown and the verge of suicide. In an attempt to start afresh, and following advice from her psychoanalyst to turn her rage into creative use, she decided to write an autobiographical novel, *Daughter of Earth*.[21] This took her several years and was published in New York in 1929 as well as by the *Frankfurter Zeitung* in instalments that year. But by 1928 she had left Berlin for China intending to move on to India. In fact, she became so involved with China and its revolution that she never reached India.

Through contacts with a German communist before she left, Agnes managed to secure an appointment as US correspondent for the influential *Frankfurter Zeitung* (in addition to the serialisation of her book) and it is for her work in China, much of it in book form, that her fame as a great reporter rests. She arrived with little knowledge of the country; what she knew she had picked up during her time with the League Against Imperialism and contact with Chinese revolutionaries in Berlin. She had a vague notion of using her position in China to link the Indian and Chinese revolutionary movements by writing news about China for publication in India and by introducing Indians to revolutionary Chinese in Nanjing. From the first she was passionately committed to the revolutionary struggle, saw the communists as the best answer to oppose the Japanese fascist threat and never attempted to conceal her fervour in her reports.

Agnes Smedley first entered China in 1928 via Manchuria, where she stayed for three months investigating social conditions as well as Japanese economic penetration and military build-up. By now vehemently opposed to the institution of marriage, she wrote about the position of women, some of whom she considered household slaves, and was particularly struck by the brutal practice of foot-binding, which could reduce an adult female foot to a mere three inches. But when she wrote about the military situation in Manchuria and the growing Japanese aggression, some of the evidence she gathered for the stories was so incredible, and so few European newspapers had proper coverage of China during these years, that at first her newspaper refused to believe her. Soon she moved to China itself and immediately contacted as many revolutionaries as possible in her quest to investigate working conditions; her great motivation was to use her writing to try and change these conditions. At first, most of her Chinese friends were western-educated intellectuals, but it was not long before she developed additional journalistic contacts; for example, she was invited to write book reviews for the *China Weekly Review* and she soon broadened her acquaintance base once she started investigating child labour, the abuse of women and the widespread poverty in China for her reports to the *Frankfurter Zeitung*. She interviewed a number of ordinary Chinese and her poignant accounts of their lives, originally a series of newspaper articles, subsequently formed the basis of her book, *Chinese Destinies*.[22] In China, for the first time in her life, she began to feel that through her work she could make a real impact on the world. According to her biographers, Janice and Stephen MacKinnon: 'Her studies of Chinese women are the most lyrical and moving pieces ... about a variety of Chinese women in the 1930s from the urban elite to the Communist guerrillas to the ordinary peasant women.'[23]

In addition to reporting, Agnes continued as a political agitator, setting up a League for Civil Rights in China and trying, unsuccessfully, to establish a birth-control clinic in Shanghai. She was not a member of the Communist Party but such involvement in revolutionary causes led to threats on her life as well as to personal attacks in the Japanese and British press. The Chinese Government even asked the German Government to have her contract withdrawn. However, her activities were soon forcibly brought to an end when, in 1932, the *Frankfurter Zeitung* was bought by I. G. Farben Industrie, who considered Agnes's committed left-wing stance ill-suited to the new fascist ideology already on the rise in Germany. By this time, Agnes was suffering from a heart complaint and she went to the Soviet Union partly for medical care and partly because a Moscow publisher offered her an advance for a book she was already working on. She remained in the Soviet Union from June 1933 to April 1934, during which time she finished *China's Red Army Marches*.[24]

Once she was stronger she returned for a brief spell to the United States, then in the grip of depression, where she tried unsuccessfully to be commissioned as a correspondent for an American newspaper or magazine. None of the major papers or wire services would employ her. Undeterred, although with extremely limited financial resources, she returned to China in 1935 determined not only to witness but also to be part of events and write about them – in books if necessary. But professionally, the next few years were not as productive as the last few had been. According to her biographers, she suffered 'swings in mood from long periods of depression and poor health to brief bursts of happiness and physical energy . . . the few articles she did publish reveal a pervasive sense of isolation and near paranoia about political persecution'.[25] Then Agnes moved out of Shanghai to the centre of the north-west region near Xi'an, invited by Communist Party leaders who knew that a showdown with General Chiang Kai-shek was in the offing and wanted a suitably sympathetic international correspondent on hand to report events. She accepted, believing that she would be able to rest there, but also because she knew that the new base of the Red Army was only fifty-five miles away. Thus it happened that she was present when Chiang Kai-shek was captured by some of his own officers and forced to have talks with Chinese communist leaders, including Zhou Enlai, about opening a united front against the Japanese. Agnes, who believed that this was a crucial development, made regular forty-minute broadcasts in English about the Xi'an incident. In a letter to a newspaper friend at the time, she described the tension and excitement as well as the bloodshed in Xi'an. Kitted out in thick riding breeches with a red sweater, a Red Cross armband and a military pass, she could work on the streets each day administering first aid in scenes reminiscent of her predecessor, Jessie White Mario; both had the ear of senior commanders and both could get near the action because of their willingness to provide medical aid. Agnes, often suffering from severe back pain herself, none the less tried to nurse hundreds of wounded men, women and children on the streets until they could be removed to a hospital:

Nearly all were poor peasants, and some had been slaves. I felt always that I was walking down one of the most tragic and terrible corridors in human history when I worked with them. The sight of poor peasants or slaves who had known nothing but brute labour all their lives, lying there with no covering, no bed, on stone floors with untended and unhealed wounds, with big hard bloody feet – no, I shall never forget that.[26]

Agnes's broadcasts from Communist Party headquarters were, for a time, the only news emerging from Xi'an. Although largely factual they caused a terrific stir when they were picked up in Shanghai and, from this time on, she was acknowledged as a figure of international repute yet also branded a communist apologist. The American press now wrote stories about Agnes herself with vivid headlines such as 'US Girl a Red Peril'[27] and 'American Woman Aids Chinese Rising'.[28] An Associated Press background report even described her as 'the one-time American farm girl who may become a virtual "white empress" over yellow skinned millions'.[29]

In January 1937, Agnes made a daring move. Keen to visit Red Army units, yet well aware that foreign journalists were prohibited from entering such strongholds, she took advantage of the confusion following the kidnapping of Chiang Kai-shek to sneak past a blockade in the back of a truck provided by a Red Army escort, and travelled to the mountain citadel of Yan'an, the new base of the Red Army. It was here that she met and had discussions with Mao Zedong, whom she never liked and found physically repulsive, and started work on a major biography of the Red Army's legendary peasant commander-in-chief, Zhu De, a man she found much more sympathetic. As ever, she involved herself in numerous other activities including building up a library for the Anti-Japanese Military and Political College. She also, finally, applied for membership of the Chinese Communist Party and was devastated at being refused. Perhaps she was considered more use as an outside journalist or perhaps the Party hierarchy recognised that she was always too wayward to be confined to one strict discipline. At all events in the autumn of 1937, although by this time in considerable pain from a long-standing back injury aggravated by a recent fall from a horse, she set off to join the Eighth Route Army as a correspondent – albeit self-appointed.

'Often I work all night long if we remain but one day or one night in that place,' Smedley wrote later. 'I can do no polishing at all. I am so weary and often in such pain that I cannot retype and at times cannot even correct.'[30] A western observer, describing her at this time, said that she looked 'woefully grim in her military uniform... [and] her face had the signs on it of suffering'.[31] Many of her despatches from the front were again published in book form in 1938 as *China Fights Back: An American Woman with the Eighth Route Army*. Yet in addition to her own pain, Agnes was acutely aware of the shortages in food and medicines facing the Eighth Route Army. She immediately wrote to the Indian leader, Jawaharlal Nehru, whom she knew personally and had corresponded with, appealing for help as a way for him to show his solidarity with the Chinese anti-fascist struggle. Nehru responded positively, sending an Indian mission of doctors and medicines for which the Chinese were eternally grateful. For months Agnes devoted most of her energies to raising funds for the Chinese Red Cross, but she also used her pen to create international awareness of the misery facing the Chinese masses. By now she was an internationally acclaimed war reporter of worldwide repute and editors from a wide range of newspapers and periodicals were keen to take her work. These included the *China Weekly Review, China Today, The Nation,* the *Modern Review, Asia* and *Vogue.* Perhaps the most significant financially, and that which brought her finally to a British audience, was the *Manchester Guardian,* which hired her as its special correspondent. The money she earned, at last, enabled her to continue with her unpaid work for the Red Cross Medical Corps and to travel again, keeping the world informed of the Chinese revolutionary struggle.

Agnes loved reporting war. It gave her a sense of fulfilment and personal worth as she saw herself acting as spokesperson for those who could not speak for themselves, the wounded in central China. In addition, she basked in the praise being accorded her journalistic work by editors at the *Manchester Guardian,* who for a time used a Smedley story almost daily. For eighteen months, from November 1938 to April 1940, she was given carte-blanche by the commanders of the New Fourth Army to travel freely around the war zone, a rare privilege for a western man or woman but granted largely because of a personal endorsement from Zhou Enlai, who had always admired her. Agnes needed the recent acclaim to boost her reserves of energy. It was arduous work visiting resistance movements and trekking up and down the hills north and south of the Yangzi river.

Hers turned out to be the longest sustained tour of a Chinese War Zone by any foreign correspondent, man or woman ... it was an exhilarating experience and probably the high point of her career as a journalist. But the conditions were rugged and dangerous and Smedley paid a price in steadily deteriorating health.[32]

In September 1940, she left China once more for urgent medical treatment, this time flying over Japanese lines to Hong Kong; then in the summer of 1941 she had to return to the United States. There she continued to write books and give lectures, shedding hitherto unseen light on Chinese history. In 1943, her powerful work describing her experiences of war reporting, *Battle Hymn of China*,[33] brought her further excellent reviews, after which she retired to a writers' colony at Yaddo, New York State. From about 1945 onwards she had trouble with editors who, if they agreed to take her work at all, wanted changes which she was unwilling to concede. Then in 1949, she found herself accused of being a paid Russian spy and on the communist blacklist, which meant that she was unable to support herself. Devastated by the accusations she wanted to return to China, but died on 6 May 1950 after an operation in London for ulcers. Her remains were taken to Peking, where she was buried with the honour befitting the heroine she was.

In America, however, she was largely forgotten for the next twenty years; remembered if at all only to be scorned and insulted. The main charge against her was not merely that she was a simple, passionate woman but that her reporting was biased and over-emotional, a not uncommon judgment on women reporters. Her work was always intensely personal and she never tried to restrain the use of auto-biography as a tool in her reportage kit, often identifying herself closely with her subjects as well. Although her sympathies were, undeniably, with the Chinese communists, Agnes Smedley never became a member of any Communist Party and even contributed a chapter to a book edited by Madame Chiang Kai-shek when she saw it would help to garner medical aid. Although she was in touch with the American Communist Party in China, she did not allow it to censor her work. Her achievements for any woman in the 1920s and 1930s, let alone one from such an ill-educated, impoverished background as hers, are remarkable.

6

The Inter-War Years: Europe

'A young lady who wants to practise being the correspondent of a foreign rag.'
GENERAL BURNETT STUART TO SHIELA GRANT DUFF

The situation in Europe during the 1930s posed similar challenges for women reporters. Fascism and communism, the twin evils bred from high unemployment, high inflation, strikes and riots, reared up to face each other in a variety of guises and for women, who could not play a physical part in the fighting, reporting was the next best thing. When Shiela Grant Duff left Oxford University in 1934, she was unambivalent about what to do with her life: prevent the outbreak of a second world war. Her father and two uncles had been killed in the Great War and this profoundly affected the way she viewed the world from her childhood. She was even tempted to leave university before finishing her course so that she could actively undertake something to temper developments on the continent: 'I remember one of my strongest impulses to leave Oxford came after the shelling of the workers' flats in Vienna in February 1934. It seemed preposterous to be living a useless life in this ivory tower while such things could happen.'[1]

Advised by Professor Arnold Toynbee that the only way to stop a war was to study the possible causes on the spot, and that the best way to do that was to work as a foreign correspondent of an influential newspaper, Shiela made an appointment to see Geoffrey Dawson, editor of *The Times*, to whom she was introduced by Toynbee. Dawson sent her to his foreign editor, who 'explained to me at once that it was quite impossible for a woman to work on the editorial side of a newspaper since it meant night work alongside men,' she recalled. 'If, on the other hand, I was going to Paris anyway perhaps I would like to send them some fashion notes. I was deeply incensed. To feel capable of stopping a world war and then to be asked to write fashion notes!' In retrospect, she recognises that she was not enough of a feminist to feel insulted as a woman; she took umbrage over the insult to her intelligence. Mr Deakin clearly had not noticed that fashion was the last thing to interest Miss Grant Duff. But the affront was not sufficient to quell her desire to go to Europe. She left anyway for Paris, relying on her two strengths in the world: a small private income of £3 a week and some good connections into the upper echelons of British society.

Shiela Grant Duff was born in 1913 to a distinguished and well-connected liberal family and spent her fatherless youth in material comfort in Chelsea, always overshadowed, it seemed, by the impending possibility of another war. She went to St Paul's Girls' School, where her education was dominated by the importance of history, and at eighteen went up to Oxford University to read Philosophy, Politics and Economics (PPE), 'a preliminary course in political journalism'.[2] Here she soon became vividly aware of a deepening conflict between her old life – she had just been presented at Court – and the new, where she was moving increasingly in left-wing, egalitarian circles. Her Oxford group included Isaiah Berlin, Douglas Jay, Goronwy Rees and two friends from school, Peggy Garnett (later Jay) and Diana Hubback; as well as the young German Rhodes scholar, Adam von Trott zu Solz, who was to play a crucial part in her life and in German history. They were a closely knit group, spending their first summer together in Austria, Moscow and Germany. When Hitler took over in 1933, they decided a holiday in Nazi Germany was unpalatable and travelled around eastern Europe instead.

But when Shiela, at twenty-one, arrived in Paris, it was for the first time. She knew no one there and barely spoke the language. Not surprisingly she blundered into staying at a hotel where most of the bedrooms were in constant use throughout the day. She had been given one introduction through von Trott and Rees and now wasted little time in visiting him. Edgar Ansel Mowrer, Paris correspondent of the *Chicago Daily News*, was by this time a journalist of world renown for his courageous reports from Nazi Germany and his book, *Germany Puts the Clock Back*. The German Government, however, was determined to get rid of him and when they arrested Paul Goldmann, the elderly Jewish correspondent of an Austrian newspaper, Mowrer reluctantly agreed to leave in exchange for Goldmann's release. 'I felt such a man could teach me a lot and I was not mistaken,' Shiela recalled.[3]

When they first met he asked her only one question: whether she knew any economics. Naturally, she said 'yes', so he told her to start work on Monday. He was not going to pay her anything, he added; she could come and learn if she wanted. So she sat in his office, back to back with his nephew who was there under similar circumstances, and learnt more about international relations than journalism. Mowrer was shocked to hear the extent of Shiela's pro-German, anti-French views when she first arrived and gave her the sobriquet, 'Hitler's girlfriend'. He set about explaining the reality of Germany's defeat in the First World War and the true intentions of its new leaders. Inevitably, Shiela acquired much about journalism from Mowrer as well. He stressed the importance of 'putting news before everything even if it meant leaving your bride on her wedding night'. Occasionally, Mowrer took her out to lunch, but she would have preferred the money so that she could have afforded to eat for the rest of the week. Her £3 did not go very far. After a few months Shiela still believed that she did not want to be a reporter, she simply wanted to prevent another world war. But then came a chance not only to witness at first hand how the new Germans behaved, but also to put her newly acquired reporting skills into practice.

In January 1935, world attention was focused on the Saar, a coal-producing region which, under the Treaty of Versailles, the French had been awarded the rights to exploit for a limited period as part of the reparations agreement. The period had now expired and the people of the Saar were being offered a choice in a plebiscite: they could return to German ownership, become French or remain under their current League of Nations Commission. The plebiscite was of considerable international significance as the first test of the prestige, power and popularity of the new Third Reich. Although the outcome was not in doubt (the population were, after all, German in nationality), it was an opportunity missed to mount some formal opposition to Hitler. The international community responded by sending 3,300 British, Italian, Swedish and Dutch troops as a peace-keeping force. An atmosphere of high tension raged for weeks before-hand as the world's foreign correspondents descended to watch the spectacle. It was here that Grant Duff met for the first time Elizabeth Wiskemann, who was working as a freelance correspondent for a number of British publications.

Wiskemann, in spite of her German name and antecedents, felt herself to be wholly British. She had been born and educated in England at a time when it was awkward to have a German name and it is possible that her lifelong sympathy for persecuted victims stemmed from this. She travelled widely with her parents in Europe, delighting as much in baroque art as in magnificent landscape. In 1918, her mother died and she went up to Cambridge to read History. Her relationship with her father was never close and, after her years at Cambridge, she led an independent life. She intended to remain in the academic world, but when her thesis was awarded an M. Litt instead of a Ph.D., she was so dismayed that she decided to make a break and went for a holiday to Berlin. It was 1928, just before the great depression, and she arrived with the presumption shared by almost all contemporary academics that Germany had been harshly treated at Versailles. From the start, she grasped the full significance of German politics and never shied away from stating her views boldly in print.

After spending several months in Germany from 1930 to 1931, during which she developed a wide cross-section of friends in intellectual, political and artistic circles, Elizabeth became fluent in the language. An introduction to Frederick Voigt, correspondent of the *Manchester Guardian*, was her catalyst. Through him she met the other English-speaking journalists in Berlin at the time: Norman Ebbutt of *The Times*, Darsie Gillie of the *Morning Post* and Edgar Mowrer of the *Chicago Daily News* – all men of great calibre who could exert significant influence. They recognised in their new colleague a winning combination of female charm and prettiness with a devastatingly acute mind. Thanks to Voigt she was taken to an early Nazi rally and experienced an address by Goebbels, who was already employing all the militarist trappings of Nazism. Through another introduction she also met the architect Erich Mendelsohn, Arthur Koestler, then a young journalist in Berlin, and the artist George Grosz, with whom she once danced at a party in his flat. 'It was daunting rather than agreeable as he was acidly drunk.'[4] She also had an introduction to Thomas Mann and his family and, on the political front, met 'Putzi' Hanfstaengl, the rich, half-American Nazi propagandist.

When she returned to her flat in Cambridge, she found coaching small groups of students in modern European history rather humdrum; she had acquired a formidable understanding of contemporary Germany and had a voracious appetite for news about the country. Within a year she had settled into a rhythm of teaching in Cambridge during the term and spending her vacation in Germany, or elsewhere in central Europe, the better to describe and analyse events there. The teaching financed a frugal life abroad and she continued thus for five years. It is tempting to observe that British readers imbibed the wisdom and understanding of Elizabeth Wiskemann on the cheap, since no newspaper was paying her travel or living expenses, not to mention a regular salary. But whether she would have wished to live permanently in Germany is doubtful. For the time being she preferred her split life, poor though it was: 'The interplay of teaching about the past and playing with the fire of the present was extra-ordinarily stimulating.'[5] Her first article was published in the *New Statesman* in April 1932 on the re-election of President Hindenburg of the Weimar Republic. Almost immediately she found that she could place at least four articles per trip.

Intelligent enough to realise that if she wanted to understand the new regime she could not confine her friendships to left-wing artists, intellectuals and Jews, Elizabeth also tried to retain contact with men on the right and often said as little as possible about her connection with the *New Statesman*. She quickly acquired other furtive habits too, such as not mentioning names on the telephone and talking in whispers in public places. Within weeks of Hitler's election in 1933, she went to Berlin, where she could not fail to notice an immediate change for the worse. Policemen shouted at her for crossing the road at the wrong time and a stormtrooper snatched a cigarette from her mouth, informing her that the Führer disapproved of women smoking. She met a Jewish lawyer who gave her sworn testimony about how his clients, by no means all Jewish, were being tortured and she tried to work the information into her articles in such a way that she would not be accused of falling prey to 'Jewish propaganda'. She was among several correspondents who knew within days of the establishment of the first Nazi concentration camp at Dachau near Munich. A German official in the Foreign Office Press Department begged her not to propagate in London the stories about concentration camps.

She returned to England on 26 March 1933 and that week went to report on her trip twice to the House of Commons in the hope that she could impress upon influential Members of Parliament the truth about Nazi Germany. She had little success; no one who had not seen for himself could believe that things were quite as outrageous as she described them and she was called a Cassandra by many. But in professional terms she was enjoying considerable success and could place almost as much as she could write in several weeklies and monthlies, in addition to the *New Statesman*. She was also invited to give lectures about Germany and continued visiting the country as often as she could.

By January 1935, Elizabeth was well prepared to cover the Saar plebiscite. She had already visited the region twice and had formed a clear impression of the efficient way the International Commission was governing the region before the Nazi propaganda machine started to blacken its reputation. She had also established contact with G. G. Knox, President of the Governing Commission, who, in spite of scrupulously observing the rights of individual Saarlanders, was labelled 'The Tyrant Knox'. He, keen to see journalists rebut the Nazi propagandists, was especially helpful to Elizabeth, lending her his car and chauffeur whenever she wanted to visit Nazi enthusiast industrialists or simply tour the region. Six months before the plebiscite she wrote a reasoned piece about the Saar, one of the first reports which was not simply a straightforward re-statement of the German case. It caused some consternation at the German Embassy in London.

Elizabeth's considerable knowledge of the story meant that she was much in demand from all the newly arrived correspondents, which she keenly resented. 'Crowds of journalists turned up who were quite new to the Saar and expected me to tell them all they did not know,' she commented later, remarking, too, that even *The Times* sent a representative, David Scott, who did not speak German. But she made a pact with him: he supplied her with transport and she supplied him with German. Shiela Grant Duff, on her first assignment, noticed this prickliness and in her case felt that it was directed personally towards her since she had been asked to report on the crisis for the *Observer*. The offer came through a journalist friend who owed her a favour. But now, also not speaking a word of German, she felt woefully inadequate and recognised that Wiskemann, or Whiskers as she and her friends called her, would have been far better qualified to handle the *Observer* report.

Shiela was at first given only two weeks in the Saar, an experience she found sadly enlightening. She was proud that she was now a 'presswoman in my own right and with my own credentials', which enabled her to move among the 'famous' correspondents of the time. Frederick Voigt proved for her, too, an invaluable guide. He not only taught her patiently about the intricacies of the situation, but also generously took her with him to the mining villages where he had myriad contacts, especially among the anti-Nazis, who would have been frightened to talk to anyone else. But if being young and feminine helped her on this occasion, the British military were less keen to assist. When she had asked General Burnett Stuart, who had been a close friend of her father, for an introduction to the British officer in command in the Saar, he had replied: 'I hardly think it would be fair to add to the responsibilities of the Chief Command . . . by planting on them a young lady who wants to practise being the correspondent of a foreign rag.'[6]

The day the result of the plebiscite was announced, the face of the Saar changed irreparably. Most of the foreign correspondents left as quickly as they had come. But Shiela, aware of the immense human suffering that was imminent, requested that she be allowed to stay longer to write about, and help if possible, the marked men who knew that they must pack up and leave immediately. For the second Sunday, Shiela's copy – less hard news than an unashamed appeal on behalf of the anti-Nazi minority in the Saar – was the lead story in the *Observer*.

Their position is pitiful. They have no work, no country and no money. They have no confidence in a police which is already the agent of a country for whom they are traitors. They have no faith in justice based on National Socialist law as defined by General Goering two months ago. They have no meeting places. Their leaders are exiled or driven into hiding and they themselves are isolated through the country. Already panic has begun to spread.[7]

There was no reason for Shiela to return to Paris immediately – Mowrer after all was not paying her – and she felt for the first time that there was something practical she could do by staying. 'While my high-powered colleagues had to earn their living and show their faces in important places, I realised that my own absurd position, above all my small private income, gave me a leeway not permitted to the established and powerful,' she wrote.[8]

She decided that she must speak personally to the *Observer* foreign editor, Hugh Massingham, and so embarked on a trip home – a third-class train journey as the newspaper did not offer to pay her fare. 'It never occurred to me to ask for it. . . . I had no idea how to approach the newspaper whose correspondent I had been on this dramatic occasion.' Voigt had given Shiela advice on terms and an introduction to Massingham, who was evidently relieved at the modesty of her request: to return to the Saar at her own expense on a freelance basis. This she did.

During the next few weeks Shiela used her position as an English journalist, which helped her cross into France, quite shamelessly to ease the escape of anti-Nazis, some five thousand of whom fled in all. Many of these were communists and among them a large number of Comintern agents. 'I was very hazy about such things in those days,' she admits now. Shiela's activities were highly dangerous and became more so as the day approached for Hitler's final takeover. On the morning itself a young boy came to her with a loaded pistol, which she hid for him in her stocking drawer, and then went out to listen to the Führer. She had by this time taught herself German and was able to take notes of his speech. While doing this she was unaware that the crowd around her had slipped away and that she was surrounded instead by Nazi stormtroopers. What was she doing, they demanded. Taking notes of Hitler's speech, she replied. On what authority? With courage surging, she retorted, on what authority did they presume to ask her questions? At that point a policeman arrived and she handed him her press card, realising with horror that the card stated boldly her address, where there was a hidden pistol. She accepted the return of her card, waited for the stormtroopers to move on and then, even though she missed hearing some of the speeches for the *Observer*, dashed for home. She disposed of the gun in the river. Shortly after, she left the Saar.

Having now started on her own, the question was, where next? Massingham proposed Warsaw or Prague, where there was a dearth of correspondents; Adam von Trott Berlin and Voigt Rome, where he said there were no good English correspondents. But Shiela herself felt equivocal: 'I dared not confess that I disliked news as such; the coming and going of statesmen, the meetings, the talk, the intrigue, the speculation left me both bored and confused. I wanted guidance to understand these meetings, not the opportunity to report them.'[9] And so she went back to Mowrer and her desk in Paris. Now that she had proved herself, he gave her an important assignment reporting on the fascist leagues there. But when she had completed this and Goronwy Rees came out to visit her, Mowrer could not understand why she was not prepared to contemplate marriage. An old-school chauvinist, Mowrer believed that there was no problem in Shiela's life which could not be solved by a man telling her what to do; he failed to understand why she was so reluctant to abandon her frugal and dedicated existence.

She decided, however, that she had outgrown her original 'job' in Paris and proposed to the *Observer* that she travel to Russia, in which she had a deep interest. Massingham declined politely, telling her, 'I really must say how profoundly I disapprove of this desire to go into journalism. It is no life for a nice young person,' by which Shiela knew he meant 'woman'. As a final resort she decided to take a holiday job as a secretary in the office of the *Daily Telegraph* in Berlin, 'a job I was even less qualified for than journalism,' she admitted. There, too, she was never treated with any seriousness, nor was she missed when she left to return to England and ponder the next stage in her life.

The months after the Saar plebiscite were equally disturbing for Elizabeth Wiskemann. She paid a further visit to Berlin and then, so as to avoid censorship, went to Prague to write up her article. Entitled 'A Land Fit for Heroes', the piece did its best to shatter the illusion which in Britain still pervaded, that Germany was settling down nicely.

'Nothing could be more disastrously deceptive than this impression,' she wrote with her usual decisiveness:

There is no possible doubt that capital industries are booming on rearmament and builders are thriving on all the new barracks.... Germany is longing for a fresh inter-national monetary crisis, under cover of which she could slip off the nominal gold standard.... Liberal and intellectual opinion in Germany is in despair over the cowardice of England. 'Can't you make your countrymen understand that we are fighting for all the values upon which European civilisation depends?' People have been saying to me every day, 'Our government hangs upon your lips, but instead of speaking the words which could help us, having waited till barbarians rule us, you come to terms with them merely, it seems, because they are strong.'... In the Germany whose respectability we have now guaranteed with the Naval Agreement, the maltreatment of the Jews is being carried to hitherto unknown lengths.

She gave many details of brutal incidents: 'The new ss weekly... makes plain to any reader that the ss is pledged to neopaganism and every sort of dehumanisation.' She concluded:

... the Führer is a Moderate only *ad hoc*. Julius Streicher is his oldest and perhaps his dearest friend and Hitler's subjective pacifism will mean peace at any price that Germany demands once the breakneck pace of rearmament has brought the goal within reach.[10]

It was a courageous piece of clear-sighted reporting, drawing on what she had seen, read and been told; it was rare in the British press in 1935 to find such a piercing exposé of the reality of Hitler's Germany. The night that Elizabeth wrote the piece, a raging thunderstorm gusted the article off the table. 'I have never paid much attention to omens... but that article was to give the Gestapo their pretext for arresting me a year later.'[11] She went on to Poland and Danzig, as she had promised four articles on Danzig to different publications, and, professional that she was, rose early to finish each one on time. 'They were all different and all published without delay.'

In 1936, she returned to Germany, first in March and again in July, aware of course that the international situation was deteriorating monthly as Hitler's aggression went unresisted. 'It was obviously increasingly perilous for a person like myself to go to Germany and it might be increasingly thankless to write articles which people at home found unpalatable. I do not remember doubting that it had to be done,' she wrote later. Quite how dangerous her own position was she could not know. By February 1936, the Bavarian political police had opened a dossier on Wiskemann which they circulated to all police frontiers and local authorities in Bavaria. This noted that in 1935 she had travelled to Germany and written two articles in the forbidden newspaper, *The New Statesman and Nation*: 'In these articles Germany and National Socialism were reviled in unexampled fashion. It seems probable that Wiskemann will come to Germany again soon. Should this writer turn up it is to be reported at once without preventing her entry into Germany.'[12] *

In July, Elizabeth went first to Berlin to talk about the latest situation with Ebbutt of *The Times* and then to Danzig again, where she visited Sean Lester, the High Commissioner of the League of Nations, reviled by the Nazi press as one who cherished Jews and other non-Nazis. She was, she realised later, watched by Gestapo agents as she went in and out of his house. She returned to Berlin, planning to spend the weekend at the estate of Count Albrecht Bernstorff, one of the most openly vehement critics of the Nazis, and return home from there. But while she was waiting for him she started 'for once, rashly,' to write her article on the Danzig crisis for *The Scotsman*. 'Then just before midday there was a sharp knock at Ebbutt's door. His German maid opened it and started back, shaking with fear, into the room we were in, followed by two men in civilian clothes. One of them showed us the words Geheime Staats Polizei on something he wore under his coat lapel.' She was ordered to go with them; they declined to give any reasons and forbade Ebbutt from accompanying her. Told to bring everything with her, including the half-written article, she found her voice simply refused to function, so terrified was she.

She was immediately driven off to the notorious Gestapo headquarters in Prinz Albrechtstrasse, her mind filled with the horror stories she had heard so much about. She was walked up to the fourth floor and then left alone for what seemed an eternity, during which time her courage overcame her natural timidity and her resourcefulness pacified her hunger. She collected her thoughts sufficiently to look

* Elizabeth Wiskemann commented in her memoirs that she saw this document only after the war when friends in the Institut für Zeitgesichte in Munich sent it to her.

around and notice that, into every room she was taken, there was a huge map of Russia and eastern Europe on the otherwise bare walls. She was also quick-witted enough, when confronted with a German translation of her article, 'A Land Fit for Heroes', and asked if she had written it, to reply that she could not possibly say unless she saw the English original. This threw her interrogator into a momentary turmoil; he then said that if she persisted in her obstinacy, she would have to see his 'chief'. This man, in full ss uniform, was a 'typical blond beast type of Nazi and quite young'. Clearly they could not find a copy of the article in English as he asked her, if she would not admit to having written it, would she accept that the sentiments were hers?

In her account of the interview, Elizabeth clearly took the upper hand, demanding specific examples. Could she for example have said that Jews were maltreated in Nazi Germany? 'Why yes, it's true isn't it?' she replied. Finally he asked her whether she could have written that Nazi Germany was dominated by brutal ss types. 'But by now I was feeling almost hilarious and was able to say, "Why not, isn't that fairly exact too?" '[13]

In spite of such outspokenness, the ss chief then explained that, in view of the imminent Olympic Games in Berlin, he was prepared to allow her to leave, providing she signed a statement confirming that she could have written the article. She agreed, and asked whether she could return to Germany another time. That, said the Nazi, was up to the German Embassy in London. She returned home in the middle of the afternoon and made immediate plans to leave the next day. Undaunted she finished the half-written article that afternoon and it was published in *The Scotsman* three days later. She wrote several more articles once she was safely back in England, some of which had editorial remarks about her recent detention by the Gestapo. It was to be several years before she returned to Germany.

In their lives, both Elizabeth Wiskemann and Shiela Grant Duff shared an overwhelming commitment to 'the cause' and, in their writing, an unashamedly partisan view. Wiskemann considered historical detachment, if taken to extremes, as moral and scientific nonsense and Grant Duff, at considerable personal risk, used her position as a reporter to help individuals in need. Both were good-looking but unglamorous with the same liberal, English educational background. Both were scholarly in their approach, although Wiskemann was the more experienced with a wider range of contacts. Both were dedicated to humane values in which they passionately believed. And, at a time when British newspaper editors were still reluctant to send women as their permanent correspondents, both risked going in any case for meagre financial rewards.

Yet they never became friends and Grant Duff is convinced that Wiskemann looked on her younger colleague with disdain while she, in turn, saw only the serious side of Elizabeth. Within a few months both women found themselves working alongside each other again, this time in Czechoslovakia, the last surviving democracy east of the Rhine and certain to be the next victim on Hitler's list.

7

The Spanish Civil War

'War was always worse than I knew how to say – always.'
MARTHA GELLHORN

In 1936, Martha Gellhorn's second book, *The Trouble I've Seen*, signalled a brilliant new talent on the international literary scene. It consisted of an eye-witness account of how the depression in America was affecting those least able to defend themselves. Martha was born on 8 November 1908 in St Louis, Missouri. Her father was an eminent gynaecologist; her mother was a graduate of Bryn Mawr College, a tireless advocate of social reform and a major influence on Martha. There were three brothers. After high school, Martha also attended Bryn Mawr. However, much against her father's wishes, she left at the end of her junior year, with an impatience to get on with her life that mirrored Shiela Grant Duff's desire to leave Oxford and a fiery independence of spirit that was essentially her own.

From then on, she proudly embraced the principle that, if you choose how you want to live, you must pay for the privilege, and promptly did so. She earned enough money from two holiday jobs in 1929 on the *New Republic* and the *Hearst Times Union*, plus some freelance work, to pay for her passage to France, where she hoped to start her career as a foreign correspondent.

'My life began in 1930,' she once wrote. With the confidence of the young she landed a succession of jobs in Paris with an advertising agency, *Vogue* and United Press and, like Grant Duff, made her base in a hotel which she later discovered was a brothel. The *St Louis Post-Dispatch* sent her to Geneva to watch the moribund League of Nations in session and to interview some notable women active in League politics. Here she immediately drew attention to herself by fearlessly shouting '*Pas d'accord*' from the reporters' gallery. 'When the men looked up, they must have seen a wonderfully angelic creature from mythology with her foot on the dragon, sword in hand and golden renaissance hair,' commented her friend and colleague Sybille Bedford.[1] Martha lived from hand to mouth in Paris, but established herself among a group of artists and writer friends. What little money she had she spent on travelling around Europe and writing about what she saw. A trip to Germany with a delegation of young French students left her profoundly disturbed.

Martha worked prodigiously, accepting no money from her family. She helped found a newspaper, called *The Struggle of the Young*, attended strikes and started writing fiction, which was her main ambition, journalism being merely the means to experience the raw material of her future novels. She was also married, briefly, to Bertrand de Jouvenel, a radical journalist with a colourful, romantic past. But in 1934, realising the depths of the depression into which her own country was sinking and believing that she could do something to help, she returned home.

She was hired by Harry Hopkins, director of the Federal Emergency Relief Administration (FERA), as a relief-investigator because, she told him, she was 'vastly experienced and very well known in Europe'. Her brief was to report on how the organisation actually operated. For the rest of the winter of 1935 she travelled the depression-worn country, interviewing hundreds of people who were suffering hunger, homelessness and despair. But Martha herself now despaired that merely writing reports about statistics would ever help. She quit her job and decided to write a book about the people she had met. *The Trouble I've Seen* focuses on four individuals of different ages from various parts of the United States. The most poignant, and possibly one of Gellhorn's best pieces of writing, was the story of Ruby, a child prostitute based on a girl Martha had come across in Hooverville, Illinois. Desperately poor, eleven-year-old Ruby begs the older girls for work. At first they let her stand guard outside an old cabin while they take their customers inside. She brings her mother peaches as a present with the money she earns. Then they let her work herself. 'And all you gotta do is think about the money and how you can get marcelles and lipstick, and go to the movies, and everything you want, afterwards. That's all you got to do. It don't last long. It only hurts the first time, really.'[2]

Harry Hopkins had already introduced Martha to Eleanor Roosevelt, wife of the President, since she was known to take a keen interest in social problems. When she read the advance copy of the book, she was ecstatic about its merits and wrote in a syndicated column:

I cannot tell you how Martha Gellhorn, young, pretty, college graduate, good home, more or less Junior League background, with a touch of exquisite Paris clothes and 'esprit' thrown in, can write as she does. She has an understanding of many people and many situations and she can make them live for us. Let us be thankful she can, for we badly need her interpretation to help us understand each other.[3]

Like it or not, Martha's looks and lifestyle were from now on to be inextricably linked with her professional career. Both book and author received widespread adulation; fulsome reviews appeared in the major New York papers and Martha's photograph on the cover of the *Saturday Review of Literature*. The English edition was similarly well received with Graham Greene paying her a backhanded compliment in the *Spectator* that summer when he wrote:

Her stories are quite amazingly unfeminine. In Joe and Pete... the tale of a union organiser... it is quite impossible to detect that a woman is writing. She has none of the female vices of unbalanced pity or factitious violence; her masculine characters are presented as convincingly as her female and her writing is hard and clear.[4]

A few months after publication, at Martha's prompting as Dr Gellhorn had died earlier in the year, the Gellhorn family decided to take a holiday. They went south to Miami and then, on impulse, to Key West. It was here that Martha, her long, blonde hair flowing around her shoulders, a ravishing smile and long, slim legs that she often revealed in shorts, caught the eye of Ernest Hemingway, at thirty-seven, nine years older than her and a writer hero since her schooldays. Just a few months previously one reviewer had written about them both: 'Who is this Martha Gellhorn?... her writing burns... Hemingway does not write more authentic American speech. Nor can Ernest Hemingway teach Martha Gellhorn anything about economy of language.'[5]

By the time Gellhorn and Hemingway met, she had already decided to go to Spain. The Spanish Civil War, which began officially on 19 July 1936, aroused the most passionate emotions of the western world. Here was a democratically elected Popular Front government being attacked by a range of right-wing forces that included aristocrats, bankers, clergy and the army. While the western democracies stood by proclaiming a policy of non-intervention, no such qualms beset the new fascist dictatorships of Hitler and Mussolini, who eagerly intervened on the side of Franco and his Nationalists. When the Soviet Union joined in – with more limited help for the Republicans – the struggle seemed to many to have converged into a single moment when the world train could be stopped in its dangerous tracks and the points changed by some mighty act of will.

Thousands of men from Europe and America went to Spain to fight on the Republican side, not out of patriotism but because they believed the democratic ideal had to be actively supported. They included many of the most famous writers and artists of the time, such as George Orwell, John Dos Passos, André Malraux, Stephen Spender and Arthur Koestler, all of whom were deeply committed to the 'Causa', as, melodramatically, Martha always referred to it. This had the effect of persuading newspaper editors that they must therefore send correspondents of the highest calibre to cover such momentous events; most of these correspondents were also passionately involved in what they were witnessing. 'Those of us who championed the cause of the Republican government against the Franco Nationalists were right. It was, on balance, the cause of justice, legality, morality, decency,' wrote Herbert Matthews of the *New York Times*.[6] The Spanish Government was not merely proud of such attention; it desperately relied on the reports of these correspondents to show the world the depths of its despair.

After *The Trouble I've Seen*, Martha had been working on a novel which required research in Germany. There she was sickened by constant references in Nazi newspapers to the democratically elected government of Spain as 'Red Swine Dogs'. Although she had learned virtually nothing about Spanish history, she knew, instinctively, which side she supported. The Nazi brutality surrounding her soon cured her of any youthful pacifism and fuelled the anger against injustice which drove her for the next sixty or so years.

'When I was young I believed in the perfectibility of man, and in progress, and thought of journalism as a guiding light,' was how she explained her ideals some years later.

If people were told the truth, if dishonour and injustice were clearly shown to them, they would at once demand the saving action, punishment of wrong-doers, and care for the innocent. How people were to accomplish these reforms, I did not know. That was their job. A journalist's job was to bring news, to be eyes for their conscience. I think I must have imagined public opinion as a solid force, something like a tornado, always ready to blow on the side of the angels.[7]

She talked about the Spanish Civil War and the anguish of the
Spanish loyalists with Hemingway, who was also preparing to go to
Spain not only as a correspondent of the North American Newspaper
Alliance (NANA), but also because he was making an important propaganda film entitled *The Spanish Earth*. But Martha had trouble finding
an editor who would give her an official reason for entering the country.
Finally, in March 1937, Kyle Crichton, an editor at *Collier's Magazine*,
supplied her with a letter announcing 'To whom it may concern' that
the bearer, Martha Gellhorn, was a special correspondent of theirs in
Spain. The fact that she had no contractual (or other) relationship
with *Collier's*, spoke no Spanish and was totally inexperienced in war
was of no matter. 'I believed that all one did about a war was go to it
as a gesture of solidarity, and get killed or survive if lucky until the
war was over.'[8] The letter was enough to help her with any authorities
who might question her presence in Spain.

So, with just a knapsack and $50, Martha made her way to Paris
and from there applied to the French authorities for whatever stamps
and papers were necessary to leave the country. She took a train south,
got off at the station nearest the Andorran Spanish border and, armed
with a map which she was less than adept at reading, walked the short
distance from one country to another. She then took another train,
old and cold, full of soldiers of the Spanish Republic returning home
on leave, and arrived in Barcelona. Finally, after lifts on trucks and
crowded cars, she reached Madrid at the end of March 1937, just
after the battle of Guadalajara had saved the Spanish capital for the
Republicans and had revealed evidence that Italian troops were actually fighting on the Nationalist side. She plunged into the midst of her
first war.

She did not find it difficult to track down Hemingway, eating in
the basement restaurant in the Gran Via frequented by almost all
correspondents in Madrid, although even at the communal table
reserved for the foreign press the food was at best meagre. Immediately
there followed a scene which disturbed Martha more than she had
allowed for. Hemingway claimed her safe arrival was in large measure
due to him. 'I knew you'd get here, daughter,' he said, getting up from
the table to put his arm around her, 'because I fixed it up so you
could.' Martha was astounded. 'What did he mean? He had fixed
nothing. This was the first of his many little attempts at self-aggran-
dizement that she began to notice.'[9]

In spite of Martha's aversion to such possessiveness, they soon
fell into an affair with little attempt at concealment from the other

correspondents, most of whom were also guests at the Hotel Florida. One night, the hot-water tank in the hotel suffered a direct hit and Ernest and Martha were seen emerging from the same bedroom. Hemingway, it seemed to others, was the one correspondent with everything: a hotel suite, extra food, transport, friends in high places, and now a mistress as well. For weeks, overwhelmed by the situation, Martha felt unable to write a sentence. 'How could I write about war, what did I know and for whom would I write? What made a story, to begin with? Didn't something gigantic and conclusive have to happen before one could write an article?'[10]

But since she was not under pressure from any editors to produce daily news stories and yet was well placed to soak up the atmosphere, she fell in behind the other correspondents, 'experienced men who had serious work to do'. She could easily have drifted in this way for months, learning a little Spanish and visiting hospitals. Another woman writer in Madrid at the time, Josephine Herbst, similarly placed as a freelance without the discipline of a daily deadline or a demanding editor, also found herself blocked. Josephine, a passionate radical with a high reputation as one of America's finest women writers at the time, had been told by a handful of magazines before she left to 'get the women's angle on Spain'. However, feeling herself almost a prisoner in Madrid, and watching dozens of other reporters sending off nightly articles from the telephone building on the Gran Via, paralysed her will to compete. 'For Josie, for long periods, there was no editor wanting anything, there was no audience, the days were empty except for pointless rambles around the city, the nights were terrifying, there was nothing to do except concentrate fearfully on staving off fear,' wrote Herbst's biographer.[11]

Doubtless Martha's personality would have prevented her falling into similar traps, but her affair with Hemingway gave her practical help in Madrid in a number of ways. One of the major problems for most correspondents was getting transport, but she travelled with him and a few other select correspondents to the fronts in and around Madrid. Eventually, prodded by Hemingway, she wrote her first article about the war, based on life in Madrid. Typed on a battered borrowed machine, she maintains that she never expected *Collier's* to publish. It did, under the heading 'Only the Shells Whine', and when it published her second piece her name appeared on the masthead. 'Once on the masthead I was evidently a war correspondent. It began like that.'[12]

From the first, Martha had a natural flair for describing the horrific unreality of war at its most basic level. How crazy it seemed to be living in a hotel, a hotel like any in Des Moines or New Orleans,

with a lobby and wicker chairs in the lounge and signs on the door of your room telling you that they would press your clothes immediately and that meals served privately cost ten pence more and meantime it was like a trench when they lay down an artillery barrage.[13]

She wrote with ease of walking to the ever-crowded Chicote's Bar for a drink at the end of the day. 'On the way you had passed a dead horse and a very dead mule, chopped with shell fragments, and you had passed criss-crossing trails of human blood on the pavement.'[14]

Her style was simple, direct, unadorned, as when she told of the old woman with a shawl over her shoulders, holding a terrified thin little boy by the hand:

You know what she is thinking; she is thinking she must get the child home, you are always safer in your own place with the things you know. Somehow you do not believe you can get killed when you are sitting in your own parlour, you never think that. She is in the middle of the square when the next one comes. A small piece of twisted steel, hot and very sharp, sprays off from the shell; it takes the little boy in the throat. The old woman stands there, holding the hand of the dead child, looking at him stupidly, not saying anything, and men run out toward her to carry the child. At their left, at the side of the square, is a brilliant sign which says: Get out of Madrid.[15]

The uncomprehending child was always for Martha the most frightening symbol of man's brutality in war.

Martha learned about war fast. With a teacher such as Hemingway she soon grasped most that was necessary about shooting, weapons, ballistics and survival and, later, fishing and boats, and remained always grateful for such useful knowledge, rarely part of a middle-class girl's education. In addition to his special privileges of a car with driver and petrol, he was also an invaluable guide, especially when they toured together the four central fronts during the last week of April; Martha impressed him with her courage and bravery in conditions of extreme tension and danger. Her lack of knowledge about warfare even worked to her advantage in that she was fearless in a way that he, understanding for example the constant danger from booby-traps, could never again be. By comparison, Josephine Herbst lost her voice in front of Hemingway in a moment of panic during a violent bombardment: 'I suspect she carried the shame of it to her grave,' surmised her biographer.[16] Hemingway described Martha as the bravest woman he had ever met. 'Since Courage had come to be the yardstick by which Ernest judged people, Martha's possession of this quality dramatically enhanced his admiration of her,' wrote one critic.[17] Martha's reporting debut was so successful that, by October, she was asked by some of the foreign networks to send out short-wave broadcasts from the soundproofed building in the diplomatic quarter. Some of these were re-broadcast in the United States, consolidating her fame there, and at the end of the year, much to Hemingway's anger at being left, she went on a lecture tour of the United States, donating her fees to Spanish medical aid.

There was always an element of competition in Martha's relationship with Hemingway. In a sense she had the easier task in that he, to an extent, found himself forced to write propaganda; he needed to maximise the loyalist victories, and the amount of German and Italian help and overlook the brutality of the communists. But the battlefield Martha chose for herself was the one true to all wars, the pain and suffering of ordinary people trying to keep body and soul together as everything else disintegrates. She could write about the hospitals, the food queues, the unemployed, almost transcribing everyday dialogue, and her reports needed little embellishment for dramatic effect. And whatever Martha absorbed from living with Hemingway, her own reputation, though not established, was already well laid on the foundation of two books and numerous articles before she met him. The Spanish Civil War brought the ghastliness of killing to the home-front towns on a scale never before witnessed and Martha's intense brand of anger for the suffering of ordinary people was perfectly suited to reporting the horror.

Noticeable though Gellhorn was in Madrid, she was not the only glamorous woman reporter in Spain. Virginia Cowles was another American, born in 1910 into a New Hampshire middle-class family, whose father was a doctor. She too was deeply influenced by her mother, Florence, who was divorced from her father and, with no alimony, forced to earn her own living by writing magazine articles. Virginia was a wilful, difficult child at school, but, after formally 'coming out', matured rapidly and went to live in New York. From then on she, like Gellhorn, survived off whatever she could earn for herself and soon found occasional work writing captions for advertising agencies. This bought her a second-hand car in which she drove across the United States, but all the while with an eye open for a chance to move into journalism. Still in her late teens, she was badgering magazine and newspaper editors with her articles and short stories, but collecting as many rejection slips in return.

In 1931, she finally landed a job at a small magazine called *Entre Nous*, enough to get started. Within two years she was taken on by Hearst Sunday Syndicate and became a regular contributor to the 'March of Events' section. Then in 1933, a legacy from her mother materialised and Virginia and her sister found themselves with a windfall of $20,000. They bought two round-the-world tickets for $500 each and Virginia managed to persuade Hearst to take her articles about the countries they were to visit. During the next five months her 'March of Events' column carried a huge variety of stories, many of them concerning women. There was a piece about the surprising independence of women in Burma, the effects of purdah on Muslim women in India, the restricted lives of Hindu married women, as well as others about gambling in China and a marriage bureau in Tokyo. On her return, Virginia wrote her first book, a light-hearted account of her travels entitled *Men are so Friendly*, and was then offered some freelance work.

In 1935, when Mussolini invaded Abyssinia, the resulting crisis shattered the world's fragile calm and Virginia suggested to her editor that she visit both Italy and North Africa for Hearst Sunday papers. Resolutely unqualified as a political reporter, she frankly admitted that 'my knowledge of foreign affairs was negligible'.[18] Although she had travelled extensively in India and the Far East, her reporting had been entirely of peaceful events. None the less, Hearst accepted and she was officially accredited as its correspondent, only to be paid, however, on publication with no guaranteed salary or expenses. It was intended that she would write descriptive stories of the atmosphere in Rome.

Exactly one week after Mussolini's invasion, a chance meeting at a dinner party led Virginia to an exclusive interview with him. Virginia was both striking and elegant but she never explains exactly how, within days of arriving in the Italian capital, she was invited to such a smart evening gathering. 'She was not so much pretty as fascinating to look at,' according to her future husband, Aidan Crawley, 'with large, brown eyes far apart which held one's own steadily, a broad forehead and mouth, tapering chin and a slender figure.'[19] She wrote in her autobiography only that 'she happened to meet' Dino Alfieri, the Minister of Propaganda, 'who told me that he and he alone had the authority to control the interviews Mussolini gave to the Foreign Press'. She begged him to arrange one for her and, much to her amazement, he rang the next morning to say that Mussolini would see her at six o'clock that evening. Virginia then grew extremely nervous and unhappy at the prospect. Never before had she interviewed an international statesman and she agonised about how to prepare the right questions. Inevitably she need not have worried since the Italian leader took command of the conversation and, after a ten-minute angry tirade, instructed her to go home and relay his views to the American people. Virginia, resentful at being told what to do, wrote instead a vivid description of his menacing tone and aggressive actions towards her.

A few days later, Dino Alfieri arranged for Virginia to visit Marshal Balbo, the new Governor of Libya. After a terrifying flight to Tripoli during which the pilot thought that he would not be able to land with the British fleet concentrated in the Mediterranean, Balbo insisted on taking Virginia for a further flight in an old aeroplane which could barely get off the ground. When it finally became airborne, its vibrations almost convinced her that it was about to disintegrate. Balbo also tried to impress her with his ability at shooting and, after a few days, invited her to spend some holiday with him and fly down to a fascinating Arab village several hundred miles from the coast. 'Nothing would have induced me to get into the same plane with the Air Marshal again, and I told him I was sorry but I had to return to Rome. He argued for some time, then shook his head sadly. "I know. The trouble is you don't like my beard," ' Virginia recounted in her autobiography.[20]

Virginia returned to New York with increased prestige because of the ease with which she appeared able to secure interviews with high-ranking male politicians and statesmen. Within six months, Spain was riven by its Civil War and Virginia pressed her editor at Hearst to send her there so that she could visit both sides and write a series of articles contrasting the two. Virginia approached the undertaking not with Gellhorn's passionate outrage to show the wrongs inflicted by one side but with the newshound's motivation to investigate what was the biggest world story. Again, she went with little or no knowledge of the situation and 'not the least idea how to set about such an assignment'. With innate confidence, she assumed a plan would evolve once she got there.

She flew into Spain in March 1937, just after the battle of Guadalajara. Her journey was swifter but no less terrifying than Martha's, leaving Toulouse at five in the morning, crossing the snow-capped Pyrenees and arriving in Barcelona one hour later. Yet one hour after that, Virginia was in Valencia, seat of the Republican Government and a mass of swarming humanity. As she walked about the town, so ill-prepared that she had no Spanish money with her, she asked a passer-by for directions to the best hotel and realised that she was attracting unfriendly stares. This was partly because she seemed to be the only person wearing a hat, but also because her suitcase, which she had owned for years, sported a red and yellow band – Franco's colours.

She made for the Bristol Hotel and introduced herself in the dining-room to a tough, young American reporter, Edward Kennedy, of Associated Press. Thanks to his efficiency, she was found a room in the already overcrowded hotel and was introduced to the Foreign Press Chief, who arranged for her to go to Madrid by car two days later. Kennedy then filled her in on the current situation and quickly disabused her of her notion that Spain was exciting. Virginia never pretended to be other than a novice in this situation, but there was no shortage of more experienced journalists to help her. Sometimes their advice was of dubious assistance as when she arrived in Madrid: 'My room on the fifth floor of the Hotel Florida stamped me as an amateur; knowledgeable people lived as close to the ground as possible as a precaution against aerial bombs,'[21] she wrote. Warned of the dangers, she soon managed to switch to the fourth floor overlooking rolling green hills, but as these were enemy held, the new room was little safer, placing her in direct line of fire.

Also staying at the Florida, in addition to Hemingway and Gellhorn, were several other British correspondents, including the seasoned journalist, Sefton (Tom) Delmer of the *Daily Express*. 'He greeted me by asking hopefully if I had brought any food from France. The fact that I hadn't, I soon realized, was an unforgivable oversight,' she recorded.[22] None the less, Delmer offered to show her the sights and explained the realities of life in Madrid. He made clear to the raw American reporter how journalists risked being expelled by either side if accused of taking up attitudes favouring the one against the other. He was now reporting from the Republican side because he had been expelled by the Nationalists. The *New York Times* had two men, one in each camp. Yet Virginia insisted her plan was to report from both sides.

At first the regular and violent bombardments of Madrid by the fascists terrified her: 'I had never before felt the sort of fear that sends the blood racing through your veins.' Ordinary people were killed every day performing ordinary tasks. The worst deprivation after the bombing was the lack of food; most correspondents felt permanently hungry. In an attempt to overcome this, Delmer's sitting-room in the Hotel Florida became a regular meeting place. He had equipped it with electric burners and chafing dishes and whatever food could be procured by any means. Every night, from eleven o'clock onwards, the press gathered there to consume whatever was on offer. The regulars included Hemingway and Gellhorn, Josephine Herbst, Herbert Matthews of the *New York Times*, 'Hank' Gorrell of United Press, Thomas Loyetha of the International News Service, George and Helen Seldes, Cowles, Delmer himself and others. Madrid was seething with reporters – 'to look at some of their recollections you would think that reporters were all there were in Spain'.[23]

They not only lived together and ate together but

they observed the same incidents together, clucked over the rubble together, and they all studied one another like crows. Contacts could be shared or not shared, rumours could be passed along or withheld, an invitation to a particular correspondent to ride along here or there with a particular official could be extended to include another correspondent or it could be reserved; it all depended.[24]

Fortunately for Virginia, she immediately became part of this intimate coterie.

Virginia remained in Madrid from mid-March to early June and cabled nothing back to Hearst while she was in Spain, waiting until she was on neutral territory before writing. Her aim, she still insisted, was not only to see both sides and contrast them, but to predict a result. From Madrid she went immediately to Paris and her first signed article appeared in the *New York Sunday American* dated 27 June 1937, just before Gellhorn's first piece for *Collier's*, but, like hers, dealing with daily life in Madrid. It was both more detailed and more matter of fact; without emotion she concluded: 'As you walk through the blackness, stumbling over shell holes, you wonder what has happened that a great European city can be reduced to such a state of barbarism.'

Her second article, bylined 'NY society girl sees Americans fighting in Madrid's front trenches',[25] had a more exciting tale to tell. In May 1937, Virginia made a trip to the Morata front, where the International Brigades were fighting to defend the Madrid–Valencia road, the last link between the capital and the outside world. This front was regarded as the most important sector in Spain and was commanded by a Soviet general. But the existence of Russian experts in Spain sent to train the Republican army was being kept secret from foreign journalists. Virginia discovered the Morata headquarters by accident. Driving to the front with a Swedish girl and a French agency journalist, they lost their way and ended up at a ramshackle mill which was serving as divisional headquarters. In the garden of the mill they were confronted by the commanding officer, a middle-aged man with a broad Slavonic face and sullen green eyes. 'His manner was cold and hostile and he curtly cut off our attempts at conversation,' Virginia recorded.[26] He refused to let them pass through the lines and sent them home. A week later, lunching as ever in the Gran Via restaurant, Virginia was approached by a tall soldier who, speaking English with a foreign accent, introduced himself as 'Santiago'. He asked if she had paid a visit to the Morata front a few days previously; if so, he added that the commanding officer wished to apologise and to invite her back for lunch. This was arranged for the following day, with Santiago as chauffeur. Naïvely unaware of the potential danger in store for her, she told no one where she was going.

When they arrived at the mill, Virginia found the commanding officer no more helpful than before, but the lunch – partridges, fresh vegetables and wild strawberries – a decided improvement on standard Madrid rations. There were eight other Russians at the lunch, two Spaniards and a Russian-born American, who acted as interpreter. General Gal, as he called himself, teased Virginia that she was too soft to go to the front. He commented on her foolishness in wearing gold bracelets and expensive black suede shoes. 'You would get tired and want someone to carry you,' he scorned, in a manner she assumed was deliberately provocative. At all events she persuaded him to make the trip after lunch in driving rain amid roaring gunfire. As the General led the way through the mud-filled trenches, they passed soldiers of many nationalities, including German, Slav, French, English and American. The men looked sick and strained; some told her that they had been in the front line for seventy-four days without a break. 'Most of them had been recruited by the Communist parties of the world and they struck me as a pathetic group... they were idealists and down-and-outs, many of them ill-suited for soldiering.'[27]

It was a sobering trip, and when they returned to the mill headquarters, Virginia tried vainly to remove the mud from her clothes and then went to Santiago to arrange about starting back for Madrid. With embarrassment he told her that the General had instructed that she was to remain for at least three days and understand the principles for which they were fighting. She was, he explained, deeply suspect as she was not a communist. 'The General wishes to convert you,' he explained. Virginia was annoyed rather than frightened. She was brought some toothpaste, a comb and a bottle of eau de cologne and shown to a small room with no windows and a hard bed with filthy blankets. Over dinner that night the General became more garrulous. Three bottles of champagne were uncorked which the General used to toast the throat-cutting of the bourgeoisie. Then he asked his unwilling companion, 'Did you ever think you would find yourself drinking champagne with a Red Army general?' During the next two days, Virginia explored the shooting-range while the men had machine-gun practice, and chatted to some of the soldiers. At night, the General enjoyed giving her lessons on Marxism. He warned her to make sure she was on the right side when the revolution came to America, which it surely would. When the three days were up, the General allowed her to leave, as promised, but not before suggesting that she join the Party secretly as a sleeper. She could be very useful, he urged. He was sorry to see her go; he had, he admitted, taken a fancy to her.

Back in Madrid, Virginia found that her disappearance had caused a flurry of excitement. Delmer warned her that, if she was under suspicion as a spy, she should take extra precautions and not travel alone by car as a road accident could easily be 'arranged'. But by then she was in a hurry to reach Valencia from where she was due to fly to Paris. She left and was under surveillance the whole way. Not until a year later, when she returned to Spain, did she discover that the question of her arrest had lain in the balance. 'Even though the press bureau was convinced I was a spy, they had finally decided the amount of publicity given to the arrest of an American journalist would do more harm than good.'[28] Being a woman in Madrid in 1937 was clearly a double-edged weapon: it helped attract her to General Gal's notice but it also drew unwelcome attention to herself.

Virginia wrote about her experiences in three articles only after she reached Paris. 'I had no line to take on Spain as it had not yet become a political story for me,' she admitted. 'I was much more interested in the human side – the forces that urged people to such a test of endurance.... I wrote about the things I had seen and heard but did not try to interpret them.'[29] After a few months she went to St Jean de Luz, a small town on the French side of the Spanish border, to try and arrange a visit to Nationalist lines. She had been warned that she had no chance of getting a visa for Nationalist Spain; no journalist who had been tainted by the Republic had ever been allowed to cross to Franco's side. But by a combination of coincidence and her skill of working up mere acquaintances until they became useful contacts – one of Virginia's outstanding strengths as a reporter – she succeeded.

The British Ambassador to Spain, Sir Henry Chilton, had a home a few miles away from St Jean de Luz. The Cowleses had known his daughter Anne in New York and through them met Franco's agent, the Count of Mamblas. 'On looking back,' Virginia wrote, 'I suppose I took unfair advantage of the Count... having met me under the auspices he did, I suppose he bracketed me as "safe".'[30] Evidently the old Count decided that a visit to Nationalist Spain would provide such a contrast to the red chaos she had previously witnessed that it could only enhance their cause in western eyes. Three weeks later the visa was granted.

By the time Virginia arrived in Nationalist Spain, Franco was in a strong position and it appeared as if the war might be over by the spring. During her two months she visited Avila, Talavera, Toledo, the wreck of Guernica and the outskirts of Madrid. Here she overlooked the streets in which, only a few weeks before, she had taken cover from the shells which were now being lobbed into the city behind her. She was shocked by the overt presence of German and Italian support and, when she was not being shepherded around by official escorts, tried to talk to everyone she could find to understand why they had come to Spain to fight. It was, she said, 'like piecing scraps of information together and trying to make a composite picture out of the whole crazy pattern'. Most of her random informants told her how important it was to destroy Bolshevism. 'The only thing the Reds like to do is destroy. You must emphasise that in one of your articles, the joy of destruction,' she was advised by one of her aristocratic guides, Captain Aguilera, a Nationalist cavalry officer.[31] When she responded to this with less enthusiasm than he expected, relations grew strained – so strained indeed that when she had returned to Salamanca and applied for travel permits to France, she was refused. 'You will remain here until you hear further from us,' she was told. Virginia suspected that Captain Aguilera had submitted a hostile report on her and she realised that she had to flee the country as quickly as possible.

Knowing that her previous trip to the Republican side could provide the basis of a spying charge against her and that other correspondents had been gaoled for less, she decided to make her way to San Sebastian, although she recognised this would be difficult without the proper travel papers. One after another, Virginia's tenuous contacts in the right places were tapped to help her escape. First she 'ran into' the Duc de Montellano, a friend of a friend, who drove her to Burgos. From there Count Cosme Churrucca, a Spaniard whom she barely knew and an extreme fascist, agreed to drive her to San Sebastian. At San Sebastian she had 'the good fortune to run into' Eddie Neil of Associated Press, who bought her a drink and updated her with the situation, and finally Tommy Thompson, the First Secretary to Sir

Henry Chilton whom she had cabled, came to her hotel and her rescue.

He decided that the only solution was to take a chance and drive her out in the official Embassy car sporting a large Union Jack on the bonnet. Virginia wrote in her memoirs:

I shall never forget approaching the international bridge ... when the Spanish guards stopped us, Tommy handed them his *salvo conducto*. They inspected it carefully and I waited for the terrible moment when they would turn to me. It never came; they nodded with a satisfied air, handed back the paper and saluted. The barriers rose slowly, Tommy stepped on the gas and we dashed across the bridge to freedom.

Once again she wrote her articles after she had settled in neutral territory, this time London, and as her contract with Hearst lasted until the end of 1937, most of her articles appeared in American publications. But her first piece for the *Sunday Times* was published on 20 October 1937 with the dateline claiming, 'Article written in the Gran Hotel, Salamanca, where Franco has his headquarters'.

As Virginia soon realised, from a journalistic point of view, she could not have chosen a better moment to arrive in London where there was a huge demand for articles on Spain. 'Conversationally, the war was almost an obsession. It was like a crystal that held all the shades of the rainbow; you turned it to the light and chose the colours that suited you.'[32] Until her contract with Hearst expired, the only way she could write for the *Sunday Times*, apart from one or two pieces by special arrangement, was anonymously or under the byline 'correspondent lately in Spain'. One such article explained how Franco acquired foreign currency to pay for petrol and supplies for his army; the Rio Tinto Zinc company was obliged to deposit the equivalent in sterling of pesetas at a fixed rate in order to obtain a permit for any shipment made abroad. In the second of her signed articles for the *Sunday Times* she was introduced by the paper as 'a young, dark, glamorous American writer who has been covering the Spanish War – from both fronts. She is now on holiday in London.' The piece was described as 'not front page news but ... exciting if you're there yourself ... the sort of things you would have experienced if you had been on the road in Spain this week'.[33]

However patronising such introductions might appear, they made known the name of Virginia Cowles. During her 'holiday' in London, she reflected on the situation she had witnessed in Spain and, in honing her views, her subsequent articles became more reflective, showing greater political understanding of the world situation. Although her own sympathies lay with the Republic, she now recognised that she did not believe, even if Republican Spain were victorious, that democracy could emerge in Spain as the Communist Party had become too strong. Franco and the Nationalists, she believed, would win and trample on it. Having seen the Germans and Italians at work in Spain, she believed the fascist menace to be far more dangerous than the communist, and, as she explained in one of her pieces for the *Sunday Times*, the Germans and Italians were far less concerned about fighting Bolshevism than in training their armies for the day when they could expand at the expense of Great Britain and France.

A copy of the article was shown, through Virginia's friend Tommy Thompson, to Sir Robert Vansittart, then Permanent Under-Secretary of State for Foreign Affairs and in a pivotal position to shape British foreign policy. He summoned Virginia to his office and told her, revealingly, that he had expected from her article a middle-aged woman with flat-heeled shoes and a man's tie. Virginia stood out in an era when it was still considered extraordinary for a woman to have both looks and intelligence. Vansittart was deeply interested to hear Virginia's first-hand account of the Nazis in Spain and it was not difficult for her to gauge accurately Vansittart's extreme concern at the growing tide of appeasement in Britain.

After this meeting, Virginia began a warm friendship with Sir Robert and Lady Vansittart and established in London a circle of close and influential friends, all the more remarkable since she herself was aware that the upper echelons of British society were a tightly knit band. 'What surprised me most about these gatherings was that everyone seemed to have known everyone else since childhood,' she wrote. But immediately on her arrival in England, Virginia's charm and extraordinary talent at blending into new situations landed her a temporary post on the *Evening Standard*, where she attracted the attention of Lord Beaverbrook, who often invited her for a cup of tea and some provocative conversation. Probably, she was introduced to the *Standard* by Randolph Churchill, Winston's son, who worked there and had met Virginia in New York many years previously. Randolph was both charming and difficult. He loved to hear Virginia's views on current affairs and, in return, introduced her around. On one occasion, after Lloyd George had referred to her unsigned article on Spain in the House of Commons, Randolph offered to present him to the author. 'When I stepped out of the car, the old man regarded me with surprise that almost bordered on resentment. I suppose it was a shock to find the eminent authority he had quoted was just a green young woman.'[34] More significantly, Randolph soon presented Virginia to his father, a prize which she used sparingly but to decisive effect in her reporting over the next few years.

Although Martha and Virginia shared several attributes and external similarities, they were essentially different creatures. Martha wrote very fast from few notes: 'I was always afraid that I would forget the exact sound, smell, words, gestures which were special to this moment and this place.'[35] Virginia preferred time to reflect and discuss, away from the heat of the moment. Martha, with a healthy cynicism for authority, never trusted the views of the generals and politicians, describing such officials as 'boring and liars and fakes'.[36] For Virginia, getting to the top man in any situation was both important in itself and valuable for smoothing her path whenever she might need their help. Martha believed passionately in being partisan; as long as you describe what you have seen accurately, why should there be a need to put the case for the other side too? Virginia, however, drew strength from her determination to give both sides a fair hearing.

Even their reasons for going to Spain were different: Martha because she saw writing as a way of doing something in a situation about which she already felt passionately; Virginia because, for her, writing was a way of understanding, but not necessarily changing, momentous world events. Martha had been prepared to travel there even without any commitment from a newspaper to take her work – a freedom she valued highly; Virginia, while not a full-scale accredited correspondent, had at least the security of a contract.

While the two American women visited hospitals and prisons together and, in each other's company, were to make several more forays into international politics, their sense of sisterhood was not always as strong as their ambition. 'There never was anywhere a more inaccurate reporter than Virginia Cowles,' Martha says today, in her mid-eighties. 'She lived on gossip and was very lazy. She did not give a damn about journalism. . . . (She was charming and fun.)'[37] This is an ironic criticism since the charge of inaccuracy could just as easily be laid at Martha's own door, given her aversion to note-taking[38] and her personal involvement in the war. Martha told one recent interviewer that she can never read a book about the Spanish Civil War because 'they might get the facts right but not capture the emotion, the commitment, the feeling that we were all in it together, the certainty that we were right'.[39]

As Phillip Knightley commented:

The drawback of reporting with heart as well as mind is that, if the cause is basically just, as the Republican one undoubtedly was, the correspondent tends to write in terms of heroic endeavour rather than face unpalatable facts, and to mislead his readers with unjustified optimism. Few resisted the temptation.[40]

Virginia Cowles strove harder for objectivity and balance, whatever she felt privately, and her emotions were not strained. Both she and Martha Gellhorn were raw and untried before Spain, but matured rapidly afterwards. Spain signified for both if not sisterhood, at least the onset of adulthood.

8

Awaiting World War

uropean tension mounted steadily in the years following Hitler's
accession to power. The western democracies seemed paralysed
as, month after month, Hitler made further outrageous
demands. By the mid-1930s, both Shiela Grant Duff and Elizabeth
Wiskemann recognised that safeguarding Czechoslovakia's independence was crucial, even if their own country's leaders did not
consider this an important British interest. Czechoslovakia was shakily
supported by a pact with the Soviet Union, but this would come into
effect only if France acted first, and the French were divided. In
addition, the three million Germans resident within Czech borders
(not all of whom lived in the Sudetenland) gave the Nazis an excuse
to exploit international guilt. In short, to clear-sighted observers
Czechoslovakia seemed calculated to explode whenever Hitler was
ready to light the fuse.

Elizabeth Wiskemann paid her first visit to Prague in 1935, becoming good friends with the Masaryk family among others, and through
her relationships with a number of important individuals from this
time on was able to build up an invaluable network of contacts on
which to base her detailed and penetrating reports of the country. In
June 1936, Shiela Grant Duff, too, concluded that by stationing herself
in Prague there was a chance she could save the country from Hitler;
being a reporter was a means but certainly not an end in itself. Shocked
at the ignorance about Czechoslovakia which she encountered on all
sides in Britain, she hoped that she could at least inform the public
and those in authority about the true state of affairs. Having decided
this, she went to the *Observer* for an interview. She was not seen by

the editor, J. L. Garvin, who was already in favour of appeasing Hitler and did not consider it necessary to meet his minor correspondents, but by Massingham. He agreed to her going, although since she was paying her own way there was little to agree to, but he told her lightly that there was a possibility they already had a correspondent in the country. 'Oh no! I think he died,' he corrected himself, 'but if you should happen to meet him just say you're "a" correspondent and not "the" correspondent of the *Observer*.' Shiela then asked what aspects of Czechoslovakia particularly interested *Observer* readers: 'Oh, cows with five legs and that sort of thing,' he replied.[1] She was still, at twenty-three, having great difficulty in being taken seriously.

Thanks to Hugh Dalton, the Labour spokesman on foreign affairs for whom she had done some secretarial work, Shiela arrived in Prague with letters of introduction to Masaryk and his successor, Eduard Beneš. She had other entrées to important artists, writers and musicians. Almost immediately she wrote her name in the British Legation book, which led to an invitation to meet Sir Joseph Addison, the British Minister in Prague. She enjoyed her lunch with him, but was dismayed at his attitude, which she found reflected by numerous officials. When she asked if he had many Czech friends, he replied in horror: 'Friends? They eat in their kitchens.' His friends were Bohemian noblemen. He went on to tell her that she was the sort of person who was ruining England by her anti-patriotism 'and that women should never have anything to do with politics because they introduce sentiment into them'.[2] Not surprisingly, Shiela was distressed by 'the complete contempt for what one was trying to do'.[3] The advice she was given from other British officials was simple: 'I hope you're not promoting war,' they told her.[4]

When she discovered that, in 1936, she was the only resident British correspondent in Prague, she began to understand the reason for the depths of ignorance in England of Czechoslovakia's economy, geography, history and culture. However, getting accurate information out was not going to be easy. In the first place, there was 'no band of helpful newspapermen as in the Saar, no established office like the ones where I had worked in Paris or Berlin'.[5] All the British Central European correspondents were based in Vienna and relied on stringers, who were mostly German émigrés in Prague. Massingham was not prepared to authorise her to have an office or an expense account. 'All the *Observer* paid for was what it cost to communicate with them and the space my copy filled.' Without her £3 a week – and a free pass on Czech railways – she could not have carried out her assignment.

She might even have come home had she not met Hubert Ripka, a man of intellect and influence, 'a real and lasting friend'.[6] Ripka was diplomatic correspondent of the independent paper, *Lidove Noviny*, and confidant of Beneš; a man of seriousness and fun, great understanding and fighting temperament. He shared many of Mowrer's views on the world crisis and took on Mowrer's role as mentor in Shiela's life. Under his tutelage she studied Czech history, geography and economics, was furnished with introductions to leaders of the principal parties and travelled around the country as much as possible, especially in the Sudeten area, talking to men of widely differing views, including members of Konrad Henlein's pro-Nazi party.

From the first, Shiela was emotionally involved in the situation surrounding her. Although this did not blind her to the political realities, the more she grasped them the more frustrated she felt at her impotence. Two items she wrote for the *Observer* in the summer of 1936, reporting on Beneš's conciliatory tour of the German districts, were spiked in London as the paper's creeping line of appeasement took hold. When an innocuous piece she sent them on Czech manœuvres was published, she realised that her position as a correspondent for the newspaper was increasingly untenable. They used this report, which could be made to fit into their position of criticising Beneš and Czech policy, under the headline 'Striking Power of the Czechoslovak Army', so that it appeared as if the Czechs, not the Germans, were the warmongers.

Shiela was deeply embarrassed by her newspaper's tone in front of her Czech friends and contacts, some of whom 'argued flatteringly that I myself was the initiator of the paper's new line, others that I was not really a journalist at all'.[7] She comforted herself with the fact that she was also now writing for the *Spectator*, but as these were unsigned pieces no one was to know. For the time being she carried on. Ripka recognised his protégée's naïveté along with her genuine commitment and took it upon himself to turn her into a serious political reporter. He did not deal with her lightly because she was a woman; on the contrary, he expected her to work as hard as he did himself. In September 1936, he took her with him to the Conference of the Little Entente (Czechoslovakia, Romania and Yugoslavia) in Bratislava, which she would not have been able to attend without his help since the *Observer* had refused her request to cover it for them.

Shiela continued to meet Adam von Trott periodically during this time. He had already proposed marriage, but her anguish over the international crisis and her belief that her work was the only way she could influence the situation was constantly driving them further apart. Then, in February 1937, when Shiela was due to meet him for the last time before he left Europe, sent by the Rhodes Trust to study in China, she received a reporting assignment from Edgar Mowrer that she might have been better equipped to deal with had she been trained in espionage. While most of Shiela's emotional energy was harnessed to Czechoslovakia and eastern Europe, it was inevitable at some point that she would be caught up in the Spanish Civil War, 'one of the great battles of human history (whose) mythic quality moved us all'.[8] She went to Paris, where Mowrer explained that she was required to go to Malaga, which had fallen to Franco, and discover how Republican prisoners were being treated – in particular, there was concern over the fate of Arthur Koestler, representing the *News Chronicle* and arrested as a Republican spy – and to learn if the fascists were fortifying Malaga harbour. Mowrer told her that he could not send any of the *Chicago Daily News* staff correspondents because they were too well known for their pro-Republican line. Shiela, he thought, would be unnoticed. The fact that, as a young girl, she was not taken seriously would, this time, work to her advantage. However, he advised her to get a new passport in Paris as her old one had a Soviet visa in it. Not only had Shiela never flown before, but she also spoke no Spanish and knew nothing about the country. Mowrer reassured her: she would approach Malaga from the south; tickets would be provided as far as Tangier and then she would make her own way to Malaga where she was to contact the American consul, adding that he was a stout supporter of the Spanish Government.

'I reached Malaga, unaided I am glad to say, in a bus from Algeciras,' she recalled later. 'To find the consul was more difficult since there were no taxis, the streets were deserted after nightfall and when I reached his house, it was protected by a huge garden wall which I had to climb.'[9] Once they met, he invited her to dine, but she quickly recognised that Mowrer had been mistaken: he was a Nationalist sympathiser as were his fellow guests. As midnight approached they invited her to watch an execution:

I felt confronted ... with a stark choice the consequences of which would stay with me forever. For a young journalist it would be a sensational coup; for a spy it was precisely one of the things I had been sent to find out; for a human being, it would be to stand and watch people whom I regarded as friends and allies being put to death in cold blood. I knew I would never be able to live with this. I did not go.[10]

Suspicious of her refusal, the following day one of the Nationalist escorts demanded to see her passport and was alerted by its pristine state to ask more probing questions about her true identity and purpose for being so close to the front. Angrily, he threatened to return that evening and have her sent to Seville for a full investigation. Knowing therefore that she had just one day, she set about her task without delay. She bluffed her way past teenage guards at the harbour gate and saw crates of rotting oranges but no fortifications being built; she attended a summary court trying Republican prisoners and saw how the sentences carried out the previous midnight had been reached. Finally, she learnt from the British consul that Koestler was probably alive in Seville awaiting investigation.

The next day she caught the first bus to La Linea and walked 'trembling but safe' into Gibraltar. She had been frightened during almost the entire escapade. There she cabled her findings to the *Chicago Daily News*, crossed over to Tangier, took a train to Oran and flew back to Paris – where Adam was waiting. But he neither understood nor shared her passionate commitment to the cause of Spanish freedom, an attitude almost as alarming as that confronting her in London, where she stayed before returning to Prague. This time her appointment was with the news editor of the *Observer*, a man who had been regularly spiking her copy from Czechoslovakia and who told her, now that she queried this, that journalists did not dictate editorial policy. From other friends she learnt that her position in Prague was becoming dangerous on two fronts: the sympathetic stories she was writing were not getting through while her meetings with Germans in Prague were leading some to suspect that she was in the pay of Germany. She returned, disconsolate, to Prague in the spring of 1937, reassured only slightly by a commission to be Prague correspondent of a New York periodical, the *Financial Observer*, as well as by an invitation to write a pamphlet for the *New Fabian Research Bureau* (NFRB) on the German problem in Czechoslovakia as a threat to world peace.

However, the New York newspaper collapsed after two editions as did her patience with the editorial line of the *Observer*. In mid-May, provoked by an article by Garvin on the problem of the German minority, she resigned. She sent him a three-page letter in which she argued her corner against his assertion that the pacts with Russia, signed by Czechoslovakia and France, threatened to drag Europe into war.

She was still writing for the *Spectator*, but, urged by Ripka to undertake more practical work on behalf of the Czech cause, returned home and made contact with Winston Churchill (initially through a tenuous family link on her mother's side with his wife, Clementine) and other political leaders. Her pamphlet for the NFRB was published to a warm response while she was in England and led to her receiving further requests for articles. Although she returned to Prague and Berlin that autumn, she felt that she could be more helpful if based in London, keeping the contact open with Churchill, making occasional forays to Czechoslovakia, and, in 1938, writing a book called *Europe and the Czechs*, one of a new series of Penguin Specials on current political issues.

Elizabeth Wiskemann, in the summer of 1936, also was in an invidious position: an acknowledged expert on Germany who could not enter the country. Not surprisingly, she turned her attention to Czechoslovakia and, two-and-half months after her arrest in Berlin, returned to Prague. Helped by her fluency in German, she immediately organised dozens of meetings with a wide cross-section of Czech, German and Slovak leaders as well as Bohemian aristocrats and social-ist workers, such as Wenzel Jaksch, a leader of the Sudeten German socialists, and Otto Strasser, whose brother Gregor had been mur-dered by Hitler.

After this visit she produced one of the most clear-sighted pieces of reportage on inter-war Europe. As ever, it was the result of hours of work – she always insisted that she never interviewed as such but asked for a confidential talk from which nothing would be quoted verbatim except statistics. She used what she had learnt and blended it with other eye-witness accounts, subjected it to the rigours of historical analysis and then extracted the essentials. In this she was both a true professional and a craftswoman.

In 'Czechoslovakia Prepares', published by the *New Statesman and Nation* on 31 October 1936, she recognised that Czechoslovakia was bound to be Hitler's next Saturday midday coup victim; it was the quickest way to attack Russia. Elizabeth understood all the nuances of the struggle:

The more Czechoslovakia rearms the more employment is provided for the Czech workmen in the big heavy industries and the more the appalling unemployment in the German glass and china industries appears to the Germans as due to malicious discrimination. . . . Inevitably while rearmament and fortification claim the Government's main attention social reform is neglected and democratic freedom tends to be curtailed. . . . Militarisation tends to require procedure by decree in place of parliamentary legislation but

there are many who believe that democracy can only defend itself today by
acting as promptly as its enemies.

In 1937, she was invited by Chatham House, the Royal Institute of
International Affairs, to write a book on the Czech–German problem,
a commission which meant relinquishing her university post and
establishing herself in a small flat near the Charles River in Prague.
By using basic methods of investigative reporting, Elizabeth discovered that Konrad Henlein, leader of the Sudeten Germans,
however charming and honest he appeared (even to many in London),
was obviously in the pay of Nazi Germany. A 'source' in the Czech
National Bank told her exactly how much foreign currency Henlein
was allowed when he went abroad. This was generally sufficient only
for one night and day lived in the style which he demanded, yet he
usually stayed away for at least a week. When not studying Bohemian
and Moravian history, she talked to everyone she could but, like Shiela
Grant Duff, was disappointed by the unhelpful attitude of the British
Legation, who made it clear 'that its staff, naturally enough, did not
care for young women who might get themselves into scrapes'. As a
result of what she was writing for newspapers, she was constantly
subjected 'to what now seem to me blackmailing reproaches about my
"unkind" attitude towards Henlein ... another form of blackmail was
to call one a hysterical warmonger'.[11]

Elizabeth came home to write her book and for four months worked
assiduously to submit her manuscript early as she felt any delay might
render it out-of-date and unpublishable. By March, once Hitler's army
had stormed into and annexed Austria, it was clear to all but the
blindest that Czechoslovakia, with its unresolved and aggravated
German problem, was to be next. Still the British Government and
others believed Hitler might stop there. *The Times*, in its leader articles,
was at pains to point out how the Viennese welcomed their Nazi
invaders. In May 1938, with no illusions, Elizabeth returned to Prague,
where she was when her book was published on 2 June. It was a
depressing visit as all the British newspapers were now arguing, from
a position of guilt towards the Germans, that Hitler should be allowed
the German-speaking part of Czechoslovakia and that this would
prevent a second European war. Elizabeth went next to the United
States and Canada for a three-month lecture tour and seriously considered remaining in America, 'since it was clearly going to be increasingly difficult to write the truth in Europe while the policy of
appeasement lasted'.[12]

Martha Gellhorn and Virginia Cowles both made further trips to
Spain in 1938, but by this time the Republican struggle was lost.
The Spaniards knew, as they told Cowles: 'Soon new things will be
happening. We are only the first.'[13] And so, in 1938, both Martha and
Virginia set off to report on the doomed situation in the forlorn
democracy of Czechoslovakia. Virginia went first in May to cover the
Sudeten Germans' election campaign for the *Sunday Times*. Together
with a male colleague from the *Daily Mail*, she was shepherded by
Herr Ulrich, Press Chief of the Sudeten Nazi Party, to see the Henlein
rallies in Aussig, a town ninety miles north-west of Prague near the
German frontier. As Ulrich got drunker during the train journey, he
let slip what Elizabeth Wiskemann had known all along: that Henlein
was a Nazi agent, at that moment with Hitler at Berchtesgaden planning the German army's assault on Czechoslovakia. They did not
spend long at the rally as they soon heard that Czechoslovakia was
mobilising in reaction to a German threat. They needed to return to
the capital to find a working telephone link with London.

Although that particular crisis passed, the Czech army demobilised
and British and French statesmen gave President Beneš a severe
reprimand. From then on every Czech knew that sooner rather than
later there would be a major showdown. Virginia believed from what
she saw that the Czechs would have fought and fought well; that,
although they knew they could not ultimately vanquish, they could
have inflicted heavy German casualties. She spent the summer months
on trains between France, Germany and Czechoslovakia recording
and trying to interpret the endless vacillations of the western powers
to Hitler's relentless pressure on Beneš. Her schedule was relieved
only in June by an enjoyable few weeks travelling around England with
Martha Gellhorn, who had just returned from Prague and was now
trying to get an idea of what ordinary working men in England thought
about the prospects of a war over Czechoslovakia.

In her autobiography, Virginia described her travelling companion
as 'A tall blonde girl with a brilliant gift for writing and a passionate
concern for the underdog, she refused to take the woes of the world
lightly'. Martha had been commissioned by *Collier's* to write about
British reaction to fascism, Hitler's aggression and the vulnerability of
the British Isles. The women talked to waiters in a Leeds café, textile
workers in the Midlands, armaments workers in Sheffield and Newcastle, and were shocked by the confusion of the replies. The most
common assumptions were that things were never as bad as they
seemed in the papers, that 'Mr Chamberlain was a fine man because

he was pledged to do everything to keep the country out of war',[14] and that the weather or racing were still the most important topics of conversation. 'Martha was infuriated by the complacency... the fact that the working man in England was not stung to fury [as she was] by the treatment of his brothers in Spain or the doom of his brothers in Czechoslovakia struck her as shameful.'[15] Soon the trip became something of a lecture tour as Martha constantly harangued her random interviewees with the facts about Hitler and his armies if they intimated that they were against war. In Yorkshire, the pair stopped for tea with Sim Feversham, then Under-Secretary of State for Agriculture, who told them that they were acting like warmongers, stirring. up the country.

Martha stated that she was going to stir up more trouble by talking to his peasants. 'In England we call them farmers,' he said. 'I know', retorted Martha, 'that's what you CALL them.' Later, they tramped across fields to meet some tenant farmers, who agreed with their master that talk'of war was rather silly.

Martha returned to Paris in early July to write up her report in a mood of fierce anger. 'I think that England is a kid glove fascism,' she wrote to her mother,[16] 'worse because of its hypocrisy and the fact that all of the people are fooled all of the time... day by day the ten per cent who rule that country are practising a cynical opportunism, which is certainly pushing off the chances of peace farther and farther, the while they deny with amusement the mere suggestion of war.'[17] In her *Collier's* article, 'The Lord Will Provide – for England', she vented her scorn at the privileged British training each other in civil defence.

When an old woman said that she did not think ten minutes was much of a warning, Martha commented:

The English are fortunate, I thought, they haven't any imagination at all. I asked the gentlewoman who was secretary of this course (and she stared at me) whether anyone here knew what was being talked about; had any of them considered Spain and China. Had anyone the remotest idea of the exhausting, persistent menace of death from the air? The poor are pretty indifferent to all this; they haven't the money to buy gas-proof rooms and have no gardens in which to sink bombproof cellars, and besides, they aren't told very much because there's no use disturbing them.

She then stated publicly what she was saying in private:

The English have always had the privilege of fighting their wars someplace else, but now England is preparing to fight in her own air, over her own fields and cities, and the prospect is pleasing to no one.[18]

She spent much of the summer in Paris waiting for war, often with Ernest Hemingway, who had by this time suggested marriage. Martha, however, was not yet convinced she wanted to change her relationship with him from lover to husband and was committed to her work, which required her to move as freely as possible between Prague, London and Paris. Her reports from Prague, written less in outrage than in sadness, were more than just impressions. After travelling to all the frontiers she was able to explain why the geography of the country was against it. It was, she described, shaped like a badly made kite with its head (the Sudetenland) resting in Germany.

'The uncertainty of all this is enough to break your heart... the Czechs are so terribly strained by these months of uncertainty and waiting and bullying that they do not much care.... '[19] Then on 29 September 1938, Chamberlain, whom Martha considered one of the most hateful figures on the contemporary stage, flew with Daladier, the French Premier, to meet Hitler in Munich and give away the Sudetenland in return for the fluttering scrap of paper offering 'peace in our time'. For Gellhorn, 'the moral of that moment in history has lasted for me permanently; never believe governments, not any of them, not a word they say; keep an untrusting eye on what they do'.[20] Gellhorn's work for the rest of her life is a testament to this conviction.

Within a week of Hitler marching into Czechoslovakia, *Collier's* cabled her instructions to go to Prague, just as the *Sunday Times*, for whom she was now a permanent 'roving' correspondent, ordered Virginia Cowles there too. 'I can do a fine story called "Obituary of a Democracy", I am wild with anger and this is my chance.... Democracy is dying. The disease is called cowardice.... Everybody's in Prague, waiting for the end,' Martha wrote to her mother.[21]

Virginia, factually, described the end:

Germany's first zone of entry was in the south, near the former Austrian border.... As we neared the Sudeten zone we passed long columns of Czech troops with artillery and machine-gun units slowly retreating from their frontier positions. We could feel the bitterness of an army which had been defeated without a shot being fired.... The Henleinist peasants, heavily armed with rifles and revolvers, had taken over the Czech road patrol, and the atmosphere was one of high tension and hostility.... After being twice held up at the point of a revolver, we were, finally, arrested by a group of belligerent peasants near the small village of Oberplan and spent the night in jail.[22]

Martha left Prague on the last civilian aeroplane and was immedi-

ately sent to do 'post-mortem' articles on France and England, judging
the response to Hitler's latest action. This time she took even less
trouble to conceal her fury at those in the pro-Munich ruling class.
She preached of the inevitability of war and 'promised them that they
would get it too, in turn; they would be bombed like Spain; they had
sold out the Spanish people and the Czechs and I was never going to
set foot on their cursed island again'.[23] In fact, she did return to the
cursed island in 1943, when she found it a different country. 'Of
course they all behaved splendidly in war,' she commented later.[24]

November 1938 found Martha in Paris again, struggling with an
article for *Collier's*, which she was calling 'Mr Chamberlain's peace'.
This time she was berating the League High Commissioner for Refugees, Sir Neill Malcolm, who 'showed up for two days in Prague and
didn't see a single refugee. But I had seen them, all of them, all over
the place and I was sick at heart and very angry.' In a letter to her
mother she described what she did next:

I went to his hotel and saw him and pounded the table as always and shouted
and pleaded and explained and described and then he said what should he
do, which kind of surprised me. I suggested he see Sirovy [General Sirovy,
Prime Minister of Czechoslovakia] at once and get the blanket expulsion
order which was sending these people back to Hitler held up.... He said
he'd see Sirovy if I'd get the American Minister at Prague to make the
appointment.[25]

She then described the complicated negotiations which followed,
including a telephone call she made herself to Sirovy pretending to be
Sir Neill's interpreter, which won her an appointment. But all to no
avail. Sirovy refused to grant a stay for the refugees. 'I'll maybe lose
my mind with the fury and the helplessness,' Martha concluded.

Spain, which was the cause closest to Martha's heart, was in an
even worse state as those who had survived the bullets were now slowly
being killed off by hunger. She witnessed many heart-rending scenes
of haggard mothers and starving children during her final visit there
in November 1938:

My work was useless, none of my articles had saved anyone. When I saw the
starved, withered babies in the Barcelona Children's Hospital and the eyes of
the silent wounded children I decided to get out. Leave Europe, leave History.
I could not help anyone; I could remember for them.[26]

Early in 1939, Martha decamped to Cuba (and Hemingway), where
she wrote a short story that encapsulated her deepest emotions about

Spain, although the setting was Czechoslovakia. 'The enemy was the same; the people were equally abandoned, alone, and related by pain.'[27] She wrote it quickly, springing as it did from such a deep well of pain, but at the same time with much pleasure. In the disaster engulfing Europe writing was all she could do:

I think, no doubt selfishly, that right now there is nothing to do about it except help one's friends. And write about it . . . as an act of faith, believing still in telling the truth . . . and also write to save one's sanity, not to think, to lose oneself in a specific problem of construction, imagination and sentences.[28]

Fiction for Gellhorn was always more rewarding but always harder than journalism. The advantages of fiction were, chiefly, that 'you had much more time, as much time and space as you want, and can go into a degree of detail which you can never do in journalism'.[29] On the other hand, there was something magnetic about the attractions of journalism; however ghastly, she had to go and see for herself. But above all, journalism was her bread and butter, it paid for her luxury, the time to write fiction. For the rest of her life she managed to keep the two more or less in symbiosis. 'In journalism you are reporting exactly what you see but your point of view and your sympathy being your own, you can use some of the skills of fiction to make it come alive.'[30]

However, the critics in 1940 were not so certain that she could rein in both disciplines. The heroine of *A Stricken Field* is Mary Douglas, an American reporter who bears more than a passing resemblance to Martha. Mary arrives in Prague in 1938 in an atmosphere of devastation created by the Munich pact. Through her friends Rita, a German refugee, and Peter, Rita's lover, Mary herself becomes involved in the destruction of the state. Reviewers tended to ignore the prescience of Gellhorn's prose, treating the book as thinly veiled autobiography. Martha admitted that the comments of the *Philadelphia Record* put the general criticism succinctly when it described *A Stricken Field* as 'a compelling piece of reporting and a so-so novel'. Sybille Bedford believes that Martha can write brilliantly about immediate experiences but less well about those further in the past. 'The talents which make her such a good journalist do not make for distilled fiction and her novels, therefore, are not on a par with her journalism.'[31]

The death of Czechoslovakia was the major story of the decade and four women reporters, all of whom felt passionately about the injustice being done to the country, did their best in different ways to bring the situation to the world's notice. Shiela Grant Duff, frustrated by her lack of influence on the newspaper for which she reported, eventually resigned and, basing herself in London, worked through her own high-level contacts and wrote a book which sold 190,000 copies. Elizabeth Wiskemann wrote closely argued newspaper essays as well as an important book on the subject, but then travelled to America to lecture in the hope of increasing her influence that way. Virginia Cowles continued writing her contributions for the *Sunday Times* as objectively as possible, but Martha Gellhorn, as well as her polemical articles for *Collier's* about what she saw as British complacency in the face of Czech despair, shared the views of Wiskemann and Grant Duff that reporting alone was an inadequate tool in such a desperate fight. Gellhorn alone used fiction to strengthen her case and *A Stricken Field* makes a more powerful, if emotional, case than her articles ever could. Later Gellhorn herself regretted the way she had blended fact and fiction in this novel. She had used 'two of my own small acts in that tragedy as part of the story. It was not my tragedy and I disliked myself for taking a fictionalized share.'[32]

9

The Beginning of War

'I'm a journalist . . . . This is how I earn my living.'
CLARE HOLLINGWORTH

In the months that followed the fall of Czechoslovakia, Europe became more tense than ever; Britain sank into a depression as most Britons accepted stoically the inevitability of war. But would Hitler now turn his attention to the Soviet Union in an attempt to destroy communism and if so, a few wondered, might he be doing the western world a favour? When the *Sunday Times* proposed to Virginia Cowles that she make a six-week trip to Moscow to write a series of articles on current conditions in that country, she viewed it as 'almost a holiday... I welcomed the chance to escape from the gloom of London.'[1]

Virginia's brief, however, in spite of her holiday spirit, was not merely to report on the goods in the shops or the artistry of the ballet companies but to dig for the political story and evaluate Stalin's intentions. Was he still interested in co-operating with the western powers? What were his relations with Poland and, above all, after the massive purge of 1937, was the Russian army capable of fighting anyone? Virginia approached her assignment with her usual open mind: 'I had no bias either for or against the Soviets; I wanted to see for myself.' In fact, she had wanted to see for herself for some time but her application for a Russian visa two years previously had been refused with no explanation. This time Randolph Churchill took her to lunch with Mr Maisky, the Soviet Ambassador in London, to whom she had also been recommended by Sir Robert Vansittart. When she arrived in Warsaw, the visa was awaiting her and she then wired to a friend in Moscow, Fitzroy Maclean, Second Secretary at the British Embassy and a fluent Russian speaker, telling him that he could now make good his promise to show her some Russian hospitality. Maclean met her at the station and, as he drove her to the Embassy followed by a car full of secret police, told her that as the Ambassador was away he was in charge. 'Altogether I was determined to enjoy myself,' wrote Virginia.[2]

Maclean was an invaluable source of information for the newly arrived American with no word of Russian. But while he could obtain statistics for her, act as interpreter and introduce her to important people, he plays down his own role: 'She was very ambitious, that was one of her great gifts – and she was unstoppable. Virginia was representative of a new phase of journalism; she got around more and went to see people right at the top.'[3]

Maclean believes the secret of Virginia's success as a reporter was that she had a light touch in her writing which concealed a sharp, if not deep, mind. 'Her methods were largely intuitive, but she didn't miss a trick,' he comments. 'She was ready to go anywhere and do anything, and by talking to a lot of people could get a good grasp of essentials in a very short time.' She also took advantage of her natural good looks. Maclean remembers how, when she kept him and his party waiting for half an hour before a diplomatic function in Moscow, he was furious. But then she looked so marvellous that he instantly forgave her and, within ten minutes, she was the centre of attention: 'She was enormously attractive and she radiated vitality.'[4]

The resulting articles covered almost all aspects of Soviet life. Virginia wrote about concentration camps she had seen from windows of her train; she praised the brilliance of the Moscow ballet; she assessed the weaknesses and the strengths of the Russian army; she noticed that often the only food on the shelves was bread, and that, wherever she went, police cars resolutely followed. But she failed in her ambition to interview the Soviet President in Moscow. 'We had great fun sending telegrams to Stalin or 'phoning,' recalls Maclean, but all to no avail. There is little in her articles about Stalin's military intentions and, although she attended a lunch at the German Embassy presided over by the Ambassador, Count von der Schulenburg, she did not take seriously the rumours of a Russo–German pact, which was announced six months later in August 1939.

After leaving Russia, Virginia travelled across Romania into Poland, where, in April 1939, she reported on the country's losing struggle to maintain its independence. She recognised that, 'despite Danzig and Gdynia, Poland has no secure access to the sea, for German military forces might close the Vistula and cut rail routes to the Baltic. Polish security therefore has been dependent on diplomacy to a greater extent than that of most countries in Europe.'[5] She concluded: 'The strong anti-Nazi feeling throughout the country and the memory of the partition that wiped Poland from the map has endowed Poles with a fiercely patriotic spirit. If Hitler's ambitions cannot be checked he will have to face war on two fronts.'[6]

On 2 September, as Hitler moved to invade Poland, Virginia paid her last visit to Berlin. This was a brave undertaking as the newspaper explained underneath her byline: 'Miss Cowles, a *Sunday Times* Special Correspondent, flew to Berlin from London on Thursday morning and left Germany yesterday. The important despatch from her that follows is all the more interesting because of the withdrawal of resident British correspondents from Berlin more than a week ago.' In her article Virginia wrote how one German in her compartment on the train to Cologne explained that, 'since it was only "police action" the Germans were taking in Poland, Britain would not be so foolish as to risk a world war. A second smiled, drew his finger suggestively across his neck and said, "After we cut Poland's throat we'll all settle down to peace." '[7]

The article, her last as a peacetime reporter, dramatically conveyed the tension of a country in crisis. She described in detail the army fighters lined up in endless rows, Hitler dressed for the first time in the field grey of the German army, and Berlin like an armed camp edged with the silhouettes of men mounting the anti-aircraft guns on the roofs of Unter den Linden. As she finally left Germany for Holland, she saw several Jews on her train arrested at the frontier, a prophetic scene with which she concluded her report.

On 3 September came the broadcast everyone had long awaited: Neville Chamberlain announced that Britain was at war with Germany. Virginia, who had just arrived back in London, decided immediately to apply for a visa for Poland. But in the five days she had to wait for the necessary travel permits, the route she had planned – through the Baltic states to Kovno and then by train to Warsaw – was closed. However, there was another option: through Switzerland, Italy and Yugoslavia to Romania. A further wait for Romanian travel papers meant that she did not arrive in the Polish frontier town until mid-September, from where, now as a war reporter for the *Sunday Times*, she wrote of the Polish struggle to repel the invaders.

But if Virginia scooped the world's press by filing the last peacetime report from Berlin, the prize for breaking the news that the Second World War had begun went to another woman reporter, Clare

Hollingworth, an unknown twenty-seven-year-old on her first assignment.

Clare's earliest dreams had been to become a reporter of wars. Her fascination with fighting was not a gruesome love of killing, but stemmed rather from an interest in history. Growing up in a middle-class family in Leicester, she had been taken by her father on regular visits to old battlefields such as Bosworth and Naseby in England, and Crécy, Agincourt and Poitiers in France. Her mother initially taught her at home until she was old enough to be sent to the local Collegiate school. There the joint headmistresses 'were dedicated to producing girls able to stand on their own feet in a masculine world without losing any femininity'.[8] In addition, her father's wish, that she finish off her education at a domestic science establishment, gave her a lifelong hatred for all housework. Yet, soon after she left she became engaged to 'a suitable young man in the county'. In spite of this nod to society and the hunt ball existence which she briefly shared with her fiancé, she was energetically seeking to fulfil her headmistresses' ambition of establishing herself in a man's world: she wanted a foothold into journalism. Her keen interest in international affairs won her a first job not as a reporter, however, but as secretary to the League of Nations Union (LNU) organiser for Worcestershire. At the same time she decided to take a course at Zagreb University in an attempt to learn a Slav language. 'Working for the LNU certainly had many advantages,' Hollingworth recalls. Because there was no work in the Worcester office during the summer, she was encouraged to take months of sabbatical leave for study and to travel on condition that she included a visit to Geneva to collect material for articles for *Headway*, the LNU magazine. This she did willingly, returning to Zagreb for several successive summers and using it as a base for touring Yugoslavia, Hungary, Bulgaria and Albania.

She made slow linguistic progress but many useful contacts, especially among the British diplomatic and press corps. 'Standards of journalism were then far higher than now,' Hollingworth comments tartly today.[9] During the annual meeting of the League of Nations in Geneva, she met Trilby Ewer of the *Daily Herald* and Vernon Bartlett of the *News Chronicle*, two of the best-known names in diplomatic journalism at the time. In between, she returned to Worcester and contributed occasional freelance articles to *Berrow's Worcester Journal*, the oldest newspaper in England. However, her engagement could not withstand this hectic international existence and, deciding against provincial life, she broke it off. Shortly afterwards she met Vandeleur

Robinson, then regional organiser for the LNU in the south-east. 'We soon discovered we had much in common, especially an interest in the politics of central and south-eastern Europe,' she wrote.[10]

They married and spent their honeymoon in Yugoslavia and Albania. But Clare was determined never to give up her maiden name and, as she explained with pride in her autobiography, went to some effort to have her passport issued under this name. 'I gather I was about the eighth woman in England to have a passport in her own name.'

Both she and her new husband were Labour Party members and, in 1937, Clare returned to Leicester to organise the peace ballot there, still undecided as to whether to make a career in politics or journalism. However, having built up a good knowledge of much of central Europe, including Hungary, Czechoslovakia, Yugoslavia, Austria and Bulgaria, she was appointed as the senior official in Warsaw in charge of the *News Chronicle* fund for refugees from the Sudetenland. She ran a small office in Katowice, in the same building as the British Consulate General, staffed by two German-speaking secretaries and a few volunteers. She went frequently to Warsaw, as she needed the help of the British Embassy to deal with the Polish authorities, as well as to Gdynia, where the Honorary British Consul helped her to obtain cheap sea transport for the refugees.

In July 1939, with the threat of war imminent, Clare was recalled to London. Although she was passionately involved in the problems of central Europe, she was pleased with her recall as she had by then resolved to be a reporter and thought that she would have to go to London and Fleet Street to secure such a job.

My husband was all for my pressing ahead in journalism but my parents were horrified and told me so in very direct terms. They had 'taken' the shock of my joining the Labour Party and even becoming a parliamentary candidate without much fuss or trouble. But they abhorred the press, apart from *The Times*, and to work for any newspaper other than that august journal was, to their way of thinking, out of the question.[11]

However, her work for the refugees in Poland and her freelance articles for the *News Chronicle* from there had brought her to the attention of the editor of the *Daily Telegraph*, Arthur Watson, who summoned her for an interview on 25 August 1939. He wanted her to go back to Poland as quickly as possible, reporting to his correspondent in Warsaw, Hugh Carleton Greene. Thrilled to be asked, she accepted with alacrity. 'I do not remember whether we discussed money', Clare wrote, 'but it had never been of particular importance to me.'[12]

She went home to make her arrangements, to tell her friends, who merely considered her an eccentric traveller, and to organise herself with a seat on the next flight to Berlin, which left from Hendon early the following morning. When she finally started packing, after midnight, she realised that her suitcases were too large for the aircraft. Ever resourceful, she rang the all-night service of Harrods, which, within the hour, delivered luggage of the correct dimensions.

Twenty-four hours later, after a terrifying period of detention in Berlin, her aeroplane touched down into a pitch-black Warsaw – the last British airliner to cross Germany before the outbreak of war. She immediately found her way to her new boss at the Europejski Hotel and, in his room over drinks, discussed their plans. One of them had to go to the German border; the eager new arrival, undaunted by any potential danger, insisted that it should be her. She assured Greene that she was quite familiar with the area on both sides of the frontier around Katowice and Krakow; he agreed, therefore, that she should go. She took the night train to Katowice and, on arrival there, telephoned John Thwaites, the British Consul General, whom she had known from her refugee work. He offered her a bed for the night and the next day agreed to lend her his official car. Clare knew that the border with Germany was closed to all but flagged cars, which enabled German officials access across the frontier. She conceived the daring idea of driving into Germany in a British official car displaying the Union Jack.

With confidence verging on madness, Clare succeeded in snooping around the German border to report on the last-minute preparations that country was making for war. Today she describes her action as that of a lunatic, or child, who has no idea of danger. She was, she supposed, too young and inexperienced to be frightened by anything she had seen in the previous few days. But at the same time she was intelligent enough to understand the significance of everything she had witnessed. The Nazi officers were, she commented later, 'somewhat surprised when they realised they had been saluting the British flag but, in fact, no one tried to stop me'.

After an excellent lunch of partridge in a small German town, she went off to buy a supply of film, wine, electric torches and soap, which were all in short supply in Poland. She then drove along the fortified frontier road through Mindenburg to Gleiwitz, past huge hessian screens beside the road, obviously intended to conceal the hundreds of tanks, armoured cars, field guns and troops massing nearby. But as

the screens blew in the wind Clare saw them all. She raced back to
Katowice and relayed everything she had observed to Thwaites, who
would not at first believe her. He was convinced only when she laid
out in front of him her purchases, whereupon he sent a top-secret
message to the Foreign Office. Next, she rang Greene in Warsaw and
dictated a story, which the *Daily Telegraph* had in London three
minutes later. 'In those days there were no bylines in quality newspapers in Britain, which was a good thing because my family would
have been worried.'[13]

She remained in Katowice until 1 September, when huge explosions
and distant gunfire pierced her sleep. From her window she saw the
dawn bombers high in the sky and the artillery fire near the German
border less than twenty miles away. After several bursts of lightning in
the park, she realised that the Polish invasion had started and war was
inevitable. She rang both Robin Hankey, Second Secretary at the
British Embassy in Warsaw, and then Greene; the first advised her to
get out as soon as possible, the second instructed her to remain as
near to the action as possible. When Greene telephoned the Foreign
Ministry in Warsaw, they told him he must be mistaken as negotiations
were still in train. But he was able to insist that his correspondent in
Katowice had seen and heard the German advance. Even as they
talked, the Nazi bombers flew over Warsaw. Greene, after telephoning
Clare's story to London, then alerted his rivals in Warsaw that hostilities had begun, first of all waking Patrick Maitland of *The Times* to
ensure his paper carried the news.

By 10 a.m., as the gunfire died down, Clare decided to visit the
frontier for further investigation. In spite of the many rumours, she
established that there was a real possibility of a night attack on Katowice and decided to drive to Krakow for the night, a frightening
enough prospect itself as she was stopped by control points in every
town and village and, for the rest of the journey, had to fight and jostle
with refugee wagons and mobilising troops. The next day she returned
to Katowice, where she 'functioned almost as a one-woman incident
room'[14] by taking notes of all she saw. But she was then forced to leave,
along with other British and French officials. She was again grateful
for the use of Thwaite's car and, although this time she was driven,
the journey was terrifying as they were strafed by Nazi aircraft swoop-
ing low to pepper the streets with bullets and bombs. Just as they
reached Krakow, they heard that Britain and France were now at war
too, and knew that they had to leave Krakow for Lublin. But Clare
drove on into Warsaw, now without the chauffeur but with two refugee

women, hoping to renew contact with her boss. He was neither at his apartment nor at the Europejski Hotel and the Consulate had closed. After a frantic search for petrol, she drove on through the night back to Lublin, fortified only by a bottle of champagne she had found at Greene's flat. Not merely dusty and dirty, she was by her own admission finally exhausted, scared and hungry.

She spent two restorative nights in Lublin and then, together with Thwaites and various refugees desperately trying to escape, squeezed into two cars between them and set off again for Lvov, across eastern Poland. A stop en route at Luck, where the Polish Government and Military had set up headquarters, offered Clare the opportunity to sleep in a monastic college in a room with three men – this a distinct improvement on some of the bug-infested beds she had been forced to use in the last few days. But then local officials found her lodgings with a Polish countess in a large house just outside Luck. After a few days there she drove on to Krzemieniec, where the British Embassy and Polish Foreign Office had lately established themselves in the one-storeyed Hotel Bono. Here she met up again with Robin Hankey and was introduced to the British Ambassador, Sir Howard Kennard. He called her a 'peculiar woman' and asked her what she was doing 'running about in the middle of all this? Love of excitement, I suppose?' – a comment he presumably would not have made to the handful of male correspondents in the combat zone also awaiting the outbreak of hostilities.

'I'm a journalist, Sir Howard. This is how I earn my living,' she replied.[15]

Peculiar or not, that evening, over a dinner of one egg and a portion of rice, Clare proposed that she return to Warsaw:

As air-raids and retreats were ceasing to be news, why should I not go back for the latest story there before the Germans took the city? . . . I was not being brave – I certainly did not feel courageous – ignorant, perhaps and naïve. My overriding feeling was enthusiasm for a good story, the story on the fall of Warsaw to the Nazi divisions. Who could resist that?[16]

Much to her surprise – she was, after all, not an official war correspondent but an enemy alien with no protection if captured – the diplomatic corps agreed to her dangerous proposal. They offered to provide precious petrol for what she herself recognised was a mad escapade. They also gave her a map, some hard rations and a bottle of whisky. But she was on her own this time, with no driver, retracing her journey towards Lublin.

However mad her actions occasionally seemed, investigating for herself rather than taking another's word for it was to be the hallmark of Clare Hollingworth's professionalism. She commented later that, although historians have often said that the German air force disabled all Polish aerodromes in the first few days, it was only by actually looking that she knew this not to be the case: 'I myself saw the Krakow Airport in use after being bombed during those first days... after a week Lublin aerodrome was still in action... lack of fuel was the reason why those Polish fighters were so seldom seen over the battle-grounds.' She survived continuous raids and roads so blocked with escaping peasants that she frequently made detours on to side roads or even across fields. She ate little more than biscuits, drank whisky and slept in her car with her revolver beside her. She passed detachments of German soldiers and, without knowing it, drove through German-occupied territory.

But shortly after Lublin, she realised that the road to Warsaw was cut off and there was no hope of continuing to the capital. She returned eventually, making her way to Zaleszczki in the extreme south-east of Poland, where she once again found her *Daily Telegraph* boss, Hugh Carleton Greene. He suggested that they go immediately into Romania, from where she could file her latest story. Together they walked down to a long, wooden bridge, which crossed the Dniester on the Polish border, into a waiting taxi on the other side. 'We must have looked an odd sight,' Clare recalled. 'Greene hugging a huge standard typewriter and I with a dirty pillowcase full of clothing.'[17] After a small bribe to a customs official, they entered Romania and drove to Cernauti some thirty miles away, where she filed her story to London on the war situation in general and her own dramatic escape from Poland in particular.

Although Hollingworth and Greene crossed again into Poland more than once in the next week, for her the next phase of the war took place in Bucharest; she then returned to London for Christmas. Her marriage only just survived the strain of her not living at home, but her husband, 'in a curious and somewhat contradictory manner',[18] encouraged her to consider a further reporting stint.

'She was afraid she would be reporting disaster all her life,' Martha Gellhorn wrote prophetically of Mary Douglas, the heroine of *A Stricken Field*. By 10 November 1939, Martha herself was on board a small Dutch ship carrying wheat for Belgium as well as anxious European refugees returning home to their families, the army or they knew not what. She was on a commission for *Collier's* to write articles on Scandinavia with special emphasis on Finland as her editor, Charles Colebaugh, thought that something was about to happen there.

The Russo–German non-aggression pact not only relieved Hitler of his fear of war on two fronts but also freed Stalin to make adjustments to the Soviet Union's borders. He wasted little time. Having absorbed the Baltic states of Estonia, Latvia and Lithuania, he then wanted to seal off all access to the Gulf of Finland, thus making sure that no other country could use Finland as a base. Finland, desperately clinging to its neutrality, bravely announced that it wished to remain outside the conflict. But, once the Russian bombs fell on Finnish soil, the Finns fought with determination as the rest of the world watched awe-struck. Within a week, 100 correspondents had rushed to northern Europe to file stories datelined Helsinki. Few people thought that the Finns could last for long and most expected that they would soon be watching another small nation swallowed by a giant neighbour.

Martha arrived in Helsinki the morning before the Russo–Finnish war began. 'Years afterwards I remembered that I was eager to go, but my letters prove that I was far from enthusiastic about this dull assignment in the frozen north.'[19] The eagerness stemmed partly from the fact that Finland was 'a highly literate nation... a good democracy'.[20] But money provided the real enthusiasm persuading her to accept a commission that took her away from the warm paradise of Sun Valley, Idaho, where she was then living with her husband-to-be, Ernest Hemingway. She hoped to make enough to devote herself to short-story writing in future. But, as she told her mother, she expected to be married to Hemingway by the spring and 'once married I'd have a swell excuse not to be separated from him. I can just say (to *Collier's*) my husband and I work together.'[21]

Martha spent fourteen days in submarine zones with ships being blasted in front of them and mines – and sometimes bodies – on every side. In her piece for *Collier's*, 'Slow Boat to War', she described the mixed emotions of the other passengers, the food 'as interesting as boiled cardboard' and the ominous sea full of mines into which they feared they would be plunged at any moment. It was during that voyage that her own views on war crystallised:

I was in on the beginning of a great war of greed, started by a madman; and it felt different... the sense of the insanity and wickedness of this war grew in me until, for purposes of mental hygiene, I gave up trying to think or judge, and turned myself into a walking tape-recorder with eyes.[22]

Her boat made it to Ostend and, on 29 November, Martha flew to Helsinki, where she stayed at the less than luxurious Hotel Kamp. It was a condemned building before the war, with rapidly dwindling supplies of food and fuel. 'She hates cold and it really hurts her,' Hemingway wrote about Gellhorn for Collier's.[23] 'But she was the first journalist, man or woman, to get to the front in the Finnish War and she wrote some fine despatches from there with the cold never above twenty below zero.' She also thrived on plenty of sleep, as Hemingway was fond of remarking, preferably twelve hours of it. 'She hates to get up in the morning,' he told Collier's readers. Yet in Helsinki, 'a frozen city inhabited by sleep-walkers',[24] she often had to wake at 5 a.m. and was on the move within half an hour to make use of the few hours of daylight. Sometimes she was driven about in the dark, over mined bridges, where skidding meant certain death, but where using head-lights was equally dangerous as it identified the car to the Russians. 'Nothing surprised me any more,' Martha wrote in her article for Collier's.[25] 'This night war in snow and ice with unending forest hiding the armies was too fantastic to be true.'

Once she was ordered back, told that her presence was 'the height of stupidity'.[26] When she asked permission to walk the extra eight kilometres to the front, she was told that it was impossible, that the 'walk went through forests where every inch of ground seems either taken up by a tree or a granite boulder and between rocks and trees the snow drifts are as high as your neck'. She tried insisting that she was perfectly prepared to walk through anything, but 'I had argued with officers before and I knew it was a losing game'. The Finns were, however, no more lenient towards male correspondents trying to get to the front line.

The following week she reported from the bomb-wrecked capital itself, a city where there was no longer time to kiss children goodbye:

... the bus was collecting children to take them away, anywhere, no one knew where, but out of the city. A curious migration started that afternoon and went on all night. Lost children, whose parents were gone in the burning buildings or separated in the confusion of that sudden attack, straggled out alone or in two and threes, taking any road that led away from what they had seen. Days later the state radio was still calling their names, trying to find their families for them.[27]

By the time that article appeared the Finns had proved, after a month of heavy fighting, that their determination, discipline and superior knowledge of the terrain were a match – for a short time – even for the vast army of the Soviet Union. The world was gripped by the valiant struggle of what many called this latter-day David against Goliath. The Finns were not only holding out but had also recaptured two eastern frontier towns. In January 1940, the *Sunday Times* despatched Virginia Cowles to report from the frozen North. Like Martha – and the other foreign journalists – she stayed at the Hotel Kamp. Like Martha, she suffered dreadfully from the biting cold; in spite of travelling in a thick suit, fur-lined boots and a sheepskin coat, she was still terribly cold. Her suitcase was filled with sweaters, woollen underwear, woollen socks, a ski suit and a windbreaker; the weather had not been so cold for years.

Virginia, charming as ever, knew that her first task was to seek out the other reporters and ply them with questions about the war. Over lunch with Webb Miller of United Press she learned that the Russian attack on the Mannerheim line had been repulsed and in a series of guerrilla actions the Finns had also halted several Russian thrusts, succeeding in wiping out entire divisions. She decided to travel north as soon as possible and see the forest patrols for herself. But when she filed an application at the Finnish Press Bureau, she was refused. Apparently, on a trip to Viipuri the day before, a Swedish woman journalist had reported that one of the Finnish press officers had made advances towards her. The authorities, exasperated, promptly ruled that no more women could visit the front. Virginia was despondent, but she finally received permission to travel to Rovienemi, the capital of Lapland, twenty-four hours away and a mile and a half from the Arctic Circle.

Her eye-witness reports made gripping reading. On 4 February 1940, she wrote in the *Sunday Times*:

The Finns have succeeded in repulsing the [Russian] onslaught with some of the most spectacular fighting in history. They have annihilated entire divisions and hurled back others thirty and forty miles to the border from whence they came. They have done it not by ordinary methods of trench warfare but by desperate guerilla fighting.... We turned a bend in the road and came upon the full horror of the scene. For four miles the road and forests were strewn with the bodies of men and horses; with wrecked tanks, field kitchens, trucks, gun-carriages, maps, books and articles of clothing. The corpses were frozen as hard as petrified wood and the colour of the skin was mahogany. Some of the bodies were piled on top of each other like a heap of rubbish covered only by a merciful blanket of snow. Others were sprawled against the trees in grotesque attitudes....

So keen were the English and American journalists to see a Finnish victory, however unlikely, and so efficient was the Finnish censorship machine at keeping their losses secret, that the reports which appeared in the West were in danger of overestimating Russian defeats.

Virginia continued her visits to the front for several more weeks, enduring night travelling in freezing conditions. Once, after driving for nearly two hours, she had just fallen asleep when she was woken by a deafening crash: the car had skidded on the glassy road and landed, still upright, against a tree. 'We had hit an empty white truck which had been left standing by the roadside with no lights,' she wrote.[28] Although the car was totally wrecked, the passengers were not hurt. But as they climbed out they were confronted with endless miles of desolate forests and frozen fields. It was four o'clock in the morning and, with little prospect of anyone passing for hours, they decided to walk as the only way to keep warm and alive. Finally they came to a barn, where they took shelter.

Virginia remained in Finland until early March, when she went to Stockholm. It was there, on 11 March, that she learned that peace talks were taking place with the Swedes acting as mediators. She and Edward Ward (later Lord Bangor), the BBC representative, were organising their return to Helsinki through the Finnish Chargé d'Affaires, Eljas Erkko, when Ward casually asked if it was true that an agreement had been reached in Moscow? To his amazement Erkko said, 'Yes.' Ward immediately rang the BBC in time for the 6 p.m. news bulletin and a world scoop. By 7 p.m. Ward and Cowles were on a flight back to Helsinki to watch the feverish rush to evacuate the areas ceded to Russia.

'The greatest difference is in the press room at the Hotel Kamp,' Virginia wrote.[29] A few days earlier it had been the scene of wild confusion; now it was almost deserted. The slate outside the door which used to announce the time that the communiqué would be released had been wiped clean. The orchestra played 'It's a long way to Tipperary' to a gloomy, almost deserted restaurant as the world's reporters abandoned Finland for a new front.

Over There

*'The inflexible rule that no women correspondents are ever allowed
to visit the Army on active service.'*

UNNAMED EDITOR TO CHARLOTTE HALDANE

In this way the Second World War had begun without a single
British woman correspondent officially accredited to cover it. Once
war was declared, those women active in reporting international
politics in the 1930s had to find other outlets for their talents or ways of
circumventing the official ruling, namely that women correspondents
were not allowed at the front. They did both. In September 1939, four
male correspondents, chosen by ballot to report on a pool basis, set
off to cover the activities of the French army near the Maginot Line.
In addition, Alexander Clifford, a former Reuters' bureau chief, was
appointed as 'Eye-Witness' to accompany the British Expeditionary
Force (BEF). A dozen or so others, nominated by the major newspapers, had to wait a month before they could leave and were then
looked after by so-called conducting officers, who, according to Phillip
Knightley, 'were outwardly polite to the war correspondents but actually hated them'. The veteran reporter, O'Dowd Gallagher of the
Daily Express, described the conducting officers as

such astounding caricatures of British Army regular officers and upper classes
as to be scarcely credible. They were either drunk half the time or half drunk
all the time. Whenever you were out driving with them it was always, 'Let's
pull up and have a snifter at that café, old chap,' or if there were no cafés,
then out came a flask from some pocket of their expensively cut uniform.[1]

It was hardly surprising, in this sort of atmosphere, that neither the
army nor the War Office was concerned to advance the cause of
women reporters who wished to cover the fighting in Europe.

In May 1940, the Germans invaded Belgium, Holland and

Luxembourg with lightning speed and success, sending the Allies rushing back towards the French coast. Virginia Cowles, at the time staying in a hotel in Paris off the Place Vendôme, had the clear feeling that she was missing the real story as she watched the city disgorge. On hearing the 'wild' stories about the German advance across France, and knowing the BEF rule barring women correspondents from the front, she went to see Sir Charles Mendl, an old friend, at the British Embassy. She asked if there were any possibility of circumventing the rule, particularly since she had already had experience of war reporting, albeit in an unofficial capacity. He could do nothing, but advised her to go to London and try to arrange it from there. She left the next day but while she was in England, making attempts to get back to France and report on the fighting, the evacuation had already begun. Instead, she went to Dover to watch the ignominious return of the defeated forces.

After the collapse of the BEF, Virginia made a formal application to go into the French army zone. The French Ministry of Information was more helpful, promising to arrange a tour of the front for her even if it could not officially accredit her. On 10 June, it instructed her to go to Paris immediately and co-ordinate the final details there; her visa would be valid for a month. But in spite of the visa, there seemed little chance of getting to France as all flights were suspended. Her travel arrangements had always been looked after by Cooks Travel Bureau, who, even in this perilous hour, did not let her down now. They rang early one morning: if she could get to the Imperial Airways office in London in twenty minutes, there was a flight from Croydon which she could catch. She pulled on a dress – in 1940 this was still considered suitable attire for a war correspondent – and bolted out of the door. She arrived, however, not in Paris but in Tours. After a six-hour wait, she caught a train to Paris arriving at 4 a.m., just hours before the Germans occupied the city.

The next problem was finding somewhere to stay, as all the hotels were suddenly filled with transient hordes while her former colleagues had, it appeared, all left. She tracked down Walter Kerr, of the *Herald Tribune*, who had a car and two gallons of petrol. He was delighted to have such a charming companion and together they toured the deserted city. In her article she wrote:

The loneliness and the quiet of Paris was almost beyond words. Occasionally we passed cars careening under the weight of mattresses, chairs and bicycles and hastening down the boulevards on their way out of the city. Every now and then we passed family groups who were starting out for their long trek on foot. One old woman was wheeling an invalid husband along. When we asked them where they were going they said they didn't know. They only wanted to get out 'before the Boches come'.... [2]

As they drove past Les Invalides they saw a fleet of 500 taxi-cabs waiting to take away government documents. 'The faces of the people on the streets showed no sign of weary resignation, only a deep and bitter hatred to think that soon German troops would be racing through the streets of their beloved city.'

No sooner had she arrived than she was trying to think of a way to get out herself. Although she drove, she could not find a single car for rent or sale in such pandemonium. Recognising therefore that she would have to be dependent on the kindness of others, she went to the American Embassy, where she was given a cool reception from the military attaché, who said that he would do his best but offered little hope. Virginia was sympathetic to his point of view, accepting that in such an emergency 'stranded women journalists were a final straw'.[3] She then spent a few hours trying to type out her story, find something to eat – apart from one cup of tea and some coffee she had eaten nothing for forty-eight hours – and organise a lift.

Eventually she managed to hitch a ride out of Paris with Tom Healey, the *Daily Mirror* correspondent, who had a Chrysler roadster. For ten hours, averaging four miles an hour, they crawled along roads and fields bursting with desperate humanity. They drove against a constant background of guns rumbling and flashes through the sky. Virginia convinced herself that, as an American citizen, she would be in no danger if the Germans overtook them, although Healey could face internment for the duration of the war. By the time they reached Tours their radiator had sprung a leak. But in this bedlam of a town she 'happened to run into' her former colleague Eddie Ward, now working for Reuters, who offered to drive her towards the coast if she could wait twenty-four hours. He told her that Press Wireless, the only means of communication with the outside world, was still functioning and that he and the Reuters' staff were remaining another day. As this looked like being her only chance to file a story – and she had little choice in any case – she decided to stay too. Reuters provided her with a bed and Eddie a place in his car to Bordeaux in the morning.

At Bordeaux the pair were lucky to squeeze on to a small, 9,000-ton cargo ship which normally carried no more than 180 passengers; that day it was crammed with 1,600 people. On board were bankers, cabinet ministers, doctors, soldiers and diplomats all rolled up in blankets on deck for the zig-zagging journey up the coast of France and across the Channel to England. Virginia herself curled up in a sleeping-bag on the top deck in a row with six fellow journalists. Volunteers were asked to stand look-out watches for submarines or to help with the preparation and serving of the small amount of food which remained. The vessel arrived in Falmouth to be met by a motherly detachment of the Women's Voluntary Service, offering lemonade and sandwiches to all. One of them handed Virginia a card stamped 'refugee'. She protested that she was not a refugee but an American journalist. 'Everyone', said the woman firmly, 'who is not English is a refugee.' Virginia nodded and signed the card.

After a year of Europe in turmoil, there were still few openings for any reporters to cover events on the continent. Virginia went to Ireland in the summer of 1940 to report on wartime life in that country. Shiela Grant Duff worked first in Toynbee's section of the Foreign Office and then joined the BBC as Czechoslovak editor in the European service. Elizabeth Wiskemann worked for the Royal Institute of International Affairs, at Chatham House, which had moved to Oxford.

Clare Hollingworth was briefly in Paris in February 1940, increasingly anxious all the while to return to eastern Europe where she was convinced the 'big' story lay, and unconcerned as to whether or not she was officially accredited. She took a train through Switzerland and Italy and then, because the border between Italy and Yugoslavia was closed, crossed on foot via a narrow bridge. Clare, with her sound grasp of political realities, understood the extreme dangers facing the Balkan nations in the wake of the fall of France and the Italian declaration of war, particularly in view of the continuing co-operation between Germany and the Soviet Union. She managed to station herself in Bucharest as not only the *Daily Telegraph* but also the *Daily Express* had told her that they would be interested in her reporting for them from the Balkans. Once there she resigned from the *Telegraph*, largely because she found their local man unco-operative and pro-German, and began working for the *Express*. She scored a notable triumph for her new paper that summer while covering a conference on the future of the province of Transylvania, which Hungary was demanding from Romania. As thirty reporters fought for one telephone box she, being small, pushed through the jostling crowd and then, on her hands and knees, crawled between legs to the kiosk door. 'From the floor, I reached up and grabbed the receiver from flailing hands and wrapped my arms around the mouthpiece so that nothing short of dislocating the entire apparatus could pull me out of the box.'[4]

She then refused the incoming call from the operator and ordered instead to be put through to her own contact in Geneva, to whom she dictated her story.

Back in Bucharest, the major events were the abdication of King Carol, the riots incited by the Iron Guard and the arrival of the Germans. But her time in Romania was running out. Early one morning the security police burst into her small flat to take her to the Prefecture of Police. 'I knew only too well what happened to British people who went there; they were tortured and frequently forced to confess sins they had never committed.' Quick thinking as ever, Clare decided on an unusual course of action: she stripped naked, rang her friend Robin Hankey at the British Legation and told the Security Police with great authority: 'You can't possibly arrest me, I'm naked.'[5] Within minutes Hankey arrived and escorted the blanket-covered reporter to the British Embassy.

Saved that time, Clare knew her situation was extremely precarious. It would not have been difficult for the Romanian Press Bureau to prove that she had been consistently flouting its censorship rules. For the past two months she had been taking her daily filing for the *Daily Express* to the Press Bureau, which passed it with the censor's stamp, but at the same time she was dictating another, quite different story over the telephone to Geneva for passing on to London. The Romanians could easily have produced a gramophone recording of this second story, as Clare was well aware. The British Legation helped her to extend her visa initially for seven days and then, over a period of six weeks, they used up one excuse after another: she was ill, she had had a car accident, she had lost her passport, until she could think of no more and the Government insisted that she leave.

During those last weeks she was subjected to several more unpleasant incidents, but she kept her nerve and continued filing. 'I'm not the sort of person who trembles with fear,' she explains. 'Nor am I frightened of gunfire. I do know what fear is but I don't experience fear in war; I just know it won't happen to me and I'll come through all right.'[6] When she was finally expelled, her own newspaper commented that, 'Miss Hollingworth, twenty-nine, earned the title "The Scarlet Pimpernel" after rescuing Czechs and Poles in danger from the Gestapo.' Then it could not resist adding, 'In private life, Miss Hollingworth is Mrs Vandeleur Robinson.'[7] By this time, the Greek war had begun and the *Daily Express* wanted her at the front, which pleased her. 'I have always tried to get more dangerous assignments because danger is exciting and usually produces good stories.'[8]

She arrived at the Greek frontier to witness the continuing dis-
integration of the Balkans at 5.30 a.m. on a dark, cold, November
morning. 'I walked across the border carrying just a rucksack and a
typewriter and found myself in the God-forsaken town of Python,'
she wrote.[9] She then boarded a filthy train that crawled along, picking
up conscripts at every station, but with no possibility of obtaining
food during the fifty-six-hour journey to Salonika. Having found a
hotel, she set off to examine the current situation and was immediately
assailed by an air-raid siren so loud it actually hurt. She was then
herded into a shelter so dank it felt like a submarine where, at any
moment, the oxygen would give out. She staggered over the sweaty
and exhausted bodies to get out but found that the shelter was locked
from the outside. When eventually she escaped into daylight, she set
about writing a story of the devastation in Salonika, but the censor
refused to pass a word except a line saying where she was. 'I begged,
stormed and tried every trick I knew but he would not yield. I tracked
down his assistant and by bribing him I got a telephone call through
to my contact in Belgrade and asked him to inform the *Daily Express*
that I was still alive.'[10]

When she realised that no one in Salonika was prepared to give her a
pass for the front, Clare decided to endure another disgusting train
journey and try her luck in Athens, where, after several arguments with
officials as she refused to get off the train at each station, she arrived at
4 a.m. There she found several other foreign correspondents, all lan-
guishing in fury at being refused permission for the front. At this point
the *Daily Express*, in the absence of any news, instructed her to leave
Athens, but she, determined as ever, decided to make one last push.

When she finally won her authorisation, she was in a party with
Henry Stokes of Reuters and his local stringer, Mr Drossos, 'who was
reporting all our movements to the Greek secret police'.[11] The journey,
much of it through the mountains, was gruelling with several stops.
At Larisa they reported to the base camp general, who gave them
papers for proceeding to Kozani and advised that the Koritza section
in the north would produce the best stories as the Italians were still
showing some resistance there. After a night in Kozani, with another
damp and bug-infested bed, she rose early, eager to see the fighting,
and dressed in her old but warm clothes – several woolly sweaters,
long scarves and a long, sheepskin coat. 'I made no pretence of an
elaborate toilet,' she wrote, pouring scorn on her Reuters companion,
'who dressed as though he were out for a walk in Hyde Park in early
spring'.[12]

At Koritza she talked to many of the troops about life at the front and bought herself some Wellington boots for tramping over the battlefields. On the roadside she now saw piles of naked Italian corpses, their clothes and jewellery removed, many of whom had been shot in the back while trying to escape. After an interview was arranged for her with some Italian prisoners at the Greek camp, she walked the last few miles to the front. No car could proceed through eight-inch-deep mud and the walking was heavy. Among the debris scattered along her route were open boxes of Mills bombs and empty tins of Italian food (devoured by the Greeks). When she looked down into the deep ravine she was walking alongside, she saw a stream of blood-stained water. At last, as she arrived at the site of recent fighting, a heavy mist descended. She tramped around in the cold and damp for long enough to see that this had been 'no front of blazing guns or well-uniformed marching men', but mountain warfare using centuries-old tactics. As she walked on alone, she became uncomfortably aware of pockets of activity above her as unaccountable bits of slate kept slipping down on to her path. She assumed these indicated some Italians getting desperate for food and clothing whom the Greeks would soon flush out, but she was not frightened.

The party returned to Koritza at dusk just as Italian bombers swooped to hit the new Greek headquarters and from there to Athens. Near Larisa they encountered an air-raid, which Clare wanted to ignore, convinced that the Italians, however low they flew, would never hit them, but which terrified Drossos, the Reuters stringer, who wanted to stop for cover. Clare was maddened by his cowardice as delaying would 'waste hours of our precious time .... I resisted because it was very important to me to get my story off before the other correspondents who were in the car following us.' Back in Athens she filed her report and found herself in great demand from two British generals who wanted details of all she had seen at the front.

After a short stay in Athens, she made another hazardous train journey back to Romania, often travelling through the night in sub-zero temperatures in a train with snow blowing through broken windows. Again, her male companions were all for stopping, especially when there was a chance of some food at Alexandroupolis, but Clare's will won out. 'When we finally reached the frontier we were very hungry indeed,' she admitted.

By the end of May 1941, she was in Mersin, on the coast of south-east Turkey, on her way to Egypt for the *Daily Express*. There she was taken on board a caique, with no accommodation for passengers, whose captain was prepared to risk crossing the Mediterranean to Egypt. The cargo was infested with fleas and bugs, which almost ruffled Clare. 'I do not mind not washing for a week or more but I do hate getting fleas in my hair,' she commented. Worse was to come, however, as the waves washed over the side, soaking all her clothes. Since it was impossible to change or get warm, she tried to sleep and waited for the scorching daytime sun to dry her out. The five days and nights on board that tiny craft – which she had looked forward to as 'an adventure ... possibly enlivened by machine-gunning Nazi planes'[13] – were in fact among the worst she had ever endured. She arrived in Alexandria, dirty but cheerful, ready to cover a new phase of the war – the war in the Western Desert.

Martha Gellhorn had bade farewell to Europe in 1940, convinced that there would be a massacre which she could not bear to watch, and reluctant to leave her home in Cuba or her lover. But, in spite of her marriage to Ernest Hemingway in November 1940, there was one assignment she was particularly keen to be given and she had been negotiating this with *Collier's* for some weeks before her marriage. 'No one then knew or cared much about the war in China, but Japan had become an Axis partner and what Japan did held a new menace,' Martha wrote. 'I wanted to see the Orient before I died; and the Orient was across the world from what I loved and feared for .... Journalism was now turned into an escape route.'[14]

Her brief was to report on the Chinese army in action and defences against future Japanese attack around the South China Sea. Hemingway, although he had no wish to go to China, liked even less the idea of Martha going without him. Years later, in a highly amusing account of the trip, she wrote: 'On this super horror journey I wheedled an unwilling companion, hereinafter referred to as U.C., into going where he had no wish to go .... That was scandalous selfishness on my part, never repeated. Future horror journeys were made on my own.'[15] But in her articles at the time she made no secret of the fact that Hemingway had accompanied her; his photographs adorned her articles.

Ernest and Martha set off in February 1941 from San Francisco for Honolulu by boat and then to Hong Kong. Martha quickly recognised that their different personalities and approach to reporting made it imperative, for all the diversion Hemingway offered, that she operate on her own, wherever possible. 'U.C. was able to sit with a bunch of men for most of a day or most of a night or most of both day and night though perhaps with different men, wherever he happened to have started sitting, all of them fortified by a continuous supply of drink, the while he roared with laughter at reminiscences and anecdotes,' she wrote years later in an extended travel article.[16] 'It was a valid system for him. Aside from being his form of amusement he learned about a place and people through the eyes and experiences of those who had lived there.' This was a picture of the stereo-typical male reporter, whose clubbiness and booziness are enough to get him a story. Women reporters, as they began to cover world events in increasing numbers, generally rejected such rituals, but went out on their own to uncover their story, often incurring either the wrath or scorn of their male colleagues for working harder or for showing unfeminine aggression. Martha frankly admitted that she was 'a novice drinker and had a separate approach to learning. I wanted to see for myself, not hear . . . much as I like conversation I like it only in bursts for a few hours, not marathons and seldom in group formation. U.C. used to say, kindly, "M. is going off to take the pulse of the nation." '[17]

And so, at 4.30 one cold and windy morning, leaving Ernest behind, Martha went off alone in an elderly DC2 which was neither heated nor pressurised, and where the only comfort thrown to the eight passengers was a rough, brown blanket and a rough, brown-paper bag. She was flying at night on a round trip over Japanese lines, which included overflying sharp, unbroken mountain ranges with peaks 9,200 feet high and no plateaux for forced landings. The weather report said 'visibility two miles, storms ahead', and soon enough they flew into the storm. In her first story of the trip for Collier's, Martha graphically described how the 'hail beat against the wings and the fuselage with a noise like a threshing machine. . . . Ice formed on the wings and the propellers . . . there is no de-icing equipment on the 'plane.' The American pilot of the China National Aviation Corporation (CNAC) aeroplane came back into the cabin and remarked that his air-speed indicators had frozen during the storm. Stopping at Chungking, they took off again for Kunming in the late afternoon, where they collected passengers and fuel and which the pilot encouragingly told her he thought 'the Japs used for bombing practice'. For the next leg of the journey the 'plane behaved 'like a runaway rollercoaster . . . [it would] drop and tip and we hung on to our chairs. I did not even see the Lashio field until we had landed on it.'[18]

After sixteen hours' flying and 1,494 miles, Martha was, by her own admission, relieved to see a wooden shack in a field where she could wash and sleep in an iron cot. She had not only been frozen during the trip but also felt ashamed at not having been braver about it. 'Soft, nothing worse than being soft,' she explained, 'because I was also flushed and my legs and arms twitched and my mind seemed peevishly dislocated and I thought with horror that I might burst into tears for no reason.'[19] Refreshed by sleep, Martha looked around Lashio, an oriental boom town with limited sight-seeing. It was soon time to return to Kunming, then Chungking and then, after three nights, Hong Kong again. The report was one of Martha's most graphic; her audience could not fail to share her alternate terror and discomfort. Without such vivid, first-hand descriptions, the serious point she makes at the end – that CNAC was China's American-run life-line for brains, money and mail – would have had no impact.

Back in Hong Kong, what Martha saw, as she set out to 'take the pulse of the nation', did not please her: opium dens, brothels, dance halls, mah jong parlours, markets, factories, the criminal courts. 'It was my usual way of looking at a society from the bottom rather than from the top.'[20] Hemingway chided her:

... the trouble with you, M., is that you think everybody is exactly like you. What you can't stand they can't stand. What's hell for you has to be hell for them. How do you know what they feel about their lives? If it was as bad as you think they'd kill themselves instead of having more kids and setting off firecrackers.[21]

Martha could not fail to notice that alongside the vast white palaces of the rich most of Hong Kong's 800,000 inhabitants lived eight or ten to a room. 'The city smells of people,' she wrote for *Collier's*. 'It smells also of Chinese cooking and of old sweaty clothes, of dust, of refuse in gutters and of dirty water in drainless houses.'[22] In fact, Martha was not alone in her views: Agnes Smedley, who was in Hong Kong at this time, felt an identical crushing burden of sympathy. Presumably, when she met Hemingway in the spring of 1941, they did not argue about the matter, since he persuaded her to write a short story for a volume entitled *Men at War*,[23] which he was editing.

In March 1941, Martha went, this time with Ernest, to the backdoor to Hong Kong, or the Canton front, one of the most important in China. In New York, when her assignment had first been mooted, reporting on the Chinese army in action seemed a rational project. Once in China it seemed absurd: the distances, poor roads and transport and communication all conspired against it. Foreigners were either discouraged or forbidden to make journeys such as the one she was about to undertake. As she wrote later, 'I now think it astounding that this trip ever got arranged; at the time, not knowing the practical obstacles, I fumed and fretted and complained of the delay. What more natural, I asked, than for war correspondents to look at war?'[24]

The first three days in Shaokwan were a portent of the horrors to follow. As they examined an unappetising bowl of water in their bedroom, Hemingway told her that she was mad if she intended to brush her teeth in it. In other ways, too, Hemingway was invaluable. 'The burden fell squarely on him; he alone had to swap compliments and reply to flowery toasts. As a woman I was expected only to smile; I was free to be a mere presence, mute and suffering, though sometimes so beside myself that I went off into insane giggles.' At least he enjoyed the rice wine, which to Martha tasted like kerosene. After Shaokwan, they travelled in an antique rusty Chriscraft, which needed regular pumping to prevent it from sinking and which towed behind it a sampan full of women, children and soldiers who made Martha retch by their continuous habit of 'hawking up phlegm, collecting it in the mouth and spitting it out'.[25] At least Martha and Ernest could make their sleeping quarters on the Chriscraft, using an unusual form of mattress – coiled ropes and boathooks. Martha hardly slept.

The next phase of the journey was on horseback, slithering up a mudbank in torrential rain. 'The gait of the awful little horses was unlike any known horse movement; there was no way you could ride them painlessly,' said Martha. They were all diminutive but hers had a particularly ferocious kick which had caused their uninformative Chinese escort, Mr Ma, to slip and fall flat in the mud. When Hemingway's miniature creature fell on him, he stretched his arm over the saddle and under the horse's belly and picked it up, muttering about cruelty to animals and started to walk with it. 'I said sharply, "Put that horse down." He said, "I will not, poor bloody horse." '[26]

Finally, they reached a sector called the Seventh War Zone, where Martha with notebook and pencil set about recording 'much now meaningless detail about the formation, training, weaponry and actions of the Twelfth Army Group, which held this sector of the front'. As ever she was more interested in the people than the hardware: 'unfortunate boys, usually barefoot with puttees on their bare legs dressed in cotton uniforms. They were paid a token wage, something like $2.80 US a month, and an even smaller rice allowance.... I alternated between pitying the soldiers most and pitying the peasants most.'[27]

Martha concluded in her article that the Japanese could never conquer China by force, 'because people who can move their capital three times, carry factory machinery and university equipment over the mountains to safety, supply a front by sampan and coolie carrier, burrow into rock and survive endless bombing, build a 1,000 acre airfield in 100 days without machinery, will endure to the end'.[28]

All the while, Martha and Ernest were quartered in a cold, stone house with the now all too familiar complement of insects. When Martha told Ernest she wished to die, he retorted: 'too late ... who wanted to come to China?' But apart from the inadequate washing and sleeping arrangements, Martha had encountered the perennial problem for women reporters: lack of facilities. In a landscape of bare rice paddies there was, simply, nowhere to go. 'The village latrine was a public monument, a bamboo tower reached by a fragile bamboo ladder. She did not know which she was more frightened of, the bamboo structure collapsing or being bombed by a Japanese aeroplane while on the lavatory.' Hemingway joked: 'Oh poor M. what an inglorious death it would have been. M. the intrepid war correspondent, knocked off in the line of duty. But where? But how, the press of the world enquires?'[29] As she climbed the ladder, Martha was left to ponder 'the unfair fact that a female cannot modestly relieve herself'.[30]

In spite of the humour, Martha recognised that war was never funny. 'But there wasn't any war here,' she wrote; there was an undeclared truce. 'I was sure this China had always been drowning in hopeless poverty and disease, war only made the normal state somewhat worse.'[31] Having seen the Chinese army, albeit not in action, Martha and Ernest returned the way they had come.

The worst part of the journey home was an enforced stopover in the unbelievably squalid Palace Hotel in Kweilin. Here they endured 'mashed bedbugs on the walls, bedbugs creeping over the board beds, peering from the wood floor .... China has cured me; I never want to travel again,' she wrote to her mother.[32] However, she could not leave the Far East immediately as she had not yet completed her commitment to *Collier's*. But before the pair could leave Chungking, Martha had to recover from China Rot, a violent disease where the skin between her fingers started 'rotting away in a yellowish ooze laced with blood'. For weeks she went around with large, white gloves covering a strong lotion which made her 'about as alluring as a leper'. China Rot notwithstanding, she and Ernest had lunch at this time with Generalissimo and Mrs Chiang Kai-shek, a lunch where Martha took some careless, casual notes about the discussion of the western press view of the Chinese communists. She did not realise at the time what an exceptional event an intimate lunch was between the Hemingways and the Chiangs. Another day they were taken secretly to meet Zhou Enlai, a meeting of which Martha was unable to remember a word, but at which she felt at home with the Chinese for the first and only time during her entire visit.

Her final article for *Collier's* was from Singapore, 'one of the few places left in the world where you can still eat fresh caviare'.[33] Although she discussed the preparations being made there for war, she was overwhelmed by an air of unreality, as though everything was merely being arranged to make an effective stage or film set. Martha maintained the filmic metaphor throughout the piece: 'In a movie of this sort there has to be drama so bring on the spies, the Japs and the communists . . . . If the plot should develop into real war the Japanese would just be picked up and put in concentration camps.' It was a long piece in which she talked about not only strategic considerations and English military snobbery, but also the economic realities of Singapore. 'And let us not forget the moral of the Singapore movie. Business as usual, or far better than usual.' Although Ernest had by now gone home, Singapore was 'a whirl of gaiety with all the charming chaps in uniform fresh from Britain to defend that bastion of Empire'.[34] She lived in such luxury, clean as a whistle and cured of China Rot, that she could not justify writing about that part of the Orient in her travel book.

Charlotte Haldane, a British reporter married to the scientist J. B. S. Haldane, had also done a short stint in China in 1938 as special correspondent for the *Daily Herald*. Three years later, in the summer of 1941, employed by the *Daily Sketch*, she was one of five British reporters, and the only woman, selected to go on a trip to Moscow and report on the Soviet Union at war. Her brief was to send a daily story on life in the capital, focusing on issues such as the availability of salted cucumbers on the vegetable stalls and the length of food queues, but also to interview leading personalities, talk to refugees from towns invaded by the Germans and to study the organisation of civil defence. Charlotte believed that the British public was thirsting for news of the Russian people. 'Never in the history of the world has the anti-fascist press through its foreign representatives had a more responsible function to carry out than it has today,' she wrote, somewhat immodestly, in a later account of the trip.[35] But Charlotte well knew that in the wake of the Russian success in pushing back the

Germans at Smolensk and Bryansk, and in spite of her meagre understanding about military matters, her newspaper also expected her to
get to the front line.

Before she left London, there had been discussions with her editor
about the 'inflexible rule of the British War Office that no women
correspondents are ever allowed to visit the army on active service'.[36]
She was convinced that in the case of the Red Army this would be
different since communist theory proclaimed total sexual equality.
Charlotte, an ardent feminist and communist sympathiser, told her
editor confidently: 'You may be quite sure that if the men correspondents are allowed to go, I shall be allowed to go with them.'[37]
But when the question of a visit to the front first arose, her Russian
hosts told her that she would, as a new arrival, have to wait; Charlotte
was appalled. She reminded the Russians that surely they could not
allow 'the fact that I'm a woman [to] disqualify me from being allowed
to do my duty to my paper'. With the Soviets, such an argument
worked. On Monday, 15 September, Charlotte was one of eleven war
correspondents who set off in eight small 10 h.p. cars along the
Vyasma–Smolensk road, frequently to be strafed by German bombers.
There was one other woman in the party, the American photographer
Margaret Bourke White (whom Haldane constantly referred to in her
later account of the trip under her married name of Mrs Caldwell).

Wearing trousers underneath an old and long, blue leather coat,
which had stood her in good stead in the trenches during the Spanish
Civil War, Charlotte took copious notes on everything she saw. The
fact that she 'did not understand much about 'planes' did not seem to
matter since the censors cut out all references to the new Soviet fighter
aircraft. For six days and nights she remained in the same clothes,
although she was fortunate enough on most evenings to be offered
some sort of bed as well as the use of a communal wash-basin. As she
spoke fluent German she was able to interview some German prisoners and her verbatim report was much in demand among her
colleagues. But when she interviewed some Russian women performing back-up duties at a military camp, she let slip an extraordinary
question from such an ardent feminist: 'Jokingly I asked them if
they also did the soldiers' washing and darned their socks . . . . They
appeared almost offended, and answered me seriously, if not reprov-
ingly, that the Red Army had a special tailoring unit which carried out
such duties for the troops.'[38]

She and her colleagues made the return 250-mile journey to Moscow
in sixteen hours, in a rush to get back for the three-power conference.

Charlotte, exhausted, went straight to bed, but suffered a twinge of uneasiness around 4 a.m. at the thought that her colleagues would already be despatching their stories. She typed her piece in half an hour. Hers was a short assignment – she left Moscow in mid-October amidst real panic of a German invasion – but the Red Army had proved more willing than the British to allow women reporters near active fighting.

By January 1940, Elizabeth Wiskemann had had enough of research work. She wanted a more active role using the reporting skills she had acquired as an observer abroad in the 1930s and, therefore, proposed to the Foreign Office that she be sent to Switzerland, which she recognised as a key position in Europe. At first she went only in a semi-official capacity, attached to the British Legation, to help prepare anti-German propaganda and to pick up whatever snippets of news she could about the atmosphere in Germany. She developed contacts with businessmen, artists, writers, actresses and especially newspaper correspondents in Berlin, who frequently returned to Switzerland to consult their editors, and she was able to send long reports home by way of couriers, usually South American, as the Swiss could not risk openly breaching their neutrality. One of the most important messages she sent home at this time concerned information about the use of concentration camps not merely as prisons but as extermination camps. 'This was a good six months before the "final solution" was adopted by the Nazi leaders, i.e. the liquidation or physical destruction of the Jews; the incurables had been the guinea pigs for the gases used,' she wrote later.[39]

But by January 1941, she felt dissatisfied with her work and, in spite of the difficulties in travelling, decided to return to London. She went from Geneva across Vichy France to Spain, constantly aware that the Germans were said to be inciting Franco to arrest Englishwomen in order to create an explosive incident and that she, as a known opponent of Hitler on the Nazi's blacklist, would be taken straight to a concentration camp. However, she arrived safely in Portugal and, after a three-week wait in Lisbon, managed to get a flight to England.

She told her superiors in the Political Intelligence Department of the Foreign Office that she did not wish to return to Switzerland unless she was accorded full diplomatic rank, an unlikely prospect only ever granted to one other woman. None the less, the Foreign Office agreed and by September she was making plans to return. By this time Hitler dominated Europe and was dangerously deep into Russia. Her brief as assistant press attaché was to collect and convey home all possible non-military information about the enemy and enemy-occupied Europe.

The small flat she found for herself in Berne was intentionally without a concierge as the nature of her work made it imperative that no one should take note of her visitors. She had quickly picked up the essentials of the espionage business: her diary contained only initials, usually inverted; her engagement book merely code names. Frequently, if meeting an important contact whose own life might be jeopardised by her messages, she took no notes but relied on memory. One contact who caused her great anxiety was Adam von Trott. He heard about Elizabeth's work and wanted to meet her; from then on he saw her whenever he came to Switzerland. She recalled: 'When he rang me up he said, in his nearly perfect English, "It's Adam speaking." Anyone listening in could be in no doubt that it was Adam von Trott zu Solz.' But when she begged him to call himself Tom, Dick or Harry, he could not bring himself to oblige.

Most of the Legation staff were not allowed to meet enemy subjects at all, a rule which had to be waived in her case. Among the most significant she was introduced to was a German Catholic journalist who worked in Berne and had regular access to the German Legation. 'Until late in the war, almost every other week, he gave me reliable information of great value; we kept our promises.'

Elizabeth, then in her early forties, travelled courageously around Switzerland, often working from five in the morning until nine at night and constantly risking her life. Frequently her meetings were with theatrical friends or picture dealers,* both of whom were a valuable source of information as they had retained links with the Berlin, Munich and Vienna theatrical and artistic worlds. In Geneva, a centre for many émigrés, Elizabeth established useful lines to Hungarians, Czechs, Belgians and Dutch, all of whom were highly informative at various times. While in Basle her most valuable source was a German married to a Jewish wife who worked at Hoffmann-LaRoche, the giant chemical firm. He regularly crossed into Germany, where he had conversations with the industrialist, Robert Bosch of Stuttgart; sometimes he even went to Berlin. Elizabeth used to meet him at his home outside Basle at night, but at least once missed the tram back and had to walk about four miles along a snowy road which ran close to the frontier. 'I was a bit scared of missing my way and running into a

---

* After the war her art-dealer friends presented her with a rare figure drawing by Piranesi 'for helping the Jews', which she proudly bequeathed to the Fitzwilliam Museum.

German sentry so I stuck slavishly to the tramlines though theirs was not the shortest route,' she wrote.[40]

'She was by nature a timid woman,' recalled Boofy Gore (later Lord Arran), a colleague who shared an office with her at this time and found her courage inspirational. However bleak the outlook, Elizabeth always retained her sense of humour and worked 'with a smile at the absurdity of her surroundings', commented Gore, also then an assistant press attaché. 'I can see her still with her little pieces of paper on which she took notes in her exquisite handwriting, bustling from one secret rendez-vous to the next aided by no one, least of all the legation staff.'[41] There were many occasions when he would worry if she was not back on time. Then she would 'rush in with her pretty legs and her pretty face – she must have been a very pretty girl – and I ask for the latest news. She tells me and we are overcome with solemnity though the laughter is always there.'

In November 1942, when the western Allies landed in North Africa and the Germans occupied the whole of France, her life became more dangerous. From then on she could only communicate with London via coded messages and the Germans fed rumours that they had cracked the code. Another persistent rumour was that the Germans, looking covetously on the Swiss factories, were about to invade. Encircled as she was by Axis-controlled countries, Elizabeth commented that she 'was by this time so absorbed by her job, that I really did not have time to be afraid'.[42]

At this point in the war there were still no women officially accredited to report on the activities of British soldiers, even though several had managed to make their way, independently on occasion, to the shifting front line wherever that happened to be. The women active in reporting international affairs in the late 1930s and early 1940s were determined to continue with their work, irrespective of any formal documentation. There was, too, a discernible change in attitude amongst male reporters from merely tolerating women, as Emillie Peacocke had been, to being admired, as Virginia Cowles was; also there were not yet enough of them to be seen by their male colleagues as a threat, which made for generally good working relationships.

Officially, the situation was little changed since the First World War, when only one woman, Peggy Hull, had been formally, if grudgingly, accredited. Unofficially, there were many women reporters trying to relay the latest news and they no longer just happened to be where the action was; they were deliberately sent there by their editors. By the time of the Finnish campaign, three of the women war correspondents (warcos) in the frozen North were veterans; Martha Gellhorn, Virginia Cowles and a much younger colleague, Hilde Marchant, had all witnessed the Spanish Civil War and knew precisely the horrors which a sustained bombing campaign could wreak on a civilian population. Of the three, only Hilde Marchant was purposely used by her editor to convey the women's angle during her extremely brief stay in Madrid and then in Finland (as Charlotte Haldane had been in Moscow) and this was, in any event, what she wanted to write about. Gellhorn ferreted out aspects of the fighting which, while not specifically 'feminine', were frequently overlooked by the men. Notwithstanding Grant Duff's university education, she suffered interminably patronising remarks; her determination to cover hard political stories was in spite of her editor's suggestion that she write about fashion.

Given that the military commanders generally disliked all warcos, it was hardly surprising that they should be especially scornful of women, who, they assumed, understood little or nothing about military tactics, might need protecting and would almost certainly be an irritant. Yet it was Clare Hollingworth, who only months earlier had been a relief worker with the League of Nations Union in Poland, who was responsible for telling the world that war had begun and who proved that women were capable of living in extremely unpleasant and dirty conditions for extended periods with few material possessions and without making a nuisance of themselves.

Of course male correspondents, living in equally difficult conditions, were scoring too. Yet a woman travelling alone in the early part of the twentieth century faced additional difficulties, especially if she did not have the backing of a major news organisation. Most of the women reporters had to work individually rather than hunting in packs or pairs as did their male colleagues. However Virginia Cowles, helped by the fact that she was extremely attractive, was always able to find willing male reporters to supply her with up-to-date background news or a lift in a car. Both Elizabeth Wiskemann and Shiela Grant Duff as freelancers had no obvious hotel used by the other correspondents in which to stay; they had to find their own accommodation, develop their own contacts and decide which stories to cover, all on a shoestring budget. Both women had small independent incomes which made this possible. But for Agnes Smedley in China, also freelancing in similar circumstances, life was often lived on the breadline. The advantage for these women reporters, including Gellhorn and Cowles too because of their position as special correspondents, was that they enjoyed a freedom to write about aspects of a story which interested them rather than always answering the dictates of an editor for hard news.

Women reporters were still, and perhaps always would be, a part of the story themselves. However, in general, the women were taken seriously by this time and were not used by their papers as stunts. Their most severe test to date was about to come in the desert, where the military commanders were determined that the presence of women was not going to jeopardise the critical battle against the Germans and where male reporters began to suspect women reporters of employing unfair advantages in the battle for news.

11

Females in the Desert

'She becomes a source of worry and embarrassment to all concerned in times of danger.'
COLONEL PHILIP ASTLEY

When Clare Hollingworth arrived in Cairo in 1941, the first thing she did was to join the Gezira Sporting Club, which throughout the war was a crucial meeting place for soldiers and reporters, as well as a centre for polo playing, tennis, golf, swimming and good meals. Life in Cairo was, especially compared with Britain, rather glamorous. There were nightly dinner dances at Shepheards Hotel – where Flora Shaw had stayed with the Younghusbands fifty years previously – no food rationing, plenty of petrol and a thriving social round among the foreign correspondents. Alan Moorehead, a young reporter on the *Daily Express*, and Alex Clifford, formerly 'Eye-Witness' in France and now with the *Daily Mail*, had arrived shortly before her and were already enrolled as official war correspondents at the British Headquarters in Cairo. According to Moorehead, this involved buying

desert boots made of suede that came half-way up the ankle, knee-length khaki stockings, shorts of khaki drill that fastened with two neat buckles at the midriff, drill shirts and the whole was surmounted by the regulation khaki sun helmet .... We were given, also, water bottle, gas masks, flat steel helmets and, for the first and only time in the war, a revolver each. The revolver, we were told, was not to be used against the enemy but against the local population in case it turned against us. Finally, we bought mosquito nets, camp beds, sleeping-bags and canvas washing buckets.[1]

The uniform also included little green tabs to be worn on their shoulders inscribed in gold, 'British War Correspondent'.

Clare Hollingworth made do with none of this. Instead, she bought a large-brimmed, straw hat in an Alexandrian market and carried her own kit of basic essentials – a suit, spare underwear, toothbrush and typewriter. After a few weeks in a hotel, she found more sympathetic accommodation in a Chummery (a large shared flat) with Christopher Buckley, correspondent of the *Daily Telegraph*, whom she had first met in Athens. Buckley, at thirty-seven, was noticeable not merely as one of the oldest reporters in Cairo, but also because of his intellectual, schoolmasterly mien. According to Clare, he was 'slim, tall, but with a slight stoop that reduced his height. He wore thick glasses and, although he was basically good looking, few women noticed him.'[2] Buckley was an expert on military history and strategy – the works of Clausewitz were favourite reading matter – and Clare spent much of her free time in his company. She was writing a book at the time about her experiences in the Balkans, and Buckley gave her considerable support and advice. He also had useful contacts with intelligence officers, to whom he introduced her and who were prepared to help her get stories where the action was. Clare was not unattractive and, more importantly, she was extremely knowledgeable and intelligent.

While in Cairo, Clare learnt, without much surprise, that her pre-war marriage to Vandeleur Robinson was at an end. They had barely communicated during her time in the Balkans, when letters could take anything up to six months. Now that she could use the army mail services, her husband informed her that he wished to remarry and, in a simple uncontested case, divorced Clare for desertion. 'There was nothing really dramatic in the failure of my first marriage,' she wrote in her memoirs. She felt no rancour as Robinson had supported her career, which ensured that they had lived apart, and so the marriage had scarcely existed. Had the beginning of the war not coincided with the start of her marriage, enabling Clare to develop her career in England, it might have been different. But Clare insists that, even without a war, she always fretted when she had to remain in one place for too long. Her impatience, together with her thirst for adventure and her hunger to be in the very spot where history was in the making, made her an uneasy companion.

Clare's relationship with Buckley was close and romantic; friends assumed that now she was a free woman the pair would marry. But she maintains that her attachment to Buckley was 'not an affaire [*sic*] in the accepted sense of the word'.[3] Some seven years younger than he, she was both forceful and energetic. Colleagues were amused by the story of how once, after lunch at a hotel on the edge of the desert, the couple walked together to the great Pyramid of Cheops. Clare then proposed climbing right up to the top; Buckley declined, so she scaled it on her own. On her return she asked him to fetch her notebook for her, which she said she had left at the top.

When she first arrived in Cairo, Clare found little difficulty either in visiting the Eighth Army or in attending background briefings and the official press conferences. Held at noon every day on the second floor of the Immobilia building in central Cairo, these were usually followed by a drink at the Churchill Bar. Although she was employed by Kemsley Newspapers, which included the *Sunday Times*, the *Daily Sketch* and a host of provincial papers, she did not have the official accreditation she required to travel openly to any of the forward areas.

'Cairo may have been the nerve centre for disseminating information, but for me the news was out there in the desert with the British troops,' Clare wrote later.[4] It was also the only active front where the British were fighting the enemy and, since it was a highly personalised battle between Montgomery and Rommel, it made for an excellent story. Clare embarked on more trips for longer and under more dangerous conditions than any other woman reporter and was often behind enemy lines, but only as a result of her forceful character being rewarded with 'special treatment' or officialdom turning a blind eye and not because she was allowed to. Since Buckley was a close friend of both Moorehead and Clifford, the three men, known in Cairo as The Trio, covered many stories together. Clare sometimes went with The Trio and camped with them in the desert. At night they would climb into their sleeping-bags around their parked truck and discuss the world's problems, treating her as one of the gang.

This situation, where non-accredited reporters received special favours, although irksome, was more or less controlled by Lieutenant-Colonel Philip Astley MC, director of Army Press Relations. Colonel Astley was a lean, good-looking officer, veteran of the First World War and the former husband of film star Madeleine Carroll. It was well known that he did not allow women in the forward areas (there was not always a front as such in the desert), but could be utterly charming to individuals. When Eve Curie, the journalist daughter of Marie Curie, arrived to report for the *Herald Tribune* Syndicate, he greeted her warmly: 'Don't you remember? We dined together at Vera M's and she gave us heaps of caviar.'[5] Eve, who had spent the day before in Cairo having her hair done and her nails painted, was invited to join a dinner in Astley's tent. But when Randolph Churchill, then in charge of British propaganda in Cairo, who loved flouting rules and who was known to be sympathetic to the demands of female reporters, took it upon himself to accompany her to the Advanced Army Head-quarters, Astley was furious.

'I am sorry to say that having successfully battled for a long time against allowing women into the desert, a precedent was unfortunately set by the arrival... of Mlle Eve Curie,' Astley wrote to the War Office.[6] Astley insisted that the other male correspondents, although they did nothing about it, objected just as strongly as he since she was able to secure interviews with senior officers which he had been unable to obtain for them. 'Apart from this the situation was most awkward for both officers and other ranks with a woman in their midst living under open conditions which of necessity exist in the desert.'[7]

The problem was, once again, how to answer the call of nature in the desert. Although a screen could be erected for a single woman, 'what of the officers and men in the neighbourhood?' asked Astley. 'In mobile warfare it is generally impossible to make adequate latrines.' As a result of Eve Curie's visit, 'at least three hundred men were unmoved for three days,' he told the War Office, prompting the following reply: 'Find your picture of unmoved men most moving.'[8]

Eve spent a few more days in the desert, presumably unaware of the obstructing effect of her visit. She gratefully accepted, 'as a special favour', the back seat of a military car to sleep in, which she padded with an inflated rubber mattress. She covered herself with a white sheepskin coat lent to her by Randolph so that in all she was, unlike anyone else in the camp, 'very warm and comfortable'.[9] But her visit was cut short when, ten days after her trip to the front, she collapsed with malignant malaria, which she had contracted in Nigeria.

Three months after Curie's sorties, another woman found her way around the British Government ruling. Clare Booth Luce, wife of Henry Luce, the proprietor of *Time* and *Life*, was taken up under the auspices of the RAF as a distinguished visitor. 'It is no part of a woman's function to usurp the prerogatives of a war correspondent in desert warfare,' Astley fumed to the War Office in a long tirade headed 'Females in the Desert'.[10] 'There are fully sufficient men for this purpose and any visit by a woman is inclined to be treated as a "stunt", thereby stultifying potential propaganda value.'

Astley, then in his forty-sixth year, was not merely parroting chauvinistic attitudes of his day. There was a particular bond that had grown up amongst the Desert Rats, necessary to achieve the single-minded will to win, and glamorous females who 'swanned around' for a few days were both distracting and unnerving. Astley understood that it was not a question of whether women were tough enough.

'Although we may deny the fact, chivalry still lies latent in all men. The woman may say she can "take it" and in fact she probably CAN. But that is beside the point. She becomes a source of worry and embarrassment to all concerned in times of danger.' So worried was he that Astley consulted with Chief Commandant Chitty, head of the ATS, who supported his view: 'Women should not be allowed beyond the point in the desert where men's interest ends and their chivalry begins,' she told him, reassuringly.[11]

Of course, some women delighted in exploiting men's chivalrous tendencies. When Dixie Tighe of International News Service (INS) arrived one day at an air station after a long flight out from London, she was greeted by a large party of officers all proffering their hands to the new correspondent. One of the officers then proceeded to outline the programme. 'First of all . . .' he began. 'First of all,' broke in Dixie in a clear voice, 'I shall need a little girl's room and a sentry.' Then with a dazzling smile at the colonel, added, 'Guess you'd do.'[12]

Astley had been wise to recognise the danger of precedent; it required only one woman to report from the front for the others to cry foul. Since 1941, Virginia Cowles had given up reporting for the *Sunday Times* and after several months writing her book, *Looking for Trouble*, to be published in 1941, embarked on a lecture tour of the United States trying to persuade her fellow countrymen to enter the war and help defeat Nazism. On her return to England, she was awarded the OBE for her efforts. Then, early in 1942, she was appointed personal assistant to the American Ambassador in London, Gilbert Winant, and it was in this capacity that she too found herself in North Africa. Winant sent her to collect material for articles which would promote Anglo-American friendship.

Before leaving, the War Office had instructed her that, in view of its regulations, she could not visit the First Army area as a 'war correspondent' but could go under the designation 'distinguished visitor'. However, on arrival she was told that, even with this grand title, it was now prohibited to visit the forward area or Allied Force Headquarters. Virginia wasted no time in writing to General Eisenhower himself. Her tone was warm and friendly – she apologised for any embarrassment she may have caused – but determined and professional. 'My position has been made even more embarrassing by the fact that Miss Margaret Bourke White has been up into the forward area for a considerable time and is immediately going to the USA on a lecture tour on which, I feel sure, my unfortunate experience will be a subject of discussion,' she wrote.[13] Eisenhower promptly cabled back: 'Miss Cowles can go where she likes; she is to be given every possible assistance; there is to be no discrimination between race, creed or sex.'[14]

Shortly afterwards she was at the front, accompanied by Captain Nigel Nicolson of the Grenadier Guards, who remembers Virginia's arrival coinciding with a moment of extreme crisis. Rommel had turned away from the Eighth Army after the battle of Medenine and struck northwards with the best part of three panzer divisions in an attempt to cut the First Army's communications by capturing Beja far beyond the Allied front line. The British hurried to stop him at the pass south of a place called Sbiba. The engagement that ensued in the valley directly below was between two armoured groups hidden from each other by a fold in the ground. It was the first time Britain's Churchill tanks had been deployed in action and the clash made 'marvellous copy' for Virginia. On the way home at dawn they were approaching a village when they came under a fierce air attack. Everyone dived for cover in a ditch, except Virginia who was taking photographs. 'That was the moment that remains most vivid in my memory,' Nicolson commented.[15] However nothing further happened and, very cautiously, they advanced.

Nicolson remembers Virginia's visit as a considerable morale booster and 'an unbelievably lovely vision on the battlefield. In Africa she was the first Anglo-Saxon woman, literally, that we had seen for months and she was there to tell our people at home something of what we were doing and suffering.' On her return she made several broadcasts and wrote a series of articles for the *Sunday Times*, some of which, much to her annoyance, appeared in its sister paper, the *Sketch*.

Clare Hollingworth knew about Eve Curie and the others but was in a rather different category herself, principally because she had not come for a short visit but was based in Cairo and had built up a powerful understanding of the local situation. She never minded sleeping rough, or being unable to change her clothes or wash properly, and never complained about lavatorial inadequacies in the desert. She maintains that she has never experienced any unpleasantness from her male colleagues because 'I obey orders, behave in a very careful way and never ask for a single privilege, never ... if there were six reporters and five beds I would volunteer for the floor.'[16] When she went into the desert, she did so with a minimum of fuss; no special screens or mattresses for her.

By her own admission, her most terrifying experience occurred during a desert sortie with one of her intelligence officer contacts, Colonel Ralph Neville. His job was to round up enemy equipment. After a few hours fruitlessly searching for German weaponry among the dunes, they decided to rest for the night and dug themselves into a body-sized, shallow trench using the sand as a blanket. After a few hours dozing, she awoke to hear the distinctly German voices of an enemy recce party no more than a hundred yards away. 'I literally sweated with fear. I had never been so frightened in my life. I could feel that sand sticking with perspiration to every pore all over my body.'[17] But that night she was lucky. The Germans never discovered the sleeping English party.

On 12 August 1942, General Bernard Montgomery (Monty) arrived to take charge of the Eighth Army. Monty was a hero to his men but Clare, warned that he was a woman hater, failed to establish any rapport with him. 'I never met him alone at this time and my contacts, who opened doors for me to report the war at close quarters, decided it was better for me not to do so,' she wrote in her memoirs. Monty absolutely refused to accept the accreditation of women war correspondents and so Clare believed that her days of quietly bending the rules would soon be over. She was therefore extremely aggrieved to learn that the Americans had persuaded him to allow Clare Booth Luce and others to join their press corps in the desert.

In January 1943, after the British capture of Tripoli and at the end of the Desert Campaign, Clare had her first brush with Monty. She had been sleeping in the back of a truck at Castel Benito, the main airport south of Tripoli, when Monty ordered her back to Cairo. She was furious. 'It seemed illogical that I should be ordered back... because I was a woman when there were thousands of other women in Tripoli; the town was full of Italian women who had not been evacuated and there were plenty of nurses based at the airport,' she wrote later.

But she did not remain in Cairo for long. 'By that time, to his eternal credit, General Eisenhower insisted on having a few experienced women correspondents around who – and this was vital – demanded no special treatment.... Many male correspondents got themselves sent back to Cairo because they could not take it.'[18] She therefore flew to Algiers and, now reporting for the *Chicago Daily News*, in addition to her work for the Kemsley group, became accredited to US operations, which were based in the Algerian capital.

Astley, although informed in advance of Clare's application to be accredited to the American forces, had been reasonably confident that this would not materialise as the Americans had assured him, 'Nothing would be done to embarrass us.'[19] 'In spite of that, the embarrassment came upon us pretty quickly,' Astley admitted. In reporting to the War Office, Astley advised that the Army Commander was equally as cross as he had been about Clare's ruse:

In no uncertain terms... [the Commander] did not propose now or in the future to allow any women correspondents in his army area.... This he did but not soon enough to stop Miss Hollingworth's arrival; however she was quickly sent back again and is now, I imagine, nursing a grievance against British Public Relations.[20]

Astley was unhappy about Clare's situation but could do nothing more. With a touch of Higginsian despair, he asked his colleague in the War Office in London: 'Why can't women be content to be treated as visitors for whom special facilities can be laid on if and when considered desirable?'[21]

Clare remained in the Middle East for the duration of the war. She caught jaundice, which was debilitating, and learnt to pilot an aeroplane, which was exhilarating. She made a point throughout her time there of attending as many briefings as possible to learn about weaponry, air power and other strategic considerations and she learnt how to parachute. She went on many bombing missions and, towards the end of the war, joined raids over the Mediterranean designed to shoot up enemy shipping. But the excitement soon palled.

In 1944, when news came through that the Germans were about to surrender in Crete, she went there as soon as possible with Geoffrey Hoare, another reporter she had met in Cairo, who was then working for *The Times*. The scoop of the main surrender at Lüneburg Heath was, however, given to Chester Wilmot, who had developed a particularly warm working relationship with Monty. Monty trusted him in a way he would never have trusted a woman. Wilmot, an Australian, who had been given much confidential information by senior British generals throughout the war, was now rewarded with the major prize. Hollingworth and Hoare arrived in Crete with a British officer and had the pleasure of forcing the senior German officers on the island to surrender. The two then commandeered two staff cars and, for the next few days, 'drove around the island like lords'.

This phase of the war proved crucial for the future of women reporters. Although the British still considered that they were not only unnecessary but a nuisance and, after the experience of Eve Curie, were more determined than ever not to change the rules, American authorities proved more amenable. Both Hollingworth and Cowles were, thanks to the Americans, given a chance to prove what men such as Colonel Astley already knew: that women reporters could be just as brave and efficient in difficult and unpleasant circumstances as their male counterparts. Even so, women reporters would have to find devious means to get on with their jobs for a few more years before they could force through a change in wartime accreditation.

12

The Home Front – and Beyond

'If they don't want to accredit you, just do it.'
MARTHA GELLHORN

The best woman reporter that ever worked in Fleet Street was, according to Arthur Christiansen, editor of the *Daily Express*, Hilde Marchant, a butcher's daughter from Hull. She was also for a time the youngest and the most highly paid.

Hilde Marchant was born in Hamburg in 1916 to an English father and a German mother. After the Great War, the family moved to England and settled in Hull, where, at fifteen, Hilde ended what had been a 'quick and violent' adolescence by becoming a telephonist on the *Hull Daily Mail*. She had shone at English at school and now used her initiative and persuasive ways to earn a transfer from the switchboard to the reporters' room. It was not long before her employers, Allied Newspapers, sent her up to London for a trial stint as a junior reporter on the *Daily Sketch*. Within months, she had cut herself loose from her family and established an independent life in London.

'She was a tiny little thing with wispy hair, never in place, but two major physical assets, a deep-toned, exciting voice and dark, beautiful eyes which seemed always to me to conceal a wistful wonder about the world and its mystery,' remembers Bernard Hall,[1] a colleague from those early days. It was an apparent vulnerability, mixed with overwhelming ambition and toughness of character, which gave the edge to Hilde's reporting; human frailty and resilience were delicately counterpoised in her articles. Never shy, within days of her arrival in London, Hilde was seen chatting to editors in the corridor, flaunting her ambitions and causing a stir by freely inviting male reporters and photographers back to her rooms in Doughty Street.

After a short time at the *Sketch*, Hilde was ready to move on. In April 1936, she turned in such a good story on the unexciting topic of a model railway exhibition in London that she attracted the attention of the legendary Christiansen, who had become editor of the *Daily Express* at the age of twenty-nine. Hilde's story had centred on a senior engine driver from the London Midland and Scottish Railway, who had just driven a morning express from Manchester to Euston and, still in his footplate rig, had hurried to Westminster to look at the miniature trains endlessly whirring round the big tables. It was written with a pace and style – focusing on people rather than things – which decided Christiansen at once. He summoned the *Express* reporter, Hall, who had written on the same exhibition, and told him that his piece was cliché-riddled by comparison. 'I am amazed we gave it space. This girl Marchant is obviously the reporter we need. I have moved at once to bring her to Shoe Lane before the *Daily Mail* get the same idea.'[2]

Hilde was just twenty when she joined the *Express* at thirty guineas a week, plus generous expenses. This was five guineas more than Cyril Morton, the chief reporter, and more than three times the salary of the junior reporter whose job she had threatened. She became a star reporter from her first day at the *Express* with regular top billing on the day's news-sheet and almost immediately pleaded to be allowed to go to Spain. Meanwhile, it was Marchant who covered the Abdication crisis for the *Express*, even following the former King Edward VIII and Mrs Simpson to the Mediterranean. Finally, she persuaded Christiansen to allow her to report from Spain. She went, according to Christiansen, because she persisted in her demands until he gave in. When she called him four times in one evening, insisting that no one was covering the woman's angle of the siege of Madrid, he said she could go for ten days.

'But remember, cut out that trick of yours which makes you start as well as end sentences with prepositions,' he lectured. 'Why should I?' she responded. 'I write as I talk and as people talk to me.' She reminded her editor that she had never been to a university and neither had most of their readers. 'If you want that sort of prose, get the *Sunday Times* literary critic to go to Spain and see what happens to the circulation.'

Christiansen, who had also left school as a teenager to start work, knew the sense of her argument. But he told her not to be so 'saucy' or she would not go at all. His final advice was: 'Don't forget that every soldier has a wife. Ask her what she thinks of war. Do the troops in Madrid come home every night? What are they using for food? How are the children standing up to it?'[3]

Although Hilde also travelled to France, Poland and Sweden on assignments, hers were never stories of trenchant political analysis, nor were they meant to be. 'The battle was bigger, more complex than I had sensed,' she admitted after returning from Germany in the wake of Neville Chamberlain's mission to meet Hitler in Bad Godesberg.[4] At the outbreak of the Second World War, she was sent to Finland and reported on the tragedy that had befallen hundreds of families in the small, wooden Finnish towns. 'The story to tell was that these mass raids did not frighten the Finns . . . . I never once saw a Finnish woman or child in hysterics,' she explained later.[5] Her strength was always in writing about people, not about political theories or events, although she was, in spite of her German ancestry, passionately anti-Nazi. She described herself as having 'a cyclops eye that could stay in the middle of my head and observe of its own accord'.[6] John Young, night news editor of the *Express* for twenty-six years, agreed: 'She could write like a saint, would always dig out the unusual and get down to the human basics of a story. The stuff she sent us back from Finland was brilliant.'[7]

Hilde's natural talent and Germanic energies would have been enough to win her a high position in Fleet Street, but, in addition, from her earliest days she had the backing of the *Express* managing editor, Herbert Gunn. Gunn soon became not just her lover but also 'her office impresario, guiding her footsteps, ensuring that she was given top-class assignments and that her copy received first-class handling on the sub-editor's table,' recalled a colleague.[8] In the days when bylines were for the very few, Hilde's was rarely omitted. She and Gunn moved into a flat together near Bloomsbury, but the affair lost Hilde several friendships and quite possibly stunted Gunn's own career.

Fêted as she was, Hilde herself never behaved like a star. Most colleagues on the paper found her a real 'office trooper', always happy to help juniors or to pitch in with any reporter caught in a late-night rush. She would act as copy-taker, if the copy-takers were inundated, or 'top and tail' copy, or 'crack a piece on to her typewriter at just the length the back table asked for. In the news trade she was a woman for all seasons, even rushing to get library cuttings for some harassed reporter.'[9]

But it was reporting from the home front on how the ordinary British working man and woman were standing up to the onslaught of war that best revealed Hilde's real talent. Of course she did not deny the Government line to the extent that she wrote more about old-fashioned pluck than doom and despair; that was what she observed. But equally she did not spare her readers the agonies of war and its aimless destruction and death.

One of her first pieces, before war was officially declared, set the tone. She had been asked to cover the evacuation of some of London's schoolchildren, a story that was causing much debate. Many argued that evacuation would split the British home, divide child and parent, and break the domestic background that was the country's strength. Hilde visited a block of flats in a working-class corner of the city and in the early morning watched a frail, cockney child walking to school. The child had a brown-paper box knocking against her thin legs. 'It was Florence Morecambe, an English schoolchild, with a gas mask instead of a satchel over her shoulder.' She followed Florence to school and watched the distressing scenes as parents wept their goodbyes to the children, who then walked in crocodile fashion to the tube and train out to the country. She went with them as the children were shepherded on to the train and then taken to their billets.

In her article, Hilde moved from the individual to the general and then back to Florence again. She recognised the anguish for all concerned, but concluded with a reminder to her readers of the gravity of the world situation which had demanded such a separation. The teachers, she pointed out, had protectively covered up a news poster which declared, 'Warsaw bombed'. That it would be London next she did not need to say.

Although she wrote about many aspects of the nation at war, it was for her coverage of the suffering capital that she won most plaudits. 'Parts of London looked like Ypres or Arras yesterday as her people came from the trenches and the basements to look into a choking dawn,' she wrote in April 1940. She then told the story of the man who said, ' "Get off me, you drunken fool" as he was pushed over ... but as he moved the man off him he found the man was dead. He had been blown out of a building.' Finally, she told her readers of 'the large bomb which hit a home for blind men. They led each other out into the same darkness but some were trapped.'[10]

'From the day the war began, Hilde waged a one woman war against [the Germans] which took her wherever the danger was greatest ... sending her pen and her newsflair into battle to defeat them,' recalled Bernard Hall. On Friday, 15 November 1940, this was to Coventry at dawn as soon as she learned of the devastating raid by the Luftwaffe on the city. Within a few hours she was walking about the smouldering rubble, gathering information and interviewing survivors.

'Amid the black horror of the Nazi attack on Coventry, which was Guernicaed all through last night, two things stand out,' she wrote in the *Daily Express*.[11] 'The great courage of the people and the devotion of ARP workers who were only stopped by death.' Such scenes were, however, nothing new to Hilde; she had tramped around a blitzed East End of London many times talking to families about their wrecked homes and lives and had witnessed similar horrors in Finland and Spain. 'Yet this was worse, for in all honesty you cannot feel so deeply about the destruction of your neighbour's house as your own. These people moved against a background of suburban villas, had English faces, used the English tongue, wore English clothes. They were our own kind.'[12]

As she contemplated the skeleton of the city, watching the bewilderment and frustration on the children's faces, she noticed most strongly the determination of the WVS workers, the ambulance drivers and the police not to allow the German action to break their spirit. Although they had to cope with almost a thousand casualties that night, the real heroes and heroines were ordinary people like Mrs Smith, who, as Hilde wrote, served tea throughout the raid.

As she toured Coventry, the air was thick and full of charred wood which blew in through her car window, biting into her throat and lungs. The city was darkened by a black fog throughout the day and the heat and smoke made everyone's eyes red and sore. Hilde insisted on climbing up a tower, which was surrounded by broken pillars with a yawning crater at its heart, the only structure of Coventry Cathedral left intact. The *Daily Express* chauffeur, who drove Hilde with difficulty for part of the day, was a First World War veteran and a man of courage. When night fell he told her that he thought they should leave the city as the Germans were sure to return for a follow-up raid. Hilde retorted that he could leave but she was staying. Even when her editor ordered her out she refused. So she and her driver stayed the night, sleeping in the car, and the Germans did come back for a second, albeit less forceful, bombing.

The following day she produced another lead story. Hilde's coverage of Coventry so impressed Winston Churchill that he ordered reprints of her report to be issued for general release to British Embassies and Legations worldwide.

Hilde was not naturally fearless. To Madrid she had taken a supply of chewing-gum to prevent her teeth from chattering during air-raids. Yet by this time she had controlled her fear – 'treating bombs as snowflakes' – and would rush out to cover a potentially dangerous assignment often without her tin hat. John Young believes that her courage was the essence of her success and helped her to forge an easy relationship with male colleagues. Getting the story fast was what mattered most and if that meant hurrying into the street without troubling to put on make-up, it did not worry Hilde.

At a time when a lot of women in Fleet Street were writing guff, she knew when to be tough and when to approach a story from a feminine point of view. She had a great sense of timing and, when needed, great sensitivity. She combined the best aspects of the male and female reporter.[13]

In addition, she always enjoyed the hours she spent drinking in the pub with her colleagues and her language among them was frequently bawdy and loud. Her regular routine during the Blitz, once she had written her piece for the next day, was to walk to the Savoy Hotel and chat to the American reporters based there. Rather than go home alone, if Gunn was still working, she preferred to go up on to the Savoy roof with the others and, however foolhardy, watch the bombs drop.

But in spite of the ease with which she struck up relationships with male colleagues, she did not endear herself so easily to other women reporters in Fleet Street. Mea Allan arrived in London in May 1938, working first for the *Woman's Friend*, but soon moving to the *Sunday Referee*. When that folded in June 1939, she was given a post on the *Daily Herald*. Mea was always passionate about writing. She came first in English at school and, unlike Hilde, approached journalism from a literary standpoint. She wrote poetry and by the late 1930s had sold enough poems to enable her to subscribe to a course in journalism.

By July 1941, Hilde's affair with Gunn was over and she felt unable to stay at the *Express*. Mea was incensed at rumours that she was to join the *Herald*. 'I suppose I must be professionally jealous', she wrote in a letter to a friend, 'as I get into a vile anger when I think of it.... If there's a brass-necked way of getting a story she'll do it that way because it's easier and her first step in a job is to fasten her claws to the man whose voice is authority and if a happy home is broken up in the process well that doesn't very much matter to her.'[14]

Perhaps Mea's jealousy was misplaced; she herself was at this time not working as a reporter but as news editor – indeed, Fleet Street's only woman news editor. In April 1941, the World's Press News (WPN) did a feature about her unique position and she glowed with pleasure at being treated, for a day, as a 'glamorous and interesting thing'.[15] In the event, the 'cursed female', as Mea referred to Hilde, did not join the *Herald* but went instead to the *Daily Mirror*. The *Express* was devastated and did all it could to keep its star including, according to Mea's Fleet Street sources, 'holding out the blackmail of contract which she says she does not have with them'.[16]

As Britain battled alone, it seemed, to keep itself free from Hitler's toils, some of the most poignant vignettes of life on the home front were written by Mollie Panter-Downes. Although a novelist from the age of seventeen, she always described herself as a reporter, claiming for herself 'no powers of invention, no ear for dialogue . . . . I have to *see* the thing for it to be real.'[17]

Mollie was born into an army family and grew up in genteel poverty as her father was killed in September 1914, when she was eight. She and her mother lived in a village on the Surrey/Sussex border, an area from which Mollie scarcely moved since. By 1935, she was married with two children and a growing reputation as a short-story writer. Even so, when she suggested to her agent that some of her stories might be good enough for the *New Yorker*, he quashed the idea immediately, telling her, 'Oh no dear, no, no get that right out of your head, they don't have any English people at all.' But she persisted, at first with some verse, then the occasional short story and an arresting piece of reportage on the Jewish refugee children arriving at Victoria Station in 1937.

The *New Yorker* was sufficiently impressed by this to send her a cable on the eve of war asking her to write a regular London letter for them. At first she declined, as she was expecting the arrival of some evacuees. But they failed to appear and so, encouraged by her husband, she accepted. Her first 'Letter from London' had to be backdated to 3 September 1939. She sent it the same way as she was to despatch all her copy to the *New Yorker* throughout the war: she would either walk across the fields, bicycle or occasionally motor to the station, hand her copy personally to the guard and have the train met in London by Western Union, who had been authorised to accept her messages.[18]

Despite the London dateline, Mollie's letters were as revealing about country life – 'the little village which we will call Mugbourne' – as that in the capital. She wrote in an elegant, disciplined style about 'willing ladies who have emerged from the herbaceous borders to answer the call of duty';[19] of BBC announcers who 'read out important news in tones that suggest they are understudying for Cassandra on the walls of Troy';[20] and of German and Austrian refugees employed as domestic servants, who, 'after unbosoming themselves of any explosives which they happened to have around . . . sped happily back to their kitchens and got on with downing Hitler by bottling England's plum harvest, which is immense'.[21] She informed her American readers that 'British reserve has cracked under stress to the extent that neighbours now chat with positively village chumminess.'[22]

Once every two weeks, she fed Americans the essence of British life, no detail being too small to convey a mood. One night she saw 'raw sirloins of beef being carried from one stately club, which was temporarily cut off from its gas supply, to another equally stately establishment, which had offered the hospitality of its old-fashioned coal ranges'.[23] Eton, she reported, had partially abolished top hats 'since they were tricky things to wear with gas masks';[24] Christmas carol singers were allowed to sing ' "And glory shone around" so long as their lanterns don't shine around too conspicuously, but they must not ring bells, which might be confused with an air-raid signal'.[25] She was struck by the method of announcing air-raid deaths in the morning papers. No mention was made of the cause of death but the phrase 'very suddenly' was always used. 'Thousands of men and women and children are scheduled to die very suddenly, without any particular notice being taken of them in the obituary columns,' she wrote.[26] Her anger, though reined in, was barely concealed when she concluded: 'All that is best in the good life of a civilized effort appears to be slowly and painfully keeling over in the chaos of man's inhumanity to man.'[27]

Mollie brilliantly conveyed the mood of wartime London at the height of the Blitz. She noticed the Business as Usual stickers that suddenly appeared on what was left of a bombed-out shop window and heard the 'we shall get used to it' phrase on everyone's lips. Hardly anyone in London had slept for a week but, she observed, however bad a night Londoners had had, they emerged with their resolve stiffened. 'The behaviour of all classes is so magnificent that no observer here could ever imagine these people following the French into captivity. As for breaking civilian morale, the high explosives that rained death and destruction on the capital this week were futile.'[28] The bravery of the ordinary people would be heart-rending 'if they didn't so conspicuously refuse to appear heart-rending', she wrote in September 1940. Her own bravery deserves mention too, for reporting from London in 1940 could be just as dangerous, if less exciting, as reporting from a war zone. Throughout the war, her sense of duty ensured that she never missed a single deadline in order to get her weekly copy to the *New Yorker*, and she continued working for them for almost fifty years.

*   *   *

Audrey Russell, another reporter who made her name on the home front, was born in 1907 into a well-connected Anglo-Irish family in Dublin. Her uncle was King Edward VIII's friend and equerry, Major 'Fruity' Metcalfe. An only child, Audrey had been stage-struck from an early age. But when, shortly after a broken engagement, she resolved to 'pull herself together' and train for the stage, her parents were implacably opposed. The fact that Elsie Fogerty, principal of the Central School of Speech and Drama, had personally offered her a place, weighed not at all; Audrey had to turn down the offer. Miss Fogerty countered by suggesting she attend part-time, in secret and with no fees. This arrangement lasted for a brief six months, but was enough to get Audrey a toe through the stage door; her first job was assistant stage manager in Rodney Ackland's play, *After October*, at the Arts Theatre for a weekly salary of £4 10s.

This occupied her for a year and eventually led to two brief appearances on stage. But by this time war was clearly imminent and she volunteered for the London Fire Brigade, later known as the London Auxiliary Fire Service (the AFS). 'I'm glad I joined early,' Audrey wrote characteristically in her autobiography, *A Certain Voice*.[29] 'It was a fairly cold, calm, methodical preparation for the storm that was about to break.' As she was attached to 'A' District, Superintendent Station at Manchester Square, just a short walk from Broadcasting House, her station enjoyed frequent visits from radio reporting teams gathering news stories about the Blitz and experiences of fire fighting and civil defence. This arrangement was convenient for the BBC, required to broadcast news bulletins night and day, and was welcomed by the station superintendent, who liked the publicity. Audrey was soon asked to give an interview on her impressions of being a woman in the fire service. 'Gradually I became a sort of tame firewoman to the BBC (unpaid), often called upon for a story.'[30]

One of her early broadcasts included a description of the night of 10 May 1941, when the House of Commons was hit. Another was heard by Air Commodore Harold Peake, who was so impressed by Audrey's cool presence and clear voice that he invited her to do six five-minute talks for the BBC on the work of the WAAF with the intention of scotching rumours that some WAAF duties were too arduous for women. This was the first time she had to write a script, rather than talk off the cuff, but it was a technique she quickly picked up and, after six interesting weeks travelling around stations of bomber, fighter and coastal command, life in the AFS seemed rather quiet. However, a few weeks later she was offered a wartime appointment as an observer

(the word then used instead of 'reporter') in the overseas service of
the BBC. With so many male members of staff called up, it was now
essential to use more women, and the BBC preferred to recruit from
those whose experience was in fields other than broadcasting. After
seven months of negotiation she was vetted, screened and hired, at a
salary of £645 a year. She was immediately sent on a three-week staff
training course, during which the art of broadcasting was hardly
mentioned but where there was much to be learned about engineering
techniques.

Audrey started work for the BBC in June 1942, aged thirty-six, just
as the offensive in the desert was reaching its climax, and was attached
to the popular programme *Radio News Reel*, a daily short-wave radio
magazine. She was extremely pretty, blonde and well-dressed and, not
surprisingly, being the Corporation's first woman reporter, found
herself initially sent out on fashion and food stories. 'There was little
or no prejudice against me among my male colleagues; they were
friendly and helpful and only slightly patronising,' she wrote. None
the less, although in her first months she had been happy to cover the
soft news stories – an economic way of getting your hair cut (the
liberty cut); the opening of day nurseries and crèches; flower shows
and dog shows – she soon hankered for more exciting assignments
describing news of greater significance.

But in 1944 as the German bombs dropped on London with increasing ferocity and intensity, the dog and flower shows petered out,
leaving one harrowing disaster after another for the BBC to report.
Peter Pooley, Audrey's editor at *Radio News Reel*, confidently sent his
new young reporter on all sorts of dangerous home assignments. For
month after month she and her team were constantly visiting areas of
danger and destruction, ack-ack sites, defence posts and barrage-
balloon stations, all the while counting dead bodies wrapped in sack-
cloth shrouds. Audrey had marvellous powers of description and,
despite her training and the inherent drama of the situation, did not
succumb to theatricality. Although much of her material was banned
for broadcasting by the censor for revealing too much, her efforts were
not entirely wasted as several reports were sent to the Home Office or
Ministry of Information for analysis to determine the morale of the
population.

Audrey was often frightened by her assignments; less by the thought
of the enemy, more lest she be criticised by her colleagues for poor
work. This competitive streak drove her, to an extent, to overcome
such ordeals as climbing a rope-ladder up the side of an American

liberty ship in a rough sea off Milford Haven to report on the duties of the WRNS boarding officers. She was given a tot of rum by the captain when she succeeded on that occasion. Audrey could nerve herself to succeed on an assignment although she never quite conquered her fear of heights. This was exacerbated by a long-standing eye problem, which left her with a severe squint. As a minor concession to vanity, she always tried to have herself photographed in profile.

At the end of 1944, the BBC applied for her to become a fully accredited war correspondent to go to Europe. Until then, the only way a British woman could report on the war with a full war correspondent's licence was, as Clare Hollingworth had learned, as a representative of an American newspaper or agency. This was not for want of trying on the part of the women concerned. The war had brought home to Britain's women journalists, many of whom had taken over men's jobs, exactly to what extent they were at a disadvantage vis-à-vis their male colleagues.

The precise incident that focused them on the need for their own support group or lobbying organisation – a women's press club based on the lines of the men's press club – concerned Mrs Eleanor Roosevelt, wife of the President. In 1943, Mrs Roosevelt paid her first wartime visit to England, but, with the exception of a handful of women magazine editors, women of Fleet Street were not given the opportunity to meet her and they were furious. In a coach returning from a Facilities Visit, 'Somewhere in England', several voices were raised in protest. Especially vociferous were Mea Allan and Iris Carpenter, both of the *Daily Herald*, and Phyllis Davies of the *Daily Mail*. Phyllis Deakin of *The Times* took the lead: 'As the men won't have us, we should have a club of our own . . . . What about it?'

On 1 April 1943, sixty-two women journalists held their first meeting at The Falstaff, Fleet Street's well-known tavern, munching on wartime sandwiches amidst the ruins of London's Blitz. The Women's Press Club got under way.

But this was hardly enough to help all those women trying to get full accreditation as war correspondents. 'The British War Office was plainly obstructive,' Phyllis Davies told the Women's Press Club after the war. 'First it grudgingly agreed, then changed its mind, then had second thoughts, then changed again.'[31] This process went on for some time, 'until it could not think of any more excuses'. Six women did take off in a bomber bound for France, shortly after the liberation of Paris in August 1944, but, as Davies recalled, they were still not granted the proper war correspondent's licence, but merely given a little pink slip which stated, 'This is a SHAEF* accommodation. It cannot be stamped outside the country.' Davies remembered arriving at the war correspondents' zone, where they 'existed for five weeks being edged further and further away from any possible chance of individual stories'.[32] But some progress had been made; they wore the official uniform – officer's tunic with British war correspondent's shoulder flashes and gold 'w' badge – and held honorary rank equivalent to captain, which permitted entry to mess facilities and accommodation.

This small group complained about their treatment, but the War Office denied responsibility and SHAEF insisted that it was not their problem. They received a much more sympathetic hearing from the American authorities, who, according to Davies, were 'magnificent and time after time kicked up shindies about the way British women correspondents were treated. General Eisenhower's aide, Harry Butcher, declared how glad he was to have them and praised them as a serious-minded set.'[33]

One of the first regular War Office and Air Ministry licences issued to a British woman reporter belonged to Evelyn Irons of the *Evening Standard*. Armed with British war correspondent licence no. 976 she went to France in 1944, just after Paris was liberated, but was furious to discover that she was assigned to cover stories about military hospitals. 'The situation was quite intolerable . . . no chance of getting anywhere near the real action,' Evelyn recalled. She tried every possible way to break the impasse – Americans, Canadians – but without success. 'Finally, I ran into Janet Flanner of the *New Yorker* in Paris and she suggested the French Army. The French? With their attitude to women? But a woman ceases to be a sex object – if she ever was one – when she gets into uniform, Flanner explained, here in France.'[34] The ruse worked. Early in 1945, Evelyn joined the Première Armée Française and crossed the Rhine into Germany with General de Gaulle. Several French correspondents were also accredited, but she was the only British. Later that year she was awarded the Croix de Guerre with Silver Star, the first woman to receive the honour, for 'not hesitating to go into the thick of the fighting to get the best description of the First French Army in action'.[35] According to the citation, 'at Phorzeim on 13 April 1945 under violent enemy fire she went in with advance troops volunteering to serve as liaison officer

---

* Supreme Headquarters Allied Expeditionary Forces under the supreme command of General Eisenhower.

taking part in the transport of wounded'. Evelyn was one of a small band of war reporters prepared to contravene regulations and carry a gun. 'The French would have none of this nonsense about war correspondents not carrying weapons,' she told Phillip Knightley, years later.[36]

Among the select group of women who took advantage of the War Office's eventual relaxation of its regulations were Phyllis Deakin, founder of the Women's Press Club, Dr Catherine Gavin of the *Daily Express*, Alison Settle of the *Observer* and Mary Munton of the *Daily Telegraph*. Mea Allan was also one of the newly accredited women warcos who flew to France in 1944 and then travelled to Brussels, Berlin, Vienna and up to Oslo. 'Was I not privileged to witness the break-up of the German Army that had menaced us all, its dismal trek to prison cages along the dusty Alle–Hamburg Road in that triumphant and blazing June? Was I not privileged to be watching the delirious home going of millions of Hitler's slave-labourers to France, to Belgium, to Holland and to Russia?' she wrote.[37] For in 1945, the defeat of Germany and the reconstruction of Europe, the impending trials of the war criminals and the settlement of the refugees were the major stories. Not surprisingly, nothing on the home front could compare in importance with these.

Early that year, Audrey Russell's foreign accreditation finally came through. Wearing her khaki battledress top that she thought looked both too smart and too new, she flew in a Dakota of RAF Transport Command to Brussels. She was, she admitted, 'pleased with the dark green and gold chevrons on the shoulders neatly indicating "British War Correspondent"'.[38] But she felt self-consciously 'new' all round as it was her first flight in an aeroplane. Since the aircraft had been stripped bare, apart from rows of facing benches for troop carrying, it was not a comfortable flight. Alan Moorehead and his wife Lucy, both in uniform, were also on the aeroplane and they introduced Audrey to an excellent restaurant that night. Later, she tried to doze in her sleeping-bag on the bare springs of a bed at the four-star Palace Hotel in Brussels.

Her first job was to visit a mixed ack-ack battery of the Royal Artillery, Battery 485 on a gun site. She went by utility truck but was not officially allowed to know precisely where she was going. Her main problem was a high wind that made recording particularly difficult, especially from a Nissen hut. The mud everywhere, ankle- and in places knee-deep, hindered movement. In addition to the wind and the mud, Audrey's bulky equipment presented her with enormous technical difficulties, which, with no engineer to help her, she tried to tackle alone, knowing that if she appealed to London, 'they would send out an identical machine thinking, "How like a woman, you see, she can't make it work" and so on'.[39]

The recording gear in question was one of the first models of a type said to be 'portable'. Audrey explained: 'It looked like an early portable gramophone with a handle to wind up the spring. With it was an issue of large blank acetate discs. The instructions said that a cutting needle was supplied as well as one to play back the recording.' As the blank discs had to be kept more or less at room temperature, Audrey resorted to wearing about half-a-dozen discs under her battledress blouse. Her resultant curious shape prompted much hilarity in the camp, but even this ruse could not make the machine work efficiently. 'What I did not know was that all the men had rejected this terrible bit of equipment and refused to use it.'[40]

Eventually, Audrey sent an sos through Army Signals to the BBC forward area unit in Eindhoven. Within forty-eight hours, a War Reporting Unit and a senior engineer, with whom she had worked during the shelling of Dover, came to her rescue. After this she was driven to Eindhoven, where there was some embarrassment at the BBC billet as she was the only woman. But the men were chivalrous and helped convert a toaster into a hair-dryer so that she could wash and dry her hair. She had not bathed or taken her clothes off for days.

Audrey chafed a little at Eindhoven when she realised that the men – chiefly the BBC's Frank Gillard and Chester Wilmot of ABC – were covering hard news and she was left with background stories. Often, however, these were just as important as the facts and figures of the German retreat. One day she visited a half-ruined factory which had become home to a motley group of just-alive people, the senile, blind, deaf, mad and old, abandoned as their relatives had fled for their lives. They were being fed by one English and one Dutch woman on scraps of anything they could find, all boiled together in one large tub and called, euphemistically, 'soft food'.

Shortly after reporting this story, Audrey was instructed to proceed to Antwerp, where the Germans were still mounting a heavy attack of flying bombs in a desperate attempt to knock out the port. This was both hard and dangerous news. Gillard, who was in charge of all BBC warcos from Normandy to Berlin, 'was against my going at all and even protested to London that it was "just too tough"'.[41] But she set off the next morning with her engineer and ran into the worst week of flying-bomb attacks that Antwerp had suffered throughout the war. They were not allowed near the port to make their recording. The bombing lasted for twenty-one hours. 'I must say, I was glad to be recalled to Eindhoven on a cold February day in 1945,' she wrote.

Then Audrey developed a throat infection, which, although not serious, was enough to prevent her from working. When she was offered the chance of home leave, she took it. By returning to Britain at that critical juncture she missed being able to report on the victorious push through Europe of the British, Canadian and American troops. She insisted in her autobiography that she had few regrets about this:

I shall always believe that there is a limit to how useful a woman war correspondent can be – in fact I have sometimes felt that it is a kind of self-indulgence to try to push oneself too much into the thick of things for the sake of being there. Indeed, I have sometimes been embarrassed by the concern shown to me by people who have possibly risked their lives to escort me to point out some hazard I hadn't spotted.[42]

In 1945, Audrey may have shed her Dublin accent but not yet the feminine reticence of her upper-middle-class upbringing. It was not long before she realised that, with the male correspondents returning from war, she would have to develop a more assertive streak if she was to keep and develop the career into which the war had accidentally plunged her.

After the war the BBC compiled a printed catalogue of recorded Second World War reports and despatches from their archives. Among the thousands of recordings there are only two by Audrey and these were UK interviews with people bombed out of their homes in air-raids. Clearly her work abroad did not cut ice with the historians of the BBC. Audrey needed formal accreditation as a war correspondent to broadcast at all first-hand from Europe. There was no other means of entry. But, keen though the BBC was to re-establish links with its audiences in newly liberated Europe, she was, in the Corporation's eyes, doing essentially the same job as she had been doing in Britain and her work was not comparable to the male reporters at the front line. As Frank Gillard explains, 'She simply could not rank, and would not wish to rank, with the BBC correspondents who spent every day within range of the German guns.'[43] This was because Belgium was liberated when Audrey arrived there and the fighting had moved on to Holland. The sort of journalistic stories to be had from Brussels and outlying areas concerned hospitals and welfare, off-duty army activities as well as tales from Belgian citizens finally emerging after years of enemy occupation.

Gillard maintains that:

There was special work for someone like Audrey to do in these rear areas ... but she was not a war correspondent in the sense of witnessing and reporting actual warfare .... Moreover her material from Belgium, by its very nature, was not strong enough for inclusion in 'War Report', the chief daily front-line news programme compiled for listeners in Britain. 'War Report' was essentially a chronicle of hard battle, covering every front. That was what listeners at home wanted. There really was little room in it for the softer behind-the-lines story ... there was no question of discrimination against Audrey. She was cultivating a different field. As a war correspondent she probably never heard a shot fired in anger while she was in Belgium.[44]

Martha Gellhorn had wanted to report from the Western Desert in 1942, but, 'for domestic reasons',[45] had not been able to go. Hemingway hated it when she went off to report the war. Instead, she settled for writing a novel at home in Cuba. But then, in 1943, *Collier's* sent her to Europe. Although Martha tried to persuade Ernest to accompany her, he did not want to go. She arrived, via Bermuda, the Azores and Ireland on 3 November and checked in at the Dorchester. One of her first visitors was Virginia Cowles, who generously shared her wide circle of London literary and political friends with Martha. Within two days she received her official war correspondent ID card and started gathering material for her reports.

Repeatedly she told Ernest that he too should be writing about the war. 'You will feel deprived as a writer if this is all over and you have not had a share in it,' she said.[46] Journalism was crucial for her because, if she did not see the facts, her imagination lacked the stimuli to function. But he remained where he was. In the middle of January 1944, she set off for the Italian front and North Africa, where she saw further depressing examples of wartime suffering and death, including a

Frenchman who had just lost his eye to a shell and a Martiniquan whose torn leg was hanging by the skin and tendons only and a dead girl ambulance driver, lying on a bed in a tent hospital, with her hands crossed on a sad bunch of flowers, and her hair very neat and blonde and her face simply asleep.[47]

At the end of January she went to Algiers, where she was invited for dinner by Diana and Duff Cooper, he being British Representative to the French Committee of Liberation in Algiers. Another of the guests was the actress, Joyce Grenfell, currently touring with ENSA (Entertainments National Service Association), who took more than a passing interest in the khaki-clad US war correspondent 'doing an enjoyable "you-make-me-shy" act with Duff Cooper. I took against her then and there but envied her divine hair.' The conversation then turned to Hemingway:

I hear her say: 'Ernest wears – because of his work' – (what in heaven's name can it be other than writing?) 'a beard and it's snow white. He is a literate who cannot stand the company of other literates' .... I thought her affected, surface bright and worthless. But after dinner, when we were girls together, she let down and the glimpses of reality were more encouraging.

Grenfell admitted that Gellhorn was 'obviously capable',[48] the sort of faint praise *Collier's* would not tolerate. To them, 'she stands out among gal correspondents not only for her writing but for her good looks. Blonde, tall, dashing and with a manner – she comes pretty close to living up to Hollywood's idea of what a big league woman reporter should be.'[49]

In March, Gellhorn returned, as promised, to Cuba and, although their relationship was rapidly deteriorating, immediately set about persuading Hemingway to return to Europe with her. This time, with appallingly bad grace, he agreed, but managed to persuade *Collier's*, the magazine which had employed his wife since 1937, to appoint him as its representative in Europe, thus totally destroying her own chances of covering the final phase of the war from the front line. As if this were not a severe enough blow, she also had to contend with the hostility of the US army's public relations officers, 'a doctrinaire bunch who objected to a woman being a correspondent with combat troops. I felt like a veteran of the Crimean War by then and I had been sent to Europe to do my job, which was not to report the rear areas or the woman's angle.'[50]

Martha returned to England in May and, within a few weeks, the Allies had launched their invasion of Europe. But by the time she heard about the D-Day crossing, it had already begun and Ernest, as one of the correspondents officially accredited for the invasion, was on his way across the Channel in the attack transport, *Dorothea Dix*. He had not covered a war for seven years and was hampered by an injured knee. In the event, he did not make it to Omaha Beach and was transferred to another ship; none the less, his eye-witness account of the Normandy landing was *Collier's* cover story. Martha however, goaded by rivalry to summon up every ounce of ingenuity, managed to do better. Having got herself, somehow, to the embarkation port shortly after midnight, she locked herself into the lavatory of a large, white hospital ship due to cross at dawn. On the night of 7 June, the stowaway emerged and, still unrecognised, worked as a stretcher bearer collecting wounded men from the Normandy beaches. Carrying them from the crowded, dangerous shore to the water ambulances, raising them over the side of the boat and then transporting them down the winding stairs of the converted pleasure ship to the wards was desperately hard work. Each case was more tragic than the next. But in spite of the constant pain, 'all of us knew that our own wounded were good men and that with their amazing help, their selflessness and self-control, we would get through all right'.[51] Her story was buried inside the magazine.

When the ship docked, Martha's papers were scarcely in order and so she was arrested by the PR Office of the American army. As punishment, she was sent to an American nurses' training camp in the English countryside with permission to cross to France again only when the nurses left for a hospital in France. Again Martha was not prepared to let the war pass her by and this time climbed over a fence to a military airfield, spun a yarn about wanting to see her fiancé in Italy and persuaded a pilot to fly her there.

Arriving in Italy, she watched the Eighth Army fight yet another battle for the Gothic line and sent *Collier's* a vivid report about 'the jigsaw puzzle of fighting men, bewildered, terrified civilians, noise, smells, jokes, pain, fear, unfinished conversations and high explosives'.[52] Her motto became, 'If they don't want to accredit you, just do it . . . . Any little lie will do. To me, all the people in the rear who make the rules, they exist to be thwarted.'[53]

Martha's bravery in Italy during the entire winter campaign surpassed anything *Collier's* might reasonably have expected of her. To gather material for a story she took a jeep along a road under constant enemy observation and spasmodic shellfire to the barracks on the outskirts of Cassino, a town where the enemy, in pockets, was still highly active. She then walked to a point where she could watch the brown smoke of German shellbursts in nearby buildings and the white-plumed bursts of American phosphorus shells. When her colleagues warned her off because of minefields, among other dangers, she retorted, 'C'mon, you creeps. If I can do it, you can,' which scarcely endeared her to them.[54]

She went from Italy to Paris and stayed at the Hotel Excelsior because Ernest was at the Ritz with a new girlfriend, fellow reporter Mary Welsh Monks. Before the war was over, he had agreed to a divorce for which, by now, Martha was intensely eager. She wanted, as soon as possible, to change her passport back to 'Gellhorn' – 'I wanted, above all, to be free of him and his name.'[55]

13

The War of the Sexes

'I'm here as a newspaper correspondent, not as a woman.'
MARGUERITE HIGGINS

The reshaping of the post-war world offered male and female reporters a wide variety of exciting and often traumatic stories: the creation of new nations, the bringing to justice of war criminals and the discovery of the magnitude of war crimes committed. But for many women who owed their break to the male absence, there were fresh difficulties as the men returned from the war and usually wanted their jobs back. Now that the principle that women could no longer be barred from covering front-line assignments had finally been won, soft options were neither acceptable nor necessarily available. As the women set out to conquer fear or justify an editor's faith, it was inevitable that accusations would be levelled against some of them for being over-ambitious, aggressive or underhand – or all three. The new war was to be the one between the sexes.

In 1945, when the German armies surrendered to the Allies, Martha Gellhorn was at the concentration camp of Dachau. 'It seemed the most suitable place in Europe to hear the news of victory,' she wrote in her article for *Collier's*. 'The group of women were like mad birds, they plucked at one's clothes and said "Where is my sister?" I remember with shame and horror all I wanted to do was get away from them.'[1] Martha felt so angry she wanted to walk round the place with a flame-thrower and destroy the evil surrounding her. 'We all lack imagination and I hadn't imagined anything like this ... nothing I had ever seen anywhere could touch it,' she commented years later.[2]

'Behind the barbed wire and the electric fence the skeletons sat in the sun and searched themselves for lice. They have no age and no faces ... ', she wrote for *Collier's* in May 1945. In the hospital hall she saw more such skeletons, 'and from them came the smell of disease and death. They watched us but did not move; no expression shows on a face that is only yellowish, stubbly skin, stretched across bone.... What had killed most of these people was hunger; starvation was simply routine,' she wrote. But she also noted the systematic violence, brutality, medical experiments, the gas chamber and the crematorium:

There, suddenly, but never to be believed, were the bodies of the dead. They were everywhere. There were piles of them inside the oven room, but the ss had not had time to burn them. They were piled outside the door and alongside the building. They were all naked, and behind the crematorium the ragged clothing of the dead was neatly stacked: shirts, jackets, trousers, shoes, awaiting sterilisation and further use. The clothing was handled with order, but the bodies were dumped like garbage, rotting in the sun, yellow and nothing but bones, bones grown huge because there was no flesh to cover them, hideous terrible agonising bones and the unendurable smell of death.

Martha Gellhorn left nothing to the imagination in this piece because she saw that the real evil of the world lay in its failure to have imagined such a hideous crime. It was one of her most powerful pieces of war reportage, partly, of course, because of the nature of the subject but also because it suited her style of repeating key words in different phrases: 'If there was to be any purpose in the last war it must be to abolish Dachau and all the other places like Dachau and everything that Dachau stood for, and to abolish it forever.'[3] Meanwhile, she had no intention of ever covering another war.

Marguerite Higgins, a pushy American reporter based in the Paris bureau of the *Herald Tribune*, also recognised the ghastly significance of reporting the liberation and discovery of the concentration camps. She cut across six miles of territory still held by the Germans in order to reach the prison compound in Dachau. Marguerite was not only extremely pretty and a talented linguist, but she also repeatedly risked her life for a good story and aroused more male animosity than any other woman reporter yet. After a degree at the University of California at Berkeley, she took a graduate course in journalism at Columbia and started working as the campus correspondent of the *New York Herald Tribune*. The month she graduated she married Stanley Moore, a Harvard philosophy professor, and was hired by the paper's city staff. The ingenuity that marked her out from the rest showed up on one of her first assignments. Asked to cover a society wedding being held in virtual secrecy in a mid-town hotel, she contrived to borrow a housekeeper's uniform and watched the entire proceedings. But her career was always more important than her marriage and the pair were soon living apart.

'Big blue eyes, a high-pitched little girl's voice and sex appeal were part of her arsenal. As a last resort she used her head,' is the description given her by a recent biographer.[4] This she did in the summer of 1944 when the *Herald Tribune* refused to send her overseas and so, bypassing the normal channels, she appealed to the feminist wife of the publisher, who interceded on her behalf. Marguerite, aged twenty-four, won her posting to Europe.

She and a male colleague were travelling in southern Germany when they heard rumours that the concentration camp at Dachau was about to be liberated. Along the way they learned that Americans were still fighting ss troops nearby and had not yet reached the prison camp itself; although one Nazi general had surrendered, they could not be certain that the guards at the camp itself would do so. But they proceeded to the camp in any case. Marguerite subsequently recounted how she got out of the jeep, walked around and looked up to see a watchtower crammed with ss guards:

They were staring intently at me. Rifles were at the ready, and the machine-gun was trained on me. God knows what prompted me other than the instinctive feeling that there was absolutely no point in running.... I addressed myself to the ss guards. 'Kommen Sie Hier, bitte. Wir Sind Amerikaner. Come here, please, We are Americans.'[5]

Twenty-two Dachau guards then came down from the tower and surrendered to her. It was not long before American forces arrived, but several of the half-starved prisoners in their frenzy threw themselves against the electric fences and, after months of starvation, died of electrocution. In the fracas, an American general tried to eject Marguerite from the compound but she refused. After calm was restored, the same general recommended her for an award for outstanding service under difficult conditions.

Marguerite went on to report the liberation of Buchenwald concentration camp, where she was shocked by the brutality of a group of American soldiers towards captured German prisoners, but recognised the importance of reporting what she had observed in spite of the unpopularity this would cause her with the us military establishment. Shortly afterwards, she drove off alone for Warsaw and, ignoring army regulations, went through the Soviet zone of Germany into Poland to report on the murderous civil war between Polish patriots and communists. In 1945, at the age of twenty-five, she was appointed chief of her newspaper's Berlin bureau; the New York Newspaper Women's Club also presented her with its award for the best foreign correspondence that year.

'What gets me is how these women find things out . . . . I think every goddam officer in Italy spends his time blabbing to women. They run this lousy war on sex appeal,' was the comment made by a male reporter in a play, *Love Goes to Press*, jointly written the following year by Cowles and Gellhorn. 'They act as if the war was some sort of special coming-out party. Want to go to the front, and scream when they get here,' complained the public relations officer, Major Phillip Brooke-Jervis. 'I'm allergic to newspaper women,' commented Joe Rogers, the tough US reporter. 'I married one once. They never stop trying to scoop you and when you scoop them they divorce you.'

It may have been, as Gellhorn later described it, a 'frivolous' play, but it accurately depicted the antagonism felt towards women reporters at the time, especially those as competitive as Higgins. She combined ambition, determination, imagination and, if required, ruthlessness. She could apply flamboyance or rely on conspiratorial scheming, 'and she always knew just when to flash those pretty eyes and turn on that sweet smile,' wrote a colleague on her own paper.[6]

Love Goes to Press was set in Italy, where a group of male correspondents were awaiting the arrival of a glamorous and well-known woman reporter, Jane Mason. The PRO decides that not only is she to have no special privileges and no hot water, but she is to be put up in a damp, cold store-room with no stove in it. Unexpectedly, Jane's colleague, Annabelle Jones, also arrives to report on this phase of the war but next morning both women, who are of course based on Gellhorn and Cowles themselves, are missing. Major Brooke-Jervis is furious as the women are his responsibility. Annabelle tries to get on a flight to Poland but is prevented by bad weather, while Jane steals out by ambulance intending to reach an American garrison during a temporary truce to collect wounded men. She also fails to get her story as she stops on the way to help a wounded officer and an hysterical actress sent by ENSA to entertain the troops.

When Jane returns, Brooke-Jervis asks her, 'Why do these insane things? You're famous enough already.' This prompts an angry tirade from Jane, who accuses him of only caring about credentials and permission and whether everyone has travel orders, which results in a volte-face from the Major. 'Yesterday . . . I had a lot of silly ideas about war correspondents'; now, suddenly, he is madly in love with her and she with him. The next day he tells her, sweetly, that she must give up being a war correspondent and travelling to the front. 'You must see it's changed. You're mine now. If anything happened to you I couldn't stand it.' Instead, he wants her to wait for him at the family home in Yorkshire, with his mother and sister, until the war is over and he can marry her. She agrees, but at the last moment backs out and makes a dash to cover the war in Burma.

The play, first produced at London's Embassy Theatre in June 1946, did moderately well, but folded overnight when it transferred to New York. Its characterisation may have been shallow, its plot unbelievable, but the intense rivalry between men and women reporters accurately foreshadowed the simmering state of affairs which exploded in 1951 during the Korean War.

Marguerite Higgins remained in Germany for five years and was one of many women reporters sent to cover the Nuremberg trials of the Nazi war criminals, which dragged on for ten months of 1946. For most spectators and commentators the strongest emotion was, inevitably, a desire for punishment and revenge, but some of the most thoughtful observations on the trial came from the renowned British writer, Rebecca West. A journalist before she was a novelist, Rebecca had written to Sir Hartley Shawcross in the summer of 1946 requesting permission to attend the closing stages of the trial and had been commissioned by the *Daily Telegraph* to write an account of the final proceedings. While accepting that the courtroom had become 'a citadel of boredom' and that the twenty-one defendants looked like murderers, she also conceded, 'the evidence was more consistently shocking than it was easy for newspaper reports to convey'.[7]

In an article a few days before the verdict was announced, she set out why

the judgment... has to answer a challenge which has been thrown down not only by Germans but by many critics among the Allies. It has to prove that victors can so rise above the ordinary limitations of human nature as to be able to try fairly the foes they vanquished by submitting themselves to the restraints of the law.

If this challenge is met, these Germans will recognise it. Their recognition will seep out into Germany through the lawyers who have acted for the defendants throughout the trial, through the German editors who are compelled to be present at the judgment. The meeting of the challenge will also warn all future warmongers that law can at last pursue them into peace and thus give humanity a new defence against them. Hence the judgment of the

Nuremberg Tribunal may be one of the most important events in the history of civilisation.[8]

Although opposed to capital punishment in general, Rebecca approved of the proceedings at Nuremberg as a way of reinstating the rule of law. She looked forward to establishing good relations with the makers of the future Germany and approved therefore of the directive forbidding photographs of the defendants at the moment when they were sentenced. Pragmatically, this was to prevent heroics, but she also recognised it as 'one of the signs that there is something new at work in this court.... A sense that there are some moments in a human being's life which he should be asked to share with no one except God.'[9]

Justice in the post-war world was a theme attracting many reporters, male and female. In 1947, one of the immigrant ships trying to dock in Israel carried a young American girl with no intention of settling in the country but a determination to discover the truth of a situation which pitched unarmed refugees against the well-trained Royal Navy. Claire Sterling, a twenty-seven-year-old from New York, had been awarded a junior Pulitzer Prize in 1945 worth $1,500 to travel abroad. Although she had hoped to live in Paris, when she was offered a job as bureau chief of a small American news agency in Rome, she decided to accept the challenge.

Claire had originally intended to make a career in politics and, while studying for an economics degree, joined the Young Communist League. At first she was wholly committed, motivated by a fierce desire to see Russia defeat Hitler. But after about two years, once she had seen the internal workings of the Communist Party, she turned passionately against it. Her aim as a student had been to become a trade union organiser and, with that in mind, she took a job in a zipper factory in Brooklyn. But she soon concluded that the Party was cynically manipulating people and felt a deep commitment to broadcast to others what she had learnt. She was expelled from the Party in a blaze of publicity and set about finding herself a new career.

Journalism, she hoped, might give her the chance to use something of the political sense she had acquired. 'I had no idea if I could write, but I saw it as a way of being exposed to the workings of politics and of understanding them better.'[10] She enrolled in a postgraduate journalism course at Columbia University – 'although journalism is something you can't ever be taught' – won the prize and set off for Rome.

She soon taught herself the language, culture and politics of Italy.

Then, in 1947, she travelled to La Spezia to cover a story about a cargo of Jewish refugees trapped in their ship, which was impounded by the British. 'I saw one man who was unmistakeably a leader from the Jewish Haganah. I broke away from the other journalists and asked him if he could ever get me on to one of these ships as I wanted to write a really important story about the whole situation.'[11]

Shortly afterwards it was all arranged. Claire went to Porta Portese, Rome's flea market, and bought the sort of old, sleazy clothes the refugees were wearing, dirtied her face and arrived at the appointed spot just north of Viareggio. The Haganah were at this time regularly sneaking refugees out of the camps, first into rowing-boats and then into the larger ships which, it was hoped, could evade the British and land the Jews in Palestine. The boat she clambered aboard was barely seaworthy, had no radio communication and was carrying 1,100 people. They went for three days and were almost in sight of land when they were stopped by the British fleet. Some of the braver souls jumped overboard and tried to swim ashore, but the British boarded the boat and there was fierce hand-to-hand fighting between the refugees, who used sticks of wood and iron bars wrenched from the hull, and the British, who soon doused the Jews with hoses until it was all over.

For several hours there was no food or drinking water and the situation grew extremely tense before the refugees were all shipped back to Cyprus. The Haganah organiser, concerned for the safety of the young American, devised a ploy so that she could continue with her investigations. He had a plaster cast put on her arm inside which she hid her American passport and some money. She pinned up her long hair into tight curls and inside several of these hid a roll of film. He also assigned her a tough Yugoslav nurse who had been in the Resistance and who insisted that no one was to remove the cast other than a Jewish doctor.

Since Claire spoke neither German nor Yiddish, the Yugoslav nurse was to do all the talking for her. When they arrived in Cyprus, Claire was flung into the prison camp with the rest of the dishevelled group. After a week – since nobody from her office or the American Embassy knew where she was, and realising there was nothing more to be gained – she decided it was time to get out. She told the British guards that she was an American reporter and she wanted to leave. Furious – there was no American Consulate nearby to help her – they put her in solitary confinement. She responded by going on hunger strike until she was released.

Within a few days she was sent to Lebanon, thence to Palestine and then back to Rome, where she wrote a dramatic series of six articles. Not surprisingly, several other newspapers picked up her story and, from then on, she was given serious attention as a journalist.

At least one other woman reporter felt the pull of Israel as an emerging nation demanding justice. Monica Dehn had always intended to be a journalist and, in 1938, she embarked on the two-year journalistic diploma course at King's College, London. Although the onset of war resulted in her completing only a year of this, she soon started work on the *Sussex Gazette and County Herald* before moving to the European service of the BBC as a news typist. From there she was promoted to being a sub in the Balkan Service. At the end of 1943, the whole office moved to Jerusalem to open a new radio station broadcasting to the Balkans – the British Mediterranean Service – and Monica went too. This entailed a six-week sea voyage to Lagos, where she contracted malaria, and a four-day flight across Africa in an aeroplane loaded with ammunition for Egypt. They flew into an electrical storm and landed on a tiny airstrip in Cairo, from where she eventually made her way to Jerusalem. Monica's job, running the English section of the station, included taking news from the wire services and then re-broadcasting it at dictation speed for the underground. She found the experience both moving and exciting and stayed until the station was closed down at the end of the war.

Many of the local staffers, Jews who had fled eastern Europe, were then sent back to their native countries. This, Monica knew, often meant returning them to concentration camps since they were anti-communist and such callous treatment of friends and colleagues shocked her profoundly. After two years her contract with the BBC expired and, although she could have returned to a post with the organisation in London, she had by then fallen in love with Roy Elston, a non-Jewish Englishman who had also been with the BBC and was now writing for *The Times* and the *Jerusalem Post*. Both were passionately interested in the Jewish–Arab struggle and Monica was determined to find a way to stay. She therefore accepted a post as information officer with the Mandatory Government, but was unhappy promoting a policy which she felt was biased against the Jews. 'You were meant to be impartial, which meant pro-Arab,' she recalled. Her reportage was always strongly influenced by a desire to inform and in order to redress the balance, as she saw it, she started to string for the *Observer* in London. 'I don't deny my sympathies,' she says today, 'but I was not writing emotionally. I saw my job as a chance to explain what was going on in the country as I felt the case was not being put very fairly by many of the other correspondents there.'[12]

From 1945 until the War of Independence in 1948 and beyond, Israel provided stories of endless drama and excitement, such as the arrival of the forbidden refugee ships, terrorist attacks and the constant tension between Arabs and Jewish settlers, which sometimes flared into gunfire on the streets. Clare Hollingworth, who married Geoffrey Hoare shortly after the war, had been living in Palestine for several months and was standing just outside the King David Hotel when it exploded on 22 July 1946. 'Over a hundred people – Britons, Arabs and Jews – were killed; we could so easily have been among them,'[13] is, for one who openly eschewed personal danger, the rather curious comment she made later. She was never able to forgive Menachem Begin, leader of the Irgun (the Jewish terrorist organisation), for the attack on the King David Hotel. 'When Begin rose to political power in the late 1970s, I often found myself in his presence. But I never greeted him. I could not shake a hand with so much blood on it.'[14]

In the last month before the end of the Mandate, Monica Dehn found herself facing similar dangers and, cut off from all food supplies, lived off mallow which grew in profusion on a grassy bank near her flat; whenever she tried to go out further afield, she was attacked by snipers. Yet she reacted far more positively to the troubles of the new country.

After 1948, Monica was offered a job in the Israeli Government Information Office, but again did not like the propaganda aspect of the job and was looking for other work when a perfect opportunity arose. Flora Lewis, the Jerusalem correspondent for *Time* magazine, was returning to the United States and asked Monica if she would like to take over her job. 'It just clicked. It was fantastic; you would suggest an idea every week and file as much as you thought would be appropriate.'[15] She wrote about everything that was being developed by the young nation – archaeology, medicine, building and political structures. In 1950, her feature about the Prime Minister, David Ben-Gurion, became a cover story, the first occasion *Time* had used a cover story by a stringer, and in 1956 she reported on the Suez War, sleeping rough in the desert on the way down to Eilat.

By 1957 her marriage had foundered and she decided to leave Israel. She was offered a job by *Time* in London, this time as a staff writer with her name on the masthead, which she considered a major triumph as the magazine boasted only one other woman foreign staffer at the time.

In spite of the dramatic copy which Marguerite Higgins filed from Nuremberg, she found her role as bureau chief in post-war Germany a difficult assignment. There were not enough important, fast-breaking stories such as the Russian blockade of Berlin in 1948, which demanded the hard work on which she thrived. For much of the time she buried herself in her job, often beset with inner panic that she might not be doing it better than anyone else could:

I felt if I made the slightest mistake my new job might be taken away from me.... For a long time when any one of my competitors produced a major scoop, I took it as a personal disaster. That sort of reaction makes for a chaotic emotional life, but it does generate lots of nervous energy. And this motivation – partly fear – kept me doggedly and singlemindedly occupied with my job.[16]

This extreme competitiveness made her unpopular both with colleagues on her own paper and rivals alike. It was one of the factors which led to her posting to Tokyo in 1950 amid a welter of accusations that she slept with men to get her reports, that she pursued fellow correspondents and then stole their stories, or that she hyped her own writing beyond its importance. However, Keyes Beech, a correspondent who worked with her and knew her well, considered that she was the victim of much unfair and untrue gossip: 'Maggie didn't need to use her sex to do a good job as a war correspondent. She had brains, ability, courage and stamina.'[17]

In the event, Marguerite's intended banishment to Tokyo was fortuitous. Just as Agnes Smedley had warned that a major world conflagration would soon erupt here, so the post-war division of Korea into a pro-Russian, communist North and pro-US, anti-communist South had been fraught from the start. On 25 June 1950, fighting began as North Korean troops crossed the border and started on their drive for Seoul. Within forty-eight hours, Marguerite was on an aeroplane to Korea with three other newspaper correspondents and became one of only four eye-witnesses to see communist troops enter the South Korean capital and to report America's entry into the conflict.

But there was trouble from the start as one of the four, Frank Gibney of *Time*, tried to dissuade Marguerite from going, insisting that Korea was no place for a woman. 'For me,' she wrote, 'getting to

Korea was more than just a story. It was a personal crusade. I felt that
my position as a correspondent was at stake. Here I represented one
of the world's most noted newspapers as its correspondent in the area.
I could not let the fact that I was a woman jeopardise my newspaper's
coverage of the war.'[18]

Nor did she. The first week of the war was almost the last and
provided some of the most dramatic and shocking copy for American
readers. Within days, disciplined communist troops nearly wiped out
the South Korean forces, many of whom were trying to flee, terrified,
and often acting independently from their American advisers. Marguerite, although horrified by the panic and confusion as they and the
raw American recruits fled south, was more convinced than ever of
the need not to censor her reports:

In the first three weeks of war I was filled with pity at the sense of betrayal –
and astonishment – displayed by our young soldiers who had been plucked
so suddenly out of the soft occupation life in Japan and plunged into battle.
Most had had only routine basic training and were far from combat ready.
Only a small percentage had ever heard artillery fire before.[19]

She was passionately concerned that the war in Korea signalled the
communist determination to resort to force of arms wherever it
believed it faced a soft target. She therefore wanted her reports to
appear as shocking as possible so that American public opinion was
not spared 'the hard bruising truth' and might be better prepared
another time.

But although Marguerite was there first and filed the original scoop
at the outbreak of war, and although she behaved impeccably and
courageously under fire in the confused exit from Seoul when two of
her male colleagues were injured, the *Herald Tribune* quickly rushed
in its senior correspondent, Homer Bigart. Bigart made it plain that
he wanted Marguerite out of the way and told her flatly that she would
be fired if she did not return to Tokyo and stay there. The dispute was
complicated by an argument over a story about American bombing
of North Korea which she had apparently filed ahead of a schedule,
thereby breaking an agreement and resulting in call-backs for other
reporters. Marguerite insisted that this was a misunderstanding as she
had never been party to any such agreement. She pleaded with head
office that there was more than enough news for two reporters to
share.

While waiting for an answer from her editor, she got on with her
job, helped by moral support from Keyes Beech as well as by the use

of his jeep, which meant that she often got closer to the front than Bigart. For many months it was the only available vehicle, while the rest of the press hitch-hiked, and she became adept at typing with her machine resting on the jeep's bonnet. But her success was not achieved without enormous anguish. Marguerite admitted suffering extreme fear on occasions that felt like 'a trapped ball of breath... pressing against her heart'. But she forced herself to overcome it, as she knew she must, to disprove the repeated comment that the front was no place for a woman. At the same time, the constant arguing with her colleagues, coupled with physical exhaustion, left her unusually vulnerable and emotional. She accepted that, as the only woman, she was inevitably the target for gossip and vicious rumours and got on with her job, driving herself to her limit. But after an exhausting three weeks in Korea, when she slept on the ground, or on a table top, woke in the middle of the night to file a story, went for days without washing and shared, uncomplainingly, the hardships of the men, she was dealt a crushing blow. In the middle of the battle of Taejon, she was ordered to leave the Korean theatre of war immediately, on the express orders of General Walton H. Walker, because 'there are no facilities for ladies at the front', a euphemism that particularly irked Marguerite since 'nobody in Korea, including the Koreans, worried much about powder rooms.... There is no shortage of bushes in Korea.'[20]

Still uncertain as to her orders from her own office, she now had to fight the military hierarchy as well. In spite of vehement protestations, Marguerite was escorted by armed guard to an aeroplane and sent back to Tokyo. But no sooner had she arrived there than she learned that General MacArthur had rescinded the expulsion order, proclaiming: 'Marguerite Higgins held in highest professional esteem by everyone.'[21] She returned to Korea.

In mid-July, she met General Walker for the first time. He told her, frankly, that he was still opposed to women at the front but that from now on she could be assured of absolutely equal treatment. 'If something had happened to you, an American woman,' the General explained, 'I would have gotten a terrible press. The American public might never have forgiven me. So please be careful and don't get yourself killed or captured.'[22]

In September, she was reporting one of the most dangerous phases of the war, the Inchon landing, a naval assault intended to bisect North Korean forces. Marguerite's request to board an assault transport 'was greeted with about the same degree of horror as might have met a leper's request to share a bunk with the admiral'.[23] Officially the problem was, as ever, a question of lack of facilities on board ship, although Marguerite pointed out that such facilities as there were would be better than the foxholes she had been occupying for the past weeks. She was told she would be relegated to a hospital ship and might not be allowed off. However, owing to an administrative blunder when she came to pick up her boarding pass, she was handed the wrong sheet. It allowed her to board any ship. She did not point out the error but rather made a dash to the staging area and spent four days on the *Henrico* in relative comfort and luxury as she was allotted an emergency cabin. This was much more pleasant than sleeping on the ground or in various flea-bitten huts and gave the lie to the alleged lack of facilities.

Marguerite hit the beach in the fifth wave of assault troops:

The first marines were now clambering out of the bow of the boat. The photographer announced that he had had more than enough and was going back to the transport with the boat. For a second I was tempted to go with him. Then a new burst of fire made me decide to get out of the boat fast. I got a footing on the steel ledge on the side of the boat, pushed myself over and landed in about three feet of water in the dip of the sea wall.[24]

Her manoeuvre was especially difficult because she was carrying her typewriter with her. All around her she could hear grenades and tracer bullets whirring and she had to wade through powerful breakers before she reached a mound on the beach for shelter. In the confusion, there was a horrifying moment as some American forces started shelling their own men. After a frantic day she returned in the evening to the fleet flagship to file her story; there on board was the original officer who had permitted her only to travel across on a hospital ship. He was furious about the mistaken papers and, grudgingly allowing her to sleep on a stretcher in the dispensary for one night, decreed that from then on women would be allowed aboard only between 9 a.m. and 9 p.m. In other words, Marguerite had twelve daylight hours to file her work; if a story broke after that, she would have to wait and would have to sleep on the front or on the docks with the troops and live off cold rations. However, the male correspondents could look forward to a warm shower and a hot meal of real scrambled eggs at the end of the day.

Despite such obstacles, Marguerite Higgins reported the Korean War for a total of eight months; both she and Bigart, who regularly fought each other for front-page billing, won Pulitzer Prizes for their efforts. She returned to the United States, not merely as one of the best-known reporters of the war, but after a tough Marine colonel revealed in a letter to her newspaper how she had administered blood plasma to the wounded while exposed to fire during a communist attack, 'completely disregarding her own personal safety',[25] she became a national heroine also.

She was fêted with many other honours and awards, was invited on several lecture tours across the United States and wrote a bestselling book, *War in Korea – the Report of a Woman Combat Correspondent*. In 1952, she married again, Lieutenant General William E. Hall, former director of US Intelligence in Berlin, in spite of the apocryphal remark often attributed to her that she would not marry 'until she found a man who was as exciting as war'. In 1955, she opened the *Tribune*'s Moscow bureau and was its chief for that year; the following year she was appointed the *Tribune*'s diplomatic correspondent in Washington. A year later, in Washington, her first child was born, a girl who died after five days. She had two more children: in 1958, a son, Lawrence, and in 1959, a daughter, Linda.

Higgins was a courageous competitor who always took as many risks as the bravest men. She even contravened the Geneva Convention – as did most correspondents in Korea – by carrying a gun on occasions. 'The enemy had no qualms about shooting unarmed civilians,' she explained. 'And the fighting line was so fluid that no place near the front lines was safe from sudden attack.'[26]

She broke new ground for women in journalism by insisting on absolutely equal treatment with men – which she did not always get – and giving the public in return stories that were every bit as revealing, dramatic and analytical as those of her male colleagues. Her assertiveness may have lost her friends among the US press corps but was vital for the battle she was fighting for herself. Like many women reporters she was consumed by pressure to work slavishly hard and she suffered genuine pangs of fear lest her writing be inferior to that of her competitors. But she was popular with the troops and with one or two of the correspondents. After Higgins, there was no longer any story an editor could deny a woman merely on grounds of precedent or danger.

14

Unfair Competition?

'She was seriously into journalism: it was what she lived for.'
ANGUS MCGILL ON ANNE SHARPLEY

Three years as a wartime reporter for the BBC proved to Audrey Russell that she no longer hankered after a career on the stage and so her appointment in 1946 to the newly formed BBC Home Service was pleasing. She was the first and, for a while, the only woman reporter on the staff. But this meant, once again, that she was sent out on minor news stories while the men, as she observed, slowly returning from the war, indulged in 'a good deal of jockeying for position in the department'.[1]

She believed that her strength in broadcasting was in making on-the-spot, unscripted reports of news unfolding; in other words, the new profession of commentating. However, she encountered little encouragement from her colleagues for this. 'Even Richard Dimbleby was prejudiced,' Audrey believed. He told her: 'Do give up this idea. There will never be a successful woman commentator. Why? They haven't got the stamina.'[2] Deciding that she knew better, she started looking for a job in the Outside Broadcast Department.

In the drabness that was post-war, utility England, one story glittered above others: the new, young royal family. In 1947, when Princess Elizabeth married Prince Philip, Audrey was lent from the News Division to report on The Royal Dress. She did not stint on her preparatory homework, mugging up myriad background details to ensure that she would be prepared with facts for every eventuality; and her informative remarks struck just the right tone. Her next big royal occasion was the inauguration of Queen Juliana of The Netherlands in September 1948.

By the late 1940s, Audrey had become a well-known radio personality and was soon describing much more than the frocks. She reported on the last day of the trial of William Joyce (Lord Haw Haw) and then, in 1951, on the Festival of Britain. 'She had style, poise, the ability to think quickly on her feet, an attractive voice, a nice turn of phrase and a most agreeable personality,' explained Frank Gillard. 'Her great secret was that she was willing and able to work hard over every assignment. She was meticulous in briefing herself thoroughly, in advance, over every detail of the event she was covering, so that she could speak with total confidence and never be caught out in emergencies and crises.'[3]

January 1952 marked Audrey's successful transition from reporter to commentator as she went on her first royal tour together with Gillard and Wynford Vaughan Thomas, both experienced broadcasters. It was a highly charged journey as, at the last minute, King George VI had become too ill to travel and Princess Elizabeth and Prince Philip had taken his place. Audrey went first to Ceylon and, after the longest flight she had yet undertaken, went out immediately to investigate Colombo and the royal apartments at the Governor-General's residence. Within hours she learned that the King had died and rushed to the main cable office to speak to London. 'I soon learned that my presence was a grave solecism. I learned that Women, especially Europeans, do not send their own cables. It is just not done.'[4]

But the situation was saved by London cabling her, telling her to return immediately to broadcast at the funeral. She found all of London in a state of mourning and was grateful to her mother who met her at the airport bearing a black dress. She then started her research for the coronation as she was commissioned to provide a weekly 'Coronation Report' for transmission on several American networks. The appetite for royal stories appeared insatiable and Audrey dreamed up one new angle after another in the weeks before the occasion; once she discussed the oil to be used for the anointing of the new Queen, another time the remodelling of the Imperial State Crown. She delved into dozens of books, documents and records to make sure that she knew every possible historical detail about coronation ceremonies. What she said about the occasion would be heard, live, by millions of people throughout the world for the first time. But it was merely a foretaste of the many magnificent royal tours and state occasions at which the voice of Audrey Russell became as familiar as it was informative.

Audrey was among the BBC team sent to cover the epic journey of the new Queen and Duke of Edinburgh when they set off round the

world to visit ten countries in the Commonwealth and two foreign
states in November 1953. But she was required to report more than
ceremonial when, in the small hours of Christmas morning in New
Zealand, she had to describe the country's worst ever rail crash. More
than a hundred and fifty people were killed in the accident caused by
torrential rain when the side of a deep crater lake broke at the top of
an extinct volcano, sending a torrent of ash-grey water gushing down
the mountain-side and sweeping away the bridge in its path.

The most romantic royal story of the 1950s was the marriage of
Prince Rainier of Monaco to the beautiful American film star, Grace
Kelly. This story, with all its fairy-tale qualities of money, glamour,
true love and high society, first captured the interest of the world's
press in 1954, although the marriage itself did not take place until 19
April 1956. Audrey was delighted to be chosen along with Richard
Dimbleby to cover the wedding, but soon found herself at loggerheads
with her bigger and better-known colleague. Dimbleby was, Audrey
admits, the most accomplished and elegant broadcaster in the BBC.
However, unlike Audrey, 'he never undertook the very long royal
tours. A royal state visit of three or four days was about his limit,'
she wrote of him later.[5] By the time the Rainier wedding had been
announced, he had achieved a certain prominence in the BBC which
allowed him to pick and choose his own assignments.

Audrey was not surprised to find Dimbleby at the Rainier marriage
as 'it suited his style and he liked going to Monte Carlo's casino
anyway'.[6] Five days before the wedding, she and Dimbleby flew out
to start their research; it was the first time the pair had worked abroad
together.

The experience was a revealing one for Audrey. Neither was actually
to see the bride except on television as they were given seats for the
service not in the cathedral itself, which was full of Hollywood stars,
but in an aquarium near the cathedral, working from a TV monitor.
The evening before the wedding Audrey had been given instructions
and was scheduled in the *Radio Times* to describe a programme of
folk music sung by local schoolchildren wearing peasant dress to
entertain the wedding couple. She had attended a rehearsal in the
afternoon, but when she arrived for the evening performance, she
found the theatre box allocated to her already occupied by Dimbleby.
'I think it will be much better for me to do this,' he told her. 'Yes, I'm
sure I'd better do it.'

'In every sense there was nothing more for me to say. I was literally
speechless and astonished at his unbounded confidence.'[7]

However, as Audrey tells the story in her autobiography, she got the last laugh, since Prince Rainier and his bride were nearly half an hour late arriving at the theatre. 'Soon I was aware of panic signals in my direction for help to fill in the gaps. This was just a little too much. He ploughed on, but as a Dimbleby broadcast it was as near as he'd get to a fiasco.'[8] The following day, with great charm, he took her out for dinner and apologised. But Audrey, fast learning the art of office politics, made sure that London understood exactly why she had not made the report. The response from the BBC hierarchy left Audrey in no doubt of her own position: 'Oh Audrey, you must realise that Dimbleby generally knows best.'

Also at the wedding, engaging in similarly fierce rivalry, were two reporters from the *Evening Standard*. Lord Beaverbrook had plunged his ace reporter, Anne Sharpley, deep into the territory of his newspaper's resident correspondent, Sam White. Beaverbrook had invited both for dinner at his nearby villa on Cap d'Ail and then watched with enjoyment as they did battle to produce the most sparkling copy. Anne's story made it to the front page, but the episode created a lifelong feud between Sharpley and White, which was never resolved.

Her relationship with Beaverbrook, however, flourished. In spite of the fifty-year age gap, some believed that Anne became his mistress. But she was never flirtatious in his company and he clearly relished her intelligent, sensible conversation, even to the point of welcoming her arguments on any topic including the Empire. ' "What Empire?" I would say. "You're only talking about a couple of islands in the middle of the Mediterranean and Hong Kong." He liked that. In fact he used to introduce me to his awful, boring Canadian Prime Ministers... by saying "This is Anne Sharpley, who doesn't believe in the Empire." '[9] On her side, Anne was genuinely fond of the old man, who remained for her always the principal reader.

'Miss Sharpley is not pretty,' stated a profile in the *World's Press News*. 'Rather, I would say, engaging, refreshing, wholesome and thoroughly nice. Some might be tempted to describe her as "radiant and her laugh as girlish. She is and wants to remain a country girl." '[10] Country girl or not, Anne Sharpley first came to London from Macclesfield, Cheshire, in 1945 aged sixteen, as a result of a competition organised by *Vogue*. She was tall and dark with a prominent nose and, if not pretty, definitely handsome. So many people commented on her resemblance to Princess Margaret that she took to saying she must have come out of the same box as the Princess. Instead of working for *Vogue*, however, her first job was as an assistant on the women's page of the *Recorder*, where she later ran her own column until Christmas Eve 1947, when she resigned, in order to explore the world.

Daughter of a regimental sergeant-major, Anne had been to four schools, three of them convents, and was expelled from one of them. Her mother had died when she was three and although an aunt stepped into the breach, with her father frequently serving abroad, Anne acquired young the habit of independence. She toughened herself against the outside world and was never seen to cry. She always enjoyed writing, but, when forced to leave school below the official leaving age, was still undecided about what to do with the rest of her life and therefore enrolled at York College of Art. Then she won the competition which brought her to London, where she stayed for two years, followed by a further two spent trekking around Britain and Europe taking on whatever jobs the moment required.

At twenty, the worldly wise Anne realised that her best prospects lay in journalism. She returned home and worked on the *Cheshire Observer* and then on the *Manchester Evening News* as Woman's Page feature writer. She stayed there a year and a day, 'which I have always thought rather poetic',[11] and then moved back to London to work first as a film publicist and subsequently as a women's feature writer for *Weekend Mail* and then *Woman's Own*. She threw in both positions after only a few months, loathing the experience of writing only for and about women.

By the time she was twenty-six, there was little Anne had not turned her hand to. But her rapid turnover of jobs ended when she joined the *Evening Standard*, finally, in July 1954. Percy Elland, the editor, had already offered her a post some months before, but, fearing to tie herself down, she had declined and set off once again on an expedition around the world. This time she only made it as far as Paris when she decided to return, flatless and friendless, to London and asked if the job were still available. 'To my surprise they said yes.'[12] She was to stay there as a full-time reporter for the next twenty years and worked for no other employer.

No education could have been better devised for a journalist than this demanding schedule of travel and experience. From the first, she was a general feature writer with the widest frame of reference, always ready to try something new; her beat covered everything from crime reporting, accounts of London life and international explosions to state occasions and royal tours. The latter was 'a star job and much prized', commented Charles Wintour, deputy editor on the paper when she joined, and editor himself from April 1959. 'Also royal tours sold papers and Anne was a loyal supporter of the paper so she never queried it. Never.'[13]

Soon, Anne's picture and byline boosted sales as she rose dramatically to become its number one reporter. For a decade she dominated the London newspaper scene and hundreds of billboards throughout the capital advertising that day's paper regularly carried pictures of Anne Sharpley writing about the main news story of the day, or – just as likely – an off-beat feature. 'She had a marvellous gift of descriptive reporting and seeing a little beyond what was on the surface,' Wintour explained. 'She had an outstanding ability to describe what she saw at amazing speed with some sort of resonance and could dictate from her notes, without pausing, a perfectly formed story... she had a full mind and she used it and an immense use of colourful phrases.'[14]

Anne explained how she approached a foreign assignment in a piece she wrote before leaving for Nigeria to cover the royal tour of January 1956: 'One rushes to the nearest map and takes a long deep look. The half-dozen things one knows about Nigeria teem through one's mind. "White man's grave", "Mungo Park", "Clapperton in Kano", "The district officer who would call it Nah-geria".'[15] She talked to friends and colleagues about Lagos, she telephoned the Commissioner for Nigeria to discuss the climate, she bought clothes and a special suitcase. But, most important of all, she undertook 'a compulsive effort of "reading up" Nigeria [which has] made me almost wild to get there and see for myself'.

It was this compulsive effort of reading which was always to make Anne's copy superior. As soon as she landed anywhere she knew exactly what trees and shrubs she would find, what they looked like and whether or not they would be in bloom. Having done her research in England, she carried a typed list with her. She also took the trouble to learn the names of the people she was likely to meet and to understand their background. Not surprisingly, what she wrote sounded authentic without ever being heavy-handed; the perfect descriptive phrase would be dropped lightly into the story. Such attention to detail was outstanding.

In an article which brilliantly evoked the atmosphere of the young British monarch in Nigeria, meeting figures of almost overpowering magnificence, Anne wrote of the Queen sitting under 'a Tamarind tree as big as anything in Windsor Forest' while the Northern Chiefs were striding proudly about in wafts of thick, sweet perfume. She was aware of the penetrating rhythm of the drums, the jangle of the Durbar klaxon calls, the delicate beauty of the gold filigree jewellery, the elegant walk of slender, white egret birds and the tired fulani cattle, 'humped, wrinkled and proud like dowagers'.[16] Using her eyes, ears and nose, no detail went unnoticed.

Later that year, when Nasser seized control of the Suez Canal, Anne was sent to Cairo for a month to report on the Suez crisis. She soon found herself arrested when she tried to interview one of Nasser's enemies, Major-General Mohammed Neguib, kept under house arrest for the previous two years. 'It was a quixotic idea but so many Egyptians had urged me to try to see him, for Neguib is a man who still commands a sort of affectionate love that must make strong armed Nasser very angry,' she wrote in her article.[17] She had driven out to his residence just after 6 a.m. hoping to miss the worst of the day's heat, but after half an hour outside the house, a jeep drew up and took her to a barracks in Cairo. There she was held alone for two hours, awaiting questioning, before being taken to be interrogated by 'a fat young intelligence officer who was having his boots cleaned'.[18] She was accused of being a tool of the British Embassy, allegedly plotting to free Neguib, but when she asked if she was under arrest her interrogators insisted, 'No.' However, as she was forcibly prevented from leaving the room she considered her point proven. Eventually, when they could get nothing out of her, she was allowed back to her hotel, only to be expelled from the country two weeks later.

From the start Anne did not like the Egyptians, whom she considered 'bargain-minded, inefficient and unstable'.[19] Even less did she like their leader and she was not afraid to make her views known. She delighted in teasing her 'minder', who continued to maintain that he was there to help organise interviews but arranged none for her. When he told her lies, she picked him up on them immediately; other times she would deliberately call out 'good morning' so that he could follow her.

As soon as she arrived in the country, she developed her own contacts in a determined bid to ferret out any story the regime did not want made known. Through these contacts she exposed a Nazi propagandist whom Nasser kept hidden in his ten-storey Ministry of Information. Anne had been given the name but not the whereabouts of the Nazi professor, but, 'by a stroke of luck', she discovered a renegade whose loyalty to the regime was wavering. He slipped information to her revealing the floor of the Ministry of Information on which the man could be found. Totally fearless, she brushed past guards in the corridors and pushed her way in. When the incumbent denied that he was Professor Van Leers, formerly on Goebbels's staff, Anne bluffed by pretending that she recognised him from a photograph. He ended by begging her not to publish anything about him, insisting that he was merely a translator. During her short trip, Anne met opponents of the Government who told her of the extreme brutality in Cairo's military prisons and she saw sworn testimony about Egyptian concentration camps in the Western Desert. She knew that she was lucky merely to have been thrown out and used all the information she had gathered in her article once she was home. She described Nasser as a military despot presiding over misery, filth and poverty and running a ruthless regime.

Although Egyptian officials were well known to be less than sympathetic to female reporters, Anne Sharpley was not alone in Cairo. Claire Sterling, now based in Rome and writing for the American fortnightly, *The Reporter*, had agonised about whether to agree to cover the Suez War. Her editor had suggested hesitantly that she might go but felt he could not ask her now that she was a mother of young babies. 'I remember that my husband and I had the most serious conversation of our married lives at this time as to exactly how far a mother of young children is prepared to go when she's trying to be a political reporter,' Claire recalls. 'At first no one knew exactly how dangerous the situation would be, nor how accurate the Egyptian bombs.' None the less, she decided she had to go – 'I couldn't be a part-time foreign correspondent and housewife at the same time' [20] – and went first to report from Tel Aviv. When she then tried to enter Cairo, with her passport stamped 'not valid for Cairo', she knew that she was in for trouble. She was stopped at the airport, told that she was on an Egyptian blacklist because of her reports from Israel and kept overnight on a straight-backed chair in an otherwise empty room. The following day she was told that she could stay after all and remained for just over a week researching her piece, which she then wrote once back in Rome.

Anne Sharpley's methods of securing a story in Cairo were typical of the way she continued to operate over the next decade in the environment of vanishing colonies and sudden, explosive tension. She never approved of the male clubbiness of the other foreign correspondents, who would meet in the hotel bar at 11 a.m., share their titbits and then, displaying much professional co-operation and brotherhood, together lope off to the daily press conferences. Anne would have none of this. Consequently, she was regarded warily by her rivals as someone not altogether to be trusted. 'My God! Where's that Sharpley?' they would say, much to her own, wry amusement. She enjoyed getting to places fast and first and, under the banner 'all's fair in love and war', was not above employing such ruses as pulling out the only existing telephone wires after dictating her own story or flaunting her sex appeal which was considerable. Male correspondents were often heard to mutter that Anne was unfair competition 'because she'd sleep with the police chief to get a story', an attitude which possibly revealed less Anne's own sexual mores than the mythology that had grown up around her. Male reporters, recognising how good she was, argued that she must be using unfair tactics. Anne, who was quite open about sex being a weapon in her armoury, took the view that men had other advantages and everyone used whatever they could in the chase for news.

Anne's competitive instincts, fuelled by a determination to beat men at their own game, were not only unleashed for riots and wars, but royal tours as well. As an evening paper reporter, she had the extra challenge of catching several editions running throughout the day and the problem of not always being able to get to a cable office while the paper was still printing in London. One manœuvre she had first stumbled on to by accident soon became a Sharpley regular: she would jump into a police car, ignoring the bus facility for the press. 'Introducing myself with all the charm I could muster and showing my passes I discovered that, as the police were doing the same job, in effect, as ourselves, they did not at all mind giving you a lift.' In India, the police car was usually a jeep, which made jumping on easier, and it usually followed directly behind the royal cavalcade, whereas the wretched press bus would be bringing up the rear. Anne would deliberately leap on while it was in motion – secure in the knowledge that to stop and throw her off would hold up the smooth flow of the procession – clinging to her typewriter because she knew that there was no point in arriving at a cable office without one; handwriting took much too long to reach an evening paper. 'Time after time it worked,' Anne wrote years later. 'Other press people were understandably enraged and . . . conceived a plan which they announced to me they were going to put into effect . . . . When I jumped on to a police jeep, they were *all* going to jump on to the same jeep, they told me.'[21] It was time to devise another trick.

When on foot, the feisty Miss Sharpley had other ruses for getting herself imperceptibly into the group immediately next to the monarch. This, she considered, was the principal skill of the royal reporter. 'There is no other way one can get the quotes and small points of observation necessary to a good story and where the goodwill of the Royal Household often comes in.'[22] Occasionally she overdid the pushiness and Prince Philip's personal detective would ask her, wearily: 'Are you acting Lady-in-Waiting again, Anne?' He apparently developed an unusual technique for dealing with her: tickling. 'As I am absurdly ticklish it would clear me off any royal scene in seconds.'[23]

After a few years at the *Standard* Anne learned always to keep a packed suitcase at the ready – a habit she continued to the end – containing the barest essentials: Dreft washing powder, hangers, drip-dry underwear and a small gadget for making tea. The newspaper recognised that in Anne they had found the archetypal new woman, the crack female reporter of the age, and they catapulted her into dangerous situations (almost) relentlessly. Not that she ever complained or wished it otherwise. She lived for her work, was extremely athletic with apparently boundless energy, stamina and enthusiasm, and was as tough physically as she was emotionally. Once, however, Beaverbrook had her dramatically hauled off a plane waiting to depart from London airport with the instruction: 'We can't send Annie to the Congo. She'll be raped.'[24] Before other missions he arranged for flowers to be sent to the airport instead.

The year after Suez, Anne undertook a number of trips, including one to the Soviet Union, where she found herself attacked in the *Moscow Literary Gazette* because of a 'slanderous series' she had written about Soviet life. But the big story was Cyprus, where a campaign for union with Greece, begun in earnest at the end of 1954, had reached a violent climax three years later. EOKA, the Greek Cypriot terrorist organisation, promised to suspend its activities only if Archbishop Makarios were freed from detention on the Seychelles. Anne had spent some time on the Mediterranean island in 1956 establishing a valuable rapport with, among others, one of the EOKA propagandists she called Andy.

Aware that in such situations no one could be totally trusted, and that many of her colleagues considered Andy a dangerous phoney, Anne none the less found him useful because of her evening paper deadlines. How could she know early enough in the morning where the night's bombings, shootings or riots were likely to be? In a piece for the *Evening Standard* on 5 September 1957, Anne encapsulated the confused situation of the troubled island by focusing on Andy, his pride in being Greek and his defiant will to win over the island for his people. Andy was gunned down by terrorists outside his own door on the morning he had promised Anne: 'There's going to be some real shooting from now on.'[25] Even after his death no one was certain about his beliefs.

But I was sure about Andy. I had seen his face, glazed with tears as he ran down the street eight months earlier. It was the rage of a man who had failed to rekindle the towering heroism of Greek mythology in the gentle, rather timid people of Cyprus. Andy wasn't a phoney, he was just a romantic.[26]

This piece had all the hallmarks of Anne's reporting at its best. It was literary and stylish, yet direct and informative; it was punchy and it was moving. Above all, it left her readers feeling that they understood, through Andy, a little about the problems of Cyprus. Whatever the issues she was sent to cover, she always saw 'the story'.

Headline-grabbing though she was when filing from abroad, several of Anne's in-depth reports on life in Britain were winning her a different sort of audience. She always worked extremely hard in the London office and was prepared to tackle any subject on offer, sometimes volunteering for two or three assignments per day. Her colleague Tom Pocock remembers how Anne would invariably be the first to arrive and the last to leave. But once he came to the office early and Anne was not there. 'I've been out on a story,' she announced when she turned up an hour later. She had been standing outside Wandsworth Gaol on execution day, interviewing the waiting relatives and ghouls. A natural mixer, Anne understood the human dilemma and had an uncommon knack of talking with, and listening to, people from all walks of life. In 1959, she wrote a series about the current tension in Notting Hill and asked, 'What does it really feel to lead your daily life there?' Carting her cheap fibre suitcase around, she knocked on landladies' doors trying to find a room. But the best offer she elicited came from an elegant youth driving a brilliant pink Vauxhall Cresta with a stuffed leopard at the back window to match the leopardskin seat covers. He suggested that she spend the night in his room, which she politely declined.

One of her most notable series of articles appeared in 1961. Not content merely to interview local West Indian immigrants about their London experiences, she went to Jamaica and joined one of the last migrant boats crammed with hundreds of bewildered West Indians hurrying to beat the new immigration rules. Having done her homework assiduously, as ever, Anne understood the many differences between the islanders, so often lumped together under the catch-all label, 'Jamaican'. 'The little islands, St Kitts, Montserrat, Antigua – them's so small that if you started running on them and develop speed you'd land up in the sea.' It was a distinction often ignored but which prompted the writer V. S. Naipaul, in his book *The Middle Passage*, to quote from Sharpley's writing:

'They're going to a dream in London, they don't know what they're going to but when they ask them in London where them comes from, these yam and breadfruit little niggers, them's got to say Jamaica, 'cos nobody heard of dem islands.'[27]

When she boarded with her ticket, the crew was shocked to find that she was white and immediately tried to move her to a better cabin: one with a porthole! She refused to budge and kept her bunk in a small cabin below the water-line with a family of Jamaican girls. One of them, a beautiful child called Ivorine, became a close friend and Anne continued to help her in England, sometimes with money, for the rest of her life. For the duration of the voyage, however, Anne acted as ship's conscience, demanding from the purser that he turn the heat up as the passengers were used to a tropical climate and had no warm clothes.

After they endured five days of cold, sea-sickness and beggary, the ship finally docked and Anne watched in trepidation, sick with the knowledge of the prejudice that lay ahead, as the West Indians disembarked:

The six hundred migrants who, in the last few days, had contrived an uneasy unity and to whom the ship had given an illusion of shelter and at least the assurance of the next meal, now faced dispersal. Some with empty pockets. Sometimes with nothing more than an address and the barest geographical knowledge of how to reach it.[28]

Anne delivered Ivorine personally to Aunt Tuts in Tottenham, but she, a hairdresser, was at work. Thinking the neighbours might be able to help, she knocked on the door to be told: 'They're niggers next door, I don't have anything to do with them. Slam. For Ivorine, and six hundred like her, the new and terrible adventure had really begun.'[29]

Another triumph was Anne's series on London's homosexual community, written as part of her newspaper's campaign to change the law and which, in 1964, was not standard newspaper fare. 'They were absolutely sensational, intelligent and sensitive,' according to her colleague, Angus McGill. 'So sensational that one of the feature subs refused to sub it.'[30] Charles Wintour's original request had been for three articles on male homosexuality, but after Anne had spent six weeks at all the gay pubs and other meeting places and talked to as many homosexuals from different backgrounds as possible, she voluntarily added articles on lesbianism as well. This was at the beginning of Anne's overtly feminist phase and she felt it was her right to insist. 'She felt the series was incomplete without that,' Wintour recalls. It was one of the few times the two clashed as he refused to publish the additional articles on the grounds that the climate was not right and they would have created too much of a sensation at that time.

In her discussions of who, in fact, are the gay people – 'a light, unwounding, inconspicuous word,' she wrote in 1964; 'gay is what they prefer to call themselves'[31] – Anne was aware how careful she had to be since her sources risked anything up to life imprisonment if caught by the police. But when she went with a male homosexual to one of the small, wooded areas in North London which was a notorious meeting ground, and he explained to her the thrill of not knowing whether he was going to meet the love of his life, a policeman or a murderer, she concluded that the injustice of imprisonment was never going to solve the problem.

Since her ambition was to do what she did, not only well but the best, she was gratified, if rather miffed, by her award in 1963 as Woman Journalist of the Year, ' . . . rather less than being Journalist of the Year', as she told Roy Plomley on *Desert Island Discs* in 1967. 'As if the judges think it's a wonder one can do it at all, like a dog.' In 1964, she was rewarded with the title Descriptive Writer of the Year. She continued into the 1960s with her unusual mix of hard news stories and human interest features, as well as undertaking more royal tours to Canada in 1964, Germany in 1965 and India in 1966. Anne had respect for the royal family, but was never sycophantic in her reporting of their activities. Eventually, however, 'she became somewhat cynical about the whole routine,' Wintour explained, 'and I received a polite request from the Palace Press Office to field another reporter who might have been less interested in some of the minutiae and more impressed by the glamour of a royal occasion. Since Anne was too good to be sidelined, she went.'[32]

It was during one of her royal tours that Anne contracted a rare tropical disease, which she kept under control more or less for some ten years, but there were some afternoons when the fever left her totally wracked. In addition to, or perhaps as a result of, the tropical bug, from about the age of forty-five Anne suffered a nervous illness which all but engulfed her. 'One day she was facing tear gas in Algiers without turning a hair. The next she was unable to face the traffic in Oxford Street,' is how Angus McGill remembers the onset of her breakdown. Mary Kenny, another colleague, recalls the occasion when Anne was covering a story about fishermen in the North Sea. When they brought the fish in, they tipped them into the nets; as she watched the fish wiggle before they died, she was hit by a panic attack and could not finish the story. The first Wintour noticed was when she was reporting on Churchill's funeral and suddenly dried up on the telephone to him, something she had never done before. 'She had a finite stock of creative energy and we'd been poaching it too drastically,' he admits today.[33] She was taken off work and sent to see a psychiatrist, who asked her to describe her daily routine. When she described how she worked to a constant series of deadlines, he, aghast, told her that similar application and removal of repeated pressure was exactly how they induced neuroses in rats.

By 1973 Sharpley had not only given up full-time journalism but had made a number of dramatic changes in her life. She discovered feminism, which until then had not induced in her much sympathy; she had believed that women's issues were rather soppy. But from 1970 onwards, when she joined Women in Media, she took a keen interest in promoting her female peers in radio and television, constantly pressing for women to be employed routinely as news announcers and in current affairs programmes. Still more dramatically she moved home, from a large, four-floor house in Balcombe Street, WI, to a small flat in an almost identical house a few doors up the road. She sold or gave away almost all her clothes and furniture and bought new, very simple, functional objects. Her wardrobe, from this time, comprised only two colours, cream and brown, and co-ordinating shades, thus dispensing with the necessity of several different accessories. Her life was to be simple and uncomplicated. It was during this minimalist, feminist phase that Anne Sharpley became a travel writer for the *Evening Standard*, a job which she enjoyed enormously and whose gentle pace suited her changed circumstances. The suitcase still remained permanently packed but now there was a need for even fewer contents since one top would go with either a long, evening skirt or daytime slacks. Tom Pocock, who became her travel editor at the *Standard*, considered that she did the job brilliantly but 'she was a dynamic person who was overworked and burnt out'.[34] She continued as a regular contributor to the travel pages until 1980, when she was hit by cancer and her health deteriorated dramatically. Although she fought it for nine years – 'Getting Over It and Getting on With It' is what Anne did[35] – she died aged sixty on 10 April 1989.

Anne had often considered the pros and cons of being a woman in her job. Once, in her attempt to get close to the leaders she was following, she pursued Khrushchev, the Soviet President, on a tour of Washington, into the gents. Even less pleasant, according to Anne – who often told the story in the days before much was known about his private life – was an attempt by President Kennedy to make a pass at her in the back of the presidential limousine, which, she claimed, she fought off in disgust. But she won out when Princess Margaret went into a harem in Zanzibar and she was the only reporter allowed to go too, with a movie camera, acting as the 'pool' facility.

In spite of her desire to outdo them and disinclination to drink with them, Anne generally got on well with the other, male reporters, much better, in fact, than with other women. She was even prepared to help out her male colleagues on occasions such as when Randolph Churchill, drunk in Cyprus, persuaded her to send a story back on his behalf. She was wholly committed to her work but would hate to be remembered as a dedicated professional and single woman. 'She had a number of serious love affairs, but she was just not seriously interested in getting married,' is Angus McGill's view. 'Perhaps she deliberately picked people who would offer her no ties. She was seriously into journalism though.'[36] Her sister believes that, although she relished the company of men, she needed her independence more than she needed the stability of marriage. 'She wanted an active and hectic career and she always put her career before her boyfriends. But she paid the price,' reflected Mary Kenny.[37]

15

Justice

'Life is splendid and it's a bugger.'
SYBILLE BEDFORD

In the mid-1950s, a new medium beckoned, if hesitantly, for women
reporters. Commercial television had been talked about with great
excitement for a number of years and broadcasting was due to
start by the end of 1955. Aidan Crawley, former MP and soldier, was
responsible for setting up Independent Television News (ITN), the
news operation that would service the various independent franchise
holders.

Lynne Reid Banks, an actress working as a freelance researcher
and journalist, went to interview Crawley before the news service
started.

He told me how this would be a completely new system, unlike the BBC news
with its po-faced newsreaders sitting in tuxedos. He wanted to use a different
sort of person, one who could report, write and read the news, to be called a
newscaster, and he wanted women included in the rest of the reporting staff.[1]

Since Crawley had been married to Virginia Cowles for the last ten
years, perhaps the latter was not surprising. But it seemed dramatic
since women news reporters at the BBC had enjoyed scant success.

Halfway through the interview, Lynne suddenly realised that
Crawley was asking her more questions than she him. So she told him
with alacrity that, yes, she would be interested in a job and agreed to
an audition the next day. Clearly her acting training stood her in good
stead as she successfully memorised her résumé of the day's news,
delivered it without any sign of nerves and was offered the position.

Also in the first intake of reporters for ITN was one other woman,
journalist Barbara Mandell – these two became the first women

reporters on British television – and three men, while the newscasters included Christopher Chataway, the Olympic runner; Robin Day, a barrister who was nearly passed over because it was thought his glasses made him look unattractive; and Reginald Bosanquet. Lynne was paid what she considered great wealth, but it was not the same as the men. 'Of course it wasn't and we didn't expect it then... there were differentials and that was that.'[2] Nor was there any question of a clothing allowance although she was always expected to look smart on the screen.

More worrying to her was that she was not sent out to cover the same sort of events as the male reporters or newscasters. 'The news editor decided what stories we were to cover and the ethos of the time was that the women went out on women's stories unless the exigencies of the rota demanded otherwise.' Once, because no one else was available, she covered an aeroplane crash in which the Turkish ambassador had been killed – a story she would never normally have been allocated. As she left the office, the news editor gave her some final advice: 'I want you to stand there with all the bodies and bits around you and let your real feelings come through. Don't try and do it like the men.'[3]

Dealing with the cameramen gave her some of her worst moments, especially at the beginning when she understood none of the technical niceties and regularly antagonised them. But she believes this was because she was a novice, not because she was a woman, and she quickly learned all she needed to know about angles and light. She knew that she had been accepted when she was sent on 'industrials'. This might include charging into a huge crowd of striking men, such as the car workers at Dagenham, and asking them to explain their grievances. She was also used regularly for a new style of reporting, the 'Vox Pop', which involved accosting strangers in the street for their opinions; 'tricky for a woman reporter since most people assumed you were soliciting,' Lynne said.

After three and a half years she was sacked. The immediate cause was an interview she had conducted with Paul Robeson, the black singer, who had had his American passport confiscated and was passing through Heathrow after a trip to Russia, where he had been invited to sing. Again, the news editor briefed her and told her that she must confront him with hard political questions. But when she arrived at the press conference Robeson's minders were insisting 'no political questions'. None the less, when the cameras started to roll, ITN's woman reporter plunged in with as tough a line as she could and

Robeson sputtered a bit, but did more or less answer what she had asked. 'His PR men were furious and I always wondered after that if they complained to the Board, and got me sacked.'[4]

Lynne Reid Banks had never been a slick, professional reporter. She had a reporter's instinct which made her want to be wherever the action was, but her strength lay in the way she asked the sort of questions ordinary people would want to ask. She was, perhaps, not hard-nosed or cynical enough for the next generation of newshounds, but her powers of observation and natural ability to communicate were to flower in her command of fiction.

At all events ITN were loath to lose her completely, so they set her writing news scripts and she managed to fit in some reporting assignments too. One of these was a trip to the South of France, which she used years later as the basis for a short story in a woman's magazine. Jennifer, the fictional heroine, is sent on a three-day junket to Cannes for the opening of the Film Festival. 'My first trip abroad for the paper.... I could have wished it was something more serious but... what the hell!... Wars and disasters for the lads, flower shows and film stars for the girls!' Jennifer is determined to do a good job on the story, 'something to make 'em sit up in the office', despite the lightweight nature of the assignment. But her excitement is shattered when she meets up with Johnny, the photographer she is meant to work with. He has just flown in from Alexandria, where he witnessed scenes of appalling carnage and mayhem caused by British bombing raids. He is furious at being asked by his paper now to take pictures of film stars. Jennifer listens to him but, with the words of her news editor ringing in her ears: 'Women can't control their emotions. Show you a good train-wreck and you'd be blubbing all over your notebook', realises that she will have to find another photographer. Although Jennifer is eventually rewarded with more political stories after the meeting with Johnny, she questions whether she really does hanker after 'tough assignments' any more.[5]

A more significant foreign assignment for Lynne Reid Banks was a trip to Israel in 1960. She had pestered the editor for months to send her there for a fortnightly slot ITN produced called 'Roving Report'. 'I fought and fought and fought for a "Roving Report" but they sent the men every time,' she recalled. When it became clear that the editor was never going to agree, she decided to take a month's holiday and pay for the trip herself. 'I had read about the country and felt very strongly about it and learnt some Hebrew before I went. So I told the editor, "I'm going anyway; why not send a camera crew for the last week as you won't have any of my expenses and can get a film on the cheap." [6]

It was a tempting offer and in this way Lynne made her first documentary film, a short, romantic piece called *Women of Israel*, which showed a sophisticated, modern country, not the pioneering backwater it was still assumed to be. But it was her last reporting job because, later that year, her first novel appeared, a bestseller called *The L-Shaped Room*, which she had written during the evenings and slack periods at ITN. It was bought for a film the following year. In 1962, Lynne Reid Banks went to live on a kibbutz in Israel, married an Israeli and stayed there until 1971 bringing up two young sons. She has continued to write novels and plays since then, more than one of which has drawn upon her period as a reporter.

Among the tough assignments shelled out to Anne Sharpley had been a spell dodging bullets in Algiers in 1962. And it was tough. 'Correspondents who had been to Algiers had returned with shaking hands,' recalled Tom Pocock. 'One friend had suffered a nervous breakdown on his return, haunted by visions of a lynch mob, convinced that he was its quarry, and finally committed suicide on Hampstead Heath. By all accounts Algeria was worse than we could imagine.' [7]

For the previous eight years, the FLN (Front de Libération Nationale), the nationalist movement in Algeria, had been fighting a bloody battle for independence from France. The situation was complicated by the involvement of the French settlers' secret organisation, the OAS. Suddenly it seemed as if total anarchy was reigning on the streets of Algiers with terrorist outrages, usually perpetrated by the OAS, a daily occurrence. Clare Hollingworth, by this time working for the *Manchester Guardian* from Paris, knew the country of old. She had been there many times in the Second World War and after 1954 had covered the opening of the FLN's attack on the French authorities, developing many good contacts among the FLN and the French. But by January 1962, the violence had reached outrageous levels with gunmen bursting into cafés and opening fire willy-nilly, marching into hotels and arresting their victims, and planting bombs. Occasionally the missiles hurled in the street would be rotten eggs and tomatoes or the contents of a chamber pot. None of this seemed to bother Clare unduly. Tom Pocock, newly arrived to cover the crisis for the *Evening Standard*, retained an image of her striding the 'blood-streaked streets like a county lady determined that the vicarage fête shall succeed despite the arrival of Hell's Angels'. [8]

Covering the Algerian scene was, Clare admitted, 'somewhat dangerous'. She was many times saved by her contacts, who not only gave her information but also tipped her off about where it was or was not safe to go and enabled her to treat the Algerian cause seriously. Since most of her FLN sources operated from the Casbah, the walled warren of twisting streets where Muslims lived well away from OAS gunmen, she went there most days. A friendly Muslim shopkeeper used the position of his shutters (up for no tension, half-way up, uncertain atmosphere and nearly down for danger) to advise her about the daily political atmosphere. On the day he was shot she avoided the Casbah completely. Another day she was walking with Pocock and, as they approached the Casbah, they stopped at a narrow alleyway blocked off with barbed wire. 'That looks interesting,' Clare said. 'Don't be mad,' Pocock replied. 'Up there we'd both be killed and for what?' Clare shrugged reluctantly and agreed, but told him: 'Something might well happen to you but I'd just get slops emptied over me.' They both returned to the Hotel Aletti, home to all the foreign correspondents, where she left Pocock. 'I . . . of course, returned alone to that street and strode into the Casbah.'⁹ When she saw Pocock later he was astounded, especially when she told him she went there every day.

If Clare ever felt twinges of unease, it was not so much because of the Muslim threat as that from the OAS, who did not like her at all. They tailed her regularly and had ransacked her room on occasions, even smashing up her typewriter. They made threatening telephone calls and left her typed notes warning her to stop writing 'treachery for the *Manchester Guardian*'. Notwithstanding she continued, took no special precautions but, she insists, no wild risks either, and even slept in the same bedroom after the OAS had rummaged through it. On another occasion she held off a gang of OAS gunmen forcing eighty foreign correspondents to stand with hands up and revolvers pointed at stomachs with nothing more than an imperious threat to use her shoe. 'This was not bravado – I was absolutely furious.'¹⁰ So was the OAS ringleader, who pushed Clare to one side and seized the *Daily Telegraph* reporter, John Wallis. 'If we cannot have the Italian, we will take you,' he shrieked. Again it was Clare's cool that saved the day. As the gunmen made for the door she shouted, 'Let's all go too, they can't shoot us all.' The journalists all poured outside in an attempt to free their hapless colleague. But just as the hostage was thrown back amongst them, they heard the click of safety catches. 'Lie down. They're going to shoot!' someone shouted. But, in fact, not a shot was fired and the attackers revved off into the night abandoning their prey. 'Whether or not John Wallis owed his life to Clare Hollingworth we will never know; certainly he did not owe it to the rest of us,' Pocock commented, crisply, later.[11]

Clare fed the *Manchester Guardian* with a continuous stream of good stories from Algiers and used to reflect with pride on the way her reporting had given respectability to Arab nationalism; latterly she felt equivocal about that since she came to view all nationalism with increasing horror. For her coverage of the Algerian War, she won both the Journalist of the Year Award and the Hannen Swaffer Prize.

The Nuremberg trials, for all the horror that they revealed, had come almost too soon after the event for many to absorb the depth of evil to which man had sunk. The world was still stunned. But the 1960s saw two major war crimes trials, by which time the world had learned enough to believe such depravity which was being made known. In 1961, the Eichmann trial took place, followed a year later by that of twenty-two former members of staff from the Auschwitz concentration camp, tried on German soil before a German judge and jury. By this time there was an intense desire to know the worst.

Several women from many nations reported the Eichmann trial from Israel, including Monica Dehn and Martha Gellhorn, both for American publications. Dehn, based in London for *Time*, was sent to Israel for a cover story, which was eventually pushed off the cover in favour of the Russian sputnik launch, although her report ran at considerable length as the lead to the international section. Gellhorn was reporting for the *Atlantic*. For three weeks the world heard from dozens of German survivors exactly what life was like under the Nazis. For many it was the first time that they had spoken about the Holocaust and they experienced traumatic pain to do so now. No reporter had any need to embellish the basic facts so horrific were they. Both Gellhorn and Dehn wrote as objectively as possible, imbued with a strong sense of purpose: Dehn convinced that 'the moment you take the first step to admit one human being is not like you, cannot have the same job as you, you've denied their humanity and it's not then a terribly big step towards the gas chambers';[12] Gellhorn, because 'the private conscience is not only the last protection of the civilised world, it is the one guarantee of the dignity of man. And if we have failed to learn this, even now, Eichmann is before us a fact and a symbol, to teach the lesson.'[13]

Sybille Bedford, who reported the Auschwitz trial both for the

Observer and the *Saturday Evening Post*, became one of the most respected trial reporters of her day. She had been consumed with interest in law courts since she was a child, stimulated by the fact that her grandfather in Germany had been a high court judge. As she matured, this developed into a zeal for justice, which some major trials in the 1950s and 1960s gave her ample opportunity to put to good use.

Born in 1911 to a German father and a half-German mother, the first four years of her life were spent in a predominantly Jewish environment and, although only one-quarter Jewish, she always felt one-third Jewish through her mother's line. Her father died when she was eight and she left Germany to live in Italy, England and France. Whenever possible her eccentric and beautiful mother arranged occasional bouts of education for her:

I never learned things that other people did – for example I never learned physical handwriting, which is a terrible handicap for a reporter. Most serious writers start with journalism and go on to books. I had to do this in reverse as I would have never got a job as a reporter.[14]

Sybille is frequently described as 'privately educated'. A more accurate description might be self-educated as well as self-sufficient. She started visiting London's law courts at the age of twelve as a form of entertainment while other children of her age were going to matinées or films. She still remembers how she would press a sixpence into the guard's hand and he would let her into the public gallery. 'I was always interested in the chase for truth and yet in English courts the truth never comes out; you hear one side put and then the other.'[15]

Much of her adolescence was spent in the South of France, where, encouraged by Aldous Huxley, she started to write – three novels which were never published. She longed to go to Oxford and read history; even today her eyes glaze over at the possibility missed. Sybille married, briefly, in 1935, but when war came she escaped from France to North America. Her first published book, *A Visit to Don Otavio*,[16] was an account of a journey to Mexico undertaken with a woman friend identified only as E., and was also a form of escape, this time from New York. Sybille insists that she did not take a single note while she was in Mexico. 'If you clutter yourself with notes it all goes away. I did, of course, send postcards to friends and when I started writing I called them in.'[17] One advantage of not being tied to notes is that she is freer to look at people's faces, which she finds often tell her more than words. From this she has developed an almost painterly technique, not

unlike creating a portrait. She believes, too, that 'what doesn't stay in
the memory is not worth recording. It hasn't gone deep enough to be
digested,'[18] a claim that has had to be modified for some of her work.

Three years later, her first novel was published; yet *A Legacy* is also
tantalisingly autobiographical, describing a marriage between a Jewish
family from upper-middle-class Berlin and a Catholic aristocratic
family of lesser wealth. It was hugely praised and, as a result, she was
asked by *Vogue*'s Penelope Gilliatt to write a feature on any subject she
chose. She elected to write on the Old Bailey. The regular reporters
did not welcome Sybille's presence and she remembers more than one
occasion with Rebecca West, a colleague and good friend, when the
two women met physical opposition from the seasoned male reporters
at The Bailey. Rebecca and Sybille had to kick down a barrier made
by the men, who had put their feet up across the passage barring their
way, and they soon realised from the frosty stares that the male press
room was out of bounds. The experience also opened her eyes to the
poor quality of most law reporting.

Sybille had already formulated clear views as to how she believed
trials should be reported: 'In the first place don't overdramatise, be
economical or you lose the drama; secondly don't underrate the intelligence of the public.'[19] From this grew a determination to report a
murder trial where the public was treated intelligently and could follow
and reach its own conclusions. Her chance came with the trial of Dr
John Bodkin Adams, accused of murdering one of his elderly patients.
So excited was she with the prospect that she rushed back from Paris
and approached first the *New Yorker* and then *Life*, both of which
turned her down. Finally, she persuaded Collins to commission a book
of the trial. It appeared in 1958 as *The Best We Can Do* and shows her
sound grasp of the ways of the judiciary and the English legal process.
It is written with a pace and style which succeeds in making the reader
feel as if he were present as part of the jury. By 1960, with three books
to her credit, the commissions started coming. 'The Trial of Lady
Chatterley's Lover', as she called her piece, recounted a criminal
prosecution against Penguin Books Limited, the publishers of D. H.
Lawrence's novel of that name which, it was claimed by the Crown,
was obscene. Although written in 1928, this was the book's first
commercial publication in an unexpurgated version.

Sybille was asked by *Esquire* to cover the proceedings and she gave
them a vintage report, parts of which read like an account of a
Victorian melodrama – the murder of a literary creation – as the
prosecution brutally flung out lists of four-letter words and counted

the number of times intercourse was described. Counsel for the prosecution was at pains to point out that girls too, 'perhaps your daughter', might read such a book, as if the idea of girls reading at all was itself shocking. There was an impressive array of churchmen, publishers and dons called as witnesses for the defence, including Dame Rebecca West (as she was by 1959), who lectured the court about Lawrence's aims as well as his shortcomings. In her deadpan retelling of the trial, Sybille devotes just one paragraph to the verdict – not guilty; true drama, she knew, needed no purple prose.

The Auschwitz trial, which opened in Frankfurt a few days before Christmas 1963, lasted two and a half years and represented a historic attempt for a whole nation to come to terms with its guilt. For Sybille, who had been born in Germany, it was obviously a deeply significant process. Her reporting technique was immediately to scrutinise the faces of the accused:

... to see, to know, to find perhaps a key to deeds that most of us on this earth have heard about and are haunted by or try to belittle or forget or choose not to believe. A few of the men here look inscrutably ordinary; the faces of the rest are dreadful – pinched, closed, hard; carved by cruelty, brutality, vacuity.[20]

In spite of her aversion to note-taking, Sybille had to succumb when reporting dialogue. She was living in the South of France while the trial was running and would organise to go to Frankfurt for two or three days every three months, sending interim reports to the *Observer* whenever key witnesses were called.

Then, in the middle of the trial, she received a sudden telephone call from *Life* magazine to report the trial of Jack Ruby, accused of murdering Lee Harvey Oswald, in turn the accused killer of President Kennedy. 'I was invited because *Life* thought no American journalist could get away with it – the trial was such a miscarriage of justice. This gave me an enormous sense of responsibility which was made worse by the enormous sum of money offered.'[21] Sybille had moments of sheer panic during the trial, having never written for *Life* before, in case she failed to deliver on time or in the style it wanted. The editor tried to reassure her that she would be paid all the same, a reassurance which made her feel even worse.

Ruby's was a six-week trial from February to March 1964, during which Sybille lived in a suite at the Sheraton Palace Hotel in Dallas. With her direct telex link to the magazine and never knowing precisely when the editor would require an account to date she felt, on occasions,

trapped as she typed out her daily notes every evening. Of course she
managed the assignment and her final thoughts – approaching eight
thousand words – summing up the whole procedure was the longest
prose piece that had yet appeared in *Life*. But it was not achieved
without anguish. Not only was she exhausted from working from 5
p.m. until dawn, but also from deep concern as to whether this was a
fair trial:

For that is all that is left, all we can hope to have now: a manifestly fair trial. . . .
We, that is the American people, are obsessed by the desire – creditable,
civilized, pathetic – to see justice done on behalf of the remaining, wretched
piece of humanity. The desire is the life ring thrown into the sea – the sop to
tragedy to our bid for order, truth, relief.[22]

Following the successful completion of her assignment for *Life*,
Sybille returned to cover the final stages of the Auschwitz trial, no
more confident of her ability to produce on paper an account of that
trial that would do justice to her thoughts and impressions, as well as
the millions killed. 'I have such doubts about my writing,' she says,
'often I would be physically sweating with terror, quite unlike my
fellow reporters.'[23] The trial finished on a Friday night and she remembers how the rest of the press pack agreed to go out on the town and
write later. Unable to socialise at such a time, she went back to her
room and started writing immediately, until it was done. She wrote
coolly, in spite of the almost unbearable emotional strain. She knew
she could not possibly recount every single tale of horror and brutality.
'To repeat it here in dry print would stun the mind . . . . Pity and anger
are inadequate. The law is inadequate . . . comment is inadequate. . . .'
And she allowed herself only a brief personal insight – scarcely judg-
mental in tone – at the end:

This story is a part of our lives and time. It is irreversible for those to whom
it happened, the unfortunate men and women who were plucked from home,
from family, from cares and habits, from the entire normal context of human
expectations. What we can do is to honour them by our memory, to mourn
them, to think of them in sorrow and in awe. And we can learn . . . . Beware
of being sheep.[24]

Sybille Bedford continued to attend trials, including three in the
1960s and early 1970s which she wrote about but never published.
The Stephen Ward trial, the Vassall tribunal and the Jeremy Thorpe
trial all remained unpublished either because her account was deemed
libellous or because she considered there had been a miscarriage of

justice. She has also written seriously and impressively about the two great loves of her life: food and travel, the former being 'one of the deepest things between men and women – offering food to loved ones is almost sacramental'.[25] She writes of these two other passions beside justice, her third, not as reportage but almost as poetry. They are very important to her and appear in all her books of fiction. Her literary output has remained small. Writing does not come easily to her and she has had to work consciously at evolving a style. She bemoans the fact that she has written so little and explains it as 'partly a question of sloth and partly fear and also that I need enormously long incubation periods and when I'm forced to be quick I'm terrified.'[26]

In 1989, aged eighty, Sybille produced an autobiographical novel, *Jigsaw*,[27] which was a brilliant example of the length of time her mind takes to distil experiences into fictional form. 'None of my novels goes beyond 1932,' she explains and *Jigsaw* magically evokes character and period in a mélange of reality and imagination. It was shortlisted for the Booker Prize and was followed a year later by a collection of her best journalism on the subjects of food, landscape and justice. *As It Was* sums up the essence of Sybille Bedford: her immense capacity to comprehend horror and tragedy coupled with her immense joie de vivre and sybaritic enjoyment of the sensual pleasures of life. 'One of my great impulses for writing is down to earth; the wonders of the visible earth – trees, landscapes, sea and water, animal noises and night smells – one writes in a way to nail down those moments and to celebrate.'[28] But alongside such celebration and pleasure are her accounts of the greatest evil man is capable of inflicting. She knows only too well that the people who perpetrated the horrors at Auschwitz are the same people who sit under a sunshade in a beautiful landscape sipping fine wine. Such juxtaposition is important for her because life contains all these elements. 'Life is splendid and it's a bugger,' she says.[29] If the much threatened trials of Nazi war criminals ever take place in England and Sybille Bedford is alive, she wants to be there reporting them.

16

Vietnam

'My reaction is a woman's reaction: how very sad it all is ... '
KATE WEBB

Less than a year after the war in Korea officially ended, Vietnam was similarly divided into a communist North led by Ho Chi Minh and a non-communist South led by Ngo Dinh Diem. Shortly afterwards 200 US military 'advisers' were sent to help Diem in his struggle against the North and the fuse was lit for the world's next conflagration.

Marguerite Higgins had been enchanted for years by Vietnam and the Vietnamese people. 'And enchanted is the precise word. For there is a kind of magic about Vietnam – the magic of that which is exotic, strange, imperfectly understood and yet deep in the emotions.'[1]

Marguerite knew the country well, perhaps as well as any Westerner can, she believed. Her grandfather had died of a wound received while fighting with the French colonial forces against the Vietnamese in the 1890s. Marguerite herself, although born in Hong Kong, had first been taken to Vietnam as a six-month-old baby suffering from malaria. The family doctor prescribed a stay in Dalat, a beautiful mountain resort in central Vietnam, where, it was thought, the clean air would help cure the child. When, in 1950, she had been covering the Korean War, she had frequently commuted to Vietnam, which she viewed as another front in the same struggle.

On 11 June 1963, the crisis in Vietnam hit the world's headlines largely because of the dramatic pictures of a Buddhist monk, Thich Quang Duc, committing self-immolation. The US State Department was by turns angry and exasperated with the Diem regime, which, it thought, should be taking a more conciliatory line towards the

Buddhists, and furious with the American correspondents who were critical of Diem and the American mission.

Marguerite was not keen to leave Washington again for Vietnam – she now had a young family and was recuperating from a severe bout of 'flu. Yet in mid-June she found herself agreeing to make her seventh trip to the country, influenced perhaps by 'a rapport of magnetic quality that draws me back again and again',[2] but also by a desire to understand the roots of a conflict tearing apart a country she loved.

However much they criticised American methods and American backing of Diem, most American correspondents at that time wanted to see North Vietnamese communism defeated and none more so than Marguerite Higgins. Working with an interpreter she interviewed dozens of people including President Diem and the hated Madame Nhu, Diem's sister-in-law, in the wake of her unfortunate remark that a monk had been 'barbecued'. Madame Nhu tried to use the opportunity of an interview with Marguerite to maintain that the real struggle was to 'wrest decent treatment of women from the reluctant, devious and often hypocritical men of Vietnam', a view which left Marguerite cold. She also talked to Henry Cabot Lodge, several Buddhist monks and American and Vietnamese soldiers in the fields. Because her assignment was for a series of articles without the pressures of daily deadlines, she could spend more time in the countryside, where the war was already destroying lives; she could visit dozens of villages, where she was sometimes shot at; and she could devote less time to Saigon, scene of suicides and demonstrations where the resident correspondents were based. Her series was, by her own admission, highly controversial; her central theme was that Diem was fighting to save his government and that the perils of betraying Diem in mid-war were greater than the perils of supporting him.

Marguerite used the articles as a basis for her book, *Our Vietnam Nightmare*, published in 1965, in which she acknowledged that the situation was so volatile that anything could happen. Whatever the outcome it would be of deep significance not only for America but also for the rest of the world. In September 1965, she set off on her tenth visit to Vietnam, continuing on to India and Pakistan. While there she contracted Leishmaniasis, a debilitating infection caused by the bite of a blood-sucking insect. She was hospitalised in November and died in January 1966, aged forty-five.

The fact that Marguerite Higgins, a woman, had reported from the thick of the battle in the Korean War was in itself newsworthy. Five years later there were dozens of women writing about all aspects of

the Vietnam conflict. For the first time there were no military barriers
to women reporters getting as close to the fighting – there were no
front lines as such – as they wished. In fact, it was often rather too
easy. Apart from obtaining a visa and buying a ticket, no special
permission was required to visit South Vietnam during the war; commercial airlines continued to serve Saigon's Tan Son Nhut airport.
Several correspondents, male and female, paid their own fare to Saigon
and arrived with no official status as correspondents. Once there, the
would-be reporter needed little more than two letters from provincial
newspapers or agencies guaranteeing to take articles from him or
her. Application for accreditation was then made both to the Saigon
Government and to MACV (Military Assistance Command, Vietnam)
and, a few photographs and forms later, an accredited war correspondent emerged. The MACV press card was all that was needed
for admission to the US daily official briefing session, held at 4.45 p.m.
and known as the 'five o'clock follies'. For those who wished to leave
Saigon and travel around the countryside to talk to villagers or inspect
a battle site, it was possible to hitch a lift on military transport with no
further official permission. If this were not available, there were rental
cars or commercial bus services.

In other words, for the first time, women reporters faced virtually
no obstacles. Of course, individual officers still made caustic comments such as the one who yelled at a women correspondent to wear
fatigues the entire time: 'We don't want women with legs down here.'[3]
Others, seeing a Marine fling himself on a woman reporter to protect
her from mortar fire, were genuinely concerned that women were a
distraction. General William Westmoreland, who took over command
of the American forces in Vietnam in August 1964, was well known
for his views on the inadequacies of the female sex. He believed that
carrying a pack or living in a foxhole without taking a bath would
be impossible feats for a woman. One woman correspondent, who
experienced severe back pain after tramping through the jungle for
five days carrying a heavy rucksack, was coolly instructed by her
captain to observe the loads the GIs had to shoulder before she should
be entitled to complain.

'When I got back to my bunker and my gear there were three black
mortar rounds strapped neatly to my pack. So I picked up the 30-
pound pack and started to walk away. "Yup. She's hard core," someone
said.'[4]

Also, the eternal canard about lack of facilities had not disappeared,
but women were less inhibited and simply squatted wherever they

could. A more serious problem, which arose towards the end of the war once the majority of American female military personnel had been withdrawn, was the unavailability of tampons. However, two UPI women correspondents, Margaret Kilgore in Saigon and Kate Webb in Phnom Penh, Cambodia, came to an arrangement that whichever of them went to Hong Kong for a rest trip would bring back sufficient supplies for the pair of them. Occasionally, being a woman was a positive advantage; some helicopter pilots were more anxious to offer rides to women than men, and a few women in Saigon claimed that their high profile in press conferences often resulted in their questions being answered first.

Life in Saigon in the mid-1960s had not yet lost all the trappings of glamour which had earned it the epithet 'Paris of the East' and, for those who stayed in the capital, there was a semblance of normality maintained at the larger hotels. At the same time, the war in the countryside was one of the most vicious and horrific ever fought; at its starkest the contrast between American military technology ranged against a backward peasant nation and no front line in between was almost incredible.

'I have witnessed modern war in nine countries but I have never seen a war like the one in South Vietnam,' Martha Gellhorn wrote.[5] After the Second World War, Martha had lived for a while in Italy, London, East Africa and Mexico since 1948 with her adopted baby son, Sandy. She was writing novels, a little journalism, but mostly short stories, 'fakes with happy endings for popular American magazines. . . . I called these stories "bilgers" and having found some of them lately, I am delighted by them; they are stylish junk and I marvel that I was once so clever.'[6] Martha was very happy with Sandy, living in a small Mexican village which she considered one of the most beautiful places on earth, but she was poor. Her 'bilge' stories had to pay the rent, support the household and pay for an annual trip to Europe. Then, in 1954, she married for the third time, Tom Matthews, the fifty-three-year-old editor of *Time*.

But fiction remained her first love and although she had long since shed all her illusions about journalism acting as the world's guiding light, she still believed that it was better than total darkness. 'Somebody has to bring the news as we cannot all see for ourselves.'[7]

It was some twenty years since she had lived in the United States, yet Martha insists that she would never have chosen to go near any war again 'if my own country' had not been so enormously involved in such a vicious war that made so little sense. Distressed by reports that catalogued 'body counts' and 'kill ratios' and by young correspondents who wrote about the war as if it were a sports event, she could not see how killing Vietnamese civilians freed them from communist aggression. 'I did not want to learn about new techniques of warfare, nor ever again see young men killing each other on the orders of old men. Finally I went to South Vietnam because I had to learn for myself . . . what was happening to the voiceless Vietnamese people.'[8]

Martha was shocked by everything she saw. She was scandalised by the hypocrisy of the lecture given to newly arrived US troops. First, of course, they were told the importance of killing VC (Vietcong), ' . . . but there's a lot more to it than that. To really and truly and finally win this war, we must help the Government of South Vietnam win the hearts and minds of the people in South Vietnam.'[9] In order to examine how the Americans were winning hearts and minds, Martha toured Qui Nhon hospital, where a team of New Zealand doctors and nurses was battling to alleviate the suffering of the starving, wounded and maimed. After taking her readers on a graphic tour of the jammed wards, past blocked latrines, dazed children and agonised parents, she concluded:

We are not maniacs and monsters; but our 'planes range the sky all day and all night and our artillery is lavish and we have much more deadly stuff to kill with. The people are there on the ground, sometimes destroyed by accident, sometimes destroyed because Vietcong are reported to be among them. This is indeed a new kind of war, as the indoctrination lecture stated, and we had better find a new way to fight it. Hearts and minds, after all, live in bodies.[10]

Martha stayed in Vietnam during August and September 1966, a brief stay that 'churned up my life until 30 April 1975 when the war finally ended'. She wrote five more articles, none of them about tactical victories, magnificent landings or military hardware, but all of them about the devastating effect the war was having on the native population. She went to a Catholic orphanage, one of ten in Saigon alone which had to deal with 80,000 orphans. Some orphans were cared for by distant relatives, but a further 2,000 orphans per month were predicted for the institutions. 'Is it not strange that we count and proclaim only military casualties? These homeless children should be listed as wounded; and wounded for ever,' she indicted.[11]

In her two subsequent articles, Martha wrote about the powerless middle class and life among the Vietcong. She also described heart-rending conditions at one of many refugee camps which had been hit by cholera and plague. The country had acquired a population of 1.3 million refugees in the previous two years alone.

These peasants had survived the Vietcong since 1957 on whatever terms, hostile or friendly, and the war however it came to them. But they cannot survive our bombs. Even the Catholic refugees did not leave their hamlets until bombs fell. We are uprooting the people from the lovely land where they have lived for generations; and the uprooted are given not bread but a stone. Is this an honourable way for a great nation to fight a war 10,000 miles from its safe homeland?[12]

The articles were refused by American newspapers on the grounds that they were 'too tough' for American readers.[13] Eventually, the *St Louis Post-Dispatch* took two of them, but only the *Guardian* would take the entire series. Nearly twenty years later Martha stated that she considered what she wrote at the time to have been 'a model of self-censorship'.[14] 'It is the only piece of reporting of which I am ashamed,' she said.[15] Knowing that only the official American version of the war was accepted as truth, she believed that, in order to be published at all, 'I had to suppress half of what I knew and gentle the rest. Re-reading the articles now, the gentling disgusts me. At the time, these reports gave some first idea of what the war was doing to the South Vietnamese people, whom we were supposedly protecting.'[16]

Martha was so profoundly sickened by what she had seen in Vietnam that she wanted to return as soon as possible and use what little power she had to alert the world to the truth of the situation as she saw it. In any case, she could not erase the images, tormenting and disorienting her, of what she had seen there. 'I remember flying north from Saigon and seeing the whole earth covered by huge deep round craters of blood red water. There was no untouched space between the craters. That was carpet bombing.'[17]

But when she tried to return, she found that she could not. She was exiled. 'After repeated, increasingly angry requests for a visa the South Vietnamese Embassy in London finally admitted that I was "on a list in our foreign office". A Blacklist. My self-centred articles were too much and too soon.'[18]

Gloria Emerson, of the *New York Times*, who arrived in Saigon for the second time in February 1970, shared Martha's brand of anger. In particular, she was irked that so many correspondents and other Americans were living comfortably, eating well and enjoying much of the Saigon lifestyle.

Since her newspaper enjoyed the luxury of several correspondents in Vietnam, Gloria was not required to write about daily battles or other military matters and could concentrate on the devastating effects of the war on society. She wrote many stories about various aspects of the war, including rehabilitation for wounded civilians, bureaucratic difficulties for war widows in Saigon, relations between Vietnamese and Americans as well as the difficulties facing new recruits. Her series of articles on refugees, which won her the George Polk Memorial Award in 1971, included the movingly understated story of a Vietnamese orphan boy living with his family in the crowded squalor of a Saigon orphanage. The family had been forced to sell many possessions, including the boy's bicycle, when they fled. 'It is the loss of his green bicycle that hurts him most, but, like most children of Asia, thirteen-year-old Than Minh Hoang does not complain.'[19]

Not all those who wrote about Vietnam's hospitals and orphanages – 'human interest reporting' – were women and one former correspondent, Richard Hughes, even gave up journalism to run four orphanages. And not all women reporters who went to Vietnam concentrated on the effects of the war on the society; several wrote about the politics, if not the strategy, of war. Frances Fitzgerald, possibly one of the most brilliant minds to analyse the Vietnam crisis, went in 1966 as a freelance intending to write a few articles about the war for a variety of American periodicals. She was never interested in day-to-day combat but made a serious attempt to understand the background and culture of the native society and the effect of the American presence and war on that society. *Fire in the Lake*, Fitzgerald's magisterial book about Vietnam, was published in 1972 and laid bare America's tragic misconceptions about the country and its people.

Mary McCarthy, the American novelist, freely admitted that when she went to Vietnam in February 1967 she was not going to report battle successes and failures but was looking for material damaging to the American interest. Not surprisingly, she found such material in abundance as the Americans saw no need to hide what they were doing. But, as she pointed out in her subsequent essay on the overpowering American presence on Asian soil, they had altered the vocabulary. 'For example napalm has become "incanderjell", which makes it sound like jello. And defoliants are referred to as "weedkillers" – something you use in your driveway. The resort to euphemism denotes, no doubt, a guilty conscience or – the same thing nowadays – a twinge in the public relations nerve.'[20] She was shocked, too, when she went to church for Sunday Mass and heard an Irish American priest making a sermon about hemlines in a service taken in English. She hated everything she saw in South Vietnam from the smog, the garbage and the snarled traffic to the clip joints and ever accommodating prostitutes. Her travels through the country left her in no doubt that there was only one solution to the problem: the Americans must get out and precisely *how* was not the concern of those who opposed the US presence. Not being a military specialist, Mary did not see it as her role to plot the logistics of withdrawing 464,000 American servicemen. Her position was simply stated: the war is wrong, therefore stop it as quickly as possible.

But although her views were supported by thousands of Americans who demonstrated against the war in 1967, she was heavily criticised for such simplistic thinking, even by those who believed America should withdraw but only after giving some commitment to the South Vietnamese and against communism. As a novelist, however, Mary was skilled at making a point and saw no need to apply the journalistic straitjacket of objectivity. She bolstered her views further the following year by visiting North Vietnam, where she was impressed by the cleanliness and the absence of refuse, prostitutes and ragged children with sores, as she wrote in *Hanoi*, her next book on the subject.[21] She insisted that her purpose in going to North Vietnam was to judge, compare and report back in the hope that this 'might dispel some of the phobic attitudes that were allowing the war to continue'. Yet once there she questioned her own ability to remain detached and was aware not only of a quickening of sympathy with the North, but also of 'a sense that my detachment and novelistic powers of observation were not only inappropriate but also a sort of alibi'.[22] One episode in particular during her stay in Hanoi troubled her deeply. After a visit to the War Crimes Museum she was presented with a ring made from a downed US aircraft and engraved with the date the aeroplane was shot down. Mary felt unable to wear the ring even for a few minutes but was not certain why she found it quite so repugnant. She felt a physical aversion to being touched by the metal and yet was unable to throw it away. She concluded that 'quite a few of the questions one does not, as an American liberal, want to put in Hanoi are addressed to oneself'.[23]

Clare Hollingworth, who is proud of being able to strip down and reassemble a machine-gun as fast as any man, was by this time an unusually experienced combat correspondent. None the less, she believed firmly that what matters in war is who is winning the battle. 'The real story is in the front line and at HQ . . . . My newspaper has never asked me to do a woman's angle story; they wouldn't . . . because they know I'd be hopeless. I'm interested in war.'[24] But perhaps this is to miss the point: why is it a woman's angle to write about war's victims? From 1963 to 1967 Clare was defence correspondent of the *Guardian*, the first woman to hold the post, and had developed a considerable knowledge of military hardware. 'I love weapons,' she told one interviewer, adding that the Americans were using 'fantastic weaponry'.[25] Although by then in her mid-fifties, she was still utterly fearless about tracking even the most dangerous action. 'I don't feel frightened under machine-gun fire ... if you know you're going to die there is nothing you can do about it,' she insists.[26]

She was unpopular with the American authorities not because she was writing stories which pointed out the tragic effects of the war, like Emerson and Gellhorn, but because she was always convinced the Americans would lose and her pessimism permeated her reports. The sort of stories she wrote during several visits to Vietnam, first for the *Guardian* and then, after 1967, for the *Daily Telegraph*, ranged from helicopter bombing missions against groups of communist guerrillas encamped beside canals; dropping supplies and visiting besieged Americans in Khe Sanh and other fortresses in the demilitarised zone; accompanying South Vietnamese and American troops on jungle forays or watching Saigon street fights. 'When the Vietcong were trying to take over Cho Lon, an outlying Chinese district of Saigon, a European military attaché took me into the middle of it. We moved from one bullet-pocked building to another and there was little danger to worry about because he had been a first-class house-to-house fighter in the 1939–45 war,' Clare recalled matter of factly.[27]

She still moved around the world relentlessly. If she was in the same place for more than three months she grew restless and was frequently absent for trips lasting between two and four months. 'When I was away ... I missed Geoffrey not only as a husband and companion but also as a colleague with whom I could discuss politics and work in general,' she wrote in her autobiography. It was during one of those extended trips that she suffered a more profound shock than anything she had seen in Vietnam. Her husband wrote to her telling her of pains in his arm similar to those he had had before succumbing to a heart attack some years earlier. He was going to see a London doctor for a check up. 'Sensing danger,' Clare explains, 'I requested my editor for permission to take immediate leave "for personal reasons" for the only time in my life.'[28]

She arrived in London within twenty-four hours, in time to see Geoffrey in hospital, cheerful after suffering a minor heart attack. Ten days later he had a further massive attack and died within a few hours. 'Life has never been quite the same since,' is the only pointer Clare gives in her autobiography to the emotional wrench she suffered.

In the spring of 1968, she returned to Vietnam and was rewarded with a front-page scoop. Through her FLN contacts in Algeria she was invited by an agent of the North Vietnamese or Vietcong to attend Mass at the cathedral the next day. Soon a man came to sit beside her and, after a few prayers, suggested they leave. He whispered that peace talks between Hanoi and Washington were about to start which would produce agreement on terms to end all American bombing of North Vietnam. In return, Hanoi would offer to withdraw one or two of its divisions from the South and a general ceasefire could follow. He gave her other details which she used in her story for the *Daily Telegraph*. But although peace talks did open in Paris within a month, the war itself was far from over.

Because the war in Vietnam was the major issue of the decade for its generation and because it was so easy to become accredited, dozens of women towards the end accompanied their husbands to Saigon, confident of finding enough work once there. As Della Fathers, a twenty-nine-year-old freelance writer whose husband Michael was sent by Reuters in 1972 discovered, the freedom of choosing their own material and not being tied to deadlines and press conferences gave them the more interesting opportunities. Inevitably these stories were what some disparagingly refer to as 'soft news' or even 'side issues'. When she first arrived Della was struck by how few reporters were investigating the damage to children, homes and ordinary lives. But towards the end of her eighteen-month stay, 'as the networks suddenly realised the importance of having a woman's byline, many more women reporters were sent'. Della considers that she, writing mostly for the *New York Times*, the *Guardian* and Reuters, about the reper-cussions of war, was in a privileged position, 'whereas the men got caught up in the day-to-day news, churning out casualty figures, and couldn't sit back to reflect on the broader picture and the rest of life'.[29]

Phillip Knightley, in his book *The First Casualty*, comments that Victoria Brittain, 'a resident correspondent for *The Times* of London, mixed straight reporting with articles on child victims'.[30] Victoria herself takes exception to the concept of 'such a mixture' since she considers that the only real war story concerns the victims of war. 'Looking back at the torrent of reporting (of Vietnam), it is in fact two series of articles, by Gloria Emerson and Martha Gellhorn, about orphans and refugees, which told the political story as all of us should have told it,' Victoria wrote years later.[31] 'Women are much closer to reality and don't put up a barrier between "my work and the rest of my life".'[32]

Victoria Brittain had emerged from a sheltered British boarding-school education with no particular ambition to write, but landed a job on the *Investors Chronicle* because she had seen the journal lying around at home. Her political awareness developed rapidly in 1968, watching Europe's students in revolt, and she soon moved to the *Daily Telegraph* and then, married with a young son, went to America. This provided her first opportunity for reporting as she was invited to write from Washington one piece a month for *The Times* about almost anything that interested her. *The Times*'s bureau chief, Louis Heren, was extremely encouraging and she was also given a weekly column for the *New Statesman*.

Whilst there she began writing about American attitudes to the war in Vietnam, but increasingly suffered from a feeling, swelled by current agitation over revelations of the My Lai massacre, that she was out of her depth. 'And then I began to have a sort of obsession that I must understand this thing. I must go to Vietnam to understand it. There was such a gap between what was in the papers and what I was being told.'[33]

Victoria returned to London in 1970 and was approached by ITN to do a three-week stint in Vietnam. By this time the Americans were mostly gone or going and the war was no longer a 'hot' news item. But Victoria was bitten by the Vietnam epic and the day she returned she resigned from ITN and asked Heren if she could be *The Times*'s stringer in Saigon. He agreed, without any of the patronising remarks she had expected, such as 'How will you manage?' since she was by this time divorced with a six-year-old son whom she intended to take with her. He simply asked her how much money she thought she would need.

Victoria went with a single ticket, not knowing how long she would stay, and about £30 in her pocket. She believes that having her son with her was a great advantage because she was forced to lead a more normal life than her male colleagues and was able to ingratiate herself more into Vietnamese life. During the day her son would attend school or swim or play with local children. 'All this meant I was perhaps more conscious of the destruction of families and communities. I was more involved.'[34]

As she explained, it was not so much a question of women showing more natural sensitivity:

Visiting orphanages and refugee camps was a wretched way to spend the day. The kids clung to any passing person like leeches, demanding a moment of fleeting attention or affection, and the repetition of their stories by women uprooted from their village by the US B52 bombers which had killed their neighbours, relations and at worst their own children, was numbing.[35]

On another occasion Victoria wrote:

But however horrendous it was to do stories about napalmed children in orphanages I would screw my courage up and force myself because it was so important. Men on the whole did not do those kind of stories and pretended they weren't important. Male colleagues would drive out to some disputed control zone and write about that or go to a press conference or talk to an ambassador. On the whole they really despised 'people' stories.[36]

One such story – revealingly *The Times* placed it in a section headed 'Features for Women' – discussed the thousands, possibly hundreds of thousands, of children in Vietnam with American fathers; 'whether their fathers were white or black Americans, the children stand out in any group,' Victoria wrote.[37] 'Their families are marked for victimisation as collaborators in any area newly controlled by the Vietcong or the North Vietnamese army.' She also described how even a relatively good orphanage was 'chaotic, filthy, and stuffed with children so starved of adult contact that the moment you step inside the courtyard your whole lower body and legs are covered with small, exploring hands'.[38] On a balcony outside, she saw a baby barely old enough to sit up lolling in a pool of urine at the top of a flight of twenty iron steps.

In order to remain sane in the midst of so much pain and suffering, Victoria soon learnt how to switch off – how to block out the routine horror of what she saw. 'War is so outside any ordinary experience that nothing can prepare you for it . . . . I was in a permanent state of outrage.'[39]

Marina Warner was another reporter who similarly learnt to quench her natural emotional response to the horrors of Vietnam. She explains: 'There was a day when nothing was happening so the journalists were all sitting around bored, with no battle to go to.'[40] Marina suggested taking a group taxi to the holy mountain of Tay Ninh as she had started researching material for a book on the Virgin Mary and there was a shrine there. The group hit first one roadblock, then another, and finally, when they reach Trang Bang, saw the village go up in black, oily flames. 'I was standing two yards away from a child who came running with no clothes on and her back on fire and next to her was this grandmother holding a baby being burnt to death and all her flesh hanging off.' And yet, Marina was not shocked as she had expected to be because at the same time she was numbed by a feeling of having seen it all before. 'Somehow, seeing it before on television took away some of the reality.... But later, when the horror sank in, I stood on the roadway exposing myself to fire when I didn't need to... it was some sort of expiation.'[41]

Marina Warner, a graduate of Oxford, was named 'Young Writer of the Year' in 1970 by the *Daily Telegraph*. She had been married just three weeks in 1971 when her journalist husband, William Shawcross of the *Sunday Times*, was despatched to Vietnam. At first she waited patiently at home. But, reading horrific headlines predicting the fall of Saigon, she became increasingly nervous and upset and decided to take leave from her own job as features editor of *Vogue* and go out and join him. She got herself accredited without difficulty by telling US officials that she was working for *The Times*.

In Saigon, Marina felt herself rather an anomaly, particularly because she was the only woman in the once grand Hotel Royale, which, for her, found itself forced to relax its strict rules on allowing women to enter bedrooms. During her two-month stay from May 1972 she deliberately maintained her status as an outsider, aware of the atmosphere among the male journalists of belonging to a men's military club. The most obvious symbol of this was that most wore full army gear.

'Some of the older correspondents really enjoyed this side of it.... It was part of a performance they gave themselves to with some kind of pleasure.'[42] As Marina points out, one could, and several women did, simply wear a flak jacket over civilian clothes with boots. She wrote three articles, which her agent placed in the *Spectator*, and a fourth which the *Guardian* published. The first dealt with the ethics of other correspondents and was 'rather a savage piece'. She pointed out the essential paradox of the war correspondents' situation in Vietnam: while they were writing against the outrage they needed the outrage to give them their copy.

However impassioned he is against the American presence in Vietnam – and many pressmen are – he does not really want the Americans to withdraw completely because it is their actions that make Vietnam a story of international concern. So the same criticism that many writers make against the Americans – that they care little or nothing for the interests of the Vietnamese people – can be levelled at the press.[43]

This was a courageous conclusion, given that the author was just twenty-six at the time.

Another story Marina tackled, aware that it was not considered 'important', concerned orphanages because she was riveted by the extraordinary number of American-Asian children sired by GIs on Vietnamese bar girls or women who had been inducted into prostitution because they had no other means of livelihood. 'Contraceptives were available free in the PX stores of the US army,' she pointed out, 'but it only needs one glance at the cots in the ramshackle orphanages of Saigon to realise that very few GIs seem to know what they are for.' It was a hard-hitting, factual piece which took the reader on a tour of the filthy, overcrowded orphanages and explained why so few adoptions were possible to western families who desperately wanted the babies. The orphans seemed doomed to stay there in ever increasing numbers suffering skin sores, eye diseases, epidemics of boils and malnutrition. 'If only ... the GIs could see the orphanages in which their children live,' she concluded.[44] Marina's third article was about the bar girls. But she was always more of a meditative writer than an on-the-spot reporter and much of the material she gathered in copious Vietnam notebooks reappeared in various fictional guises, some of it as recently as 1992.

Of the more than seventy women correspondents who reported the Vietnam War, at least two were captured by enemy forces. Elizabeth Pond took a 'temporary' job as a copy girl at the *Christian Science Monitor* after she graduated in International Relations from Harvard and was immediately captivated by journalism. 'At the beginning I didn't get the same promotions as male colleagues; that was part of my reason for going to East Europe as a freelance in the sixties.'[45] Elizabeth became a political writer who specialised in trenchant analyses of the political situation in Vietnam and was first sent there by the *Monitor* in August 1967 to cover the South Vietnamese elections. After this she remained in the country as a special correspondent for the paper.

On 7 May 1970, Elizabeth was driving in Cambodia, reporting on the situation following the US invasion, with colleagues Richard Dudman of the *St Louis Post-Dispatch* and Michael Morrow of *Dispatch News Service International*. 'Don't shoot, we are international journalists,' shrieked Morrow when two men with rifles, one Vietnamese, one Cambodian, stepped from behind a tree and forced them to stop as they were driving along Highway One between Saigon and

Phnom Penh. What happened next was particularly shocking for Elizabeth because she considered herself 'a woman whose reporting in Vietnam has tended to be dispassionate rather than committed to a point of view,' she wrote afterwards. 'Personally I had been deeply dismayed by the American decision to send troops into Cambodia.'[46]

The three reporters were ordered to drop their belongings, empty their pockets and walk westwards with their hands in the air. When they were made to run, Elizabeth fell behind the others until she was lent a bicycle. Finally, they ended up at a village where they were searched and interrogated in an atmosphere of mounting hostility and turmoil, '... such that a kangaroo court could have flared up at any moment'.[47] Later, discussing those chaotic first few hours, one State Department official told her that possibly the only reason all three were not killed was the fact that one of the captives was a woman.[48]

But Elizabeth was not at first treated gently. Separated from her colleagues, she was left blindfolded in a room for crowds of people to come and jeer at her. However, after the first week the atmosphere grew more relaxed as the captors started to believe the three when they insisted that they were not spies but journalists, and objective ones at that. The reporters and their captors spent another month either playing chess or indulging in ideological discussions about the nature of revolution. Although they were well cared for, they were forced to travel a total of 200 miles and stay in ten different homes. Then, after five-and-a-half weeks, they were returned to Highway One and released.

In a series of subsequent articles, Elizabeth Pond questioned her luck. Since at least twenty other reporters were still missing in Cambodia, she felt that her own freedom posed 'serious moral issues for a journalist who has been released'.[49] The questions centred on the extent to which it was acceptable for the captives to compromise their own views to ensure their eventual safety. But she was adamant that the three of them never said anything they did not believe, nor were they ever asked to sign statements written by others. She concluded: 'There is no ethical code for journalists in situations of this sort, and I am not sure that any could be established.'[50]

Almost a year later Kate Webb, a New Zealander, suffered a similar fate. Kate started her working life in Australia writing about ANZAC troops being sent to Vietnam for the *Sydney Daily Mirror*. She believed that Australian and New Zealand coverage of the war was seriously inadequate since so many ANZAC lives were at risk. She determined to reach Saigon herself, optimistic that she would be offered journalistic

work once there. She saved enough money for the trip together with
living expenses and took what she thought would be a five-week
vacation. In Saigon, she pestered the UPI bureau chief to hire her as a
stringer, which, after giving her a number of odd jobs, he eventually
did. As she was hard-working, eager and spoke French, she soon
impressed the local team with her ability to cover political stories. In
November 1967, they sent her to Cambodia to cover Jackie Kennedy's
visit to Prince Sihanouk.

Nothing had prepared Kate for such a war and she was honest
about her reactions to it. As she told Phillip Knightley,

The first time I went out, there was a bit of a firefight, and I was so scared
that I wet my pants. I hoped the GIs would think that it was sweat and that
no one would notice. Then I saw that some of the GIs had wet pants, too,
and it didn't matter any more.[51]

By 1971, Kate had been promoted to Phnom Penh bureau chief.
One April day in 1971 she set off, with her interpreter and some
reservations, to investigate reports of a new offensive along Highway
Four. Suddenly a burst of gunfire came from all sides and they dived
into a ditch along with four other newsmen. Then they had to run
through the jungle and Kate felt embarrassed at her unsuitable clothes:
white jeans and a short-sleeved sweater.

At 11.30 a.m. the next day their hands shot up involuntarily as they
encountered the muzzles of two AK-47 assault rifles. The group were
then tied individually and roped together in a human chain and forced
to march. 'With six guards pushing us swiftly along a winding jungle
trail it was the worst of our many walks, which were never short. We
were still parched with thirst from our day of trying to elude the
Communists,' Kate wrote later.[52] The worst torment was that their
shoes were removed from them and Kate's feet soon became badly
bruised and lacerated. Eventually, they arrived in a North Vietnamese
mountain camp, where they set about the crucial task of persuading
their interrogators that they were journalists. Kate was both bored and
scared and in pain from her feet, although a young doctor did treat
her injuries.

When they asked her to describe the worst atrocities she had witnessed, she agonised over her response. She did not want to incrimi-
nate any of the other prisoners by writing about South Vietnamese
savageries nor did she want to provide her captors with propaganda;
but there was no point in antagonising them by recounting North
Vietnamese atrocities. Finally, she referred to My Lai, since the mass-

acre was already public knowledge. Kate found her constant interrogations tough and worrying, but she tried to tell her guards honestly what she believed in and to lend as much humour as she could to her answers. Within a short time she was weak, thin and suffering recurrent fever. In addition she needed tampons, a commodity the North Vietnamese were unable to supply. Puzzled by her demands, they supplied her with a field dressing and some white parachute silk.

After two weeks the US press reported Kate as dead since a body had been found and wrongly identified as hers. But on the day this article appeared, she and her five companions were released. After an elaborate ceremony, they had to endure two further nights of walking 'our march to freedom.'[53] They were set free finally along a lonely stretch of Highway Four – the same road on which they had first encountered captivity – just before dawn.

'We hurriedly shook hands with the Vietnamese and whispered farewells. "Tell the truth about us," our guards said, and melted into the dark.'[54]

Kate went to Hong Kong to recuperate not only from her badly damaged feet but also from malaria. However, by September she was back at her desk in Phnom Penh. In an interview shortly afterwards she remarked: 'I still don't lean towards one side or the other in this war. My reaction is a woman's reaction: how very sad it all is, what a bloody awful waste.'[55]

17

Equal Opportunities

'You can't betray the strains you are under.'
PATRICIA CLOUGH

Newspaper, television and radio editors of the 1970s, confronted by the daughters of the post-war bulge flooding on to the job market, found that most of them were strident, determined, confident and, above all, well-qualified. In addition, they were now backed by vociferous support groups such as Women in Media, set up in 1970, arguing not only for equal pay but also for much wider opportunities for women to progress in all parts of the media.

Although since its founding in 1907 the journalists' trade union had specified in its rule book equal treatment for both sexes, too many women had found this not to be the case. By the early 1970s, they were not afraid to argue their case in public and hardly a day passed when the subject of sex discrimination in general was out of the newspapers. None the less, in spite of intense lobbying for a change in the law, old prejudices were slow to die among men and women and the law did not reflect the new attitudes until 1975.

Cecil King, a key figure in Fleet Street for many years, believed that 'an influx of women journalists, photographers and executives would give the national press a new look and a new lease of life'. None the less King, a former director of the *Daily Mirror* and, since 1963, chairman of IPC which controlled the *Daily Mirror*, the *Sun* and the *People*, felt in 1972 that 'ordinary news reporting is a hard life for anyone and perhaps too hard for women'. Explaining his view to a group of women journalists, he said that for women the news of interest was personal or expressed in personal terms: for example, a general election would be reported by a woman as Heath vs. Wilson not Conservatism vs. Socialism. However, he commented that human stories were much more popular with readers than political stories. 'People sometimes say that this view of women's attitudes is contemptuous or at least patronising. This is not so; it is merely realistic.'[1]

Some women, too, still had their doubts. In an article welcoming the new possibilities opened up by local commercial radio stations, Jill Evans, a producer for BBC Radio London of a programme called *Women in Town*, wrote that even in local radio few women were attracted to news. 'The reasons are complex,' she argued, 'but it may be that many women like to be able to plan their day in advance, which you cannot do with news. They may also prefer to delve long and hard into a subject, an interview or a person, concentrating on the human interest.'[2]

Olga Franklin, the veteran writer and broadcaster, was convinced that,

in my business they discriminate in *favour* of women.... If an editor has to choose between his best woman reporter and his best man for an exciting assignment, say, a visit to Stalin or to cover a Kennedy assassination... he will choose the woman. For obvious reasons her story, even if it's weaker, will have that much edge over a rival paper's story. It is more of a talking-point for everyone; it is more daring, more dashing (and some readers like it chatty). If the girl happens to be good-looking that is an added bonus, whereas the male reporter's appearance is hardly newsworthy.[3]

Olga, although small and plump herself, could speak with the voice of authority. In 1939, at the outset of war, she had begun her journalistic career with a junior position at Reuters. She was fluent in several languages, including Russian, and soon moved on to the *Oxford Mail*, followed by the *Newcastle Evening Chronicle*, the *Daily Graphic* and the *Daily Sketch*, before settling at the *Daily Mail* in 1956. There she remained until 1971, with her own column called 'Frankly Yours'. But at the time of her tirade against Women in Media, she was freelancing and writing books.

Olga knew that she was courting trouble when she insisted that a girl who enters journalism can hardly go wrong.

She may make a quick killing and marry the editor; she may land Gregory Peck like the French girl reporter, or President Kennedy like Jacqueline Onassis, or end up with Anthony Crosland like Susan Barnes.... Or perhaps, most unfair of all, she may rise straight from the top editor's bed into Fleet Street, with hardly any qualifications at all, as I did myself, and as I know some of my colleagues also did (but I do not want to libel anybody).

According to Olga, it was not absolutely essential to be pretty. Even plain girls got noticed or, being fewer, stood out from the rest.

At all the big political or international conferences I always felt sorry for the men reporters. They never stood a chance. It was always the girls who caught the eye of Khrushchev or Kennedy or of the cameramen and TV crews.... But the nice thing about men is that they bear no grudge, no malice, no spite. 'Good luck to her,' they say. They don't even see that once again, they have been discriminated against.[4]

Not surprisingly, Women in Media were disdainful of such comments. In a letter signed by Anne Sharpley, Mary Kenny, Mary Holland, Margaret Howard, Jill Tweedie, Mary Stott and Joan Shenton, criticising Franklin's 'tiresomely silly piece', they pointed out how the popular image of the Ace Girl Reporter or the Glamorous Women's Magazine Editor had done much to obscure the real discrimination that most women working on newspapers suffered and to prevent women from wielding real power at high editorial level.

The profile of women in journalism is, in fact, remarkably similar to the profile of women in professions such as medicine or the law; some individuals succeed but, for the majority, a special ghetto has been carved out for females which means that they may participate at a certain level but they stick where it doesn't matter.[5]

In 1975, the British Parliament passed the country's first Sex Discrimination Act and, at the same time, the five-year-old Equal Pay Act became enforceable. Women in Media, which by then numbered more than three hundred members, had worked hard to promote these reforms and now organised a writers' co-operative venture and an information pool. It also set up an offshoot group women's lobby and worked with existing women's rights organisations to run an advisory centre for women and to produce a regular news report. In spite of these efforts and the change in the law, nine years later, when a subsequent survey was conducted, Fleet Street remained a male preserve. At the *Guardian*, for example, out of thirty-five general news reporters only nine were women; at the *Daily Mirror* there were three women general news reporters out of thirty-two; at the *Sunday Times* there was not one woman in the general news reporting team of nine and of eight foreign reporters only two were female. Bleakest of all was the picture at the *Sun*, whose team of forty general news reporters included just three women while its fifty-five sports reporters were all male. The *Financial Times* employed thirty-seven women out of a staff complement of 300, but only one of the thirty-seven was in a position to oversee other journalists.[6]

In spite of such statistics, few women were deterred from trying to work as reporters and there was, as ever, scope for talented individuals. Notwithstanding Jill Evans's observations, local radio was the single most important factor in opening the floodgates for potential women reporters. By 1970, there were still only a dozen stations (twenty years later there were 200), but the number was rising steadily and all of them needed staffing. Editors were desperately looking for large numbers of people, most of whom, it was accepted, would not already be trained. Women seized the opportunity and usually found themselves working in newsrooms where the atmosphere was much freer than at the BBC and where those in charge generally did not take the traditional view of who was, or was not, a suitable person to be working in a news operation.

As the younger generation emerged, a few old hands found that being a pre-war star reporter could not guarantee success for life in this fiercely competitive era. Hilde Marchant, after a stint at the *Daily Mirror*, had joined *Picture Post* as a staff writer. The magazine suited her style as she could produce articles of depth and detail which had never been possible in her newspaper days. But the growth of nationwide television put *Picture Post* out of business in June 1957 and Hilde, in poor health and suffering from a lifetime's excess of alcohol, became a pathetic 'has been'. The enormous courage she displayed in wartime London now seemed to have abandoned her and she was often to be seen at the bus stop outside St Bride's Church in Fleet Street, if she could afford the fare; or, more commonly, her elderly, bedraggled figure was spotted staggering up Fleet Street to the Wig and Pen Club. Sometimes she begged money off her old friends, most of whom did not recognise her at first, so wizened and frail had she become. Anything they might have given her was spent immediately at the Wig and Pen, where the proprietor, who had admired her journalism, was kind and hospitable to her.

If former colleagues tried to draw her out, she declined to answer their questions or tell them where she lived. 'Her one evident desire, to be anonymous to her past,' Bernard Hall concluded.[7] On 3 February 1970, she collapsed under a railway arch, where she was found hours later and taken to Charing Cross Hospital. There she died, destitute. Although she had married a journalist called Cyril James, there was no family to pay for or to organise her funeral; staff on the *Express* and other colleagues from better times chipped in to a fund so that Hilde Marchant could, at least, be decently buried.

Another sad and lonely death of a once great reporter occurred a year later. On 5 July 1971, Elizabeth Wiskemann, aged seventy, committed suicide because she feared that she was going blind and would no longer be able to read and write. Elizabeth, referred to in obituaries as a scholar-journalist, was also historian, author, diplomat and travel writer. In 1965, she received an honorary degree from Oxford University and was described as a 'Cassandra who had lived to record the war she had foretold'. After the Second World War, she had taken up an appointment as Rome correspondent for the *Economist*, but relinquished this in order to write a book about Italy. In 1958, she was appointed Montague Burton Professor of International Relations at Edinburgh University and, in 1961, Tutor in Modern European History at the University of Sussex. From 1945 until her death, she contributed to a variety of journals and newspapers as well as writing books and travelling widely.

Although she did not marry, she was rarely short of friends and had several affairs. Those who knew her well believe that the commitment of marriage scared her because it implied a loss of independence; given her overriding fear of being controlled, this was insupportable for her and explains why her suffering at the end was so intense. 'Perhaps she never found a man who appreciated her for what she was,' believes Franca Magnani, the journalist and writer who was a lifelong friend.[8] 'She could be pretty and delightful and very feminine but, above all, she had a great charm which she sometimes had to use to hide her intelligence in front of men.'[9]

But many veteran women reporters who had made their names in the Second World War were still active in the 1970s and in demand for their wisdom and experience. Clare Hollingworth went to Peking in February 1973 as the first *Daily Telegraph* resident staff correspondent in China. Being there at such a pivotal time in the nation's history gave her a lasting interest in and deep understanding of the country. So much so that when Mrs Thatcher, as Leader of the Opposition, was considering whether to pay a visit to China in 1975, Clare was consulted.

Although Clare returned to London in 1976 as the *Sunday Telegraph*'s defence correspondent, the Far East remained her favourite area of study. For the past few years she has spent at least six months writing and lecturing in Hong Kong, and making regular forays into China. The rest of her time is divided between France and England.

With her global outlook and wide experience she is saddened by what
she perceives as a lack of interest in foreign news today. 'There seems
to be a concentration on one big story with very little about the Far
East or India in the British press. We shouldn't be looking at the world
through such narrow spectacles.'[10]

Martha Gellhorn published nothing from January 1969 to May
1975. Anguished by the suffering she knew to be happening in South
Vietnam, she was afflicted by

a writer's block made of solid concrete.... Not that I spent those years in a
dark room with my face turned to the wall. I spent them like a Mexican
jumping bean bouncing around for no reason except perpetual motion to
Turkey, Greece, Russia, Denmark, Holland, Sweden, Italy, Switzerland,
Yugoslavia, France, Costa Rica, Malta, always to Africa, always in and out of
London, where I bought a flat with a view, still my one durable base.[11]

In desperation, rather late in life, Martha even took cookery lessons.
Suddenly, when the war in Vietnam was over, her life picked up and
she started writing again – books at first, then articles. When Franco's
death was only hours away, the editor of *New York Magazine* asked
her if she wanted to go to Spain. 'There was no assignment I wanted
more; there was nobody I wanted dead more than Franco.'[12]

On the day Franco died, 20 November 1975, Martha Gellhorn
returned to Madrid and wrote a vividly nostalgic piece for *New York
Magazine*. Staying, 'for memory's sake', at the Palace Hotel, she could
hardly believe that it had been the largest military hospital in Madrid
with piles of used bandages in the corridors and blood on the marble
steps.

The clientele was very young then, though pain ages the face, and wore
shabby pyjamas, scraps of uniform.... The surgeons used to work by
the light of two cut-glass chandeliers. Fancy Edwardian show cabinets, for
displaying jewelry and crocodile handbags, held their tools. The room seemed
to have vanished. Then, while watching Franco's funeral in the walnut-
panelled TV room, I stretched back to rest from that curious TV spectacular
and saw above me the chandeliers and the stained glass skylight and knew
this was it. In this room, filled with Franco's devoted followers – old men
wiping their eyes at the sight of the coffin, ladies sniffling into delicate
handkerchiefs – soldiers of the Spanish Republic had pieces of steel cut from
their bodies, had their legs and arms amputated.[13]

Martha's filmic technique worked brilliantly. She moved on, after
reminding a new generation of readers of the devastation and suffering
in Madrid in 1937, to a discussion of the future of Spain without

Franco. In the course of a few weeks she spoke to Basque shopkeepers, Jesuit priests, active communists and a right-wing industrialist opponent of Franco's regime who was confident democracy would come to Spain. Only when she found a grey-haired taxi driver who had fought in and was wounded in the Civil War did she feel at home again, 'and after that I talked to all grey-haired taxi drivers and they had all been in the war and we were instant friends'.[14]

Far from diminishing as she grew older, Martha's sense of passionate outrage increased with age. 'Infuriating and shabby' was how she described the 1980s. 'I can think of at least six more adjectives but might then give the impression of foaming at the mouth.'[15] She fulminated against both Ronald Reagan and Margaret Thatcher in equal measure, both of whom she described as 'apostles of the belligerent Selfish Society.... But there are gallant generous-minded minorities, in both countries, who fight defensive actions against the worst abuses of Thatcherism and Reaganism, and I put my hope in them.'[16]

Martha's most important piece of reportage in this period concerned torture in El Salvador. She visited the country in 1983 and wrote a piece for *Granta* based on a document given to her by the Commission of Human Rights of El Salvador detailing the unbelievable torments inflicted on a young Salvadoran called Miguel. It was a powerful, sickening piece in which she explained how the previous year the Human Rights Commission recorded the fate of 6,952 Salvadorans who were seized, disappeared or assassinated. This document concerned just one victim and was unique because the victim survived to tell his tale.

Shocking though that was, Martha admitted that some of the worst violations perpetrated against him were unprintable. Not for the first time Martha had used her reporting skills to inform the world of facts they preferred not to see. But this was one occasion when she wished she were more famous,

to use fame as a means of being heard.... I wished I had the VIP standing to call a press conference and talk of Miguel's testimony and of thousands of others who could not testify condemning with all my force the Salvadoran Government and its support by the American Government.[17]

By this time, aged seventy-five, Martha lived mostly in Wales in a cottage amid serene and hilly farming country. She wrote about British society whenever her temper was aroused, as it was for the women of Greenham Common – 'I am dazzled by their fortitude' – or on behalf of the striking British miners in 1984–5. 'The TV strike spectacular made me sick at heart,' she explained. 'Britain was going down the drain, had become as mean and nasty as anywhere else.'[18]

Finding herself merely an hour's drive away from a coal mine, she went to talk to the Welsh miners and their wives, introducing herself merely as a foreign journalist who lived in Britain. The resulting piece, printed in the *Guardian* on 'the unimportant women's page', asked whether anyone had thought about coal and the future. 'The next generation may regard as madness the stockpiling of indestructible deadly nuclear waste, and demand coal – but where will the miners be found, a vanishing species?'[19]

Martha's erstwhile colleague, Virginia Cowles, had also been unable to resist the lure of Spain without Franco. After her marriage to Aidan Crawley she gave up reporting in favour of supporting her husband's political career, bringing up their three children, and producing an impressive array of biographies – including one, in 1949, of Winston Churchill which won her much acclaim. In the 1950s and 1960s, she and her husband travelled the world together, making documentary films mostly about the developing Commonwealth countries and then, from 1974, they divided their time between London, France, Spain and Italy.

But for some years Virginia had been noticeably short of breath. Emphysema had been diagnosed and, too late, she gave up smoking. In 1983, her doctor warned her that she had only weeks to live. They were in Spain, driving one day from Madrid to Bordeaux, when she asked to leave the main road and go via Sierra Guadarama, which she had known during the Spanish Civil War. This entailed a diversion along narrow, twisting roads, but eventually they stopped in Biarritz for lunch. Their journey resumed, and Virginia fell asleep. The car hit a bump, a soft patch, and turned over. Crawley, who was half-conscious and had badly damaged his neck, managed to lift Virginia on to the back seat only to realise that there was no hope for her. She had been killed instantly by a brain haemorrhage. It was a tragic end to a brilliant career.

Typical of the new breed of university-educated reporters, prepared to put career before marriage and work abroad alone, was Patricia Clough. Patricia read languages at Bristol University and was near fluent in French and German. On leaving she applied for a job with Reuters, but was told to return in a year with more experience. The latter she duly gained at the *Bolton Evening News* as a cub reporter and then, a year later, reapplied to Reuters. This time she was told that Reuters had a job for only one woman reporter, covering fashion shows, weddings and royal babies; however, as the woman reporter thus employed was on leave for a year, she could have the job on a temporary basis. This was in 1960 and Patricia, aged twenty-two, was thrilled. In fact, when the other woman came back, Reuters found space for them both. After two years, she applied for a posting abroad and was sent to Geneva – at the same time turning down a proposal of marriage because she was determined to develop her career first. After a year and a half she moved to Bonn, where the main stories she covered were the Queen's visit and the Auschwitz trials. She recalls a typical incident when Chris Bonington and Dougal Haston were climbing the north face of the Eiger. The pack of reporters at the bottom, impatiently waiting for days, started to climb up to meet them. Patricia was wearing the wrong shoes and kept slipping, so one of the sweaty mountaineers picked her up and carried her back down on top of his rucksack. As soon as she could, Patricia dictated a story, recounting Bonington and Haston's exploits, but her bureau chief put his own gloss on events. The story that went out on the Reuters' wires led with how, after a perilous climb of the Eiger, a British mountaineer carried a woman reporter down. The female reporter was still a significant aspect of her own stories.

After eighteen months in Bonn, Patricia was posted to Rome in 1966, quickly learning Italian and getting a grasp on relations between Church and State to handle the many stories about divorce, abortion and the Vatican at that time. But soon after marrying an Italian journalist and the birth of their daughter in 1971, she had to leave Reuters – the nightshifts and weekend work were unacceptable to her husband – and started freelancing for the *Baltimore Sun*, *The Times* and the BBC. As her marriage rapidly deteriorated so work became increasingly important. She soon realised that she could not patch up the relationship and that it was time to leave and take her young daughter with her. She set up on her own in Rome. 'As a middle-class English girl who was not geared to standing up for herself, I learned through this experience to fight and get enough income to stand alone.' Faced with the responsibility of earning enough to support her child as well as herself (although she received some maintenance from her husband), Patricia ended up working harder than ever especially over the summer months, when everyone else was away. On one occasion, she found herself feeding Italian news to a major chunk of the British media.

After eleven years in Rome, *The Times* invited Patricia to become its correspondent in Bonn. An appointment as bureau chief in a major European capital was a tempting offer for a woman still under forty. But if she took her daughter out of the country, she knew that she would, henceforth, be solely responsible for each of their upkeep. What followed was unquestionably the toughest period of her life. 'I worked so hard – harder than I needed to – it was a very challenging job and at the same time I was trying to be the full-time mother of a small child. I don't know how I did it; it's just that when you have to, you do,' she recalls today.[20]

Patricia remembers many agonising moments when she was under tremendous pressure at work, writing to a deadline, but would have to go out in the middle of the story to deliver her child somewhere and then return to the office to file:

You just can't tell London what is going on in your life, you can't betray the strains you are under and say 'I don't want to go to Munich because my child is sickening for something', so you just go ... but I remember feeling absolutely fraught the whole time and a couple of times at least I forgot to collect her, after Brownies I think.[21]

Then after five years in Bonn, *The Times* closed down for a year. Patricia had been due to leave Bonn in any case but when the newspaper started up again, rescued by Rupert Murdoch, she was offered the number two position in the Washington office. This she turned down, thinking that, after running her own office, it would be difficult to be anyone's deputy. Instead, she was sent back to London, where she found herself doing a number of home-based reporters' jobs which were even less to her satisfaction. For four years she wrote 'mindless stuff about Princess Diana and spotted socks', desperate to earn enough to pay for her child's education yet longing for the day when she could report something exciting again.

Meanwhile in Rome, after twenty years' reporting from trouble spots around the world, Claire Sterling was now involved in investigative research for books. *The Reporter* magazine, short of funds, had folded in 1968 and Claire, who had covered North and West Africa, the Middle East, Czechoslovakia, Poland and western Europe, was worried that she would never again find such a sympathetic job. Instead, she used her reporting skills to write what she called mystery thrillers with political implications. Her first was a study of the Czech leader, Jan Masaryk, in which she tried to discover the truth about his death in 1948. She interviewed several people in Prague, including Masaryk's nieces, who had not talked about his death for twenty years.

But this became increasingly difficult after the Soviet invasion of Prague and when one of her interviewees went to gaol shortly after their meeting, Claire decided to rely on Czech exiles in Europe for information. The book, published in 1969,* was enough of a success to convince her to continue with this form of extended reportage. She had never been happy under the pressure of a daily deadline and working for *The Reporter* had enabled her to spend several days at a time on one story.

Claire believed that she had two valuable assets which would help her with future in-depth reporting for books; one was her knowledge of the workings of communism, which enabled her in the Masaryk book to understand how the 1948 coup had been mounted. 'It was an area where my own early experience gave me extremely valuable keys.' The other advantage was in being female:

In spite of some extremely unpleasant encounters, being a woman has been much more of a help than a hindrance to me, even in Arab countries. Most of my interlocutors did not think that a woman had any political brain or was capable of understanding what they were talking about. I am a very good listener – an ability I have developed over the years – and am capable of sitting for hours listening to a useless, droning conversation. In all this I can say how interesting and let them talk with one ear half open in case a single word might drop which is useful to me. I'm constantly amazed at how much people will tell you when they don't have to.[22]

Elizabeth Pond found exactly the same male assumptions working to her advantage in Japan when she overheard some sensitive telephone conversations in Diet offices that MPs and their staff would never have conducted in front of a male reporter.

Recognising this critical advantage Claire Sterling spent the 1970s and 1980s engaged in writing books about international terrorism, the plot to kill the Pope in 1981 and the Mafia; these involved her in years of painstaking research, some danger, much fame and considerable unwelcome controversy.

She insists that the research is the pleasurable part and that, especially in the case of the Mafia, she was given many details by adherents 'because it wouldn't cross their minds that a woman was capable of writing anything about the Mafia that was not soppy, sentimental trash'.[23] Nor did she believe that she was exposing herself unduly to danger because she kept a low profile, documented everything she wrote about and did not betray secrets. Her book on terrorism

* Claire Sterling, *The Masaryk Case* (Harper & Row, 1969).

caused her more worry and while writing this she was forced to take precautions such as changing airline tickets at the last minute and using false names in hotels. But the aspect of her work that she finds hardest to bear are allegations that she is a CIA agent, involved through her reporting in some high-level, right-wing, worldwide strategy. 'The whole purpose of my professional life has been to write as honestly as possible and to be as totally independent of any political pressure as I could be and to be able to uncover stories. I have been my own boss, able to choose my own sources and able to write things which have proved to be true; that is my pride and so to be attacked there is where it hurts most,' she said recently.[24] Her work as a reporter has, of course, left her with a tough outer shell. None the less, she concedes that she has been deeply hurt by such accusations, recognising that some mud always sticks.

18

Modern Times

'Most people would rather talk to a woman.'
EDIE LEDERER

In the 1990s, the majority of trainee journalists are women. Whereas in 1981/2 forty-one per cent of all entrants into newspaper journalism were women, ten years later this figure had risen to fifty-two per cent. Radio and television however, rather than print journalism, seem to hold particular appeal for women; at some colleges which specialise in broadcast journalism women fill as many as eighty per cent of the places. There are now women bureau chiefs, women 'firemen' reporters – home-based to be catapulted into the world's major trouble spots – and women general reporters, who are expected to cover every story from a financial crisis to a soccer match, from murder to civil war. There are still women who report on the fashion scene and write features about family life, but there are also men who do that today.

Women have been particularly successful as newsreaders – something which seemed impossible until recently as women, it was believed, could never have the gravitas to convey important news. But in spite of the success of such women as Sue Carpenter and Carol Barnes of ITN, and Francine Stock and Sue Cameron of *Newsnight* who conduct interviews and report the news in addition to merely reading it, they are still subjected to magazine articles which discuss how they look. According to one critique, in order to look 'serious', women involved in news on television are virtually forced to cut their hair into a severe helmet shape. 'Hat hair is a definite anchorwoman stamp,' the article explained, blaming the whole process on Angela Rippon, one of the first successful British anchorwomen, who 'was so determined to look serious that the hairspray seemed to have been applied right over her facial muscles'.[1]

Individual women have reached some of the highest positions in the world of news. Jenny Abramsky has been BBC Radio's editor of news and current affairs since 1987. Diane Nelmes, appointed editor in 1992 of the current affairs programme, *World in Action*, amid a welter of publicity, was a few months later promoted to take charge of all Granada Television's factual programmes from current affairs to sport, positioning her as one of the most powerful women in independent television. Three national newspapers have, or have had, women editors: Eve Pollard, first at the *Sunday Mirror*, then at the *Sunday Express*, Patsy Chapman at the *News of the World* and Wendy Henry at the *People*; and, at the end of 1992, two of the BBC's five controllers were women: Frances Line at Radio Two and Pat Ewing at Radio Five.

The obvious success of talented individuals such as these helps explain the dramatic rise in the number of female applications to journalism courses. The glamorous few attract, magnet-like, the as yet unfocused school-leavers. Yet in spite of the large numbers of women recruited, there has, as in most other fields, traditionally been a significant fall-out rate somewhere between the usual child-bearing ages of twenty-four and thirty-four. And although it may be generally agreed that there is no longer anything in the field of news which women are not able to cover, there are still few of them at the top. No 'serious' British newspaper has yet appointed a woman editor, and the BBC, having set up a Corporate Equality Department in 1990, has difficulties in persuading enough women to enter news reporting at a senior level.

The BBC aim is to raise the number of women in senior management from ten to thirty per cent and in middle management from eighteen to forty per cent. It is targeting that, by 1996, sixty-six out of the top 200 jobs will be filled by women. Yet in spite of this positive approach, those involved in recruiting women as reporters at a senior level find that the majority of applicants for these jobs are still men. The reasons are not clear, but informal discussions have revealed that too many women are still put off by what they perceive as the cut-throat nature of the news business, which, they fear, would be incompatible with personal and domestic responsibilities. There is also a belief among some women that BBC news demands a commitment above and beyond what they could possibly give.

A BBC spokesman pointed out that these perceptions were no longer valid and that the Corporation has been making strenuous efforts, at least in the last two years, to make it easier for women with children to drop everything and rush off to cover a disaster. There is an emergency childcare scheme, which offers qualified nannies to take over at a moment's notice, term-time working (available to both women and men) and some job sharing. Yet, so far, few women reporters have taken advantage of these schemes, perhaps frightened that to do so might lead to repercussions on their careers, while other women are known to delay having a baby for several years for the same reason.

In 1992, Anna Ford, one of the BBC's most outspoken newscasters, attacked the Corporation for failing to take its women journalists seriously. Ford, a presenter of the Six O'Clock News, was particularly critical of the fact that there was no BBC anchorwoman in the studio during the 1992 general election campaign coverage. 'I thought it was perfectly disgraceful,' she said. 'We make up fifty-two per cent of the population. We might have put different questions from those of the middle-aged, middle-class, white, Anglo-Saxon Protestant men.'[2]

Anna was publicly supported by the BBC's social affairs editor, Polly Toynbee, who agreed that women were side-lined on important news stories in what was still a male-dominated profession. Perhaps the real issue here is why there are so few women news editors at the BBC. At the end of 1992, out of eleven editor/managers in the reporters' area, only one was a woman. Yet it is these people who make crucial decisions both about long-term strategy and short-term coverage.

Notwithstanding the validity of Anna Ford's comments, male bastions are crumbling all the time. War apart, two areas of reporting which have been particularly slow to accept women are sport and politics. Women's ability to report on parliamentary matters was extremely restricted even after they received the vote in 1918 and in spite of Emillie Peacocke's breakthrough in 1906. Reporters who sat in the Press Gallery were highly regarded among their peers and women, it was believed, simply did not possess the necessary acumen and grasp of political affairs. In 1984, Julia Langdon became the first woman political editor in Fleet Street when Robert Maxwell appointed her at the *Daily Mirror*, fulfilling something of Northcliffe's original vision for the paper. Julia had started her journalistic training aged seventeen at the *Portsmouth Evening News*, but made her reputation at *Labour Weekly*, where she was the main news reporter for six years, building an impressive armoury of contacts. In between she worked at the *Guardian* in the number two position as political correspondent.

Working for Maxwell was extremely stimulating. 'He was an easy man to manipulate because he was so vain... he liked women and especially intelligent women. I got on with him because I stood up to him and never wrote anything I didn't want to say.'[3] From 1986 to 1987, Julia was the first woman to chair the 102-year-old lobby group in Parliament. At the end of that year, aged thirty-nine, she had her first child and, to her relief, found Maxwell 'a very good equal opportunity employer. I was on full pay for almost as long as I wanted.' But in 1989 she moved on to become political editor of the right-wing *Sunday Telegraph*, keen to show that being a member of the Labour Party did not cloud her reporting skills. Two years later she discovered that she was pregnant again, aged forty-five, only this time she was not able to return to the same job quite so easily. She admits that being pregnant in her mid-forties sapped her energy, but believes that her absence gave the management an opportunity to run the department with someone younger, cheaper and less experienced.

Today Julia juggles with two young children and a variety of free-lance political reporting jobs from home, including some television work and 'Crossbencher' at the *Sunday Express*.

Working in British politics is particularly difficult for women with children because of parliamentary hours; nothing happens until about 3.30 p.m., which is just when children return home. There is reform in the air, largely as a result of pressure from women MPs who want more morning sessions. Yet, according to Julia, there is one advantage of being a woman political reporter: male MPs, who are alone for weeks on end, are more than happy to go out for dinner just to talk. 'Men turn to you because you're brought up to be a good listener. It's very respectable.'[4]

Julia Langdon's career was paralleled by another woman, Elinor Goodman, formerly at the *Financial Times* until her appointment as political editor at Channel Four. In the 1980s, Langdon and Goodman were often the only two women political reporters in the corridors of Westminster – although by the 1990s there are more. Physically, they do not resemble each other yet several male MPs regularly confused them. 'It's such a man's world that we were treated as one – rather like being Japanese in a western society,' Julia comments wrily.

There is, of course, no obvious reason why women should not be as adept at describing a sporting event as men, yet sports reporting has proved a particularly vicious arena for women in the last fifteen years. Women claim that unless they are allowed equal access to men's changing-rooms immediately after a match, they are being denied equal access to the best quotes, always made in the heat of the moment, and put at an impossible disadvantage in their trade. For many years, women sportswriters had been content with cajoling individual players, wrapped in a towel, out into a corridor for a few hurried quotes. But it soon became clear that this method, or else lying in wait for the clean, showered team on their way home when they were too tired to say anything of note, was not comparable to the atmosphere and excitement their male colleagues could conjure up from being in the locker-rooms.

Twelve years ago in the United States, where the issue is particularly virulent, a Federal judge ruled that women sportswriters had a constitutional right to go into the locker-rooms as long as they did not mind the nudity. This followed a case brought by Melissa Ludtke, a young reporter for *Sports Illustrated*, and her employer, *Time* Inc., claiming that Miss Ludtke had been excluded from the clubhouses during the 1977 World Series and that the exclusion had been based solely on her sex, thus violating her right to pursue her profession under the equal protection and due process clauses of the Fourteenth Amendment.

However, winning the court decision was not the open sesame women sports reporters had hoped for. Many male columnists subsequently accused women reporters of wanting to get into the locker-rooms mainly to ogle naked athletes. One male sportswriter suggested publicly on television that women sportswriters gave sexual favours to athletes as a means of getting news. B. J. Phillips, a female sportswriter who had reported from Vietnam, Ireland and the Middle East before she covered sport, commented in 1979: 'It kills me that my peers treat women writers with an attitude that says they're something between a pariah and a sex-crazed thrill seeker. It hurts privately. I don't think anybody knows the price we're paying.'[5]

Some ten years later, the issue flared up again when Lisa Olson, a twenty-six-year-old reporter for the *Boston Herald*, claimed that she had suffered sexual harassment in a locker-room of one of America's professional football teams. She described graphically how she was sitting on a bench after a game when five naked players came by and positioned their genitals close to her face and made lewd suggestions. 'A couple of players had decided to teach me a lesson,' Lisa said afterwards.[6] 'That if I was going to be in their locker-room they were going to give me what they thought I was in there for.' She said that several players were egging on one player to insult her saying, 'Give her what she wants, make her look, that is what she is here for.'[7] The issue now has become whether it is fair to send male or female reporters to interview naked athletes.

In England, the locker-room battle has been waged more gently. In 1973 one editor, explaining why he preferred to hire men, said that he needed journalists who could cover every story: 'We tend to ration ourselves simply because women are not interested in sport and sport has to be covered in some places as part of the normal routine.'[8] Adrianne Blue was an American reporter for *Time Out*, who had written a number of profiles of sports personalities and was particularly known for her coverage of motor-cycle racing. In 1978, the magazine asked her to interview the English cricket captain, Mike Brearley. As she knew nothing about the game she decided to take along a cricket expert. She had arranged with Brearley in advance that she would meet him in the locker-rooms at Lord's after the match, but when she presented herself the officials refused to let her in, insisting that 'ladies' were not allowed. Blue explained that Brearley himself had authorised it and eventually they gave way. 'It was a fascinating sight; there were all these naked and steaming bodies either emerging from or going into the shower but I backed out and we had the interview somewhere else more convenient,' Adrianne recalled.[9] Inadvertently she had become the first woman, let alone woman sportswriter, to enter the men's locker-rooms at Lord's. 'I could have stayed if I'd wanted, but I didn't see the issue as a matter of principle.' The resulting article, however, reached only as far as the lay-out stage since a strike at *Time Out* prevented publication. Shortly after, Adrianne went to work for the *Sunday Times* as its motor-cycle racing correspondent and began to cover other 'macho male sports' such as weight-lifting, judo and athletics, 'because I didn't want to get stuck in the women's ghetto'. She had more than a passing interest in sport generally and what she did not know she soon learned from reading books, on-the-job training and asking questions, 'which is what we were trained for'.[10]

Being a woman reporting male sports was, she considers, an advantage because men 'may talk to you as an imbecile but they give you lots of fascinating background information assuming you know nothing'. Today, Adrianne specialises in writing about women and sport because, she believes, 'the great sports story of the nineties is the emergence of women champions'.

Four women reporters working today who have broken through the serried ranks to reach the top of their profession are Edith (Edie) M. Lederer of Associated Press, Patricia Clough at *The Independent*, Diana

Goodman of BBC Radio News and Kate Adie, chief news correspondent, BBC Television.

In 1975, Edie became the first woman to head a foreign bureau for
AP when she was appointed to Peru. But that assignment lasted only
five months as she was expelled by Peru's military government for
reporting on a failed military exercise. She was subsequently sent to
run the Caribbean bureau and, in 1991, was named AP's bureau chief
in Dhahran during the Gulf War. She celebrated her twenty-fifth
anniversary with the agency in Kuwait City, cutting a celebration cake
with the bayonet of an AK-47 rifle.

Edie joined AP in March 1966 after gaining a Bachelor's degree
from Cornell University and a Master's in Communications Studies
from Stanford. Before that, she had travelled around Europe and spent
time working on the *San Francisco Chronicle and Examiner*. She is
petite (5'1"), blonde and glamorous to the point of maintaining her
beautifully painted nails even in wartime. She always wanted to be a
journalist, assuming that she would specialise in women's issues as
there were few opportunities for women who wanted to write hard
news. However, she found herself 'hooked' on hard news. 'I think I
was very lucky; at the time I started, the news business in America
was very dominated by men but women's liberation was fortuitous for
me because I was given plenty of good stories.'[11]

This being the late 1960s, her work included reporting riots, demonstrations and political gatherings. Then, in October 1972, aged
twenty-nine, she was assigned to Saigon. Edie had always wanted to
go overseas as a foreign correspondent but knew that she could not
until she had worked on the foreign desk. This appeared to be impossible since women were never appointed to the foreign desk. The
Saigon bureau chief managed to circumvent this rule by insisting on
having a woman work full time in Vietnam.

Edie's mother was distraught. 'But I wrote her a letter explaining
how it was the biggest story of the decade, or more, and that it was an
incredible opportunity which I was not going to miss.' Recognising
how little her education and upbringing had prepared her for war, she
went for two days to the Moffat naval base to study aeroplanes,
warships and guns, learning to fire both a 38 and 45 calibre pistol
before she left the States.

One year later she was plunged into her second bout of hostilities
when she was sent to report the Yom Kippur War from Egypt and
Syria. She was extremely close to some of the major tank battles
throughout, but when the war ended and Israel and Egypt were due

to sign a peace treaty, she was aware that being a woman reporter could be a distinct advantage. The Israeli military had agreed to fly some journalists down to cover the peace negotiations. Edie and another AP colleague duly reported to the aircraft, but when a rival agency complained at there being two of them she was told she would have to get off as she did not speak Hebrew. 'As I was walking away', Edie recalled, 'the cockpit door opened and the pilot motioned me to come up and sit there. He was great; when we landed, he wouldn't open the back door for the others until I'd got out. He wanted me standing there when it opened and refused to tell them how I'd got there.'[12]

From 1978 to 1981, Edie was based in Hong Kong and in June 1980, six months after the Soviet invasion of Afghanistan, she disguised herself as a rug buyer in order to get into the country and report on events. In 1982, she joined AP's London staff and has been constantly on the move since then. She covered the Falklands War and in 1989 returned to Afghanistan, where she experienced one of the most frightening experiences of her professional life. She was in her hotel room, writing about the rocketing of Kabul, when a powerful rocket ripped through the roof of the building and started a fire within minutes.

A wide variety of stories followed, from the Romanian revolution to the marriage of the Duke and Duchess of York and then, in October 1990, after undergoing compulsory US physical fitness training, she was sent to the Gulf for five-and-a-half months. This was the first major US military venture since Vietnam and, to Edie, one of the most incredible aspects was that every single major news organisation in the US had sent at least one woman in a very senior position. In contrast to Vietnam this was not just because they were women,

but because they were good... : . The *Washington Post* had three women out of a staff of four. British news organisations don't do that and it's very noticeable. Women journalists in Britain simply have not come as far as we have in the US and they are still the exception rather than the rule.[13]

Edie was the only woman in the Gulf who had also reported Vietnam, a fact which made life easier for her. 'When I was out in the field talking to some senior NCOs, once I said I'd been in Vietnam, they talked to me in a different way and told me things they'd never told anyone else.'[14] Although based in Dhahran, she would make overnight trips to aircraft carriers and sometimes stay in air bases. She was sleeping in a tent at the largest US air base in Saudi Arabia when the war began. Within minutes she pulled on her combat fatigues and desert boots, grabbed her notebook and tape-recorder, and was racing to the flight line. Edie and David Evans of the *Chicago Tribune*, the print representatives on the pool, were desperate to file the story that the war had begun, but there were no telephones. Eventually, the pair persuaded a friendly colonel at the base to open up a construction trailer some way away where telephone lines were installed. Within minutes of the scoop, Edie realised that the base was under a full chemical attack and, although she had brought her gas mask, she had left her chemical suit in the tent. She survived, despite frequent alerts of one sort or another for many days after. So much time was spent in gas masks and carbon-lined chemical suits that everyone was coated in a semi-permanent black film.

After ten days, Edie returned to Dhahran, but she was back at the air base when the ground war started. Within days it was all over and she headed to Riyadh with other correspondents to write about the end of the war and the ceasefire.

Those first few days of euphoria in Kuwait are etched forever in my memory – the young Kuwaiti girls at a street party who came over to hold my hand, the mother whose baby started squealing the instant she put it in my arms to take a picture, the Kuwaiti soldiers who screeched to a halt when they saw me and begged me to pose with them.[15]

Edie believes that in reporting a war it is important to give the news about breaking battles fast and accurately, 'but at the same time not to get hung up on equipment, casualty figures and battle scenarios . . . the human dimension must not get lost'.[16] Although she faced some harassment as a single woman working in Saudi Arabia, she was, in general, able to circumvent this. 'Once I was told to stop and cover my hair, but I didn't, and before I could travel at all I had to get an "I-am-not-a-whore" letter from the authorities, otherwise single women cannot travel or stay in hotels.'[17]

Immediately after her assignment in the Gulf, Edie was sent to Bangladesh for a further four weeks, returning to London in June. But she is still enthralled by her lifestyle and her work. 'I've always been an adventurer,' she says. 'I'm fascinated at watching the unfolding of a big story, but war is only one segment. I love being able to participate in history and help to write it.'[18] There are some years when she is away for almost the entire twelve months, rushing from one crisis-point to another; others which are more evenly split, six months here, six abroad. She believes this lifestyle has made marriage and domestic responsibilities impossible. 'What man would put up with that sort of schedule. . . . I've seen a lot of men travelling around the world whose wives are foreign correspondents, but I have yet to meet women travelling with foreign correspondent husbands.' Edie sees an inherent difficulty here: 'There are not many women who have my kind of experience and I don't see that that will change quickly.' She was particularly aware of this in the Gulf, 'where many of the papers sent women ... who knew a lot about the Middle East but knew nothing about military matters, which was a problem'.[19]

Patricia Clough, living in London as a single mother in the 1980s, has managed to work as a newspaper bureau chief (not a fireman reporter) and maintain domestic responsibilities, but it has not always been easy. In 1986, with much fanfare, a new broadsheet newspaper was launched in Britain and, from the first, *The Independent* hired a number of female reporters to write on its foreign pages. Patricia joined immediately and was posted to Bonn for the third time, the newspaper's only female bureau chief at first. It was to be the happiest period in her life personally and the most fulfilling professionally, reaching a high point in 1989 with her coverage of the destruction of the Berlin Wall.

Two weeks before the East German regime collapsed, Patricia had the distinction of being the last correspondent to be thrown out of East Germany. She had gone there on 8 October 1989, ostensibly for the anniversary of the country's founding and President Gorbachev's visit, but she also wanted to talk to East Germans pressing for reform. The atmosphere was extremely tense as she entered on a tourist visa for a day, as she always had, and then, having checked into a hotel, tried to obtain a working visa. After two hours on the telephone, a silver-haired man in a pin-striped suit knocked on her door and introduced himself as the protocol chief of the hotel. 'He sat on the edge of the chair', Patricia recalls, 'and said, "I've been instructed to tell you that your presence in East Berlin is not desired and I must ask you to accompany me to the state border (Checkpoint Charlie)." '[20]

Patricia was both amused by the situation and 'a little bit churned up'. She guessed she would have to leave eventually, but decided to fight in the hope at least of delaying her departure. She telephoned the Foreign Ministry, who denied any responsibility, and then insisted on contacting the British Embassy, where she was advised to attend. But as soon as she entered the hotel foyer on her way there, she found herself surrounded by threatening types who refused to let her leave the hotel. She returned to her room and eventually someone from the

Embassy came to see her; they agreed that there was nothing further to be done and she was despatched to Checkpoint Charlie in a chauffeur-driven limousine, shunted through the border control at record speed and dumped on the other side. Patricia went to a local hotel, made a statement and found herself part of the swiftly changing events as several German newspapers came to listen to her story and take her photograph.

Gorbachev's visit took the inevitable process several stages further down the line when he proclaimed that those who did not move with history would be destroyed by it. Within days, East German chief Erich Honecker fell and the situation turned from confusion to chaos after it was announced at a press conference that East Germans could leave directly if they had a visa. On the night of 9 November, the British correspondents could not yet be sure what it all meant. They watched as candles were put on the Wall and demonstrations continued into the small hours. Unable to sleep, Patricia came down to the hotel lobby at 1 a.m. and decided to go out with another British reporter and investigate. 'We charged down Unter den Linden and saw there was a lot of activity at the Wall. With the light coming from the West you could see people walking on the Wall going up to No Man's Land. Previously you'd have been shot for that but the guards had no guns.'[21]

Suddenly groups were running in all directions, claiming to have come from the other side. There was much beer drinking, laughing and celebrating. In the wake of the television announcement, thousands of East Germans had drifted towards the Wall and said, 'Please let me out.'

'Someone gave the order that it was okay, let them go,' Patricia recalled. 'The guards were laughing and I couldn't believe my eyes. Even more incredible was the way people were coming to and fro. It was so moving.' She did not cry at the time, 'but afterwards, as I wrote the story, I couldn't stop the tears flowing. It struck me most of all that it was like a fairy tale.'[22] For four days Patricia Clough's copy made the front page of *The Independent*. 'The day that few had thought they would live to see', she wrote, 'burst upon the city at 7 p.m. on Thursday evening with the impact of a gigantic stun bomb. At first neither the East nor the West German television and radio announcers appeared to grasp quite what the news meant . . . "to think that it could happen in my lifetime," said a middle-aged man at Checkpoint Charlie, blubbing uncontrollably.'[23]

The following day, writing a story with an all-Berlin dateline gave her a wonderful sensation. Then she watched as the mechanical diggers tore into the Wall and was shocked that this grotesque symbol of division, which had dramatically kept East and West apart, was so pathetically flimsy. 'It was made of little air bricks and was just like cutting a birthday cake which immediately crumbles. Everyone wanted to grab a bit,' she recalled.[24]

'The collapse of the Berlin Wall was the story of my life,' Patricia says today – a view echoed by several reporters including Elizabeth Pond, of the *Christian Science Monitor*, who, after working in Indochina, had been living in Germany for several years. 'It was the day no one ever thought they would live to see. And yet it was so difficult to write about because of the emotion of it; it was something I felt for days afterwards.'[25]

Patricia Clough readily admits that emotion informed her writing at this point. But although 'writing emotionally' is a charge often levelled at women reporters, in this case the deep sense of joy at freedom being granted and history being re-made which Patricia experienced did not cloud her vision but gave her accounts an important, extra dimension. She was also well aware of the difficulties that would ensue in the future, that

there was a distinct feeling among East Germans that they had lived in vain. They had thought their leaders were idealistic until they discovered how corrupt they had been and, on top of this, came the realisation that their economy was a shambles. And there was a feeling that they were somehow being taken over by the West.[26]

Within a month she was on the move again. During her time in Germany she had begun a relationship with a Canadian diplomat. Luckily for them both, however, they were able to arrange a mutually compatible posting, this time in Warsaw. In January 1990, Patricia was appointed East European correspondent for her newspaper.

Being a reporter of either sex is not easy in Warsaw. The telephone system is archaic and delays of twenty-four hours in putting a call through are not infrequent. As few people speak English, Patricia worked with an interpreter. At the beginning of 1990, the rapidly developing East European story meant that there was plenty of hard news as well as interesting feature writing. In addition to covering elections and interminable constitutional discussions, Patricia wrote a major piece for *The Independent* on gypsies. Two-thirds of Europe's gypsy population live in eastern Europe and, in order to find out what life was like for them in a post-communist world, she spent weeks one summer driving around Czechoslovakia, Hungary and Romania. She needed more than an interpreter for this and travelled with a gypsy guide who could, crucially, introduce them. Patricia also took presents, mostly sweets and alcohol, and her daughter, then in her early twenties, who was invaluable for playing with young children, which made for a more relaxed visit.

'Being a woman made it much easier to break the ice and talk about everyday problems,' says Patricia.[27] Gypsies are notoriously wary of outsiders, yet she managed to talk to them about crime (in Prague sixty per cent of all crime is believed to be committed by gypsies), fortune telling, music and education, and how they regret the passing of communism when life for them was much safer.

According to Patricia:

Women who do this job do it for the challenge of finding things out and because of the human interest involved, the feeling that you can persuade people to talk to you. It's certainly not for the thrill of interviewing a prime minister for example – although men might enjoy the power of doing that – nor for the glamour – anyone who says that doesn't realise the amount of trudging about and standing in the rain.[28]

After two and half years, the wave of revolutions ended and the world wearied of the Central/East European story. Patricia was posted back to Rome to write again about Church and State and off-beat Sicilian punishments for unfaithful wives. While she welcomed the change of scenery, she was sad on a personal level since it involved a temporary parting from her diplomat partner. But she could not continue in Warsaw as there was no longer enough news and her life as a foreign correspondent had never been predictable.

In 1990, when she moved to Warsaw, she discussed with Head Office the difficulties for one correspondent in covering all seven countries of the former communist bloc. Once they had broken away from Moscow they had their own problems and each required considerable specialist knowledge. Patricia was therefore allotted Poland, Hungary and Czechoslovakia. 'These were the most important countries but I realised I was potentially losing a big story in Yugoslavia.'[29] She was ambivalent about this since she had never covered a war and felt in some ways that it was a part of her foreign correspondent's wardrobe that was missing. But in others she was relieved; her maternal instinct is strong and since she had been effectively a single parent for her daughter, felt an even greater urge towards responsibility. Although she has been in potentially dangerous situations, Patricia Clough is grateful never to have been faced with the choice of whether or not to report a war.

Diana Goodman, one of BBC Radio News's most successful reporters and its first woman foreign correspondent, has also found that the demands of a peripatetic professional life can clash with private life. Diana made headlines herself when, aged thirty-three and by then divorced, she was appointed to run the BBC Bonn bureau. So great was the assumption that the next incumbent would be a man that the welcoming note left by her predecessor read: 'Your wife might like to know where the local shops are. . . . '

Diana was born in Christchurch, New Zealand, and knew from an early age that she wanted to be a journalist. She left school at seventeen and enrolled at Wellington Polytechnic for a two-year journalism course. Shortly after this she moved with her family to the Cook Islands, where she got a job with the local radio station which involved, among other things, transcribing the incoming BBC World Service for use by local newspapers. 'I found myself typing out names of people and places I had often never heard of. But I realised years later that this was where I first experienced the magic of the BBC.'[30] This passion for her work has not left her; although her second job was with a newspaper, as a cadet reporter with the *Dominion*, from then on she was determined to find a job that satisfied her craving for radio, and worked briefly for the New Zealand Broadcasting Corporation.

In 1975, she left New Zealand to tour the world and, after several months in England, wrote to every single local radio station asking for a job. Radio Trent in Nottingham hired her and it was there that she met her first husband, also a journalist. Soon both moved on to Manchester, he with a commercial radio station, she with BBC local radio. In 1981, Diana went to London on a three-month attachment as a network reporter – covering national stories for Radios One, Two, Three and Four. She was obviously a success as they soon offered her a permanent job and she became the youngest reporter in the BBC radio newsroom.

It was at this time that Diana first became aware of being in a significant minority – there were only two other women reporters out of a general pool of twenty-five – and how frequently hostile were her male colleagues' reactions to her.

I covered all types of stories, from IRA bombs to bank holiday weather reports, and worked all the shifts and I never had any problems with the management side. But the male reporters seemed to have a real problem in accepting that a woman could do the job as well.... They thought we couldn't and hoped we couldn't.[31]

Clearly, the managers saw that she could, as in 1984, aged thirty-two, she was sent to Beirut during some of the worst shelling the country had yet seen.

She said soon afterwards:

You don't really think about the danger, I just thought 'how wonderful – a really challenging foreign assignment'. When you're there you get a terrific rush of adrenalin. It's frightening, but also very exciting. You're in the middle of a story that's making headlines right round the world.[32]

The Corporation received several letters of complaint at this time about how outrageous it was to send a woman to war, or even that she might be endangering her male colleagues if they felt they had to put themselves at risk on her behalf.

That's quite ridiculous since I'm just as big and strong as several of my male colleagues. Whenever I've been to dangerous places I've often found that women are among the bravest and men can be quite cowardly. Of course there are exceptions but it's so insulting to generalise.[33]

In Beirut, Diana did not stop to think about being a woman doing what was still seen as a man's job. But on her return, several female colleagues congratulated her for proving that a woman could do war reporting. However, such frequent absences from home together with her rapid success were telling on her marriage, which now broke under the double strain. 'My husband couldn't cope with my being away for that length of time,' Diana explains.[34] By 1986 she was divorced.

Diana admits that she has always worked extremely hard, burdened partly by the feeling that she is doing her job not only for herself but also for all the other women who will follow in her footsteps only if she succeeds. This feeling was particularly strong in 1986 when she was appointed Bonn correspondent, the first time the BBC had sent a woman to run a foreign bureau. Then she felt as if she were on trial for future generations of women. 'The irony is you know you'll work like a maniac and then they'll say you're a workaholic, haven't you got a private life?'[35]

Although based in Bonn, principally covering German stories, Diana also went quite frequently to the Soviet Union, sometimes for as long as six months. She also covered the election of the Austrian President, Kurt Waldheim, in 1986 and spent Christmas

1989 reporting the Romanian revolution, one of the most dangerous situations she ever confronted.

A total of forty BBC staff from radio, television and World Service news and current affairs were sent into the battle zone over Christmas. Many of them found themselves not only in the thick of fighting but, as foreign journalists, prime targets for the Securitate. Diana, abandoning plans for a Christmas lunch with friends and family, flew from Frankfurt to Belgrade and then drove down through the night past several roadblocks into Timisoara.

She dumped the car and walked into the centre of town, where there was a lot of shooting going on.

It was mayhem [she commented later]. People, some of whom had been shot and wounded, were fleeing in cars with bullet-shattered windscreens. Gangs of armed revolutionaries wearing head and arm bands were manning road-blocks while soldiers driving tanks were trying to track down Securitate snipers who were firing from the tops of buildings.

At this point two male colleagues decided to turn back, but Diana went on. 'Of course I was frightened,' she recalls today, 'but you feel so hyped up that your natural sense of curiosity becomes more intense.'[36] She soon realised that a crowd of angry locals had gathered around a Securitate man they had cornered under a bridge and were threatening to lynch him.

This made for one of the most dramatic reports of the Romanian revolution and the BBC account included the sound of its female correspondent running for cover, stumbling, with bullets firing off around her. With notes of the horrific scene, Diana then drove herself out of town as quickly as possible to the hotel across the Yugoslav border where several journalists were staying. She found a telephone, which she later realised was less than private, and fed London an update. Weeks later she was shown press cuttings of the same story filed by the two newsmen who had not wanted to go with her into the centre of Timisoara. She was amused to read how they too had apparently watched in horror as a crowd threatened to lynch a Securitate policeman.

With one international telephone line in the hotel for 300 journalists, finding a telephone was one of the worst problems of covering the brutal Romanian conflict. Consequently she and her colleague, Jane Peel, spent much of their time at the reopened radio station in Timisoara and at the telephone exchange, both of which were targets for snipers. On Christmas night the two women tried to sleep on the dirty floor of the exchange, unable to leave because of the gun battle outside.

From Romania Diana Goodman went straight to East Berlin, charged with setting up a new East European bureau covering eight countries. In January 1990, after the collapse of the Wall, she moved into the fourteenth floor of a high rise near Checkpoint Charlie and had to cope with brown bath water, polluted tap water and an archaic telephone service, among other aggravations. She could have chosen to live in the west of the city but did not want to be too far, literally or metaphorically, from the people she had to write about.

Diana was not in Germany to cover the fall of the Wall as she was at Cambridge University on a press fellowship. None the less, she insists that

tracking the disaster of unification has been just as important. It's a wonderful time to be here. However, the most upsetting story is reporting on the continuing disappointment and disillusionment felt by East Germans about what freedom means for them. Perhaps their expectations were unrealistic but the worst thing is to see how West Germans behave towards them; they despise them.[37]

Diana herself has felt a profound sense of disappointment, betrayal almost, in watching the recent rise of Neo-Nazism in Germany and produced a half-hour, sobering assessment of the situation for *Special Assignment* in September 1992. She canvassed a wide range of views for the piece and, while remaining deeply sympathetic towards foreigners and asylum seekers, carefully avoided expressing her own opinion.

I have been in Germany since 1986 and spent much time explaining to friends in Britain that Germany was a true democratic nation and that there was nothing to fear from it. I sincerely believed that when I was in Bonn. What is really distressing now is to have to admit that there is such widespread xenophobia in Western Germany ... and I was wrong. Germany is no longer the predictable and utterly stable nation that it was.[38]

In November 1991, Diana married again; this time her husband, also a journalist, moved to where she was working. She travels as much as ever, sometimes being away for two-thirds of the year, but at least she believes that she does not have to go on proving herself. 'We've proved that women can do it, but there are huge battles still to be fought,' she says. One of her concerns is that the younger generation of women reporters do not see a need to press for any improvements in women's conditions because they believe the fighting has been done and total equality exists. 'We're hanging on by our fingertips because there are still people out there dying for women to fail.'[39]

Kate Adie, a colleague and good friend of Diana Goodman's, has often felt the need to prove herself because she is a woman. She is one of the most successful reporters of her generation, responsible for inspiring many girls to pursue a career in news, yet she maintains that she is a 'dreadful role model' because she never intended to be a reporter, never trained as a journalist, but fell into it by accident. She receives scores of letters from parents of daughters who, she feels, have little idea of what the job really entails. Some of them think she has a hairdresser who accompanies her to war. Kate feels strongly that they should be aware of how little glamour and how much sordidity she is constantly exposed to.

Adie is unhappy with the present situation in British television where only a few talented women have made it to the top, without the back-up of a large number of women working in the middle echelons, as she believes this encourages male innuendo.

Of course, things have changed radically in the last fifteen years for women reporters. They are now taken seriously in public at any rate, largely because of the sheer number of American and European journalists working. Certainly nobody jokes as you come into the room any more whereas twenty years ago I couldn't make it into a union meeting on Tyneside without raucous laughter breaking out. But most male journalists still believe that you're fluttering your eyelids and that you opened your legs to get the job or the story. Or did you use your tits? It's quite amazing.[40]

Unlike Anne Sharpley, who thought such tactics were fair game, Adie is genuinely shocked at the loss of professionalism implied: 'It's just not on,' she insists. But even today, given the high professional regard in which she is held, she knows she is still the butt of snide comments. 'I've been in and out of Libya several times and I know that every single sniggering remark about Colonel Gaddafi has got to do with, "Has he tried it on with you?" I still have that. Oh yes, yes.'[41]

Kate grew up in a middle-class family in Sunderland, the only child of a pharmacist and his wife. She went to the local church high school, where she is remembered for being an outstanding pupil, and then, having always wanted to become an actress, spent three years at the National Youth Theatre with Helen Mirren and Timothy Dalton. But she was not prepared to put up with the long periods of boredom for the sake of declaiming one line per play and so enrolled at Newcastle

University to read Scandinavian Studies. Fluent in Swedish, German and French and with a smattering of Norwegian, Danish and Dutch, she spent nine months in Lapland, where her title was English Language Adviser to Southern Lapland. After teaching in the Arctic and not knowing precisely what she wanted to do, Kate answered an advertisement for trainee producers with Durham local radio, which was just starting up. She believes that, as she offered no suitable qualification, she only got the job by promising to do anything.

After Durham, she moved to Bristol local radio, where she spent four years as a documentary producer. 'And then I was sacked out of a job and told to go to Plymouth as a television reporter.'[42] The way Kate later reflects on her career, the move to Plymouth and the switch from producing to reporting were totally against her will. However she went and clearly remembers the first news story she did: 'I was sent to a rabbit farm and tried to memorise my lines but I couldn't do it. Then the cameraman gave me a rabbit to hold and I clutched it so hard it was half-dead by the time we'd finished; we had to do about five takes I was so nervous.'[43]

Kate considers she was appalling as a regional reporter because she was so bored by the stories she was allotted, almost all local and of questionable interest. But she was soon sent to London at weekends to work for national television whenever there was a shortage of reporters. 'That's when I realised I had at last found something. It was the speed, the immediacy and the relevance I loved.' Hard-news reporting at a national level inspired her and she joined the BBC news team as a full-time reporter. Kate believes that, in those days, she worked twice as hard as her male colleagues 'because as a woman you never give up on a story. You go the extra mile, especially when you're younger, you feel you have to prove yourself because THEY are waiting for you to fail.'[44]

Her breakthrough came in 1980, aged thirty-five, when, by chance, being the reporter on duty she was sent to cover the Iranian Embassy siege in London. There was another woman in the pool, Frances Coverdale, who could have been sent. Crouching dramatically behind a car door, Kate delivered her account of events with bullets flying past her head just as the SAS moved in. Ad-libbing the whole time, she never dropped the cool, crisp voice which later became her trademark. In 1980, many viewers were surprised that the voice describing the siege was a woman's. It was the first time on British television that a woman had been used to broadcast live from such a potentially dangerous situation, and she scored over the opposition, some of whom were hiding behind the building. As the Embassy shook with the sound of gunfire, Kate was to be seen crawling along the pavement yelling for a microphone. She recognises today that the disturbing element in this kind of reporting is that 'it is just like the movies'. Inevitably, viewers come to expect their news increasingly to be served up as entertainment and a woman television personality – especially a pretty one – witnessing the danger is particularly effective in lending to the excitement an additional frisson. Twelve years on Kate accepts this as a dangerous development which must be resisted. But her role is to tell the news as she sees it. 'I certainly don't construct the stories to be exciting.'[45]

After the siege, Kate became a personality. Among the dozens of fan letters was a long one from Audrey Russell, then in her mid-seventies and still appearing occasionally on chat shows to talk about her memories of the royal family. 'I have had my battles at the BBC,' she told Kate, whom she never met, adding that she was thrilled and proud to see another woman blazing the same trail at the BBC. Four years later Audrey Russell wrote an autobiography, published only after some difficulty as the public had, by then, forgotten her. She was ill for the last few years of her life and died in 1989.

After a brief stint in Northern Ireland, when she had acid thrown at her, Kate continued further along Audrey's path when, in 1982, she was made BBC court reporter, a period chiefly remembered for a clash with the then Buckingham Palace press officer during a tour of Italy by the Prince and Princess of Wales. Kate and her team had managed to get pictures of the royal couple at an event for which no photographer was expected. The press officer demanded that she share the photos with ITV but Kate, adamant that this was her exclusive, refused. However, royal stories 'are not really me', she explained some years later.[46]

Kate herself hit the headlines in April 1986, when, as one of BBC Television News's special correspondents and, after eight visits to Libya, something of an expert on the country, she was sent to cover the US bombing of Tripoli. During her eleven-day assignment she produced fifty-six highly dramatic reports about the bombing. Once Libyan Ministry of Information officials tried to prevent her sending back a film. 'She was magnificent,' commented Godfrey Grima of *Today*, who was watching her:

I have a lasting image of her shouting at the top of her voice, red in the face with anger, hands waving as she told the officials that they were not going to tamper with her film . . . . It was an incredibly dangerous situation, we were virtually being held captive by the Libyans. Some of us tried to humour them. But not Kate.[47]

Seven months afterwards, the then chairman of the Conservative Party, Norman (later, Lord) Tebbit, outraged most journalists and several politicians when he attacked BBC coverage of the American bombing as biased. Kate herself was not mentioned by name in Tebbit's dossier – probably because it was recognised that she was too popular with the British public – but the BBC coverage in general was criticised as 'a mixture of news, views, speculation, error and even propaganda for Libya's Colonel Gaddafi'.[48]

Kate was incensed. 'There are much greater issues at stake here than what I said and how I said it. I am standing by every word that I broadcast.'[49] The BBC defended its correspondent vigorously, pointing out how she made seventy references to the reporting restrictions imposed on her in Libya and refused to use film of mutilated corpses in the streets because they would have helped Gaddafi's propaganda machine. In one report her closing remark had been theatrically dramatic: 'We've had no word from him [Colonel Gaddafi] about the death of his daughter,' she said. 'She's already been buried.' This, it was alleged by Conservative Central Office, was emotive and sympathetic to the Libyan position. The BBC retorted that these were 'simple unvarnished facts of news significance'.[50]

However, when the *Daily Express* accused her of providing news coverage sympathetic to Gaddafi's regime as a result of which 'she allegedly obtained facilities and favours which were not made available to other broadcasters and journalists',[51] she sued and won 'substantial' undisclosed damages. Unquestionably, in the public eye Kate emerged victorious from the encounter with Tebbit and The Royal Television Society presented her with its International News Story of 1986 Award for her Tripoli reportage.

For the next three years she was remorselessly plunged into the world's trouble spots – 'I'm like a bullet; they fire me and off I go' – from Armenia to Afghanistan, Africa, Libya again and Zeebrugge. She takes only a small holdall of hand luggage but does not keep it permanently packed as she never knows what climate she will face. She does now take curling tongs with a worldwide voltage adaptor after receiving one too many offensive letters about the state of her hair.

In 1989, the major world story was the student revolt in China's

Tiananmen Square and Kate was quickly despatched to report on the tragic uprising. Clare Hollingworth, then aged seventy-eight, was also in Beijing reporting on events as they unfolded. But the two did not meet until two years later when they were interviewed together on a television chat show.

Kate's graphic eye-witness reports of the suppression and massacre of Chinese students in May and June 1989 shocked viewers. Working under intensive strain – often she and her crew went for seventy-two hours without sleep – she admitted on her return to Britain that being in Tiananmen Square had been one of her most terrifying experiences. 'I was in one of the roads leading up to the Square – where most of the killings took place. There was a string of sustained firing. I saw the whole crowd running backwards away from the line of soldiers. It was a panic-filled couple of minutes so many people went over.'[52] As the bullets whizzed past, everybody within 100 yards was caught in their devastating trail. Then a bullet grazed Kate's elbow.

'I felt the skin burn, then it hit a man two feet away. He flinched into the air and dropped dead at my feet. I crashed over him as I fell and saw three others lying in agony.' Kate dismissed her injury as minor – 'really, just a graze' – but admitted that her emotional state at the time was stretched almost to breaking-point. 'I remember a quite definite moment when I did not know what to do.'[53]

Kate maintains that, unlike some male reporters, she does not feel any excitement in such a situation.

I just grit my teeth and say 'this is serious; let's do it'.... In Tiananmen Square, in five hours we had seen hundreds of dead bodies but only one camera. It's not a question of excitement, it's a determination to get the story, get it out so the world knows about it, and stay alive.[54]

John Simpson, BBC diplomatic correspondent, who worked along-side Kate during the massacre, recalled how, after a month in Beijing watching the student occupation develop in the Square, he felt drained of all emotion.

After a long and difficult night of watching it all I did a good old BBC stiff upper lip piece – I just said what happened to mask my own feelings. At the time friends of mine told me ... that Kate Adie's piece was horribly emotional, dreadful and hysterical, yours was this, that and the other and I rather thought that was true.

It was only six or eight months later, when he saw both pieces for himself, that he changed his mind:

I still thought my piece was fine ... nothing wrong with it, it told you what had happened. But Kate went to the hospital and she gave you a real feeling of the awfulness of it. You felt how frightened she was, as indeed most of us were and I thought she gave a damn sight better account by seeing the aftermath than the real thing.

With hindsight, he concluded that both approaches were equally valid and the most important aspect was balance.[55]

As a reward for her cool, courageous coverage of the Chinese story the BBC created a special job for Kate, with the title Chief News Correspondent. She won a salary increase, too, but even so was still rumoured to be earning less than £40,000, relatively low compared with other media personalities of comparable fame. For Kate was now a definite media personality, a role which she does not relish when it involves her in chat shows and which has played havoc with her private life. Occasionally she returns to her modest maisonette in West London to find tabloid photographers lying in wait to see who accompanies her home.

Tiananmen Square was a watershed in other ways; for the next two years one major world news story overtook another and Kate was rarely at home. In July 1990, she went to Trinidad to report an attempted coup; 'very funny but very dangerous'. Then she flew directly to Jordan and did a number of stories about UN negotiations and Palestinian refugees. From there she went to Baghdad but had just arrived when her mother died. She returned home for three weeks and, by November, was back in Saudi Arabia, which was starting to make preparations for war. She was in England for six days in December – two of them spent with her father, the other four attending briefings on the forthcoming Gulf War and gathering equipment. The next four months were spent in the desert.

It is generally agreed among media commentators that Kate drew the short straw in the Gulf since she saw relatively little action with the troops in the desert while her colleague, John Simpson, was in Baghdad where the hard news was. She is dismissive about such comments: 'It was obvious he should go to Baghdad; he was the diplomatic editor whereas I was the one who knew the military and I do the fighting stuff.'[56] But, as the 'Mother of all Battles' unfolded and the expected land assault failed to materialise, her role became increasingly difficult as she was transformed and thereby trivialised into a sort of forces' sweetheart, used to relay messages home from the troops. Her reports were criticised for being empty of news. 'Kate really didn't have much to say at all,' wrote Sandra Parsons in *Today*, 'but she delivered her words as if she were the Kenneth Branagh of the airwaves. . . . The men were busy, she said. It was a starry night but there was no moon. All the time, Kate rolled her head around and stared, wild-eyed, at we knew not what.'[57] It was a cruel attack, since it was hardly Kate's fault that the activities of the Seventh Armoured Brigade were not the main focus of the Gulf War. Even more irksome were stories in the popular press about her having lost one of her famous pearl earrings and the British army spending hours searching for it in the sand. 'It was a pure invention, look here I am wearing them still. I don't know who dreamed up that one.'[58]

But if Fleet Street was determined to overplay Kate's womanliness, the Seventh Armoured Brigade made no allowances for it. 'I had to go to the loo in front of 2,000 blokes,' she recalled, laughing uproariously at the memory. 'Although there were other women in the desert, I was the only woman in my unit and I just had to find somewhere to pee in the open desert and bury my Tampax in the sand.'[59] Nor, in spite of her television appearances, was she given any extra water for washing her hair, 'and one litre per day in the desert for drinking and washing does not go very far. In the end I just "moved" my dirty hair around for the cameras, but I couldn't wash it.'[60]

Kate, then forty-five, admits that she found the physical strain of marching with an army exceptionally heavy.

I had to dig trenches every day and once I was up all night on an exercise and was very tired and just could not dig the next day. The major who saw I wasn't up to it let me off not as a concession because I was a female but because they were very kind. The British Army were more interested in making sure you could cope psychologically rather than physically.[61]

In April 1991, her hectic year continued with a two-month stint in Kurdistan reporting on the refugees. This was little improvement on living conditions in the desert: 'We slept in an abandoned bungalow with turds on the floor which we had to scrub off before we could sleep on it.' In June, not surprisingly, she picked up a 'foul disease', Congo Crimea Haemorrhagic Fever, and was despatched back to Britain and the Hospital for Tropical Diseases. By July, 'because I have the constitution of an ox', she was working again, this time in Yugoslavia. After a brief tour of duty there she spent four weeks in the Baltic states – Latvia, Lithuania and Estonia – reporting on their struggles for independence. In September and October, she was in Romania and Yugoslavia, which was particularly violent, and finished the year in Libya, interviewing the Lockerbie bomb suspects, where she contracted hepatitis.

Of all the places she has worked, Yugoslavia was by far the worst: 'It's a nightmare, beats anything in terms of danger.' Kate readily admits to having often experienced real fear and believes it is those who cannot acknowledge it who ultimately break down. 'I've been so scared and frightened I would have betrayed my best friend,' she owned, recalling horrific incidents in Belfast and Libya. 'But in Yugoslavia that autumn I didn't think I would get through the night. There were mortars, rockets and shells every second and I found myself unable to breathe properly. In the end I curled up in a foetal ball under the kitchen table and then buried my head under a blanket in the dark with the fleas and mosquitoes.'[62] Eventually, she conquered her fear by slowly counting, as one might during labour, every shell as it came over and saying, 'right, now let's get through the next one', and of course she did. Her immediate reaction on leaving Yugoslavia in the autumn of 1991 was that she was never going to go there again. 'But then I made myself go back to Osiek under fire. I knew I'd suffered shellshock and I made myself do it to prove to myself I could.' In addition, as she acknowledged, 'I am the chief bunny and if I don't hop....'[63]

Although the conflict in Yugoslavia is more dangerous than almost any previous war, several women reporters were drawn to it seeking not danger but truth. Maggie O'Kane, award-winning correspondent of the *Guardian*, found dealing with the suffering worse each visit she made to Bosnia. 'As I'm about to go back I'm really scared but the urge to know what's happening is stronger.' The day-to-day life was not only dangerous but arduous, with extreme shortage of water one of the most serious deprivations. One month was about the most any journalist could stand in the circumstances and the only way to cope during that month was by developing an element of detachment. 'In spite of the fact that I really do care about the situation there ... if I was too personally involved I'd be overwhelmed by the suffering.'[64]

Janine di Giovanni, an American writer for the *Sunday Times* and the *Spectator*, had a struggle to convince her editor that she should go to Sarajevo, but then managed to make an account of the horrors there almost amusing. She left no one in any doubt that a woman reporter's life was, in 1993, totally devoid of glamour – if indeed there had ever been any. Living in an unheated room with most of the windows blown out and replaced by plastic amid temperatures of minus 14 degrees, she wore the same clothes every day – two pairs of thermals, a pair of jeans, two t-shirts, a polo neck, a jumper, another jumper, a Gortex anorak, three pairs of socks, hiking boots, gloves, a hat and a scarf. 'I took off the gloves only to eat and type. I took off the anorak only to sleep and then it was stretched over my sleeping-bag.' All this deprivation greatly influenced the rules of seduction, she explained. One of the most memorable offers she received was from a Bosnian whose mother had hoarded enough water to give her a bath. 'Unfortunately I was led to believe that the offer included the condition that I marry the son.'[65]

In the 1990s, is there any moral justification for keeping women away from such situations of extreme danger? Or are editors deliberately pandering to the extra excitement viewers undoubtedly derive from watching a woman thus exposed? Kate Adie claims to play down the dangers whenever possible, for example by refusing to do what are known as 'twitch' pieces to camera, i.e. ducking frequently to avoid apparent shells. Nor will she take extra risks just because she is a woman, in a desire to prove her sex is capable of reckless feats. 'I am there to get the story, not to be a heroine.'[66] She wears bullet-proof vests and feels in some ways more protected than a radio or newspaper journalist because at least she has a camera crew with her and is therefore not alone. Nor does she try to turn herself into a glamorous film star. She is attractive – tall (5'7") and blonde with penetrating blue eyes – but more as a girl-next-door type than Hollywood star.

But while admitting to the real dangers, she is annoyed by suggestions that war is any less suitable for a woman than a man.

I have never been in a single riot or war or any other dangerous situation where half the people present weren't female. Who is providing the food, clearing up, looking after the victims, consoling the relatives? It's always women. Usually it's the men who are the only people with power: the army, police, security people – the ones with the guns.[67]

The idea that women should be kept away from reporting wars is one she finds truly insulting since wars kill, maim or frighten at least as many women as they do men. If women do not have sufficient power to prevent wars, being a woman reporting them may be the only area where women can exercise some influence over the course of events.

Kate sees quite clearly that the risks for today's reporters of both sexes are infinitely greater than at any time in the past. In the Yugoslav conflict, up to the end of 1992, nearly thirty reporters had been killed, no longer caught in the crossfire, but increasingly a target in their own right. 'We are seen as participants in the struggle or instruments of a foreign power,' Kate explains. Now that the reporters in many cases have their own portable satellite equipment with generators and are no longer required to transmit their reports through the host government, thus rendering censorship more difficult, totalitarian governments look for other ways to disable journalists. Latest technological developments in weaponry, too, make for further dangers as 'the front line' no longer exists, and reporters can get as close to the story as they wish. In a civil war there is usually no military commander to restrict their movements. While a journalist may consider it an advantage to witness everything first-hand, this also means being much nearer to the danger. Apart from the self-evident risks of being closer to the firing line, such an existence means that there is rarely any quiet time to rest, no retreat to a warm hotel room with clean sheets, no chummy, comfortable bar to congregate around at the end of the day, no good food conjured up by a hotel chef. Instead, the reporter forages around for whatever he or she can find and cooks it by whatever means, and finds shelter wherever possible. With inadequate sleep and sustenance and the need for constant vigilance for his or her own safety, or in response to head office constantly demanding updates, the pressures are enormous and it is a situation which inevitably leads to more accidents.

Robert Fox, veteran reporter of the Falklands campaign and the Gulf War, sees this situation as one which holds particular pitfalls for a female reporter:

The female personality reporter covering dramatic world events is part of the package which even Britain's serious newspapers are currently offering their readers . . . . They are using the female personality reporter as a vehicle and it's deliberately thought out, there's no doubt about that.[68]

By cultivating the woman's star status the newspaper encourages the reporters to write as much about their personal impressions of events as the facts. 'But this is very dangerous for women reporters because they will quickly reach their "sell-by" date.' More critical, perhaps, is that once the woman reporter finds herself part of a cycle of events whereby she is herself reported on in the media, 'then she becomes far more exposed than someone anonymous with a notebook and pencil'.[69]

Fox praises Adie as 'a very good reporter, very straight who wants to find things out'. But he believes she now faces a particularly difficult predicament because 'everything she does is a celebrity appearance – not of her own making. Even when John Major visits the troops in the desert it is she who is mobbed.'[70] In Fox's view, the most serious difficulty facing any woman reporter in war is how to pierce the tight male bonding that exists between young soldiers, especially in the forward fighting units.

It means they just don't find things out because they don't fool around with the boys in the same way as we can. A young soldier when he is preparing to fight and possibly to die ... relies on his buddy. He fears being wounded, rather than being killed, more than anything and it's a moment of great intimacy and stress; any invasion of that moment will be prevented at all costs.[71]

Fox recognises how unfashionable it is to say that male soldiers working together won't open up to a woman reporter, but insists not only that he has seen it happen but also that it is a development which makes the military deeply uncomfortable. 'Whether the boys are going to do it is crucial and the presence of a female reporter in their unit could be an inhibiting factor.'[72] Fox considers warfare itself is a big enough social experiment and there is little premium, editorially, in adding to that risk by sending women to report on it.

Now in her late forties, Kate Adie does not see herself reaching her sell-by date yet. After all, as she pointed out, Robert Fox and Robert Fisk are also her age while BBC colleagues Brian Barron and Martin Bell are in their early fifties. And she clearly relishes the job. 'How else would you meet such interesting and different people?'[73]

But she is propelled by another, deeper motivation. There are those who believe that because she has not married, she has sacrificed her life to the BBC; that she has put career before motherhood, thus denying herself fulfilment and a private life. Kate herself dislikes discussing the subject, but insists that since many of her male colleagues do the same job with children, it would have been perfectly possible. 'The key is not just commitment in the marriage but money. Money so that you can organise your life with the chores taken out of it.' Kate does not seem like a victim who has sacrificed herself, but rather one who has chosen her lifestyle in a positive sense; getting married and having a career is, she insists, a personal decision. Horrified by the sight of friends who are 'bored stiff by their children', she aspired to do something more interesting, as she saw it, with her life. 'My ambition was to get out of Sunderland, not to end up like all the other women there, losing their looks tied into failed or boring marriages with increasing numbers of children. I knew, once I went to university, that I was out.'[74]

After the Gulf War, Kate had her share of problems. In April 1992, Libya's Foreign Information Ministry telexed the BBC to withdraw her on the grounds that she 'never hesitates in insulting and scolding our representatives as if they are her own slaves while they are trying to give her facilities.... She is causing us more and more trouble.'[75] Eventually, she came back to the UK when she and her superiors concluded that the situation, journalistically, had become untenable and unsafe for her and her crew.

At home she is now occasionally criticised for her graphic, eye-witness style of reporting when the current trend is towards more analysis. 'She may startle you on the day, but John Simpson is needed later to explain things,' commented an anonymous profile writer in *The Independent*.[76] Those who castigate her for an over-emotional approach never fail to mention her three years' drama training, yet at the same time she is reproached for her stridency. For some years now her nickname at the BBC of 'The Screecher' has been an open secret. But her loud voice is a result partly of long-term deafness; she hears only eighty per cent of her own voice. The fact that she can be direct, demanding, aggressive and occasionally arrogant when she feels she is being thwarted is ranged accusingly against her. But a man displaying similar characteristics would be praised. There is an undeniable paradox in that those who criticise Kate Adie for being over-emotional and therefore overly feminine might in another breath accuse her of being over aggressive and therefore too masculine. She is in a bind which, with luck, her formidable energy and determination will help her escape from.

In one sense the emergence of Kate Adie as a 'personality reporter' is nothing new. Flora Shaw's expedition to discover the facts about the Klondike was itself considered newsworthy irrespective of anything she might have discovered and reported on and Lady Florence Dixie was quite blatantly used by her newspaper, the *Morning Post*, since her editor knew what good copy could result from an attractive, aristocratic woman in the thick of a bloody, masculine war. More recently, Virginia Cowles's articles were often given the additional byline, 'from an American society girl', as if her social standing made a difference to the mayhem or carnage she was describing. Similarly Agnes Smedley, who approached news from a radically different perspective, also suffered from finding herself part of the headlines, one of which described her as a 'red peril'.

By the end of the Vietnam War, several newspapers and agencies recognised the importance of having a female byline and a female angle on the war and suddenly Saigon was full of women reporters. Yet ten years later, when the Argentines invaded the Falkland Islands, not a single woman reporter was sent with the British Task Force except for the official war artist, Linda Kitson. Max Hastings, now editor of the *Daily Telegraph* who reported on the Falklands campaign for the *Evening Standard*, believes that even if Britain had sent a woman reporter, it would not have made any difference to the overall reporting as it was not a war where civilian casualties played a major part.[77]

By the time of the Gulf War in 1991, Women and War was clearly still an issue, making it inevitable that even those women reporters accepted alongside their male colleagues, and expected to do the same job, still found themselves becoming part of the story themselves on occasion. Hence Kate Adie and the 'lost earring'; if it did not happen, someone had to invent it. Fidelma Cook, an experienced and senior reporter for the *Glasgow Sunday Mail* who had frequently reported on the British army from Northern Ireland, had her application to go to the Gulf turned down by British authorities because 'there are no facilities for ladies' on board the ship she was to travel on. Although she and her editor fought the decision, they lost. But if the *Glasgow Sunday Mail* was forced to cover the conflict without its own reporter, at least it made good play of the story that its own woman reporter had been refused permission to go to war. Meanwhile, a reporter from the women's magazine, *Mirabella*, gave many of her colleagues a bad name because she 'spent much of her time writing about the sex lives of female soldiers and drugs used by medical units'.[78]

But at the same time there were several British women reporters covering the Gulf War from various datelines who got on with their jobs bravely and professionally without anyone drawing attention to their activities; these included Barbara McCann and Louise Bevan for TV-am, Linda Duffin for Sky News, Carol Walker for BBC Television, Liz Donnelly and Caroline Kerr for ITN in Israel and Jordan.* It is, perhaps, no coincidence that most of these women work for television. Television, of course, magnifies the extent to which the woman reporter is part of the story. Where the picture is all, it is inevitable that complex analysis is occasionally sacrificed in favour of the horror and danger brought incongruously into our comfortable living-rooms

---

* Clare Hollingworth spent several nights sleeping on her bedroom floor to prepare herself for the privations of war but no newspaper sent for her. She was, at eighty, too old.

every night. The person telling the story is an important element.

'If you don't have the bang bang pictures you don't get on air. You need a certain amount of injury and running around or people lose interest,' explained cameraman Mohammed Amin of Visnews.[79] 'The soap opera syndrome' is how *The Times* recently described it. 'The world's war zones are chock-a-block with would-be Kate Adie's risking their lives for minor stations in the hope of landing the big story because they know that what the major networks want is a front-line account from a (preferably pretty) woman in a flakjacket.'[80] In the former Yugoslavia, a number of female reporters covered events for television, radio and newspaper; many of them relatively young – fitness is of prime importance – and not unattractive, but sent because they were the most qualified for the job. It is not that the women reporters, or at any rate the experienced ones, wish to play along with this game. It is, after all, a game played at their expense since the job of a reporter is made harder once anonymity is lost. But it is difficult to see how it can be prevented when there are high calibre women reporters whom the public enjoys watching. Perhaps it will only change when society matures and the numbers are such that male reporters become an oddity.

In 150 years, the rules of the game have changed considerably. Women do, more or less, have open access to any story today; they will not be expected to nurse the wounded or cook for their male colleagues; they enjoy the same training as men and are paid the same rate for the job; their views are listened to and taken seriously and they are just as likely to be killed or wounded as a male reporter. They will not, however, have anyone to carry their bags for them and they will be expected to drive themselves to the action and operate any machinery if required.

What have not changed are the qualifications for the job. A high degree of ambition characterises almost all those who succeed as women reporters today, just as it did in the mid-nineteenth century. Perhaps this is the only generalisation that can be made about the women in this book: whether because they felt a passionate desire to do something about the world situation or because they were ambitious for their views to be aired and for themselves to succeed in a male world, they were, and are, all highly motivated. In most cases, attractiveness has helped too – after all most employers are men, still. Stamina, energy, tenacity also remain essential prerequisites. Even though political opinions are not a qualification, a majority of the women in this book have stood on the left of the political spectrum.

Perhaps this is no coincidence because left-leaning individuals are intrinsically more likely to agitate for change as an essential part of their credo whereas a conservative is by nature less likely to feel a need to disturb the status quo. But there is no reason for a woman reporter not to represent the radical right; it seems in practice, however, that few do.

Kate Adie, Diana Goodman and Patricia Clough have all reached the top of their profession but with a clear sense of their paths having been littered with obstacles. Edie Lederer, as an American, has not had to fight quite the same battles. But all four recognise that women in disaster zones, primitive societies or war can face additional difficulties in carrying out their jobs effectively even if they freely admit that they also possess certain innate advantages over their male counterparts.

Edie Lederer articulates what almost every other woman reporter in this book has described in different ways:

Since men never expect you to know anything at all, you are perfectly free to ask all those basic questions which need to be asked, and you can get away with it, which a man can't. But also, men put up guards with other men. Most people would rather talk to a woman than to a man.[81]

Notes

INTRODUCTION

1 Public Record Office, Ancient Petition No. 4058
2 Margaret Bateson (ed.), *Professional Women upon Their Professions*
3 Arnold Bennett, *Journalism for Women: A Practical Guide*
4 Phillip Knightley, *The Times*, 21 January 1991
5 Quoted in Marion Marzolf, *Up from the Footnote: A History of Women Journalists*
6 *Wall Street Journal*, 21 April 1992
7 Radio Four *Woman's Hour*, 3 November 1992
8 Shulamit Hareven, letter to author, 3 November 1991
9 *Ibid.*
10 Sybille Bedford, interview with author, 8 May 1991
11 Quoted in Marzolf, *op. cit.*
12 *The Times*, 21 January 1991
13 Victoria Brittain, interview with author, 13 March 1991
14 Claire Sterling, interview with author, 2 October 1991
15 Isabel Allende, letter to author, 5 June 1991
16 Martha Gellhorn, letter to author, 3 November 1992
17 Diana Goodman, interview with author, 23 October 1992

1 SISTERS, WIVES AND NURSES

1 *The Times* Archive, 14 March 1859
2 *The Times* Archive, 7 August 1861
3 The St James's Budget, quoted in Margaret Drabble, Introduction to G. Krishnamurti (compiled), *Women Writers of the 1890s*
4 *Daily News*, 7 November 1856
5 Quoted in Andrea Viotti, *Garibaldi*
6 Quoted in Emillie Peacocke, unpublished autobiography
7 Jasper Ridley, *Garibaldi*
8 *The Nation*, 15 March 1906
9 Elizabeth Adams Daniels, *Jesse White Mario – Resorgimento Revolutionary*
10 *Printers Register Supplement*, 6 February 1891
11 *Ibid.*

2 THE FIRST PROFESSIONALS

1 *The London Figaro*, quoted in Brian Roberts, *Ladies in the Veld*
2 Leonard E. Naylor, *The Irrepressible Victorian*
3 'English Opinion at the Cape', *Morning Post*, 17 March 1881
4 *Morning Post*, 19 May 1881
5 *Ibid.*, 28 July 1881
6 Naylor, *op. cit.*
7 *Morning Post*, 18 October 1881
8 *Vanity Fair*, 25 October 1884
9 *Englishwoman*, 1899

10 Maria Taylor, *Some Old Letters from North Africa* (reprinted by Desire, Rome, 1889)

11 *Ibid.*

12 *Journalism*, March 1888

13 I am indebted to Fred Hunter for much of this information, to be published shortly in *Victorian Periodicals Newsletter*

3 THE REMARKABLE FLORA SHAW

1 E. Moberly Bell, *Flora Shaw*

2 Helen Callaway and Dorothy O. Helly, *Crusader for Empire: Flora Shaw*, in Nupur Chaudhur and Margaret Strobel (eds), *Western Women and Imperialism: Complicity and Resistance* (Indiana University Press, Bloomington and Indianapolis, 1992)

3 Margery Perham, *Lugard, The Years of Authority*

4 Moberly Bell, *op. cit.*

5 *Ibid.*

6 *Ibid.*

7 *The Times* Archive, 12 August 1892

8 Information contained in Instructions from *The Times* to Bankers, 28 July 1893

9 *The Journalist and Newspaper Proprietor*, 14 April 1894

10 *The Journalist and Newspaper Proprietor*, 17 February 1894

11 R. W. Stallman, *Stephen Crane: A Biography*

12 Letter quoted by Stallman in *ibid.*

13 *Ibid.*

14 Flora Shaw, 'An Address to the Royal Colonial Institute, London,' 31 January 1899

15 Flora Shaw, Series of Letters to *The Times*, commencing 27 August 1898

16 Moberly Bell, *op. cit.*

17 Quoted in Valerie Hall, *Women and Journalism: A Sociological Account*, unpublished thesis, Fawcett Library

18 Quoted in Moberly Bell, *op. cit.*

4 THE NEW WOMAN

1 Lady Sarah Wilson, *South African Memories*

2 *Morning Post*, 29 October 1909

3 Thomas Pakenham, *The Boer War*

4 Quoted by Robert Wilkinson Latham in *Victorian War Correspondents and their Campaigns*

5 Quoted in A. Ruth Fry, *Emily Hobhouse, A Memoir*

6 *Ibid.*

7 Bateson (ed.), *Professional Women upon Their Professions*

8 Emillie Peacocke, unpublished autobiography

9 *Ibid.*

10 *Ibid.*

11 *Ibid.*

12 Fred Hunter, *Victorian Periodicals Newsletter*

13 Peacocke, *op. cit.*

14 *Ibid.*

15 *Ibid.*

16 *Tribune*, 26 April 1906

17 Peacocke, *op. cit.*

18 *Ibid.*

19 *Ibid.*

20 *Ibid.*

21 *Ibid.*

22 *Ibid.*

23 *Morning Post*, undated memo circa 1909, Brotherton Library Papers, University of Leeds

24 Madame Rose to Mr Dunn, 1 September 1902, Brotherton Library Papers, University of Leeds

25 Mrs Cecil Chesterton, *In Darkest London*

26 *Ibid.*

27 *Ibid.*

5 WAR AND ITS AFTERMATH

1 Wilbur Forrest, *Behind the Front Page*

2 Emillie Peacocke, unpublished autobiography

3 Phillip Knightley, *The First Casualty*

4 Emily Hobhouse to C. P. Scott, January 1915, The *Guardian* Archive, The John Rylands University Library of Manchester

5 C. P. Scott to Emily Hobhouse, 31 January 1915, The *Guardian* Archive, The John Rylands University Library of Manchester

6 Emily Hobhouse to C. P. Scott, date unclear, The *Guardian* Archive, The John Rylands University Library of Manchester

7 *Daily News*, 4 September 1916

8 Enid Bagnold, *Diary without Dates*

9 Quoted by Knightley, in *op. cit.*

10 *Ibid.*

11 *News of the World*, 29 June 1919, News International Archive

12 Mary Stott, unpublished memoir

13 *Ibid.*

14 *Ibid.*

15 *Ibid.*

16 Mary Stott, interview with author, 31 October 1991

17 Stott, unpublished memoir

18 *Ibid.*

19 Mary Stott, *Forgetting's No Excuse*

20 *The Nation*, 28 November 1923

21 Agnes Smedley, *Daughter of Earth*

22 Agnes Smedley, *Chinese Destinies: Sketches of Present Day China*

23 Janice and Stephen MacKinnon, *Bulletin of Concerned Asian Scholars*, February–March 1975

24 Agnes Smedley, *China's Red Army Marches*

25 Janice and Stephen MacKinnon, *Agnes Smedley: The Life and Times of an American Radical*

26 Agnes Smedley to Randall Gould, 19 May 1937, quoted in *ibid.*

27 *Kansas City Star*, 9 January 1937

28 *New York Post*, 7 January 1937

29 Associated Press release, 8 January 1937, quoted in MacKinnon, *Agnes Smedley*

30 Agnes Smedley foreword to *China Fights Back: An American Woman with the Eighth Route Army*

31 Evans Carlson diary, quoted in MacKinnon, *Agnes Smedley*

32 MacKinnon, *Agnes Smedley*

33 Agnes Smedley, *Battle Hymn of China*

6   THE INTER-WAR YEARS: EUROPE

1 Shiela Grant Duff, *The Parting of Ways*

2 *Ibid.*

3 *Ibid.*

4 Elizabeth Wiskemann, *The Europe I Saw*

5 *Ibid.*

6 Grant Duff, *op. cit.*

7 *Observer*, 20 January 1935

8 Grant Duff, *op. cit.*

9 *Ibid.*

10 *New Statesman and Nation*, 13 July 1935

11 Wiskemann, *op. cit.*

12 *Ibid.*

13 *Ibid.*

7   THE SPANISH CIVIL WAR

1 Sybille Bedford, interview with author, 8 May 1991

2 Martha Gellhorn, *The Trouble I've Seen*

3 Eleanor Roosevelt, 'My Day', syndicated US column, September 1936

4 Graham Greene, *Spectator*, 1936

5 Lewis Gannett, 'Books 'n Things', syndicated US column, 24 September 1936

6 Quoted in Phillip Knightley, *The First Casualty*

7 Introduction to Martha Gellhorn, *The Face of War* (Rupert Hart-Davis edn, 1959)

8 *Ibid.*

9 Quoted in Bernice Kert, *The Hemingway Women*

10 Gellhorn, *The Face of War*

11 Elinor Langer, *Josephine Herbst: The Story She Could Never Tell*

12 Gellhorn, *The Face of War*

13 *Ibid.*

14 *Ibid.*

15 *Ibid.*

16 Langer, *op. cit.*

17 Kert, *op. cit.*

18 Virginia Cowles, *Looking for Trouble*

19 Aidan Crawley, *Leap Before You Look*

20 Cowles, *op. cit.*

21 *Ibid.*

22 *Ibid.*

23 Langer, *op. cit.*

24 *Ibid.*

25 *Sunday Times*, 4 July 1937

26 Cowles, *op. cit.*

27 *Ibid.*

28 *Ibid.*

29 *Ibid.*

30 *Ibid.*

31 *Ibid.*

32 *Ibid.*

33 *Sunday Times*, 26 October 1937
34 Cowles, *op. cit.*
35 Gellhorn, *The Face of War*
36 *The Times* interview with Martha Gellhorn, 5 October 1991
37 Martha Gellhorn, letter to author, 11 May 1991
38 *The Times* interview with Martha Gellhorn, 5 October 1991
39 Quoted in Knightley, *op. cit.*
40 *Ibid.*

8   AWAITING WORLD WAR

1 Shiela Grant Duff, *The Parting of Ways*
2 Shiela Grant Duff to Adam von Trott, quoted in *ibid.*
3 Shiela Grant Duff, interview with author, September 1991
4 *Ibid.*
5 Grant Duff, *The Parting of Ways*
6 *Ibid.*
7 *Ibid.*
8 *Ibid.*
9 *Ibid.*
10 *Ibid.*
11 Elizabeth Wiskemann, *The Europe I Saw*
12 *Ibid.*
13 *Ibid.*
14 Virginia Cowles, *Looking for Trouble*
15 *Ibid.*
16 *Ibid.*
17 Martha Gellhorn to her mother, Mrs Edna Gellhorn, 4 July 1938, quoted in Afterword to Martha Gellhorn, *A Stricken Field*
18 Martha Gellhorn, *Collier's*, 1 September 1938
19 Martha Gellhorn to her mother, 25 August 1938
20 Afterword to Gellhorn, *A Stricken Field*
21 Martha Gellhorn to her mother, 7 October 1938
22 'Tragic Days in Prague', *Sunday Times*, 9 October 1938
23 Afterword to Gellhorn, *A Stricken Field*
24 Martha Gellhorn television documentary, *Omnibus*, BBC, October 1991

25 Martha Gellhorn to her mother, undated, probably November 1938, quoted in Afterword to Gellhorn, *A Stricken Field*
26 Afterword to Gellhorn, *A Stricken Field*
27 *Ibid.*
28 Martha Gellhorn to her mother, 18 March 1939
29 Martha Gellhorn television documentary, *Omnibus*, BBC, October 1991
30 *Ibid.*
31 Sybille Bedford, interview with author, 8 May 1991
32 Afterword to Gellhorn, *A Stricken Field*

9   THE BEGINNING OF WAR

1 Virginia Cowles, *Looking for Trouble*
2 *Ibid.*
3 Fitzroy Maclean, interview with author, 7 December 1991
4 *Ibid.*
5 *Sunday Times*, 2 April 1939
6 *Ibid.*
7 *Sunday Times*, 3 September 1939
8 Clare Hollingworth, *Front Line*
9 Clare Hollingworth, interview with author, 23 July 1991
10 Hollingworth, *Front Line*
11 *Ibid.*
12 *Ibid.*
13 *Ibid.*
14 Richard Collier, *The Warcos: The War Correspondents of World War Two*
15 Hollingworth, *Front Line*
16 *Ibid.*
17 *Ibid.*
18 *Ibid.*
19 Afterword to Martha Gellhorn, *A Stricken Field*
20 Martha Gellhorn, *The Face of War*
21 Letter quoted in Bernice Kert, *The Hemingway Women*
22 Gellhorn, *The Face of War*
23 *Collier's*, 4 March 1944
24 *Ibid.*
25 *Collier's*, 20 January 1940
26 *Ibid.*
27 *Collier's*, 27 January 1940
28 *Sunday Times*, 21 January 1940
29 *Sunday Times*, 17 March 1940

10 OVER THERE

1 Phillip Knightley, *The First Casualty*
2 *Sunday Times*, 16 June 1940
3 Virginia Cowles, *Looking for Trouble*
4 Clare Hollingworth, *Front Line*
5 *Ibid.*
6 Clare Hollingworth, interview with author, 23 July 1991
7 *Daily Express*, 1 October 1940
8 Clare Hollingworth, interview with author, 23 July 1991
9 Hollingworth, *Front Line*
10 *Ibid.*
11 *Ibid.*
12 *Ibid.*
13 *Ibid.*
14 Martha Gellhorn, *The Face of War*
15 Martha Gellhorn, *Travels with Myself and Another*
16 *Ibid.*
17 *Ibid.*
18 *Collier's*, 31 May 1941
19 Gellhorn, *Travels with Myself and Another*
20 *Ibid.*
21 *Ibid.*
22 *Collier's*, 7 June 1941
23 Ernest Hemingway (ed.), *Men at War*
24 Gellhorn, *Travels with Myself and Another*
25 *Ibid.*
26 *Ibid.*
27 *Ibid.*
28 *Collier's*, 28 June 1941
29 Gellhorn, *Travels with Myself and Another*
30 *Ibid.*
31 *Ibid.*
32 *Ibid.*
33 *Collier's*, 9 August 1941
34 Gellhorn, *Travels with Myself and Another*
35 Charlotte Haldane, *Russian Newsreel: an Eyewitness Account of the Soviet Union at War*
36 *Ibid.*
37 *Ibid.*
38 *Ibid.*
39 Elizabeth Wiskemann, *The Europe I Saw*
40 *Ibid.*
41 Memorial Address for Elizabeth Wiskemann, given by Lord Arran (Boofy Gore), 21 October 1971
42 Wiskemann, *op. cit.*

11 FEMALES IN THE DESERT

1 Alan Moorehead, *A Late Education*
2 Clare Hollingworth, *Front Line*
3 *Ibid.*
4 *Ibid.*
5 Eve Curie, *Journey among Warriors*
6 Astley Private Papers, 9 December 1941
7 *Ibid.*
8 War Office to Colonel Philip Astley, Astley Private Papers, 30 March 1942
9 Curie, *op. cit.*
10 Astley Private Papers, 8 March 1942
11 *Ibid.*
12 Quoted by Iris Carpenter, *No Woman's World*
13 Virginia Cowles to General Eisenhower, 12 January 1943, used in unpublished memoir of Virginia Cowles, written and kindly lent me by her husband, Aidan Crawley
14 Quoted by Aidan Crawley in *ibid.*
15 Nigel Nicolson to Aidan Crawley, 26 November 1987
16 Clare Hollingworth, interview with author, 23 July 1991
17 *Ibid.*
18 Hollingworth, *Front Line*
19 Colonel Philip Astley to War Office, Astley Private Papers, 5 March 1943
20 *Ibid.*
21 *Ibid.*

12 THE HOME FRONT – AND BEYOND

1 Bernard Hall, letter to author, 14 September 1991
2 *Ibid.*
3 Arthur Christiansen, *Headlines All My Life*
4 Hilde Marchant, *Women and Children Last – A Woman Reporter's Account of the Battle of Britain*
5 *Ibid.*
6 *Ibid.*
7 John Young, interview with author, 19 September 1991

8 Bernard Hall, letter to author, 14 September 1991
9 *Ibid.*
10 *Daily Express*, 16 April 1940
11 *Daily Express*, 16 November 1940
12 Marchant, *op. cit.*
13 John Young, interview with author, 19 September 1991
14 Letters to 'May', 2 July 1941. Unpublished correspondence intended for publication by Mea Allan, 'A Daily Account of her Life in Fleet Street', Imperial War Museum
15 *Ibid.*, 11 March 1941
16 *Ibid.*, 12 July 1941
17 Mollie Panter-Downes to Nicola Beauman, quoted in Introduction to Mollie Panter-Downes, *One Fine Day*
18 Introduction by Nicola Beauman to *ibid.*
19 *New Yorker*, 3 September 1939
20 *New Yorker*, 10 September 1939
21 *Ibid.*
22 *New Yorker*, 17 September 1939
23 *New Yorker*, 21 September 1940
24 *New Yorker*, 8 December 1939
25 *New Yorker*, 22 December 1939
26 *New Yorker*, 30 August 1940
27 *Ibid.*
28 *New Yorker*, 14 September 1940
29 Audrey Russell, *A Certain Voice*
30 *Ibid.*
31 Phyllis Deakin, *Press On: An Account of the Women's Press Club of London*
32 *Ibid.*
33 *Ibid.*
34 Evelyn Irons, letter to author, 14 February 1993
35 Deakin, *op. cit.*
36 Phillip Knightley, *The First Casualty*
37 Deakin, *op. cit.*
38 Russell, *op. cit.*
39 *Ibid.*
40 *Ibid.*
41 *Ibid.*
42 *Ibid.*
43 Frank Gillard, letter to author, 25 June 1992
44 *Ibid.*
45 Afterword to Martha Gellhorn, *Liana*
46 Martha Gellhorn to Ernest Hemingway, 12 December 1942, quoted in Bernice Kert, *The Hemingway Women*

47 'Visit Italy', *Collier's*, February 1944
48 Joyce Grenfell, *The Time of My Life – Entertaining the Troops – Her Wartime Journals*
49 *Collier's* editorial, 4 March 1944
50 Martha Gellhorn, *The Face of War*
51 'The First Hospital Ship', *Collier's*, June 1944
52 *Collier's*, September 1944
53 Martha Gellhorn television documentary, *Omnibus*, BBC, October 1991
54 Sybille Bedford, interview with author, 8 May 1991
55 Quoted in Kert, *op. cit.*

13   THE WAR OF THE SEXES

1 Martha Gellhorn television documentary, *Omnibus*, BBC, October 1991
2 *Ibid.*
3 *Collier's*, May 1945
4 Julia Edwards, *Women of the World*
5 *Ibid.*
6 Obituary, *New York Herald Tribune*, 4 January 1966
7 *Daily Telegraph*, 27 September 1946
8 *Ibid.*
9 *Daily Telegraph*, 1 October 1946
10 Claire Sterling, interview with author, 2 October 1991
11 *Ibid.*
12 Monica Dehn, interview with author, 16 December 1991
13 Clare Hollingworth, *Front Line*
14 *Ibid.*
15 Monica Dehn, interview with author, 2 October 1991
16 Marguerite Higgins, *News is a Singular Thing*
17 *Notable American Women: A Biographical Dictionary*
18 Marguerite Higgins, *War in Korea*
19 *Ibid.*
20 *Ibid.*
21 *Ibid.*
22 *Ibid.*
23 *Ibid.*
24 *Ibid.*
25 *Ibid.*
26 Quoted in John Hohenberg, *Foreign Correspondence: The Great Reporters and Their Times*

14 UNFAIR COMPETITION?

1 Audrey Russell, *A Certain Voice*
2 *Ibid.*
3 Frank Gillard, letter to author, 16 June 1992
4 Russell, *op. cit.*
5 *Ibid.*
6 *Ibid.*
7 *Ibid.*
8 *Ibid.*
9 Quoted by Tim Heald, *Weekend Toronto*, 26 May 1979
10 *World's Press News*, 9 November 1956
11 *Ibid.*
12 *Ibid.*
13 Charles Wintour, interview with author, 12 March 1992
14 *Ibid.*
15 *Evening Standard*, 23 January 1956
16 *Evening Standard*, 17 February 1956
17 *Evening Standard*, 10 August 1956
18 *Ibid.*
19 *Evening Standard*, 9 August 1956
20 Claire Sterling, interview with author, 2 October 1991
21 Royal Cavalcade, undated article
22 *Ibid.*
23 *Ibid.*
24 Quoted by Tim Heald, *Weekend Toronto*, 26 May 1979
25 *Evening Standard*, 5 September 1957
26 *Ibid.*
27 *Evening Standard*, 26 October 1961
28 *Evening Standard*, 27 October 1961
29 *Ibid.*
30 Angus McGill, interview with author, 6 May 1992
31 *Evening Standard*, 20 July 1964
32 Obituary by Charles Wintour, *The Independent*, 17 April 1989
33 Charles Wintour, interview with author, 12 March 1992
34 Tom Pocock, interview with author, 30 May 1992
35 Obituary by Angus McGill, *Evening Standard*, 17 April 1989
36 Angus McGill, interview with author, 6 May 1992
37 Mary Kenny, interview with author, 28 January 1992

15 JUSTICE

1 Lynne Reid Banks, interview with author, 28 February 1991
2 *Ibid.*
3 *Ibid.*
4 *Ibid.*
5 *Woman's Realm*, 1989
6 Lynne Reid Banks, interview with author, 28 February 1991
7 Tom Pocock, *East and West of Suez*
8 *Spectator*, 19 October 1991
9 Clare Hollingworth, *Front Line*
10 *Ibid.*
11 *Spectator*, 19 October 1991
12 Monica Dehn, interview with author, 16 December 1991
13 Martha Gellhorn, *The View from the Ground*
14 Sybille Bedford, interview with author, 8 May 1991
15 *Ibid.*
16 Sybille Bedford, *A Visit to Don Otavio* (Folio Society, 1990)
17 Sybille Bedford, interview with Bruce Chatwin, Introduction to *ibid.*
18 Sybille Bedford, interview with author, 8 May 1991
19 *Ibid.*
20 Sybille Bedford, 'The Worst That Ever Happened', reprinted in Bedford, *As It Was*
21 Sybille Bedford, interview with author, 8 May 1991
22 'Selecting the Jury for the Trial of Jack Ruby', *Life*, February 1964
23 Sybille Bedford, interview with author, 8 May 1991
24 Bedford, 'The Worst That Ever Happened'
25 Sybille Bedford, interview with author, 8 May 1991
26 *Ibid.*
27 Sybille Bedford, *Jigsaw*
28 Sybille Bedford, interview with author, 8 May 1991
29 *Ibid.*

16 VIETNAM

1 Marguerite Higgins, *Our Vietnam Nightmare*
2 *Ibid.*

3 Quoted in Virginia Elwood-Akers, *Women War Correspondents in the Vietnam War 1961–65*

4 Jurate Kazickas, 'Vietnam Vignettes', *Eugene* (Oregon) *Register-Guard*, 1 May 1969

5 *Ladies' Home Journal*, January 1967

6 Martha Gellhorn, *The View from the Ground*

7 Martha Gellhorn, 'The War in Vietnam', reprinted in Gellhorn, *The Face of War* (Virago Press edn, 1986)

8 *Ibid.*

9 Gellhorn, 'A New Kind of War', *Guardian*, September 1966, reprinted in *The Face of War*

10 *Ibid.*

11 Gellhorn, *The View from the Ground*

12 Gellhorn, 'The Uprooted', *Guardian*, September 1966, reprinted in *The Face of War*

13 Quoted in Phillip Knightley, *The First Casualty*

14 Gellhorn, 'Vietnam Again', 1986, reprinted in *The Face of War*

15 Martha Gellhorn, address to Cheltenham Festival of Literature, 9 October 1992

16 Gellhorn, 'Vietnam Again'

17 *Ibid.*

18 *Ibid.*

19 *New York Times*, 11 May 1970

20 Mary McCarthy, *Vietnam*

21 Mary McCarthy, *Hanoi*

22 *Ibid.*

23 *Ibid.*

24 Clare Hollingworth, interview with author, 20 September 1991

25 Quoted in Knightley, *op. cit.*

26 Clare Hollingworth, interview with author, 20 September 1991

27 Clare Hollingworth, *Front Line*

28 *Ibid.*

29 Della Fathers, interview with author, 11 February 1991

30 Knightley, *op. cit.*

31 *Guardian*, 7 February 1991

32 Victoria Brittain, interview with author, 13 March 1991

33 *Ibid.*

34 *Ibid.*

35 *Guardian*, 7 February 1991

36 Victoria Brittain, interview with author, 13 March 1991

37 *The Times*, 5 June 1972

38 *Ibid.*

39 Victoria Brittain, interview with author, 13 March 1991

40 Marina Warner, interview with author, 28 April 1992

41 Quoted in Knightley, *op. cit.*

42 Marina Warner, interview with author, 28 April 1992

43 *Spectator*, 1 July 1972

44 *Spectator*, 12 August 1972

45 Elizabeth Pond, letter to author, December 1991

46 *Christian Science Monitor*, 22 June 1970

47 *Ibid.*

48 Elizabeth Pond, letter to author, December 1991

49 *Christian Science Monitor*, 26 June 1970

50 *Christian Science Monitor*, 25 June 1970

51 Quoted in Knightley, *op. cit.*

52 *New York Times*, 13 May 1971

53 *Ibid.*

54 *Ibid.*

55 *Newsweek*, 24 May 1971

17   EQUAL OPPORTUNITIES

1 *Woman Journalist*, Spring 1972

2 *Woman Journalist*, Summer 1972

3 *Spectator*, 20 May 1972

4 *Ibid.*

5 *Spectator*, 3 June 1972

6 Survey conducted by National Union of Journalists, Summer 1984

7 Bernard Hall, letter to author, 14 September 1991

8 Franca Magnani, interview with author, 1 October 1991

9 *Ibid.*

10 Clare Hollingworth, interview with author, 23 July 1991

11 Martha Gellhorn, *The View from the Ground*

12 *Ibid.*

13 *New York Magazine*, February 1976; *Observer*, March 1976

14 Gellhorn, *The View from the Ground*

15 *Ibid.*

16 *Granta*, April 1984

17 Gellhorn, *The View from the Ground*
18 *Ibid.*
19 *Guardian*, December 1984
20 Patricia Clough, interview with author, 17 October 1991
21 *Ibid.*
22 Claire Sterling, interview with author, 2 October 1991
23 *Ibid.*
24 *Ibid.*

18 MODERN TIMES

1 *Tatler*, November 1992
2 Anna Ford at charity lunch, quoted in *Daily Mail*, 23 September 1992
3 Julia Langdon, interview with author, 2 October 1992
4 *Ibid.*
5 *New Yorker*, 9 April 1979
6 CBS, *This Morning*, quoted in *The Independent*, 7 October 1990
7 *Ibid.*
8 Letter to Valerie Hall, 13 February 1973, quoted in her unpublished thesis, *Women in Journalism* (1978), Fawcett Library
9 Adrianne Blue, interview with author, 3 December 1992
10 *Ibid.*
11 Edie Lederer, interview with author, 20 July 1991
12 *Ibid.*
13 *Ibid.*
14 *Ibid.*
15 *AP House Magazine*, Summer 1991
16 Edie Lederer, interview with author, 20 July 1991
17 *Ibid.*
18 *Ibid.*
19 *Ibid.*
20 Patricia Clough, interview with author, 17 October 1991
21 *Ibid.*
22 *Ibid.*
23 *The Independent*, 11 November 1989
24 Patricia Clough, interview with author, 17 October 1991
25 *Ibid.*
26 *Ibid.*
27 *Ibid.*
28 *Ibid.*
29 *Ibid.*
30 Diana Goodman, interview with author, 23 October 1992
31 *Ibid.*
32 *Company*, November 1984
33 Diana Goodman, interview with author, 23 October 1992
34 *Ibid.*
35 *Ibid.*
36 *More Magazine*, interview with Lindy Stout, March 1991
37 Diana Goodman, interview with author, 23 October 1992
38 *Ibid.*
39 *Ibid.*
40 Kate Adie, interview with author, 4 March 1992
41 *Ibid.*
42 *Ibid.*
43 *Ibid.*
44 *Ibid.*
45 *Open to Question*, BBC 2 television interview with Kate Adie, 3 March 1992
46 *Observer*, 22 February 1987
47 *Today*, 20 November 1986
48 *Daily Mirror*, 6 November 1980
49 *The Independent*, 1 November 1986
50 *Daily Telegraph*, 6 November 1986
51 *Guardian*, 14 June 1988
52 *Daily Mail*, 20 June 1989
53 *The Scotsman*, 20 June 1989
54 Kate Adie, interview with author, 4 March 1992
55 Response to question from author at Cheltenham Festival of Literature, 9 October 1992
56 Kate Adie, interview with author, 4 March 1992
57 *Today*, 19 January 1991
58 Kate Adie, interview with author, 4 March 1992
59 *Ibid.*
60 *Ibid.*
61 *Ibid.*
62 *Ibid.*
63 *Ibid.*
64 *Options*, February 1993
65 *Spectator*, 23 January 1993
66 Kate Adie, interview with author, 4 March 1992
67 *Cosmopolitan*, June 1990
68 Robert Fox, interview with author, 14 October 1992

69 *Ibid.*
70 *Ibid.*
71 *Ibid.*
72 *Ibid.*
73 Kate Adie, interview with author, 4 March 1992
74 *Ibid.*
75 *Evening Standard*, 23 April 1992
76 *The Independent*, 3 March 1990
77 Response to question from author at Cheltenham Festival of Literature, 9 October 1992
78 *The New York Review*, 30 January 1992
79 *Eye of the Storm*, BBC 2, 7 November 1992
80 Peter Millar, *The Times*, 21 August 1992
81 Edie Lederer, interview with author, 20 July 1991

Select Bibliography

Enid Bagnold, *Diary without Dates* (William Heinemann, 1918)

Margaret Bateson (ed.), *Professional Women upon Their Professions* (H. Cox, 1895)

Sybille Bedford, *A Visit to Don Otavio* (Folio Society, 1990; originally published as *The Sudden View*, E. P. Dutton, New York, 1953)

Sybille Bedford, *Jigsaw* (Hamish Hamilton, 1989)

Sybille Bedford, 'The Worst That Ever Happened', reprinted in *As It Was* (Sinclair-Stevenson, 1990)

E. Moberly Bell, *Flora Shaw* (Constable, 1947)

Arnold Bennett, *Journalism for Women: A Practical Guide* (John Lane The Bodley Head, 1898)

Lucy Brown, *Victorian News and Newspapers* (Clarendon Press, Oxford, 1985)

Iris Carpenter, *No Woman's World* (Houghton Mifflin, Boston, 1946)

Mrs Cecil Chesterton, *In Darkest London* (Stanley Paul & Co., 1926)

Arthur Christiansen, *Headlines All My Life* (William Heinemann, 1961)

Richard Collier, *The Warcos: The War Correspondents of World War Two* (Weidenfeld & Nicolson, 1988)

Virginia Cowles, *Looking for Trouble* (Hamish Hamilton, 1941)

Aidan Crawley, *Leap Before You Look* (Collins, 1988)

Eve Curie, *Journey among Warriors* (William Heinemann, 1943)

Elizabeth Adams Daniels, *Jesse White Mario – Resorgimento Revolutionary* (Ohio University Press, 1972)

Phyllis Deakin, *Press On: An Account of the Women's Press Club of London* (Henry E. Walter, 1984)

Shiela Grant Duff, *The Parting of Ways* (Peter Owen, 1982)

Julia Edwards, *Women of the World* (Ivy Books, New York, 1988)

Virginia Elwood-Akers, *Women War Correspondents in the Vietnam War*

1961–65 (The Scarecrow Press, New Jersey and London, 1988)

Frances Fitzgerald, *Fire in the Lake* (Atlantic-Little Brown, 1972)

E. H. Fleming, *Lady Colin Campbell – Victorian Sex Goddess* (The Windrush Press, 1989)

Wilbur Forrest, *Behind the Front Page* (D. Appleton-Century Co., New York, 1934)

Robert Fox, *Eyewitness Falklands* (Methuen, 1982)

Olga Franklin, *Steppes to Fleet Street* (Victor Gollancz, 1968)

A. Ruth Fry, *Emily Hobhouse, A Memoir* (Jonathan Cape, 1929)

Martha Gellhorn, *The Trouble I've Seen* (Puttnam, London, 1936)

Martha Gellhorn, *The Face of War* (Rupert Hart-Davis, 1959; Sphere Books, 1967; Virago Press, 1986)

Martha Gellhorn, *Travels with Myself and Another* (Eland Books, 1983, UK, US and Commonwealth edns)

Martha Gellhorn, *A Stricken Field* (Virago Press, 1986)

Martha Gellhorn, *Liana* (Virago Press, 1987)

Martha Gellhorn, *The View from the Ground* (Granta Books, 1989)

Robert Giddings, *Echoes of War* (Bloomsbury, 1992)

Joyce Grenfell, *The Time of My Life – Entertaining the Troops – Her Wartime Journals* (Hodder & Stoughton, 1989)

Charlotte Haldane, *Russian Newsreel: An Eyewitness Account of the Soviet Union at War* (Secker & Warburg, 1942)

Ernest Hemingway (ed.), *Men at War* (Crown Publishers, New York, 1942)

Marguerite Higgins, *War in Korea* (Doubleday, New York, 1951)

Marguerite Higgins, *News Is a Singular Thing* (Doubleday, New York, 1955)

Marguerite Higgins, *Our Vietnam Nightmare* (Harper & Row, New York, 1965)

John Hohenberg, *Foreign Correspondence: The Great Reporters and Their Times* (Columbia University Press, New York, 1984)

Clare Hollingworth, *Front Line* (Jonathan Cape, 1990)

Bernice Kert, *The Hemingway Women* (W. W. Norton, New York, 1983)

Phillip Knightley, *The First Casualty* (André Deutsch, 1975)

G. Krishnamurti (compiled), *Women Writers of the 1890s* (Henry Sotheran, 1991)

Elinor Langer, *Josephine Herbst: The Story She Could Never Tell* (Atlantic-Little Brown, 1983)

Robert Wilkinson Latham, *Victorian War Correspondents and their Campaigns* (Hodder & Stoughton, 1979)

Mary McCarthy, *Vietnam* (Weidenfeld & Nicolson, 1967)

Mary McCarthy, *Hanoi* (Weidenfeld & Nicolson, 1968)

Janice and Stephen MacKinnon, *Agnes Smedley: The Life and Times of an American Radical* (Virago Press, 1988)

Hilde Marchant, *Women and Children Last – A Woman Reporter's Account of the Battle of Britain* (Victor Gollancz, 1941)

Marion Marzolf, *Up from the Footnote: A History of Women Journalists* (Hastings House, New York, 1977)

Alan Moorehead, *A Late Education* (Hamish Hamilton, 1970)

Leonard E. Naylor, *The Irrepressible Victorian* (Macdonald, 1965)

Thomas Pakenham, *The Boer War* (Weidenfeld & Nicolson, 1979)

Mollie Panter-Downes, *London War Notes 1939–45* (Longman, 1972)

Mollie Panter-Downes, *One Fine Day* (Virago Press, 1985)

Margery Perham, *Lugard, The Years of Authority* (Collins, 1960)

Tom Pocock, *East and West of Suez* (Bodley Head, 1986)

Jasper Ridley, *Garibaldi* (Constable, 1974)

Brian Roberts, *Ladies in the Veld* (John Murray, 1965)

Trevor Royle, *War Report* (Mainstream Publishing, 1987)

Audrey Russell, *A Certain Voice* (Ross Anderson Publications, 1984)

Agnes Smedley, *Daughter of Earth* (Coward-McCann, New York, 1929)

Agnes Smedley, *Chinese Destinies: Sketches of Present Day China* (Vanguard Press, New York, 1933)

Agnes Smedley, *China's Red Army Marches* (Vanguard Press, New York, 1934)

Agnes Smedley, *China Fights Back: An American Woman with the Eighth Route Army* (Vanguard Press, New York, 1938)

Agnes Smedley, *Battle Hymn of China* (Knopf, New York, 1943)

R. W. Stallman, *Stephen Crane: A Biography* (George Braziller, New York, 1968)

Mary Stott, *Forgetting's No Excuse* (Virago Press, 1989)

Ann and John Tusa, *The Nuremberg Trials* (Papermac, 1983)

Andrea Viotti, *Garibaldi* (Blandford Press, 1979)

Lady Sarah Wilson, *South African Memories* (Edward Arnold, 1909)

Charles Wintour, *The Rise and Fall of Fleet Street* (Hutchinson, 1989)

Elizabeth Wiskemann, *The Europe I Saw* (Collins, 1968)

Notable American Women: A Biographical Dictionary (Harvard University Press, 1980)

The Faber Book of Reportage (1987)

Index

DOROTHY L. SAYERS:
HER LIFE AND SOUL

Barbara Reynolds

Dorothy L. Sayers is one of the twentieth century's most fascinating women: greatest of all the golden age detective writers, religious thinker and medieval scholar.

Using her access to Dorothy L. Sayers' papers and photographs, many of which have never before been seen, and her own memories of her subject, Barbara Reynolds has written the most readable and the most definitive biography to date of this fascinating woman.

'Biographies of Dorothy Sayers have been published already, but this is the most authoritative by far'
Penelope Fitzgerald, Observer

'A tinglingly vivid portrait of a brilliant, quirky, combative, energetic, comical and fascinating woman . . . superb biography'
Piers Brendon, Daily Mail

'The achievement of this lucid and absorbing biography is to make you wish you had known a woman who could inspire bishops in a dozen languages and giggle like a girl'
Frances Fyfield, Sunday Express

'Barbara Reynolds's achievement is to make us not only admire but like this astonishing woman'
Jenny Uglow, Independent on Sunday

∫

SCEPTRE

HENRY JAMES
THE IMAGINATION OF GENIUS
a biography
Fred Kaplan

'Kaplan is thoroughly at ease with the 19th-century
European culture in which James made himself so
preeminently at home. He is also naturally authoritative on
James the American, and one of the strengths of his book is
that it conveys the creative tension between these two
overlapping elements . . . Kaplan is equally good on James's
sexual identity . . . His comments on the novels are
intelligent and perceptive, sensibly brief . . . no further
biography of James is necessary'
Alan Judd in The Sunday Telegraph

'Excellent . . . a compelling portrait of a life of extraordinary
sweetness, self-repression and loneliness . . . The real
triumph of Kaplan's book is the extent to which it makes one
care for James'
Caroline Moore in The Times

'It never flags, but glides, like its subject, to a polished end . . .
One of the many strengths of Kaplan's biography is the way
in which he identifies what made James run'
Roy Hattersley in The Sunday Times

'A good up-to-date one-volume life of Henry James was
long overdue; Kaplan has done that job splendidly'
Miranda Seymour in The New York Times Book Review

'May even be superior to Edel'
James Buchan in The Spectator

SCEPTRE